W9-BCM-482

. . . and the Desert Shall Rejoice
Conflict, Growth, and Justice in Arid Environments

. . . and the Desert Shall Rejoice
Conflict, Growth, and Justice in Arid Environments

Arthur Maass and Raymond L. Anderson

The MIT Press
Cambridge, Massachusetts, and London, England

Copyright © 1978 by Arthur Maass, except chapters 7 and 8

All rights reserved. No copyrighted part of this book may be reproduced in any form or by any means, electronic or mechanical, including photocopying, recording, or by any information storage and retrieval system, without permission in writing from the publisher.

This book was set in IBM Press Roman by To the Lighthouse Press and printed on R & E Book by The Alpine Press, Inc. in the United States of America.

Library of Congress Cataloging in Publication Data

Maass, Arthur.
    . . . and the desert shall rejoice.

    Includes index.
    1. Irrigation—Case studies.   2. Irrigation districts—Case studies.   3. Water-rights—Case studies.   4. Arid regions—Case studies.
I. Anderson, Raymond Lloyd, 1927– joint author.   II. Title.
HD1714.M3   333.9′13   77–17866
ISBN 0–262–13134–X

Contents

. . . and the Desert Shall Rejoice
Conflict, Growth, and Justice in Arid Environments

1 Introduction

Irrigation is man's response to drought; by this means he reduces radically the uncertainty that nature presents to human settlement in an inhospitable environment. To succeed for any length of time, to capture and distribute available water, and to control the amount of land placed under irrigation, farmers must develop self-discipline and a high level of community organization. We have observed these forces operating in a number of the world's deserts, especially those of southeastern Spain and the western United States.

The six irrigated areas we have chosen for study—the *huertas* (intensively irrigated areas that surround or adjoin towns) of Valencia, Murcia-Orihuela, and Alicante in Spain and the South Platte-Cache La Poudre, Utah, and Kings River valleys in the United States—are typical, in their variety, of irrigated systems over the world. Precisely what are the differences and similarities among their operating procedures and what do these mean? In Valencia, for example, the dominating principle of the procedures is that water is married to the land and cannot be divorced from it, whereas in nearby Alicante water is auctioned weekly by the irrigation community itself and is sold daily by individual holders. Time priority—first come, first served—has greater power in determining who gets the limited water supply in Colorado than in Utah. How are the operating procedures related to the governing institutions and to the objectives of the irrigation communities that have adopted them? The purpose of this book is to understand the institutions and the procedures, to discover the objectives, and to evaluate the institutions and procedures in terms of how well they satisfy the communities' goals.

The objective functions of irrigation communities vary, of course; but most of the systems studied, and probably most in the world, share common goals, although these are assigned different values in different systems. They include orderly conflict resolution, popular participation, local control, increased income, justice in income distribution, and equity. These objectives may be complementary within certain levels of achievement, in the sense that pursuit of one goal does not interfere with that of another; but many objectives will be competitive—the pursuit of any one is constrained by the others. Each irrigation community somehow decides on tradeoff values among its several objectives, thereby establishing a composite objective function that represents its will.

CONFLICT RESOLUTION

One objective of irrigation communities is to maintain order and certainty, and to this end to discourage and resolve conflicts over water use. Water conflicts are notorious in the history and mythology of world civilizations. Witness, as diverse examples, rivalries over the wells of Beersheba between Abraham (and later, Isaac) on the one hand and the Philistines on the other; over the river

Loire, between Rabelais's father and a neighbor, which became the model for the war between Gargantua and Picrochole; and gun fights over the ol' water hole, which is a staple of TV westerns.[1] The word "rival," as a matter of fact, evolved from the Latin *rivalis,* meaning "one living on the opposite bank of a stream from another." And the words for rival and rivalry in the several Romance languages are similarly derived.

A keen observer of early irrigation practices in the western United States, the engineer Elwood Mead, remarked—with some exaggeration perhaps—that until they learned to create strong institutions for settling disputes, "there was either murder or suicide in the heart of every member" of an irrigation community.[2] There is no evidence that the Catholic farmers of Valencia have considered suicide, but murder, yes. The stone and clay banks that support the turnout structures of several of the major laterals of the Moncada canal are pocked by bullet pits, evidence of irrigators shooting at canal guards to get them to open the gates in times of extreme drought. Any local farmer will tell you this. For several delicious accounts of medieval water disputes in this area, with appropriate emphasis on gallantry and the offended honor of women all told in the language of the court records, see Thomas Glick's study of irrigation and society in Medieval Valencia. He found that "violence lay ever just below the surface, ready to erupt, especially against officials, if provocation should be given. The medieval irrigators were extremely excitable about their rights being 'disturbed,' and millers and cultivators alike were ready to fight in an instant if they felt that their water supply was jeopardized in any way."[3]

Why is water so conducive to this conflict? Principally because it flows, its unregulated flows are likely to be erratic, and in arid country the consequences for any user unable to capture water the moment it is needed are likely to be dire. The location of a farmer's headgate on a water distribution channel very largely determines his social relationships with members of the irrigation community, as well as with those outside the community who use the same water source; and these relationships are potentially disruptive. Also, the unpredictable character of stream flow can create a tense environment of uncertainty that is disruptive of social relations. In more formal language, certain features of the technological or production function of water use such as flow and stochasticity give rise to social conflict and to the objective of controlling it.

The objective, then, is to provide order and predictability so that water users can realize their other goals related to increased income, popular control, and social justice. To this end irrigators will adopt operating procedures and institutions that discourage conflicts and settle those that arise. For most of the regions we have studied potential and actual conflicts among members of a community are resolved within the community itself on the basis of principles, rules, or regulations to which all members have consented. The several irrigation communities of southeastern Spain have their own ordinances that govern almost all water questions arising among their members. The purpose of the ordinances is "to end cavillation and litigation," as is said in those governing the New Almoradí canal of Murcia-Orihuela.[4] The irrigators characteristically enforce the ordinances, and disputes among members that do not yield to self-control are settled in special popular courts.

Irrigation districts in the Central Valley of California have written rules and regulations that are distributed to all members in the form of printed pamphlets, but these are narrower in scope than the Spanish ordinances, so that irrigators rely on the state water code and the ordinary state courts to supplement their institutions for resolving conflicts. Many irrigation communities of Utah and Colorado do not have written ordinances but depend on custom and tradition, as well as state water codes.

Conflicts between the members of an irrigation community and an outside party—typically an upstream community—are a different story. The consensual basis for conflict resolution may be weaker and political and economic power may play a stronger role. The most widely used principle for settling such disputes in the regions we have studied is that first possession or occupation creates a superior right. The "first in time, first in right" principle has been accepted, apparently, because of a widespread belief that man is entitled to the product of his own labor and therefore to protection against late-comers of land he has worked. Although this rule may seem obvious, since seniority is used frequently where a general rationing rule is needed (such as queuing for admissions to theaters or buses), it is not the rule followed for water in all parts of the world. In the Berber areas of Morocco, for example, the principle for settling water disputes between irrigation communities is one of location rather than prior occupancy. The upstream users always have preference over those below them on the watercourse.

In the western United States intercommunity disputes are settled by water commissioners, water rights boards, state engineers, or state courts in accord with provisions of state water codes that incorporate the principle of time priority or by voluntary agreements among communities that want to avoid the costs and possibly adverse decisions of courts and bureaus, again according to seniority. In Spain they are decided by ministerial or administrative orders based on the national water law, which validates the principle of time priority in the familiar form of prescription, or by voluntary agreements similarly based.

POPULAR PARTICIPATION AND LOCAL CONTROL

Community members should participate in determining procedures for operating their distribution systems and for ordering relations between these systems and other systems and authorities. They should be free from arbitrary authority of their own officers and from control by outside organizations. These related objectives have been pursued with remarkable intensity by irrigators in the United States, Spain, and probably throughout the world.

To illustrate some of the problems involved in the administration of their own systems, assume that community A requires all farmers to share a water shortage in proportion to their normal consumption, whereas Community B denies water in periods of drought to all farmers in a sector of its service area that was the last to have been put under irrigation. A's procedure may oblige the community to employ a large number of guards and to give them considerable discretionary authority to police the distribution of water as it becomes increasingly scarce, whereas B's is relatively self-enforcing and therefore requires fewer guards and much less discretionary authority in their hands. On the other hand, the water users of Community A may enjoy a high degree of popular participation, voting periodically on their rules, whereas those of Community B are governed by a set of priorities that was established by custom in an earlier century and encased subsequently in a series of court decisions.

It is in its relations with other systems, particularly higher authorities, that a community's objective of popular participation and local control is put to the test. Karl A. Wittfogel, in a well-known study of hydraulic societies, concluded that irrigation agriculture has led to strong centralization of political power, even to "oriental despotism." [5] Hydraulic agriculture requires great cooperative effort, organizing capital and labor to build dams and canals, for example, and this has been provided typically by an all-powerful "agromanagerial" bureaucracy. Political and hydraulic leadership and control have come to rest in the same hands, and these hands for this reason have been uniquely powerful.

Our observations of irrigation systems in Spain and the United States do not confirm Wittfogel's thesis, and we are unclear on the extent to which Wittfogel applies his thesis to these areas. [6] To meet the demands for cooperative effort in hydraulic agriculture, which are indeed great, the water users of Spanish and U.S. systems have shown a genius for inventing operating procedures that avoid centralized and despotic political power. Systems that were in existence before the central government invested money and technical expertise have to a remarkable extent protected their autonomy and even defied national policies that are supposed to accompany national money if these policies have been a serious threat to local custom. When, for example, the national government undertook construction of the Generalísimo Dam near Valencia, it guaranteed that its actions "will not alter nor diminish the rights nor the free administration" of the irrigation communities, which "will continue to exercise these in accordance with their respective ordinances, statutes, rules, customs, or concessions." No actions "may modify these rights in any form whatsoever." [7] In Murcia-Orihuela the canal communities have thus far failed to alter their traditional methods of taking water from the river although national policy requires them to do so, especially when the river's flow has been regulated by the construction of storage reservoirs. And the irrigation communities of the South Platte–Cache La Poudre of Colorado and of the Kings River in the Central Valley of California have opposed successfully the U.S. government's policy of limiting to small farms only the use of water from reservoirs that the government has financed.

Wittfogel has posited that the need for capital and technical expertise leads to centralized and despotic power in irrigation regions. Others have suggested, in a similar vein, that the need to control conflict, which is always close to the surface in these regions, leads to strong central authority. But here, as in the case of the Wittfogel thesis, what may appear to be logically compelling is not the case.

Avoiding foreign and arbitrary power has been one of the objectives of water users that, to be sure, they have had to compromise in order to achieve satisfactory levels of efficiency and security, but, as we shall see, the consequences of the tradeoffs these irrigators have made among their objectives have not included despotic rule.

ECONOMIC GROWTH

Greater income or efficiency is obviously a principal goal of irrigation communities. Even where nonefficiency objectives are important, a community will want to achieve them at a minimum forfeit of efficiency benefits; and in any case the community will need to establish a tradeoff between its desire for more income and any conflicting objectives. Economic growth, however, is in the case of irrigation agriculture so competitive with other objectives that farmers typically refuse to treat water as a regular economic good, like fertilizer, for example. It is, they say, a special product and should be removed from ordinary market transactions so that the farmers can control conflict, maintain popular influence and control, and realize equity and social justice. Furthermore, since progress is commonly associated with efficiency, to the extent that irrigation communities, limit efficiency by pursuing other objectives they have been "unprogressive."

After a thorough study of irrigation in the Utah Valley, James Hudson concluded that although present laws permit a free market in water, social attitudes in the valley forbid it. Attempts to convert it to an economic good by selling surplus water to the highest bidder are regarded as "water profiteering"; attempts to acquire large additional supplies are regarded as "water hogging." [8] Irrigators in northeastern Colorado can sell water to neighboring farmers at any time during a season when they find they will not need it themselves. After studying these transactions, Raymond Anderson concluded that community pressure does not allow the market price to reach the level that farmers who are short of water would be willing to pay; and significantly, the farmers say that they are "renting" rather than selling the water.[9] The historian Pedro Díaz Cassou, who knew the mind of the Murcia farmer better than any other writer, interpreted the passion of these men and those of Valencia for keeping their water tied to their lands in this way: to separate land and water may be more efficient, but it paralyzes agricultural development by promoting great antagonisms among water users.[10]

Very generally, an efficient operating procedure allocates marginal units of irrigation water to those farms that can produce with it the greatest net benefits, efficiency benefits and costs being measured for this purpose in terms that relate to the irrigation community as a whole, not necessarily to the individual farms.

The achievement of efficiency in these terms requires institutions that can forge a particular balance between flexibility, which is necessary if water is to be transferred from less to more efficient uses, and certainty, needed if farmers are to make the investments of labor and capital that are consistent with economic growth. There are, as we shall see, persistent problems in establishing and maintaining this balance.

DISTRIBUTION OF INCOME

A community's concept of social justice is normally the basis of one or more objectives that irrigation communities seek when they determine their operating procedures and institutions. Social justice, when related to income, refers to its distribution as well as its size. A typical goal of government programs is to redistribute income from the wealthy to the poor or from a wealthy and developed region to a poor and underdeveloped one or, alternatively, to preserve an existing income distribution that is considered just or simply to promote or preserve a process for transferring income that is considered just. Thus an irrigation community's objective for water distribution will depend on the group's basic attitude toward distribution of wealth and the process by which any given distribution is achieved and on its tradeoffs between this goal and others, such as economic growth, that may conflict with it.

Assume that communities A and B have similar patterns of land distribution with great differences in size of farms and that the different operating procedures they have adopted are well designed to achieve their objectives. The procedure of Community A requires that all water users share the burden of drought, but in proportions that increase progressively with the quantities of water normally used, so that a large landowner will suffer a greater percentage loss of water than a small one. Community B requires all water users to share the burden of drought in a fixed proportion to their normal water use. Assume further that B's procedure for meeting the drought is more efficient for the community as a whole than is A's (although this need not be the case). Community A, then, puts a heavy weight on its concept of what is socially just relative to economic efficiency. Community B either places a heavier weight on efficiency vis-à-vis income distribution than does A or its concept of social justice is to maintain the present distribution of income rather than redistribute it in the direction of equality, resulting in a procedure that is fortuitously more efficient than A's.

EQUITY

The irrigation ordinances of southeastern Spain state typically that their purpose is to achieve equality and equity in the distribution of water. By equity they mean fairness, avoiding unreasonable inequality in the treatment of individuals who are in the same situation or category. Equity is to govern the exercise of any discretion that canal officers have when they enforce orders and regulations for water distribution and to govern the legislators' discretion when they fashion these rules from formal concepts.

The goal that all members of a class be treated equally applies to more than economic gain; it also applies, for example, to convenience. Except where the sun is punishingly hot, a farmer does not like to irrigate at night because he needs to be present at his farm headgate, under most systems, when the water is turned into it, whence he both follows the water and moves it from furrow to furrow, borderstrip to borderstrip, or field to field. An operating procedure that always delivers water at night to the same farmers is likely to be considered inequitable, therefore, and the community may introduce considerable complexity into an otherwise simple procedure to avoid this inconvenience.

An important reason for investment in dams and other river regulation structures may be to achieve such convenience in water use. Since the Generalísimo Dam was completed in the 1950s, the farmers of Valencia have spent fewer of the sleepless nights that the readers of Blasco Ibáñez's novels have come to associate with their lives.

KNOWING OBJECTIVES

We discover the objectives of an irrigation community principally in the legislative history of its ordinances, rules, and regulations, supplemented by court records of controversies between the community and outside groups. We look also at the physical works themselves, for as David and John Major have suggested, the objectives that governed the construction and operation of large public works can be inferred to some degree from the design of the completed projects, provided one knows the community's framework of decision making.[11] Finally we examine certain results of the procedures used, namely, crop production and farm income of the system as a whole, and the distribution of this production and income among individual farms. In this we must be careful, for results of operating procedures will be indicative of the irrigators' objectives only where the irrigators have had sufficient knowledge of the relations between alternative procedures and their results in terms of objectives. Thus before we derive objectives from the observed consequences of the operating procedures themselves we examine the decision process by which the procedures were adopted, just as we do for the ordinances when we study their legislative histories and the physical works when we observe them.

As a supplement to these sources for objectives, it would be useful if we had for each irrigated area a consistent set of farmer opinion surveys taken over a significant historical period. These do not exist. But we have available and make use of extensive contemporary observations of each region (the three regions of Spain and California by Maass; Colorado and Utah by Anderson) and of recorded observations by some keen eyewitnesses of earlier periods. Some of the observers used are Maurice Aymard and Baron Jaubert de Passa in early nineteenth-century Valencia, Pedro Díaz Cassou in late nineteenth-century Murcia, Rafael Altamira in early twentieth-century Alicante, Frank Adams and Carl Grunsky in the Kings River during the early twentieth century, David Boyd and Elwood Mead in Colorado at the turn of the century, and George Thomas and Elwood Mead during the same period in Utah.[12]

We believe that taken together these sources of knowledge about goals are sufficient. As David Fisher points out in his essay on historical method: "There can be no primary direct evidence of any past motive. But there is a tacit logic of inference which can attain a high degree of probable accuracy. It is a logic which in its very nature appears to commit the fallacy of the consequent (in the form 'if X, then possibly Y; Y, therefore probably X'). But this form of reasoning is a useful tool of empirical inquiry." [13]

SIMULATION AND BASIC DATA

We have developed an elaborate simulation program to measure the results achieved in crop production and farm income for the use of any operating procedure in any environment. Because this program has proved useful not only for the analysis in this book but also for irrigation managers who have an opportunity today to choose from among alternative operating procedures, it has been published separately as a bulletin by the U.S. Department of Agriculture. The bulletin includes an essay by Anderson on the responses of different crops to alternative sequences or regimens for supplying them with irrigation water. We have not reproduced the simulation program in this book, but each chapter includes, in an appendix, a concordance that explains how the program is used to simulate the operating procedures described in the chapter.

The bulletin is available without charge by writing to the Office of Communications, Department of Agriculture, Washington, D.C., 20250, requesting Raymond L. Anderson and Arthur Maass, *A Simulation of Irrigation Systems,* Technical Bulletin No. 1431, Revised September 1974.

In some instances we have used alternative forms for presenting the physical data of the six irrigated areas because by doing so we are able to help the nonexpert to understand the significance and use of such data. Thus, for example, the stream flows of Valencia and Murcia-Orihuela are given in tables of monthly means, with their standard deviations, whereas those of the Utah Valley are presented in monthly probability hydrographs. Data for the Spanish chapters are in metric units, those for the American, in U.S. customary units. Conversion equivalents for the units used most frequently are shown below.

The data base for the Spanish huertas terminates in 1968 and that for the American systems in 1969. Developments since these dates are not included in this study, except in occasional notes.

There have been many studies of irrigation, some of them focusing on one or another aspect of operating procedures, some developed for specific regions, southeastern Spain, for example. We have referred to Wittfogel and Glick and

U.S. to Metric

inch (in)	2.54	centimeters
foot (ft)	30.48	centimeters
mile (mi)	1.61	kilometers
acre	0.40	hectares
section	259.00	hectares
acre-foot	1,233.49	cubic meters
cubic foot per second (cfs)	0.028	cubic meters per second

Metric to U.S.

centimeter (cm)	0.39	inches
meter (m)	3.28	feet
kilometer (km)	0.62	miles
hectare (ha)	2.47	acres
cubic meter (m^3)	0.0008	acre feet
cubic meters per second (m^3/s)	35.31 cubic feet per second	

shall note others in the chapters that follow. To this day the best general analysis is that of the French geographer, Jean Brunhes, written in 1902.[14] With respect to irrigation systems, Brunhes looks for relations between geographic forms on the one hand and forms of economic development and administrative organization and regulation on the other. He concludes that natural environment influences the type of irrigation system that man creates, but only indirectly, through the intervening variable of the psychology or state of mind of the individuals or groups involved. There is a necessary relation between natural environment and psychological state; irregular natural conditions that menace an individual or group will create a psychological state of insecurity, a state that will vary with the degree and character of nature's irregularity. But there is no necessary relation between the psychological state of insecurity and the resulting irrigation system. Faced with insecurity, men can act in ways that are either harmonious or contradictory; and how they act in any given situation will depend in good part on their attitudes or dispositions toward cooperation and extreme individualism. The disposition to cooperate derives, in turn, from local combinations of ethnic, historical, legal, and political influences. Thus, although it is common for men to seek to free themselves from a psychological state of uncertainty, they do not invariably do so, for this requires that they associate under fixed rules that may be quite rigorous. For sociological, historical, and personal reasons they may not be prepared to do this.

Brunhes was obviously trying to protect himself against that gremlin of geographers, geographical determinism; and to do so he used a psychological concept that may appear primitive today. At the same time his observations on the water distribution systems that we know are accurate and perceptive; and although we shall not use Brunhes's general theory as such, it does, when applied to specific cases, offer useful insights. Thus Brunhes's variations in the attitudes of different peoples toward cooperation when they suffer from psychological insecurity will be reflected in our variations in objective functions—although we take these as given without searching for their underlying causes. As with Brunhes, similar natural environments will not produce necessarily similar irrigation systems, for the latter will depend in part on community objectives.

2 The Huerta of Valencia

The plain (*vega*) of Valencia is one of several rich irrigated areas in southeastern Spain, formed by stream deltas that are defined on three sides by mountains and on the fourth by the Mediterranean Sea.[1] That part of the vega of principal interest in this study, the inner and ancient huerta of Valencia, is a triangular space with a base near the coast, 27 kilometers (km) in length, a height along the channel of the Turia River of 11 km, and, until recent urban growth reduced its size, including approximately 16,000 hectares (ha) (40,000 acres) of irrigated land, all within 10 to 15 km of the city.

The huerta's climate is characterized by hot and sunny summers and nearly frost-free winters, so a variety of crops can be grown in various rotations, producing two or three harvests a year. The principal crops are potatoes, onions, corn, and vegetables, of which celery, spinach, cabbage, cauliflower, lettuce, beans, and artichokes are important varieties. In addition there are smaller hectarages of melons, peanuts, citrus, and rice. Between late December and April or May approximately half the area is planted to early potatoes. In spring and summer onions and corn each occupy approximately one-third of the area and late potatoes, one-quarter. Vegetables are planted in about one-third of the huerta on the average over the year and the remaining crops occupy little more than a twentieth of the area. The Valencians have developed operating procedures that allow each farmer great freedom to select from among this variety of crops those he wants to cultivate.

The farms are small. Eighty-three percent occupy less than 1 ha and virtually all of them occupy less than 5 ha. This extreme fragmentation of farmland is the consequence principally of two factors that have operated with increasing acceleration over the last hundred and fifty years: the laws and practice of inheritance and purchase of farms by tenants. As a result of tenant purchases tenancy, which was typical in the nineteenth century, has declined considerably, so that for Spain a relatively high percentage of proprietors work their own lands. Burriel has described long-run trends in farm size by comparing the units used by the irrigation communities as a basis for collecting taxes: in the thirteenth century it was a *jovada* (3 ha); in the eighteenth and the first half of the nineteenth centuries, a *cahizada* (half a hectare); in the present century, a *hanegada* (one-twelfth of a hectare).[2]

The area's rainfall is scant and irregular; it is supplemented by river water distributed to farms by eight principal canals (*acequias*) and, to a considerably lesser extent, by groundwater abstracted with wells and pumps. The canals divert water from the river by low diversion dams (*azuds*), the dam of the last canal of the inner huerta being 8 km downstream from that of the first. The canals run alternately on the left and right banks of the river, four on each side, as shown in figure 2.1. Their course is generally perpendicular to the river, while that of their principal laterals, which draw from the downstream sides of

President of Valencia's Water Court consults a colleague before passing judgment. A large audience is usually present at the Apostles' Door of the Cathedral of Valencia where the court meets every Thursday, unless there are no cases.

Bronze cap of staff carried by the court's bailiff, surmounted by a sign in both Castillian and Valencian that court will hold no trials today. This is posted on Thursdays when there have been no denunciations in the previous week.

Two adversary farmers (lower right) being questioned by president of the Court (seated lower left).

Valencia's Water Court, engraved by Tomas Rocafort, 1831. The judges use a bench rather than chairs.

Valencia's Water Court, sketched by Gustave Doré, 1862.

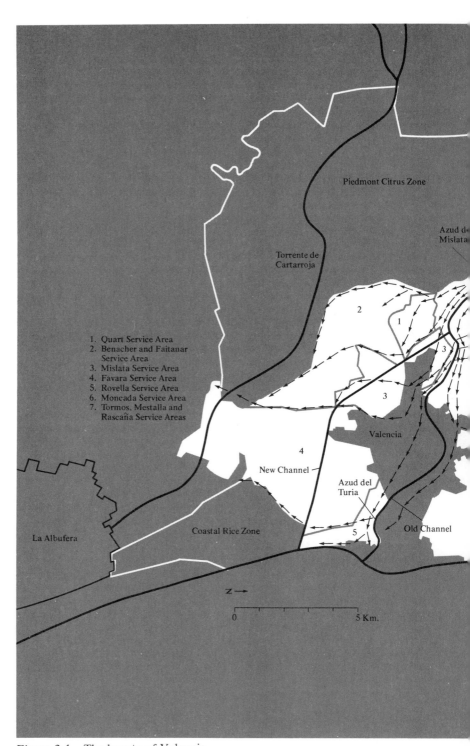

Figure 2.1   The huerta of Valencia.

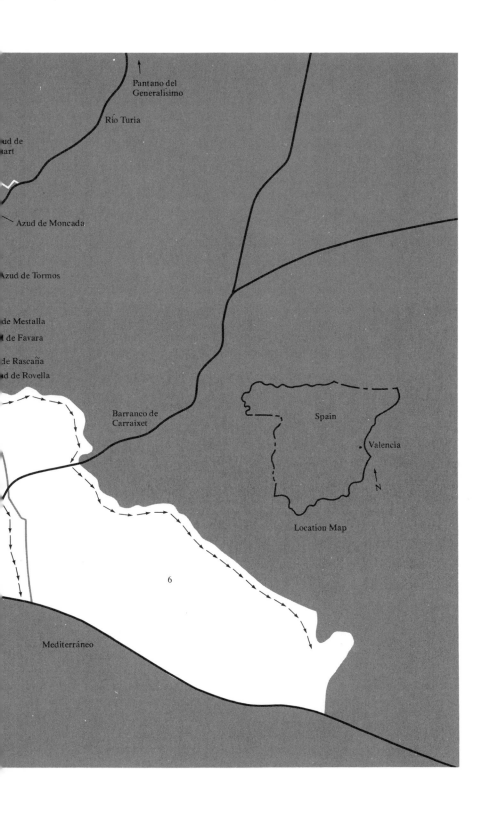

Pantano del
Generalisimo

Río Turia

ud de
art

Azud de Moncada

Azud de Tormos

de Mestalla

de Favara

de Rascaña

d de Rovella

Barranco de
Carraixet

Spain

Valencia

N

Location Map

6

Mediterráneo

the canals, is parallel to the river. Thus the return flows and excess water of the laterals of one canal flow into the next downstream canal and the whole system has an intricate and delicate unity.

The regime of the Turia River is irregular, both seasonally and overyear, and prior to 1950 there was only one relatively small storage dam on the river to modify this regime, the Buseo Dam, completed in 1915, with a 7.5 million cubic meter (m³) capacity. Minimum flows occur in summer and early autumn, which is also the period of maximum temperature, minimum rainfall, and maximum irrigation requirements, so that in an average year prior to 1950 there was a seasonal drought during which little or no water reached the sea. In addition, overyear fluctuations in stream flow have brought frequent, serious, and extended droughts, as well as destructive floods.

These basic hydrologic facts, shown in detail in table 2.1, have been of central importance in determining the traditional operating procedures of the irrigation communities of the huerta. The procedures recognize three conditions of water availability—abundance (*abundancia*), seasonal low water (*estiaje ordinario* or *mitjanía* in Valencian), and extraordinary drought (*sequía extraordinaria* or *necesitat gran* in Valencian)—and they prescribe different rules for each.

In 1951 the Generalísimo Dam, with a storage capacity of 228 million cubic meters (Hm³), began operating 100 km upstream from the river's mouth; and subsequently the Lorguilla Dam, with a capacity of 71 Hm³, was built downstream, principally as a reregulating facility. These works provide seasonal and overyear water storage for urban uses, principally in the city of Valencia, and for irrigations supplementing the water supplies of the huerta of Valencia and certain smaller huertas upstream on the Turia and providing water for a new irrigated zone approximately 45 km north of Valencia. In addition the Generalísimo Dam and its reservoir provide electric power and some storage to protect the city from floods. Table 2.2 and column (3) of table 2.1 demonstrate crudely how river storage has been used to redistribute natural flows, making them available when needed. This has, as planned, radically reduced the occasions on which the huerta's irrigation communities have needed to use their operating procedures for seasonal low water and exceptional drought.

Groundwater is readily available under most of the inner huerta and for centuries it was tapped by means of *norias* (waterwheels moved by horsepower) placed in shallow wells about 6 meters (m) deep. The norias were used principally to supplement river water when the river was low. They were found most frequently near the peripheries of the canals' service areas, where the lands are entitled to canal water only when it is abundant. The norias have largely disappeared, but in the two decades before the Spanish civil war many large wells with motor-driven pumps were dug for the same purposes. A typical well was drilled to a depth of 40 m, was operated by a 50-horsepower electric pump, and had a capacity of 2500 liters (l) per minute. In many cases these wells were the product of private initiative. A group of landowners would organize a company and sell shares to raise the capital necessary to drill the well and install the

Table 2.1 Monthly and annual stream flows entering the huerta of Valencia and monthly precipitation.

	Stream Flow, Station 25, Aguas Potables, Turia River						Precipitation at Valencia, Station 398
	(1) Means (m³/s)		(2) Standard Deviation (m³/s)		(3) No. of years of drought in certain months[a]		(4) Means (mm)
	1911–1950[b]	1951–1965[c]	1911–1950	1951–1965	1911–1950[b]	1951–1965[c]	
Jan.	16.06	14.80	6.26	7.59	—	—	26.6
Feb.	18.30	16.58	7.32	7.72	—	—	26.4
Mar.	19.56	16.94	9.32	8.02	—	—	34.3
Apr.	17.32	15.48	8.52	6.12	4	1	34.1
May	17.54	14.73	10.62	4.69	6	2	27.9
June	17.60	15.66	10.91	5.47	4	1	28.9
July	10.54	15.55	5.63	4.64	13	1	7.9
Aug.	10.60	15.85	5.52	5.60	14	0	21.3
Sept.	14.55	14.97	7.62	4.97	6	1	37.9
Oct.	14.43	12.56	7.32	3.85	3	2	59.9
Nov.	16.06	13.54	8.57	5.54	5	3	29.6
Dec.	16.87	14.45	8.09	6.06	—	—	35.4

Sources: Columns (1)–(3) adapted from Ministerio de Obras Públicas, *Resumen de aforos,* Vol. 8–Cuencas del Júcar (1966); and subsequent annual reports. Column (4) Ministerio de Obras Públicas, Centro de Estudios Hidrográficos, *Necesidades hídricas de los cultivos en los planes de regadío integrados en la cuenca del Júcar* (Madrid, December 1967).

[a] Drought exists when the mean monthly flow is less than 8 m³/s.
[b] Observations are missing for parts of 1933-1934 and 1934-1935.
[c] Observations are missing from October 1957 to September 1960.

Table 2.2 Months and years in which discharges from Generalísimo Dam exceeded inflows, 1952–1968.

	1952	1953	1954	1955	1956	1957	1958	1959
Jan.						X		
Feb.								
Mar.		X				X		
Apr.		X	X	X		X		
May		X	X	X			X	
June	X	X	X				X	X
July	X	X	X	X	X	X	X	X
Aug.	X	X	X	X	X	X	X	X
Sept.	X	X	X		X		X	
Oct.	X	X		X	X		X	
Nov.	X	X		X				
Dec.						X		
Annual	X	X	X					

Source: Ministerio de Obras Públicas, *Resumen de aforos,* Vol. VIII–Cuencas del Júcar (Madrid, 1966) and subsequent annual reports.

motor. Having developed the groundwater, they would sell it by the hour to themselves as shareholders and to other farmers. Profits were distributed among the shareholders. In other cases the irrigation communities themselves developed the groundwater. There are no reliable data on the quantity of groundwater extracted, but it is small in relation to the amount of river water.

The canals' diversion dams in the river have been damaged or destroyed by floods and subsequently rebuilt many times. In response to the last major flood, in 1957, which inundated a large area of the city, caused eighty-two deaths, and left some 20,000 people homeless, the national government adopted a scheme, the so-called Plan Sur, to relocate that sector of the river channel that flowed through the city. A new channel, some 12 km in length and between 175 and 200 m wide with a capacity of 5000 m³/s, has been built south of the city, entering the Mediterranean 3 km to the south of the river's natural outlet. The abandoned channel in the city is being developed for transportation and other public uses as part of an urban renewal plan. These works have involved considerable disruption of the huerta's traditional irrigation distribution systems. Several diversion dams have been replaced, sections of several of the canals and laterals have been realigned, and 400 ha of irrigated land have been taken out of production for the new channel.

The inner huerta of Valencia is surrounded by irrigated lands that are quite

1960	1961	1962	1963	1964	1965	1966	1967	1968	Total
							X		2
	X	X				X			3
	X		X			X			5
	X			X					6
	X		X	X	X		X	X	10
	X	X	X	X	X		X	X	12
	X	X	X	X	X	X	X	X	16
X	X	X	X	X	X	X	X	X	17
X	X	X	X	X	X	X	X	X	14
			X	X				X	8
				X				X	5
X									2
	X		X	X			X	X	8

different in their crops, water supplies, operating procedures, and organization. To the west and north in the piedmont slopes above the level of the canals, a large area is planted almost entirely in oranges and irrigated with groundwater. This area has grown remarkably over the last twenty years. The crop is grown largely for export to Western Europe and is the basis of an important regional agribusiness. The farms are on the average three times as large as in the huerta, but approximately half the area is in large estates of 2.5 to 20 ha.

Water is supplied from large wells. For estates larger than 10 ha the landowner will normally own and operate his own well. The vast majority of farmers, however, obtain their water from a well company, in which they are likely to own shares. Such a company typically operates one well that supplies water to 25 to 75 ha.

Some 2500 ha of the Turia basin that lie to the southeast of the old huerta are devoted to rice culture, requiring special methods of water management. Fields must be flooded during several months of the year and drained periodically—in February, June, and September. From 65 to 70 percent of the land is in farms of less than .5 ha, and only 5 percent is in properties larger than 5 ha.

THE CANALS OF THE OLD HUERTA

Each of the canals of the old huerta has a defined service area and abstracts a fixed proportion of the river flow to supply this area. The service areas and the

Table 2.3 Service areas and water supplies of the canals of the huerta of Valencia.

(1) Canal	(2) Service Area, 1828. Lands with rights only (ha)	(3) Service Area, 1965 (ha)		
		(a) Lands with Rights	(b) Lands without rights	(c) Total
Moncada	3,190	3,190	3,810	7,000
Cuart[a]	1,540	1,526	—[b]	1,526
Tormos	913	945	—	945
Mislata	847	769	—	769
Mestalla	1,159	900	—	900
Favara	1,552	1,054	2,056	3,110
Rascaña	784	720	580	1,300
Rovella	515	415	93	508
Total	10,500	9,519	6,539	16,058

Sources: (See note 1, chapter 2 for full citations.) Columns (2) and (5): Borrull, *Tratado de la distribución,* especially p. 38, n. 49. Column (3): Registro general de aprovechamientos, Comisaría Central de Aguas, Ministerio de Obras Públicas, Madrid, 1967. The data for Moncada are provisional, the others definitive. Column (4) Burriel, *La huerta de Valencia,* pp. 134–143.

[a] Includes service areas of Benacher and Faitanar canals.
[b] Approx. 438 ha in Manises and Aldaya, which are not under jurisdiction of Cuart canal, are served from Cuart turnout.

proportions of river water were defined in the Middle Ages. The water alloca-tions were related to the needs of each canal—for irrigation, mills, and certain urban uses in Valencia—and they have remained constant to this day. The service areas have been remarkably stable for long periods of time. However, two of the canals, because of their location, have been under constant pressure to expand their service areas: Moncada on the left bank and Favara on the right. From early times these canals have provided water to certain zones that were not within their original confines. These "new" farmlands, however, have not had the same rights to water as the original ones; they receive only "excess" water (*sobrantes*), that is, water in excess of the needs of old lands.

The careful definition of canal service areas sets apart lands entitled to irri-gation water (*tierras de regadío*) from adjacent dry lands with no such rights (*tierras de secano*) and from lands with rights to excess water only (*extremales*). Canal water cannot be sold or otherwise transferred from regadíos to other lands. In Valencia water is tied to land.

Column (2) of table 2.3 shows the service areas of the eight principal canals as reported in 1828. The total for the huerta, 10,500 ha, is approximately the

(4) Service area, 1967. Right bank canals; lands with rights only (ha)	(5) Water Supply	
	(a) Withdraws from right or left bank of river	(b) Percentage of river flow
—	Left	34.75
1,414	Right	10.15
—	Left	7.25
570	Right	7.25
—	Left	10.15
883	Right	10.15
—	Left	10.15
300	Right	10.15
—	—	100.00

same as a figure reported in 1653; and the 1830 data were repeated in studies published subsequently in 1864, 1884, and 1944. In about 1965 the Ministry of Public Works in Madrid recorded in its official register the service areas of these canals as of that time, and those figures are given in column (3). The figures, however, fail to account for the recent, dramatic, and destabilizing impact on the huerta of the urban growth of Valencia. In 1967 Burriel made a painstaking study of the official land registers of the canals on the right bank of the river. He found that almost 30 percent of their traditional service area had been absorbed by urban growth and the new river channel. His data for the right bank canals are given in column (4) of table 2.3. The closer the canal to the city, the greater the percentage loss of land. Although we have no detailed information for the canals on the left bank, it is clear that the march of urbanization does not apply equally to their service areas, for the city has expanded on the opposite bank and the new channel is located there. Nor do these factors apply to the rice and citrus zones on the periphery; citrus has expanded rapidly over the same period.

Some officials and commentators believe that the Turia River dams have eliminated for all time the necessity for procedures for extraordinary drought, but such a prediction is optimistic in our view, if drought is defined, as it has been in Valencia for some time, as a flow of less than 8m³/s at the Moncada canal.[3] It may be, however, that the recent diminution in the huerta's area means that this definition is too high, that the huerta does not suffer if it receives less than this quantity of water. In this case there has been an important reduction in threat of drought, which is due to urbanization as well as to upstream storage. [Extraordinary drought procedures were, in fact, put into effect in 1975.]

GOVERNING INSTITUTIONS

The irrigators of seven of the canals have formed irrigation communities whose governing institutions, which determine and carry out the canals' operating procedures, are similar but not identical from one canal to the next. In addition, the irrigators have formed a committee and a court (*Tribunal de las Aguas*) that enable them to act cooperatively on certain matters and to coordinate their joint actions with those of the Moncada community, which does not belong to the inner huerta coordinating groups and is governed by an internal organization that varies somewhat from the others. The principal characteristic of these institutions is local autonomy in formulating operating procedures and in choosing administrative officers.

The typical irrigation community includes all holders of land with rights to water in a canal's service area. Each landholder—but no farmer who is a renter or sharecropper—is entitled to one vote in the community's legislature or general assembly (*junta general*), although his right to canal water and his share of the community's expenses for maintaining and operating the canal are measured roughly in proportion to the land he owns. The assembly, which meets every two years, votes on proposed changes in the canal's policies, rules, and regulations (*ordenanzas*) concerning water distribution, canal maintenance, and other matters; on taxes for major replacements and new construction; and on officers to administer the canal's affairs.

The assembly elects an executive committee (*junta de gobierno*) to conduct the canal's business until the assembly meets again. This committee consists of four to eight delegates (*electos*), each representing the users of a given lateral or zone of the service area. In the past, landowners who resided in the city of Valencia, frequently absentee landlords, were permitted to elect several delegates in each community in recognition of the central importance of the city to its huerta, but this practice is no longer followed. To avoid conflicts of interest, the delegates may not be in debt to the community or involved in a lawsuit with it and in some cases they may not be irrigators served by other canals lest the interests of the two canal communities conflict. Thus, for example, officers of the Favara community, which in certain of its zones uses runoff and return flows from the Rovella canal, may not own irrigated land in the Rovella service area.

The executive committee is chaired by the canal's chief administrative officer, its syndic (*síndico*). The syndic is elected by a majority of the general assembly for a period of two years and he frequently is reelected. He must be a landowner who works his farm in the canal's service area and he cannot own a mill that uses canal water. The syndic is chief regulator of the distribution of water to the supply laterals of the network and ultimately to its farms. He works within the norms established by the ordinances and the executive committee, but, as we shall see, he has considerable discretion in times of extraordinary drought.

The executive committee interprets the canal's ordinances, determining the specific operating procedures to be used in given situations. Committee members from each zone give special advice on the application of these procedures to the areas they represent. The committee has supervisory responsibility for canal maintenance, especially annual silt removal, and decides when the canals will be shut down for this purpose and who is to do the work. It sets the annual assessment rate for the canal's operation and maintenance. Finally, the executive committee hears complaints of users against the canal's employees and in some cases the committee apppoints these employees from names proposed by the syndic.

The syndic represents his canal community in questions common to it and other communities of the huerta, especially the division of river water among the major canals. The principal institution for this purpose is a commiteee of the syndics of the seven canals (frequently called *Tribunal de Acequieros de la Vega*), which normally meets on Thursdays in Valencia at the conclusion of sessions of the water court, on which the syndics also serve. In this committee the syndics decide when to institute operating procedures for seasonal low water and for extraordinary drought, and thereafter they cooperate in the actions necessary to put these procedures into effect.

Finally, the syndic, as a member of the water court, is a judge. The Tribunal de las Aguas is what the Spanish call a popular court, to be distinguished from the ordinary courts that compose the judicial power of the state. As such, the court's jurisdiction is limited and its forms and procedures are unconventional.

The jurisdiction of the water court is defined by the ordinances of the several canals, which specify precisely the categories of actions to be judged as violations (for example, taking water out of turn, flooding a neighbor's field, or installing an unauthorized canal check) and the penalites to be imposed.

The court's authority is confined for the most part to controversies between farmers of the communities that are members of it, to questions concerning water and its use, and to questions of fact, not law. Its power does not extend to questions of property—the farmland itself, but since water creates property values in an irrigation environment, this restriction is less limiting than it might appear to be. (In rare cases the court's jurisdiction extends to third parties who infract community ordinances.)

Accepting the jurisdiction of the water court is not obligatory. Farmers who have been charged with violating a canal's rule can elect to be tried in the ordinary courts. But they rarely do so, preferring the less costly and more informal procedures of the popular court. Once farmers choose to be tried by the popular court, however, as almost all do, they cannot appeal its decisions.

As for the court's unconventional forms and procedures, the judges are not legal professionals, but men of the soil (*hombres del campo*), elected by fellow farmers. The court is free, there are no lawyers, and except for a small charge for the serving of a summons and occasional fees paid to expert witnesses court expenses are not charged to the parties. The proceedings are oral in the Valencian language and conducted in public. The jurisdiction is summary—decisions are handed down immediately after evidence has been presented.

Actions against those who violate the ordinances can be brought before the water court by a canal's guards or by a farmer whose crops have suffered damage. The complainant takes his accusation first to the canal community's syndic, who inspects the site immediately, frequently in the company of experts previously designated by the community. If the infraction affects several farmers, the syndic will try to reconcile their interests. If he cannot do so or if the infraction affects the broader interests of the community, he will order the guard to instruct the accused to appear before the court on the following Thursday. The ordinances require that charges be made shortly after an alleged violation—ten days in Favara, three in Mislata—so that evidence will be available to establish facts and assess damages.

The Tribunal de las Aguas meets every Thursday morning at 11 o'clock outside the Apostles' Door of the Cathedral of Valencia to hear all charges made in the preceding seven days. The president conducts the interrogation if the alleged violation occurred in a community on the opposite side of the river from the community that he represents; otherwise the questions are put by the vice-president, who represents a community on the bank opposite that of the president. The presiding officer first questions the complainant and then the accused, trying to determine the facts. He may interrogate witnesses or experts if either party so requests and he may question the syndic of the relevant canal about his on-site inspection (*visura*) of the alleged violation. The facts having been developed in this way, the judges, excluding the syndic from the canal in question, confer immediately, without leaving the bench, and give the court's decision. Although the decision process takes place in full public view, we have never met an observer who has heard and understood what the syndics say to each other when they confer. (In rare cases the court suspends judgment so that further site inspection can be carried out.)

If the court finds the accused guilty, it sentences him to pay fines and damages according to the particular ordinances of his community. The fines are small, since they remain those that were prescribed in the ordinances several centuries ago, but the amount assessed for damages may be considerable. The court also will require that the guilty party repair any canal he has obstructed or otherwise damaged. The sentence, although not the proceedings, is recorded subsequently by the secretary of the court.

The sentence is enforced by the canal's syndic; and guilty farmers almost invariably pay the fines and damages and take other required measures without the need of any further action by authorities. If for any reason a farmer does not conform, the court, through the relevant syndic, has adequate enforcement powers. The syndic can turn off the farmer's water until he complies or he can take the farmer's property in payment and sell it at public auction; but no official today can recall a recent case in which either procedure has been necessary.

In addition to the syndic, the following officers and employees of a canal community have important duties in connection with operating procedures for distributing water. Guards (*guardas*) regularly patrol the canal and its laterals to ensure that the channels carry the maximum water available and needed by the irrigators. On orders from the syndic, they operate the canal's principal control structures on the river. They close floodgates when the river is extraordinarily high. In times of low water they set headgates to ensure that their canal gets its proper share of river water and inspect the control structures of the other canals to ensure that they are not taking more than their due. Guards also operate the control structures of the principal laterals, opening and closing them on the days they are to receive water. It is principally the guards who cite irrigators for violating the canal's rules. They appear as accusers before the water court, where their testimony on the facts is given great weight. The principal guards are likely to be permanent, full-time employees, and the ordinances of one of the canals provide specifically that guards may not be cultivators of land. The job is frequently passed down from father to son. Extra guards may be employed in times of drought.

Ditch riders (*atandadores*) assist the syndic in distributing water when it is in short supply, instructing one farmer when to close his headgate and the next when to open his. These men are farmers along the laterals, or in the zones, that they serve. Although they are responsible to the syndic, their nomination is frequently left to the irrigators of their areas, who for this purpose form a special assembly. Each canal also has a secretary and a part-time lawyer.

The ordinary expenses of each canal community are covered by a uniform annual assessment on each unit of land that is entitled to irrigate, whether or not it does so. Extraordinary expenses for major works of improvement are assessed in the same way, but these must be voted by the canal's general assembly, whereas ordinary taxes are set by the executive committee. A supplementary source of income are the charges the canals collect from industries and other commercial interests in return for permission to build over water channels and to discharge waste water into them.

SHORT-TERM OPERATING PROCEDURES

The basic operating procedure of the canal communities is that for ordinary low water. Procedures for abundance and extraordinary drought are modifications of it.

Periods of Ordinary Low Water

In periods of ordinary low water all farmers share water shortages in proportion to the number of hectares with rights to water that they irrigate. This is accomplished by lengthening the time between deliveries of water. When the water reaches a farmer he takes what he needs, but he will have to wait longer than in periods of abundance for the water to return for the next irrigation of his fields.

When the committee of syndics institutes the regime for ordinary low water, each of their canals can abstract from the Turia only its assigned share. This procedure is enforced by requiring that the canals take water only through their principal control structures and by setting the gates of these structures so that they divert fixed proportions of the river flow. Normally it is the syndics of the three lower canals—Favara, Rascaña and Rovella—who propose instituting this regimen, while those of the upstream canals tend to oppose it. Once the regimen is voted the syndics of the three lower canals assemble at a place on the river below the Moncada canal, where they measure the water. They then proceed downstream, setting the headgates of the canals to correspond to the river flow. The other syndics meet them, each at his own canal. The gates of the last two canals—Rascaña and Rovella—remain completely open; they divide the water that remains in the river after the others have taken their shares. Dividing the river among the canals in this way is called *reparticiónes de agua*.

The water is subsequently divided and further subdivided into many separate streams by means of canal divisors (*lenguas*)—permanent and frequently ungated structures built in the canal bed. With the aid of this control device, which is typical of the Valencia huerta, thirty or more fields located in different parts of a canal's service area can be irrigated at the same time and the canal's water, whatever its quantity, is divided automatically into fixed proportions that are related to the areas served by a large number of laterals.

In addition, a number of canals practice rotations among principal sectors and laterals of their service areas. Typically these canals are divided into three sectors. All laterals that are supplied from the first sector of the canal and all farms that take water directly from the canal in this sector will irrigate on Mondays and Tuesdays, for example, those in the second sector, on Wednesdays and Thursdays, and those in the third, on Fridays and Saturdays. The time allotted to each sector is roughly proportional to its service area. Such rotations, or waterdays (*tandas, jornadas*), are especially important on a long canal, for without them water, even when it is abundant, may not reach the end of the canal with a sufficient head to ensure efficient delivery to laterals and farms.

In the canals that do not irrigate by sectors, there may nonetheless be a rotation among the principal laterals, each with assigned waterdays, or with certain days or hours when a lateral may not open its headgate. Such rotations are also practiced in some instances among sectors of the principal laterals.

In canals that practice rotations there are frequently some laterals, called *corribles*, that are always open, taking water whenever it is available in the channel. If they are located in the first sector of the canal, they will have continuous water. If they are in the last, the right to remain open means only that the lateral will receive, in addition to full flow on the days when the rotation is with its sector, any surplus flows not used by upstream sectors on their waterdays.

To effect rotations, control structures must be gated, unlike the divisors that typically are always open. Gated structures (*partidores*) are padlocked and only the canal's guards have the keys and the authority to open the principal laterals, whereas ditch riders open the secondary channels and close them when the last irrigators have taken their water.

The two methods of dividing water among laterals and canal sectors—repartition and rotation—and the control structures associated with each are used frequently in intricate combinations to distribute a canal's water supply. To illustrate, the Bennager canal is part of the Cuart system. The first laterals that draw from this canal are two small ones, with rights to continuous water, serving approximately 13 ha each. Shortly thereafter the water encounters its first lengua by which it is divided into two continuous streams in two laterals. The right lateral receives one-third of the water and is called *Terç,* meaning one-third in Valencian. With the aid of a gated control structure, Terç then supplies two regions. Water is run in a lateral to Alacuás on Wednesdays and Thursdays and in one to Picaña on the remaining days of the week.

The two-thirds of the water that flows into the left lateral of the first divisor is separated subsequently into two equal streams by a lengua called the White Cross. Immediately the left one of these streams is further divided into two equal parts, and each of these then supplies smaller laterals and farms by turn, one after the other. The right lateral at the White Cross supplies four channels that run water in succession, one day each.

This system is interrupted every Thursday for sixteen hours when all the water available at the White Cross is diverted to a single lateral called Thursday (*Dijous* in Valencian) that serves 12 ha and irrigates at these hours only. For two weeks in a row the sixteen hours are those after sunrise on Thursday; for the third week they are the hours before sunrise on Friday, an arrangement designed to distribute the burden of irrigating at night. For the remaining eight hours on Thursdays the water is divided normally at the White Cross, but that flowing into the right lateral is given each week in succession to one of the four channels served by that lateral in order to preserve the proportions and the timing used normally in that service area.

Finally, canal officers may, in periods of ordinary low water, transfer water from one or more of the smaller laterals to another. Their discretion in this regard is prescribed by a general criterion for action and certain specific constraints. The general criterion, which is stated in different ways in the several ordinances, provides that water may be transferred if the farms served by one lateral need water whereas those in another would not suffer if deprived of it. This criterion is derived from a more general principle, also to be found in the ordinances, that all farmers have an obligation to give aid to those who have the greater need. The transferred water is called favor water (*agua de gracia*).

The constraints, which are used in different combinations in the eight canal communities, are the following. Canal officers must consult with the users of all affected laterals or with their representatives before acting. Favor water is given only to laterals practicing rotation among themselves. If a lateral has irrigated lands without rights in the current or preceding rotation of its regular water, it is not entitled to favor water. Favor water may not be used on lands without rights. Favor water is limited to one-third of that available in the donor lateral or laterals.

On days when water is running in a lateral (or sector of a canal) those farmers who want to irrigate will take it in turn (*por turno*), generally in order from the head to the tail of the channel. Once a farmer opens his headgate, he takes all the water he needs, without any restriction of time; and he defines his own needs, principally in terms of the water requirements of the crops he has chosen to plant. The only limitation is that he may not waste water. If a farmer fails to open his headgate when the water arrives there, he misses his turn and must wait for the water to return to the farm on the next rotation. When a lateral operates in rotation and all users who want water at at given time cannot be served before the rotation passes to another lateral, distribution will begin, when water returns, at the point where it previously terminated.

In the huerta of Valencia lands on one side of a lateral or canal frequently are higher than those on the other. To serve these high lands (*alteros*) it is usually necessary to install canal checks (*paradas*) that raise the level of the water in the canal and to limit withdrawals to the high lands only while the checks are in place. The operating procedures specify the days or hours when high lands can be served.

In the regimen of ordinary low water, lands without water rights may not be irrigated. If a farmer who owns both types of land applies canal water to any of his fields that are without rights he will be fined, denied the right to use favor water, and, in some canal communities, denied all water in the following turn. It is at this time that owners of lands without rights will start up their standby well pumps if they have them.

Favor water need not be distributed in regular turns, however; it goes to those fields most in need, regardless of the normal order. Canal officials make the decisions here, but they are subject to the several constraints mentioned above. There are specific fines for misusing favor water, and in the Favara canal, for example, a farmer who does this can be deprived of further right to favor water for one month. For a second offense he will be deprived of this right for a period determined by the canal's executive committee.

Periods of Extraordinary Drought

For periods of extraordinary drought the water users of Valencia have devised ingenious steps to enable the canal communities to continue distributing water according to the basic principle of the huerta: that water is supplied to each farmer in proportion to the area of land he irrigates, modified by the water requirements of the crops he has planted on this land, these requirements to be defined by the farmer subject to surveillance by the canal's officers. As drought becomes more and more extreme, however, the effective discretion of the individual farmer to define his requirements becomes more limited, and ultimately the rule that water is supplied in proportion to land has to be abandoned.

Distribution to the canals of proportionate shares of river water, initiated in the regimen of ordinary low water, continues in drought. When the syndics of the seven canals declare a regimen of extraordinary drought, three additional steps are taken, however. The first is designed to increase the utility of the limited water available in the river channel below the Moncada canal. It requires that the canals on the right and those on the left banks of the river alternate in taking water, each bank irrigating for two days at a time. This measure does not increase the volume of water that would otherwise be abstracted by each canal, for while it doubles the water in the canal at any time it halves the time it is available. It does ensure, however, that farmers will receive more of this volume in usable irrigation water than they would otherwise. Without this measure it would be difficult to raise the canal's water to the level of farm turnouts and to reach turnouts at the ends of delivery routes. This measure is applied, the Valencians say, to double the water (*doblar el agua*). To initiate *la dobla,* the syndics flip a coin to determine which canals—those of the right or of the left bank—are to receive water for the first two days.

Once the syndics have doubled the river, they effect a second measure, this one designed to increase the volume of water available to the seven canals of the inner huerta. Since the fourteenth century Valencia has had a right during drought to limit water abstractions by certain small upstream communities, known as the *pueblos castillos.* Under this procedure, called a *tandeo,* the pueblos open their headgates for four days, during which Valencia receives, as in other seasons, water in excess of the needs of upstream users. But the pueblos must close their gates for the subsequent four days so that Valencia will receive all river water. This limitation on upstream diversions was imposed initially because of factors related to both time and location. The upstream huertas developed and expanded later than Valencia's and their upstream locations give them better access to water at all times.

Although the ordinances of Valencia's canal communities direct the several syndics and guards to mount the river and close down the headgates of the pueblos once the syndics have decided on a rotation of the river, the procedure cannot in fact be enforced so simply. Valencia must petition and obtain the support of higher authority, initially the king's representative in the region, subsequently various provincial officers, today the national government's watermaster (*comisario de aguas*) for the Júcar and Turia rivers. These authorities have had to settle conflicting claims of downstream and upstream interests concerning the need to initiate a river rotation.[4]

The third supplementary step taken by the assembled syndics in time of extraordinary drought is designed to redistribute river water within the huerta—between the first canal, Moncada, and the four most downstream canals, two on each river bank, that suffer most severely when the river is low. This rule, also an ancient one, called *tablones de Moncada,* provides that on Monday and Tuesday of each week Moncada is to give up one-quarter or one-half of its water, depending on the severity of the extraordinary drought. For this purpose water is measured at Moncada's control structure and that part that is for the downstream canals makes its way there through a drainage channel that discharges into the river downstream from the diversion dams of the three huerta canals not entitled to this water. As there is no automatic criterion for deciding whether Moncada must give one-quarter or one-half of its water and because Moncada does not participate in the committee of syndics that decides to institute this procedure, enforcement of the rule has given rise to numerous controversies between the downstream canals and Moncada. These were frequently settled in the past by provincial authorities, but for some years now the national government's watermaster has been the decisionmaker, as in the case of the pueblos castillos.

The canals that practiced rotations among their laterals during ordinary low water continue to do so in extraordinary drought, but they may need to alter their procedures because the canals will receive water only on alternate two-day periods. At this time and for this purpose the Favara community, for example, divides its canal into two sectors. The first distributes water to all its laterals on the initial two-day period. When water returns to Favara and other canals of the right bank, after a two-day lapse, it will be restricted to the laterals that irrigate from the second sector. Moncada similarly divides its service area into two sectors; the sector nearest the river irrigates on the two days when Moncada passes a portion of its water downstream, the farther and longer sector, on the remaining five days when water is more abundant.

The authority of canal officers to transfer water among laterals is used more frequently in drought than in periods of ordinary low water. The canal syndic, the delegates who represent different areas on the executive committee, and the ditch riders of the relevant laterals make a reconnaissance of the comparative water requirements of the laterals' service areas and transfer water to those with the greatest need. In estimating need, however, the criterion governing the canal officers' discretion is defined more precisely and additional constraints are added.

As the water supply diminishes, the time between successive irrigations may become so long that the normal procedure, allowing each farmer to take all that he needs when the water reaches him, will have to be modified if all or most farmers are not to lose their crops. Valencia's first modification has been to impose a time limit—typically fifteen minutes for each half hectare. This procedure, called *quart per cafisá,* is enforced by the ditch riders, who open and close all farm turnouts, clock in hand. On any given day of drought, time limits may be operating in some canals and not others and in some laterals of a canal and not others.

As a quarter-hour of water is not sufficient to irrigate a half hectare, farmers must concentrate all of the water to which they are entitled on a portion of their farms, on those crops that would suffer the greatest losses if they were not irrigated. To make this decision farmers must consider the following factors: the net market values of the crops, their stages of development (for example, if certain crops can be harvested after two or more irrigations whereas others that are generally more valuable require several more waterings, the early harvest crops might be favored, since future supplies are highly uncertain), the capacities of different crops to withstand water shortages (for example, if certain crops would become total losses without their proximate irrigations whereas others would lose only 20 percent of their marketable value, the former might be irrigated), and long-term losses as a consequence of crop failure (for example, loss of fruit trees represents a greater long-term economic cost than that of annual crops).

A second modification of the normal operating procedure for distributing water among farms has been to give priority to certain crops and in any rotation to deny all farmers water for nonpriority crops so long as any one of them has not had the opportunity to irrigate those in the preferred class.[5] If there is insufficient water to meet the needs of all farmers for their priority crops, preference is given to those priority crops that, based on inspection by canal officers, are in greatest need of water. When crop priorities are in effect, canal officers, in transferring favor water, are not to leave in any lateral sufficient water to irrigate nonpriority crops as long as another lateral does not have enough to irrigate those with priority. The crops that traditionally have been given priority vary somewhat from community to community, but they include the crops of greatest economic value, meaning that the marginal returns of applying water to these crops and denying it to others are believed to be greater for the canal's service area as a whole than if the classes were reversed. To put it another way, the economic loss of failing to apply water is believed to be greater for priority than for nonpriority crops. In recent years it has not been necessary to use these procedures that limit time and crops, but they remain in the ordinances and can be called on at any time.

During periods of drought the permanent rules against wasting water are enforced more rigorously and an additional rule is put into effect: no farmer may irrigate unless he has built ridges (*caballones*) in his fields.

Finally, certain special uses of canal and lateral water are given absolute priority over crop irrigation as follows. The Rovella canal supplies water for sanitation in the city of Valencia and the ordinances provide that however great the drought in the river a given quantity of water must be delivered for this purpose. When wheat is threshed on stone or concrete floors, it is necessary to keep these wetted down, and water for this purpose is to be made available as needed. After a farmer harvests hemp, he cures it in a water-filled concrete basin on his farm, and water to fill these basins has high priority. (There is little hemp in the huerta today.) Farmers have authority, under the national water law, to take water at any time for domestic uses, provided they do not use mechanical devices to withdraw it.

Table 2.4 Simulation of Valencia irrigation system, with adequate seasonal water supply and full production.

	Farm				
	1	2	3	4	5
Crop Production (q.m.)					
Early potatoes	48.0	240.0	168.0	240.0	192.0
Peppers	21.5	0.0	21.5	107.5	0.0
Cabbage	30.0	60.0	0.0	150.0	30.0
Onions	0.0	270.0	0.0	240.0	60.0
Oranges	0.0	25.0	0.0	50.0	0.0
Late potatoes	0.0	75.0	15.0	150.0	45.0
Corn	11.2	56.0	33.6	16.8	22.4
String beans	0.0	8.0	4.0	20.0	8.0
Water used (m^3)	1,481	9,924	4,131	12,893	5,387
Crop value (ptas.)	42,595	264,525	88,985	362,205	122,990
Total costs (ptas.)	24,900	117,200	46,400	183,600	57,800
Net value (ptas.)	17,695	147,325	42,585	178,605	65,190

Periods of Water Abundance

Basically when water is abundant all principal canals, all their supply laterals, and all irrigators on each lateral take the water they need approximately when they need it. And since abundant water is likely to be in excess of the needs of lands with rights, fields without rights can also be supplied.

Even where water is abundant, however, the distribution network may not be sufficiently large or elaborate to serve all farms that demand water at the same time. Some form of operating procedure, or scheduling, is required because of the mechanics, or more properly the hydraulics, of distribution. Thus in some canals the procedure of rotations and repartitions among laterals that is common during ordinary low water is continued when water is abundant; in other canals this procedure can be relaxed. In most cases farmers along a lateral will continue to take water in turn, but the waiting period between successive turns will be short (seven to twelve days). Thus operating procedures for periods of water abundance may be complex, but this should not obscure the basic characteristic of water distribution in this season, namely that farmers get the water they want approximately when they want it.

An important question is how frequently each of the canals uses the procedures associated with each of the three regimes. Unfortunately, data for a pre-

| Farm | | | | | |
6	7	8	9	10	Total
72.0	48.0	48.0	24.0	72.0	1,152.0
0.0	43.0	43.0	21.5	21.5	279.5
30.0	30.0	90.0	60.0	90.0	570.0
60.0	0.0	90.0	120.0	120.0	960.0
0.0	0.0	0.0	0.0	25.0	100.0
30.0	30.0	0.0	15.0	15.0	375.0
11.2	5.6	16.8	11.2	11.2	196.0
0.0	0.0	4.0	4.0	8.0	56.0
2,587	2,082	3,335	2,865	4,425	49,110
69,795	59,735	112,455	95,795	136,720	1,355,800
31,600	35,400	59,700	45,600	67,700	669,900
38,195	24,335	52,755	50,195	69,020	685,900

cise answer are not available. Prior to 1950 there was seasonal low water or drought almost every year, and some or all of the procedures associated with drought regimes were used in several canal communities. Since then river regulation, combined with reduction of service areas due to urbanization, has reduced drastically the necessity for using these procedures, but they remain on the books and they can and likely will be used occasionally in the future.

Simulation of Short-Term Procedures

To demonstrate the effects of Valencia's several procedures on the production and income of huerta farms, we have used the simulation program, with many simplifying assumptions about cost and benefit functions and operating procedure details. The basic data on farm size, crop patterns, yields, costs, and returns can be found in the appendix to this chapter. We assume that farms 7 through 10 are without rights to water—they are extremales—and that early potatoes, vegetables, onions, and oranges are priority crops, while late potatoes, corn, and stringbeans are nonpriority. Table 2.4 shows crop production, water use, and gross and net farm income when the turn distribution procedure is used and there is sufficient water to achieve full production of all crops, that is, a regimen of abundance. Table 2.5 reports the results when there is a moderate

Table 2.5 Simulation of Valencia irrigation system with moderate water shortages. Extremales, farms 7–10, are not watered during periods of shortage.

	Farm				
	1	2	3	4	5
Crop Production (q.m.)					
Early potatoes	48.0	240.0	168.0	240.0	192.0
Peppers	21.5	0.0	21.5	107.5	0.0
Cabbage	30.0	60.0	0.0	150.0	30.0
Onions	0.0	270.0	0.0	240.0	60.0
Oranges	0.0	25.0	0.0	50.0	0.0
Late potatoes	0.0	75.0	15.0	150.0	45.0
Corn	11.2	56.0	33.6	16.8	22.4
String beans	0.0	8.0	4.0	20.0	6.8
Water used (m³)	1,481	9,924	4,131	12,893	5,297
Crop value (ptas.)	42,595	264,525	88,985	362,205	122,150
Total costs (ptas.)	24,900	117,200	46,400	183,600	57,800
Net value (ptas.)	17,695	147,325	42,585	178,605	64,350

shortage of water that occurs during several irrigation periods—overall 12 percent less water than is delivered for full production. Under the procedure of ordinary low water, farms 7 through 10 may not irrigate on any turn until farms 1 through 6 have been watered. The regional or total net income of all farms is reduced by 26 percent, almost all of which is borne by the nonpriority farms 7 through 10.

Table 2.6 is based on a 20 percent water shortage and simulates drought conditions. Both farm and crop priorities are in effect. Water is given first to priority crops on the farms with rights to water, next to nonpriority crops on these farms, and thereafter, if any remains, to the farms with rights to excess water only. (We have not simulated the additional drought constraint that all farms are limited to fifteen minutes of water for each half hectare, but the final results would not have been significantly different had we done so.) The net income of all farms is 39 percent below full production. Nonpriority farms 7 through 10 all show net operating losses, and they account for 90 percent of the regional reduction of income below full production. Farms 1 through 4, on the other hand, achieve full production. The reductions in income of farms 5 and 6 are due in part to their location in the distribution system, for it will be observed that they lose production of early potatoes and onions as well as of nonpriority crops.

Farm					
6	7	8	9	10	Total
61.2	23.5	0.0	4.1	33.3	1,010.1
0.0	34.4	34.4	18.3	16.3	253.9
30.0	26.3	72.9	54.0	90.0	543.2
54.0	0.0	0.0	0.0	108.0	732.0
0.0	0.0	0.0	0.0	19.1	94.1
30.0	0.0	0.0	9.6	11.4	336.0
9.0	0.0	0.0	5.7	1.8	156.5
0.0	0.0	2.9	3.4	1.4	46.5
2,587	1,127.43	821.67	1,576.5	3,528.83	43,367.43
63,111	33,667	45,285	38,607	103,851	1,164,981
31,600	33,100	52,900	40,850	65,900	654,250
31,511	567	−7,615	−2,243	37,951	510,731

LONG-TERM OPERATING PROCEDURES

Water shortages are of two types: short term, caused primarily by climatic conditions in one or several successive growing seasons, and long term, caused principally by increased demand for water in response to continued expansion of the irrigated area. Proportionality is, as we have seen, the basic principle of Valencia's short-term operating procedures. But if limited water is distributed in proportion to land holdings, then of necessity there will be a restrictive definition of lands that can be served, for otherwise water would come to be divided into parts so small as to be useless. Thus the benefits of the short-term operating procedures are enjoyed by those who hold lands with water rights. Irrigable lands without rights but within reach of a canal's distribution network enjoy only the uncertain benefits of excess water and adjacent lands out of reach of the canal's laterals are either dry or irrigate exclusively with wells.

Priority, based on time of settlement, is the foundation of the long-term operating procedure. Generally the extremales and *secanos* are without regular canal water because they were developed as farm fields at a date later than those with rights. Valencian tradition since the thirteenth century has regarded the huerta as fixed by the limits adopted in the time of the Moors. In 1368, for example, the king, at the request of the jurates (municipal administrative

Table 2.6 Simulation of Valencia irrigation system with drought conditions. The first five crops are priority crops and are watered first on farms with rights. Extremales, farms 7–10, receive water only after farms with rights are fully watered during periods of shortage.

	Farm				
	1	2	3	4	5
Crop Production (q.m.)					
Early potatoes	48.0	240.0	168.0	240.0	165.1
Peppers	21.5	0.0	21.5	107.5	0.0
Cabbage	30.0	60.0	0.0	150.0	30.0
Onions	0.0	270.0	0.0	240.0	55.5
Oranges	0.0	25.0	0.0	50.0	0.0
Late potatoes	0.0	75.0	15.0	150.0	45.0
Corn	11.2	56.0	33.6	16.8	17.9
String beans	0.0	8.0	4.0	20.0	6.8
Water used (m³)	1,481	9,924	4,131	12,893	5,287
Crop value (ptas.)	42,595	264,525	88,985	362,205	109,823
Total costs (ptas.)	24,900	117,200	46,400	183,600	57,800
Net value (ptas.)	17,695	147,325	42,585	178,605	52,023

officers) of Valencia, ordered compliance with a previous stricture against widening the Moncada canal.[6]

Given the Valencian principle that marries land to water so that water cannot be transferred from lands with rights to the other classes, the key to long-term growth or other adjustment of irrigation is the development of a larger water supply. Pressure for measures to accomplish this has come from outside the canal communities, from landowners who want to convert their extremales and secanos into regadíos, and also from within the communities, from those members who own both fields without and with rights.

The Valencians have sought over the years to enlarge their water supply by limiting upstream diversions from the Turia River, such as those of the pueblos castillos, promoting the construction of works to divert water to the Turia basin from the Júcar River on the south, promoting the construction of storage works on the Turia, and tapping groundwater as was done in the inner huerta by the wells dug in the 1920s and in the citrus regions of the piedmont by more recent industry. Interest in these measures has run high in drought years, tapering off when the rains returned. Thus, with regard to the major works in particular, it has been difficult to sustain sufficient interest to carry them through the typi-

6	7	8	9	10	Total
44.1	0.0	0.0	3.3	0.0	908.5
0.0	31.0	31.0	17.4	15.5	245.4
30.0	25.0	81.0	49.9	72.9	528.8
54.0	0.0	0.0	0.0	0.0	619.5
0.0	0.0	0.0	0.0	19.0	94.0
20.4	0.0	0.0	0.0	0.0	305.4
6.4	0.0	0.0	0.0	0.0	141.9
0.0	0.0	3.0	0.0	0.0	41.8
2,527	385	1,478.33	536.5	364.17	39,007
53,323	24,409	46,550	27,544	42,705	1,062,664
31,600	31,600	52,900	38,450	57,700	642,150
21,723	−7,191	−6,350	−10,906	−13,995	421,514

cally long periods of surveying, planning, and negotiating that precede the start of construction.

Plans for works to transfer water from the Júcar to the Turia were drawn and considered in the Middle Ages.[7] During a drought in the 1370s the city council and jurates of Valencia appointed a commission and also hired levellers to locate a diversion dam and interbasin canal. The survey report, completed in 1376, was favorable and the council, having heard arguments for and against it, adopted the report and resolved to proceed to the next steps: to obtain a concession from the king to invade the Júcar, to reach agreement with the "lords, villages, and residents" of the places through which the canal was to pass, and to negotiate agreements among prospective beneficiaries of the project, principally the farmers of the huerta, on apportionment of costs and on operating procedures for water distribution. In 1393 the king granted the city the right to take water from the Júcar at the town of Tous and conduct it to the Turia for irrigation purposes so long as the landowners on the route of the proposed canal were reimbursed for their confiscated property. There followed numerous efforts to conclude the subsequent agreements, but these did not succeed and in 1401 the project appears to have been abandoned. It was restudied and considered seriously again in the sixteenth century, several times during the seventeenth, and subsequently.

In the middle of the twentieth century construction began on a vast project designed on the premise that the water resources of the Júcar and Turia basins should be considered together. This project includes storage dams on the Júcar and its tributaries and on the Turia and an interbasin canal to transfer so-called excess water in the Júcar to the Turia. Thus, after six centuries of planning, Júcar water is about to penetrate the Turia basin; but at this late date it is no longer much needed in the ancient huerta of Valencia. The regulating reservoirs on the Turia, combined with the shrinkage of the huerta, have reduced its needs. The new water will be used instead on lands surrounding the huerta and on others that are some distance from it in Liria and Sagunto. (Actually, water diverted from the Júcar will enter the Turia below the Turia's storage reservoirs and will be used in the Valencia huerta in exchange for Turia River water that will then be diverted to the newer zones.) In some cases it is to be used to convert dry lands to irrigation and in others to firm up existing surface water supplies or to substitute surface water for groundwater. Some of the citrus growers, however, prefer their groundwater to the promised canal water. Although it requires capital to develop and is on an annual average more expensive than canal water, groundwater is highly dependable where the wells are deep, the well owners have access to their water supplies at all times, and they can sell any excess water. Unlike surface water, groundwater is not tied to the land in Valencia. Furthermore, the citrus zone, unlike the ancient huerta, has no irrigation communities. The supply and distribution of irrigation water, which are the business of such organizations elsewhere, are handled in the orange orchards by private well companies.

Although the Valencians showed some interest in the Middle Ages in capturing the waters of two spring-fed lakes in the headwaters of the Turia—one at Tortajada, the other at Santa Cruz—serious plans for building storage reservoirs on the river that feeds their huerta were developed only in the nineteenth century. They were not brought to a head at that time in part because foundation conditions at the site proposed for a mainstream dam were considered inadequate.

In the late 1920s proprietors and others interested in the development of lands close to the huerta, especially in the plain of Liria, organized to promote the construction of a large storage dam on the Turia. At the same time the city of Valencia was seeking additional water from the river to meet the needs of its growing population. The huerta's irrigation communities opposed both efforts initially and a lengthy negotiation ensued, its principal phase brought to conclusion in 1933 with inauguration of construction of the Generalísimo Dam.[8] The negotiations involved various organizations of water users and potential users of the Turia River, the city and the province of Valencia, the Ministry of Public Works in Madrid and its regional hydraulic office in Valencia, the council of ministers, and others; and at each stage the huerta was effective in promoting its interests and protecting them from outside influence and control. Thus the several royal and ministerial orders that authorized construction of the dam and abstraction of water by the city pending the dam's completion protected the irrigators' rights and gave them a high priority for the stored water, which is used today, in order of precedence, for domestic purposes in Valencia, irrigation of lands with rights in the huerta of Valencia and certain existing upstream huertas, irrigation of lands without rights in these huertas, and new irrigation zones, although little water remained for this last purpose until the Loriquilla Dam was built downstream. In case of drought for which the Generalísimo reservoir has insufficient water to meet all of these needs, the newly converted lands are to be deprived of water before the older lands suffer much more than inconvenience.

Thus the principle of priority by time of development was preserved, for the rights of the lands newly supplied with full canal water are inferior to those of the old regadíos. The short-term procedures described have also been preserved. What has changed is the probability of having to use the procedures of extraordinary drought and ordinary low water.

COMMUNITY OBJECTIVES

We should be fortunate if we had for the purpose of this discussion the results of a historical set of farmer opinion surveys. Lacking this, there is nonetheless sufficient evidence to justify conclusions with regard to irrigation community objectives. This evidence is found in the ordinances and other official documents of the canal communities, the published reports of visitors to the area, and Maass's observations.

Equality

The canal communities say that their regulations are for the purpose of ensuring that all members enjoy the benefits of irrigation water with equality (*igualdad*) and equity (*equidad*). They use equality in two senses. Insofar as it refers to participation of landowners in determining the canals' operating procedures, the meaning is absolute equality—one man, one vote. For convenience this aspect of equality is discussed below as a separate objective. When the term is used in reference to the quantity of water provided to farmers, however, it means proportionate equality. The procedures are intended to guarantee that all users are favored equally in case of abundance and that all suffer equally in drought; but equal in this sense means in fixed proportion to the relative needs of crops in the farms and service areas of the several laterals and canals. Stripped of its refinements, the basic technique used to enable all farmers to share the costs of drought in this proportion is to lengthen the intervals between successive irrigation turns as the water supply gets shorter and shorter.

When equality is viewed in this way, one can ask if proportionate equality has much to do with social justice. Is it not more directed toward increasing the income of the huerta—efficiency, that is—than toward distributing or redistributing this income according to a chosen criterion? The basis of proportionality is, after all, the needs of crops, not those of men or their families. Since all landowners of Valencia have an equal voice in determining their operating rules, one might expect them to adopt a procedure that aims directly to equalize income. Whether or not they do this, however, is likely to depend, among other factors, on the initial distribution of wealth, or as a surrogate for this, of irrigated land. For when farms are of equal size, the distribution of water by proportionate equality can be at the same time efficient, in terms of increasing income of the region, and just, in terms of how this income is distributed. We have seen that variation in the size of irrigated farms is remarkably small in Valencia—over 99 percent of them are less than 5 ha, so that either or both objectives could be the intended meaning of igualdad.

It could be argued that small holders are likely to prefer a procedure that ignores inequalities or even promotes them if they have high hopes of becoming large holders. Given conditions for owning and transferring property in land and water in the old huerta, such hopes would be unreal today. But there are opportunities in the piedmont that surrounds the huerta on the northwest, and some huerta farmers have acquired orchards in this area and as a consequence appear to be less attached than they were previously to the old huerta's procedures.[9]

Equality thus defined applies to members of the irrigation community only, and for them only to those of their lands that have rights to water. Whereas proportionate equality is the basic principle of the short-term procedure, security, based on priority of development, is a key to the long-term one; and the tradeoff that Valencians have set between equality and security is represented by the three classes of lands with differentiated rights. There is ample evidence that Valencians consider the form of security that has evolved to be just and proper.

Equity

Equity is used in Valencia as a standard for administrative conduct. It means that canal officers, wherever they have discretionary authority, should be guided by a general sense of fairness, apart from specific provisions of the ordinances. As for the steps of the short-term operating procedure, the transfer of water among laterals would appear to relate to equity by its very name: agua de gracia. To justify the procedures for favor water, the ordinances say that all farmers and all laterals have an obligation to aid each other, giving water always to those who have the greater need. Similarly, several of the requirements that must be met before the canal officers can transfer water—the receiving lateral may not have irrigated lands without rights in the current or preceding rotation, it must be practicing rotations with related laterals, the canal officers must consult with the users of both the giving and receiving laterals—are motivated by fairness. The criterion of need in extraordinary drought, that the water requirements of the most valuable crops must be met before other crops can be irrigated, has the sound of efficiency rather than equity, to be sure. But if it or some similar criterion were not used because it was not considered equitable, all farmers would lose almost all of their crops, which would be a perverse achievement for equity.

Efficiency

There is little demonstrated concern for efficiency in the written and oral traditions of Valencia. Although the operating procedures do in fact foster efficiency, efficiency is infrequently made explicit as a community objective. No one admits to believing that the best procedure is one that maximizes income for the region.

Procedures intended primarily to extract a greater duty from water are obviously efficiency oriented. The dobla, for example, simply delivers water in a more efficient way. To a significant degree the procedures for rotation of water among the principal laterals of a canal are for the same purpose. Proportionate equality, the basic criterion for most steps in the short-term operating procedure, serves efficiency, as do time limits and crop priorities, the criteria to which the communities have switched in the past when drought was so extreme that large numbers of farmers would suffer nearly complete loss of their crops if proportionate equality were continued.

It may be that Valencians make no distinction between social justice and efficiency, that they equate efficiency with justice so completely that they do not find it necessary to demonstrate any connection between the two, for there is no tradeoff between them. Variations in farm size are not great in the huerta. Income redistribution is not an objective in the allocation of irrigation water. When the ordinances say that water should be distributed with equality and equity, they may mean simply with efficiency, laced by fairness.

On the other hand, there may be a different reason that Valencia's farmers fail to mention efficiency, even though they practice it, a reason that has its origin in their antagonism to market institutions. If farmers could sell water for individual turns, for a crop season, or without a time limit, the water market would direct the transfer of water among canals, laterals, farms, and crops; and if it operated properly, the market would do this efficiently. But the sale of water or of the rights to water is anathema to Valencians, where water is married to land and cannot be divorced from it. Spanish communities that allow divorce are both benighted and immoral in their view. The farmers attach considerable importance also to their claim that water is "free" in their huerta, compared to other "less fortunate" areas where water is sold.[10] Valencians, in other words, prefer elaborate administrative procedures in the short run and prohibitions against water transfers in the long run to an efficiency-oriented market. They fear market imperfections, especially that moneyed men who are not resident farmers could buy sufficient water to be able to control its price and the destinies of irrigators.

What about groundwater in this context? There are private wells in the huerta and its environs, and their owners sell water in violation of the Valencian rite. In part this is due to the technology of producing irrigation water from underground. In most countries the rules and rights relating to groundwater differ from those for streams, as they do in Spain's national water law. It would be interesting to know, however—and we do not know—to what extent the irrigation communities have shut their eyes to private development and sale because they believe that the dangers of market imperfections are less for well water than for surface water or that the efficiency benefits of private vis-à-vis public development and control of groundwater are great enough to outweigh the dangers of monopoly and speculation in it.

The long-term procedure, also, may be compatible with efficiency over a larger area. Applying Ricardo's land law, one can assume that the most productive lands were settled first and that, in the absence of a free market to allocate water, an administrative procedure to protect the water rights of the old lands is efficient. Apart from the specifics of the administrative procedure, the principal question relating to this assumption is whether technological developments since early settlement have changed the relative productivity of the old and new lands. On the one hand, the huerta lands have not been exhausted by a millenium of cultivation, Valencian farmers have a great reputation for fertilizing their fields, and the river water has been rich in soil nutrients. On the other, the old lands are more highly parcelized than those recently settled and this has made it difficult for huerta farmers to take advantage of machinery and new farming techniques. A simple comparison of the sales prices of the several classes of land would not show their comparative productivity as farmlands today, unfortunately, because the value of water rights is capitalized in the value of lands that enjoy them, because huerta lands are being converted increasingly to urban uses, because groundwater is being used increasingly, but not uniformly, outside of the huerta, and similar factors. Given these complications, we do not have the data to make the more elaborate analysis necessary to determine if the long-term procedure has been efficient as well as just in the sense of offering security to those who first invested their labor and capital.

Conflict Resolution

A principal objective of Valencia's farmers in determining procedures for allocating and distributing irrigation water and in establishing institutions to operate these procedures has been to mute conflicts among neighbors—that is, among users of the same canal, among the several canal communities of the huerta, and between huerta and upstream users. With regard to conflicts among neighbors, the organization and procedures of the canal communities, including their common water court, have controlled the disruptive tendencies inherent in a situation of chronic uncertainty of water supply. The community organizations have successfully embodied individual irrigators' needs for cooperation. The close collaboration of the syndics of the seven canals in the water court has facilitated the resolution of conflicts and potential conflicts among the communities that they represent. The Tribunal de Acequieros, as the syndics frequently call themselves when meeting as an administrative body rather than a judicial one, has for centuries spoken with a single, strong voice for the inner huerta.

As for relations between the inner huerta and surrounding communities, the Valencians have had great success in promoting as the basis for conflict resolution the concept that customary users, particularly those of traditionally autonomous groups, are entitled to preference in water use. This principle has helped solve conflicts with the pueblos castillos, with those who would irrigate the Liria plain, and with other upstream users, as well as with the Turia canal and additional groups of users downstream. It has not helped solve conflicts between the inner huerta and the first upstream canal (Moncada), however, for Moncada's rights are also ancient; and until recently conflicts between Moncada and the seven canals of the water court have been among the most persistent ones in the region.

Popular Participation and Control

We have seen that all landowners have an equal vote in a canal community's general assembly and that this assembly approves the canal's operating procedures, elects the executive committee whose members represent the principal service areas of the distribution network, and chooses directly or indirectly the canal's administrative officers. Furthermore the farmers of each lateral constitute a limited community, with equal votes, to choose ditch riders and special guards. Attendance at the general assemblies varies greatly, as one would expect. In times of extraordinary drought and controversy it may be a considerable percentage of the qualified voters, but normally it is small.

The short-term operating procedures for Valencia, both the normal procedure of proportionate equality and the extraordinary procedure of crop priorities, have subjected the farmer to considerable arbitrary authority of canal officers, according to several keen observers of the area. Andrés Llauradó says that division of water in the huerta of Valencia is characterized by the continued intervention of the syndic's agents, who are called upon to value the state of need of the harvests as well as the supplementary (favor) water needed to alleviate them. Maurice Aymard notes that Valencia's farmers pay a high cost for their freedom to choose their own crops. They are subject to the constant supervision of canal officers because an operating procedure consistent with a variety of crops requires considerable flexibility; it cannot work automatically. Jean Brunhes has likened the drought procedure of crop priorities to the declaration of a state of siege by a military commandant, in this case the canal syndic—a true dictatorial situation.[11] And others have noted the large number of canal officers —guards and ditch riders—needed to administer the procedures.

These judgments exaggerate, we believe, both the quantity of discretion in the hands of canal officers and the extent to which the discretion can be exercised aribtrarily—that is, outside of popular influence and popular control.

In the first place, the adjustment of the operating procedure to increasing drought is gradual, taking place through many small steps, the last few of which only can be considered to require discretionary authority. Even in the case of extraordinary drought canal syndics may not have to resort to crop priorities, which Brunhes describes so harshly or even to a great amount of transferring of water among laterals. The measures taken by the syndics to increase the quantity of useful water in the principal canals—rotation of canals on the right and left banks of the river, aid for the huerta from the upstream pueblos castillos, aid for the most downstream canals from Moncada—and the imposition of time limits within each canal community may satisfy the needs of the moment with little loss of freedom to the huerta's farmers.

Second, the farmers participate in selecting the officers and in applying the procedures. The syndic (Brunhes's commandant) is an elected farmer. Before ordering the transfer of water among laterals, the syndic consults the representatives on the executive committee of the affected zones. When strict conformity to rotations and turns becomes necessary, the syndic appoints special ditch riders, who are farmers nominated by their peers in the zones where they serve. This gives the farmers within a lateral, where some must come to the aid of others, a sense of collaboration and collective responsibility.[12]

Third, the criteria and the constraints controlling the canal officers' discretion become more, rather than less, specific as water becomes shorter and the potential effects on the farmers of the exercise of this discretion become greater. We have seen this in the case of rules relating to water transfer.

Fourth, the ordinances control in considerable detail the general conduct of canal officers. They specify the fines that are to be assessed against officers and employees for failure to perform their assigned duties. And there are numerous other controls.

Fifth, the institutions for appeal by a farmer against the actions of a canal officer become more active as the potential effects of the exercise of discretion become greater. The ordinances of the Favara canal provide, for example, that the executive committee of elected representatives must meet twice weekly during periods of drought so that farmers can bring in complaints and receive prompt satisfaction for any that are legitimate.

Sixth, the many steps of the short-term operating procedure are so consistent with each other that the whole has a remarkable harmony. While it is true that the procedure is complex and elaborate and requires a number of canal employees to carry it out, its coherence and integrity open the way for easy comprehension, and therefore control, by the farmers.

The irrigators of Valencia consider it important in terms of self-government that land and water cannot be divorced in the huerta, and there is in fact a relation between the form of water rights and the objective of popular participation and control. The owners of lands with water rights can organize local, autonomous water institutions without challenge from those who do not own such lands because the latter cannot own or acquire any interest in the water itself.

Can the farmers maintain this popular participation and control when the state enters to finance and build a major storage dam that changes the regimen of the river? According to Wittfogel's thesis, a major public work like this should bring dictatorship from the center and the suppression of local influence and control. The experience of the huerta of Valencia, with water made available as a result of construction of the Generalísimo Dam, presents an excellent opportunity to test the thesis.

In the first place, the dam, by storing water that was previously wasted to the sea in wet periods, has reduced drastically the need for invoking the procedures for ordinary low water and extraordinary drought, and to this extent it has reduced the probability that farmers' freedom will be limited by officers of the huerta's irrigation organizations. Their freedom has been enlarged.

To evaluate the huerta's participation in and control over decisions relating to the construction, finance, and operation of the dam, we discuss both the general Spanish procedure of hydraulic administration and the special procedures used in the Turia Valley.

By the beginning of the twentieth century and more than one-third of a century before the United States proclaimed many of the same principles in creating the TVA and in the Flood Control Act of 1936, the Spanish had developed a hydraulic policy (*política hidráulica*) that included the following concepts: public ownership of water, but not necessarily of the right to use water (this had been written into the national water law of 1866, a law modeled largely on the principles and procedures of the Valencia huerta); multiple-purpose planning and development of water resources; unified responsibility in one government agency for the planning and development of water resources; decentralization of this responsibility by major and related river basins—one river, one problem; and reciprocal and mutual cooperation between the national government and organized local interests in the planning and development of water resources.[13]

Our interest focuses on the last of these, which the Spanish have sought to implement by a hierarchy of representative organizations. On the broad base of irrigation communities and syndicates of industrial and municipal users of water, the hydraulic policy has proposed to build supercommunities (*sindicatos centrales* and *mancomunidades*), formed with representation from the lower level, for the administration of hydraulic works whose influences exceed the jurisdictions of the first-order organizations, and hydrographic confederations, again with representation from the lower levels, in each of the regional offices through which the national government conducts its water resources development activities.

Turning to the Turia River basin, the council of ministers gave its opinion in the preamble of a 1927 royal order that the most efficacious way to ensure harmony and good order in the Turia would be the formation of a hydrographic confederation. In 1934 a confederation was organized for the Valencia regional office of the Ministry of Public Works, which had jurisdiction over the Júcar and certain other streams, as well as the Turia, but Valencia's irrigation communities did not join. Nor did they form a separate confederation for the Turia, although the ministerial order establishing the Júcar confederation included a provision to encourage this. The Valencians were suspicious of a new and additional level of representation. They preferred to rely on their capacity to influence river basin development through direct relations with professional personnel in the regional offices and in Madrid and direct influence on representative political institutions in the provinces and Madrid.

In an order of 1931, the minister of public works called for the creation of a supercommunity, representing all prospective users of the newly authorized Generalísimo Dam, to assess the costs of building the dam and regulate the distribution of water stored by it. Given this more specific purpose and their growing support of the dam, the Valencia irrigators helped to organize a supercommunity, the *Sindicato de Regulación del Río Turia*. It took them three years to reach agreement with the other interests on the organization and rules of the community, however; and the most striking characteristic of the regulations that were adopted are the repetitive provisions for protection of the rights of existing irrigation communities and for preference to them in the use of "new" water to be stored behind the dam. In the community's general assembly, for example, delegates from irrigation communities of the old huerta were given one vote for each unit of land, whereas those from communities in the proposed new zones were to have one vote for each two, and in some cases six, units.

When the president of the Republic came to Valencia in April 1932 to inaugurate construction of the dam, he signed a decree confirming the autonomy and jurisdiction of the Tribunal de las Aguas and recognizing its administrative authority over water that as a consequence of construction of the dam would flow into the canals of the inner huerta. On the same day he signed a decree naming the dam Blasco Ibáñez after the Valencian writer whose novels on the huerta and its water court, especially *La Barraca,* were known throughout Spain and the world. The name Generalísimo was given to the structure after the civil war.

The supersyndicate has been concerned more with the financial than the operating procedures of the dam. For the latter purpose, and after the dam was completed, the regional hydrographic office in Valencia established a committee on reservoir operations with representatives of irrigation communities and of hydroelectric and other users, as well as the administration. This committee, presided over by a representative of the government, recommends how much water should be released through the dam, given the operating norms relating to preferences and the hydrologic situation and forecast. The chief engineer of the regional office has the authority to release the water, however, and he need not necessarily follow the advice of the committee. Furthermore, he receives this advice more typically by direct communication with users than as a consequence of committee meetings. At their weekly sessions after the water court, the huerta's syndics frequently discuss and reach agreement on the current needs of their canals for reservoir water and communicate this directly to the *confederación*.

In conformity with the first principle of hydraulic policy, that river water is public property, the national government developed a program for recording and controlling all abstractions from Spain's major streams. The water law of 1866, which incorporated this principle, provided that existing users were entitled to continue their withdrawals in accordance with traditional methods and forms. Thus, although the government made no serious efforts to record abstractions from the lower Turia River until the Generalísimo Dam was in operation, there has never been any question that Valencia's inner huerta canals have preferred rights for the use of river water. But there has been in recent years profound disagreement between the canal communities and the government over the form in which these rights should be recorded and controlled.[14] The government's procedure is to specify a community's right in terms of a fixed quantity or flow of water—in liters per second (l/s). Their experts determine the water requirement for irrigating a typical hectare, given the crops that typically are grown; and they multiply this by the size of the service area. For Valencia the water requirement has been figured as 0.7841 liters per second per hectare (l/s/ha), and the service areas that have been recorded are those given in table 2.3, column (3).

The Valencia canal communities, except Moncada, have opposed the government's efforts to limit their rights to specific quantities of water. As ancient users, they argue, they are entitled, by authority of both the water law and the orders that authorized construction of the dam, to continue to withdraw water from the river by the method they have always used, that is, by aliquot portions of river flow measured at the Moncada diversion dam—specifically, those given in table 2.3, column (5). However, Moncada canal joined the opposition, the government, in this matter; so the contest has been between the seven canals represented on the water court on the one hand and the government and Moncada on the other. The reason for this can be discerned from the data presented in table 2.3. By its traditional right, Moncada withdraws approximately one-third of the river's water for approximately one-third of the huerta's lands with rights; but if lands without rights are included, Moncada's third of the water must serve over 40 percent of the lands. Under a concessional system that recorded rights for both regadíos and extremales, Moncada's water would be exactly proportional to its service area.

The supreme court settled the matter in 1963 in favor of the government, and the government has proceeded to record canal rights, or concessions, as they call them, in liters per second. By 1969 the Ministry of Public Works had registered concessions for lands with traditional rights, the regadíos in table 2.3, column (3a), and was prepared to amend these to include the lands that do not enjoy old rights, the extremales in column (3b), as soon as the canal communities began to pay their assessments for dam construction, which are for the provision of firm water to this latter class of lands.

The concessions have been registered, then, but they have not been enforced. The canals continue to withdraw water from the river by the traditional technique. In order to enforce a system of withdrawals based on fixed quantities of water, it is necessary to rebuild the canals' ancient turnouts, installing in them modules that measure and control water in liters per second. The concession documents include a provision that the government reserves the right to require the installation of such modules "when it considers it to be opportune to do so"; but the canal communities have resisted any tampering with their turnouts. The Plan Sur has made it necessary to relocate the turnouts of the last three of the inner huerta's canals as well as that of the Turia canal. The national government's initial plans called for replacing the several canals' individual turnout structures and principal channels with two canals, one on each side of the new riverbed, each new canal serving all laterals and lands within its reach in a rational and efficient manner and without regard to the canal communities to which the lands had belonged. The communities protested that these plans infringed on their ancient concessions, so the government, with its plans to modernize and rationalize the irrigation distribution system, collided squarely with "all of the weight of an organization that is ancient, popular, and considered to be just and almost perfect." [15] Needless to say, the plans were changed. The government has reproduced as nearly as it can in the new river channel the conditionals that prevailed in the old one.

The national government is also finding it difficult to enforce its policy on concessions for the lands that have been without rights. The extremales of the Favara canal, for example, more than 2000 ha on the east or downriver side of that canal's service area, have never been registered in the canal community's official books and have never paid taxes to the community. The government wants the Favara community to register these lands, collect taxes from them, and reimburse the government for the benefits provided to these lands by the Generalísimo Dam. The community is prepared to register the lands under certain conditions, but it will not agree to assume an obligation to pay charges that accumulate before the owners of the excess lands begin to pay taxes to the community. The owners of the extremales have resisted joining the canal community, for they have been receiving the benefits of the dam without doing so.

Viewing these events in Valencia can we say that the farmers have been subjected to the demands of a Madrid agromanagerial bureaucracy over which they have no control? Clearly not. Through years of monarchy, republic, and dictatorship; of codification in the civil law tradition and systematic destruction of local privileges (fueros); of the national government's indifference toward, and concern for, water resources development in the region local influence and control have remained great. Wittfogel's thesis does not apply to Valencia.

Brunhes has argued that the high degree of farmer control he observed in Valencia at the turn of the century, greater he judged than that in many other regions of Spain and North Africa, was due in part to the lack of good dam sites near the huerta. Where dams are built, he said, water is likely to be separated from land and farmer control over water distribution eroded.[16] A comparison of Valencia 1968 with Valencia 1900 does not support the Brunhes thesis any more than Wittfogel's. We shall return to this thesis, however, when we study more of the data on which Brunhes based it (particularly, the Huerta of Alicante, where a dam was operating in 1900).

Alice Foster, an American geographer who studied Valencia in the early 1930s, suggested a modification of Brunhes's thesis, namely, that the construction and operation of dams will erode or prevent farmer control over water distribution, but only if the dams are built before the farmers have had the opportunity to establish autonomous and stable institutions and procedures for water control.[17] This modified thesis is a good fit for Valencia; but is it necessarily true that farmers cannot acquire a large degree of control over water distribution in regions where irrigation has always depended on the delivery of reservoir water? Since she studied Valencia only, Foster cannot answer this.

APPENDIX: SIMULATION OF IRRIGATED FARMS IN THE HUERTA OF VALENCIA

Simulation Procedures

The basic distribution rule used in Valencia is the Turn, in which each farmer, once the water reaches his turnout, takes all he needs for the period before the next farmer is served. If delivery is interrupted, the turn commences again where it last terminated.

Turn is one of the basic procedures of the irrigation simulation program described in our USDA Technical Bulletin No. 1431. It can be used in combination with several other procedures, which is the case in Valencia.

When in ordinary low water and in drought, water is denied to lands without rights, this is simulated by assigning priority to all farms that have rights. Non-priority farms do not receive water until all priority units have been irrigated.

When in drought, water is provided for certain crops only, this is simulated by assigning priorities to the crops, which are then watered in order of priority until the water supply for the period is exhausted.

Where farms use well water to supplement their entitlements to lateral water, this is simulated by using Demand procedure in combination with the Turn procedure. The farmer can vary his demand for groundwater from one irrigation period to another.

Program Designations With reference to table 9, Principal Distribution Rules, of Bulletin 1431, the following programs are used to simulate Valencia operating procedures:

Water Supply	Description of Procedure	Procedure Code
A. Surface water		
Abundant	Turn	2
Ordinary low water	Turn *subj. to* Farm Priorities	6
Extraordinary drought	(Turn *subj. to* Farm Priorities) *subj. to* Crop Priorities	16
Abundant in early season, becomes ordinary low water	Turn; turn *subj. to* Farm Priorities	6 (Farm priorities activated when shortages occur)
Abundant in early season, becomes extraordinary drought	Turn; (turn *subj. to* Farm Priorities) *subj. to* Crop Priorities	16 (Farm priorities and crop priorities activated when extraordinary drought occurs)
B. Surface water plus well water		
Abundance	Turn + demand	4
Ordinary low water	Turn *subj. to* Farm Priorities + Demand	7
Extraordinary drought	(Turn *subj. to* Farm Priorities) *subj. to* Crop Priorities + Demand	17
	(Turn *subj. to* Farm Priorities + Demand) *subj. to* Crop Priorities	17 (Replan)

Basic Data

The simulation uses twenty-six two-week periods corresponding to a calendar year's operation of the system. Table A2.1 shows the water supply distribution over the year. The farm sizes used in the simulation runs are given in table A2.2. The crop pattern for the huerta as a whole is shown in table A2.3; the distribution of these crops among the ten farms used in the simulation is shown in table A2.4. The yields, costs, and returns used in the simulation are given in table A2.5. These represent area averages for this region of Spain during the mid-1960s.

Table A2.1 Irrigation water supply used in simulation.

Irrigation period	1	2	3	4	5	6	7	8	9	10	11	12	13
% of water	6	3	7	3	8	5	4	6	4	3	3	3	4
Irrigation period	14	15	16	17	18	19	20	21	22	23	24	25	26
% of water	3	5	4	4	3	2	4	3	4	2	2	2	3

Table A2.2 Farm size used in simulation related to distribution of farm size in huerta of Valencia.

Actual Farms		Simulated Farms	
Irrigated ha	% of all farms	Farm no.	ha
Less than 1	83	1	.3
1–5	16	2	2.0
Over 5	1	3	.8
		4	1.0
		5	.5
		6	.7
		7	.4
		8	.7
		9	.6
		10	.9
Total	100		7.9

Table A2.3 Typical crop pattern in huerta of Valencia.

	% of hectares	
Crop	Early	Late
Potatoes	50	25
Onions	33	—
String beans	—	15
Corn	—	35
Peppers	13	—
Cabbage	—	20
Oranges	4	4

Table A2.4 Initial crop pattern on simulation farms (in hectares planted).

Crop	Farm 1	2	3	4	5	6	7	8	9	10	Total
Early potatoes	0.2	1.0	0.7	1.0	0.8	0.3	0.2	0.2	0.1	0.3	4.8
Late potatoes	—	0.5	0.1	1.0	0.3	0.2	0.2	—	0.1	0.1	2.5
Onions	—	0.9	—	0.8	0.2	0.2	—	0.3	0.4	0.4	3.2
String beans	—	0.2	0.1	0.5	0.2	—	—	0.1	0.1	0.2	1.4
Corn	0.2	1.0	0.6	0.3	0.4	0.2	0.1	0.3	0.2	0.2	3.5
Peppers	0.1	—	0.1	0.5	—	—	0.2	0.2	0.1	0.1	1.3
Cabbage	0.1	0.2	—	0.5	0.1	0.1	0.1	0.3	0.2	0.3	1.9
Oranges	—	0.1	—	0.2	—	—	—	—	—	0.1	0.4

Table A2.5 Yields (in quintals) and costs and returns (in thousands of pesetas) for crops used in simulation of Valencia.

Crop	Yield	Preharvest cost/ha	Harvest cost/ha	Gross return/ha	Full production net return/ha
Early potatoes	240	20	10	72	42
Late potatoes	150	20	6	48	22.75
Onions	300	20	10	105	75
String beans	40	15	6	28	7
Corn	56	16	6	33.6	11.6
Peppers	215	60	15	107.5	32.5
Cabbage	300	60	10	107.25	37.25
Oranges	250	45	25	130	60

3 The Huertas of Murcia and Orihuela

As in Valencia, the quantity of water available at any time in the principal canals of Murcia is not fixed; it varies with the flow of the river. As a general rule, the principal canals of both systems are always open and receive fixed proportions of a variable river flow. The practice of rotations among the principal laterals or sectors of a canal is, however, more common in Murcia-Orihuela than in Valencia. The fixed days or hours of these rotations are determined principally by the areas to be served but also, and with considerable variation between the canals of Murcia and those of Orihuela, by topographical and soil factors that affect the procedure of irrigating and by time of land settlement.

It is in the delivery of water to farmers from the laterals that the operating procedures of Murcia-Orihuela and Valencia differ principally and this in a way that has an impact on how farmers share the costs of water shortage. In Valencia each farmer takes what he needs when the water reaches him and he cannot take again until all others have had an opportunity to irrigate and the water returns to his headgate on the next rotation. Under this procedure, called a *turno,* the farmer knows how much water he will receive when his time arrives, for he can keep his gate open until he satisfies his needs; but he does not know with certainty when the water will be available, for this depends on the requirements of his fellow farmers and on how rapidly these can be met, which depends in turn on the flow in the canal and lateral and on the weather. The farmers, therefore, by lengthening the interval between successive rotations, share any seasonal shortage of water in proportion to the needs of the crops they have planted. At a certain point this interval becomes so long, however, that most farmers would lose their harvests if the turno continued; and it is at this point that Valencia switches to an extraordinary procedure that gives preference to certain crops and uses.

In Murcia-Orihuela each farmer (in some cases group of farmers) has an assigned time period in which to irrigate. He takes the water that is available in the lateral at that hour, or whatever part of it he needs, and he cannot take again until his hour returns on the next rotation. The canal rotations are of fixed duration, frequently biweekly, but in the huerta of Orihuela, especially, certain canals have return periods that exceed three weeks. Under this procedure, called a *tanda,* the farmer knows when he will receive water, but he does not know with certainty how much he will get in his assigned hour, for this depends on the flow in the lateral at that time. He may receive enough water to satisfy the needs of his crops or he may receive much less. In the latter case he must decide how to use the insufficient water—on which fields and which crops. And his decision is based on his estimate of the availability of water in future rotations and his knowledge of the capacities of different crops to tolerate shortages and of the crops' relative market values.

The Contraparada, a diversion dam in the Segura River, which supplies the two distributor canals of Murcia.

The Barreras distributor canal, which delivers water to laterals in the southern part of the huerta of Murcia.

A variety of crops in the huerta of Orihuela.

The Huertos canal in Orihuela, with a typical sector canal check.

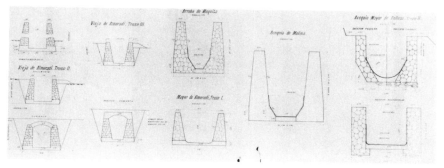

Cross sections of several canals in the huerta of Orihuela.

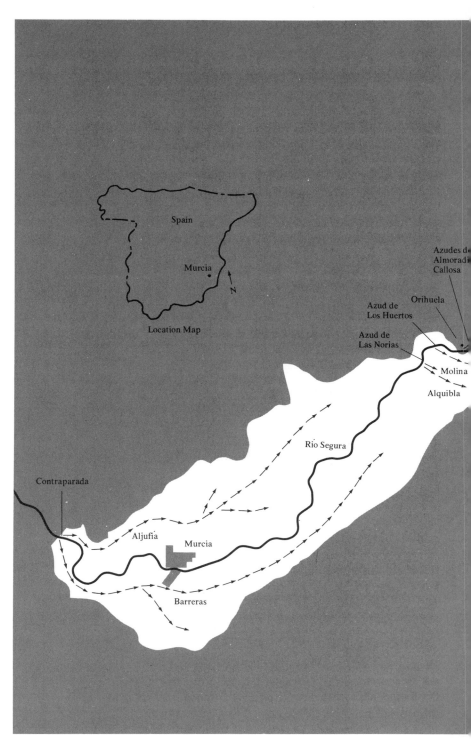

Figure 3.1   The huertas of Murcia and Orihuela.

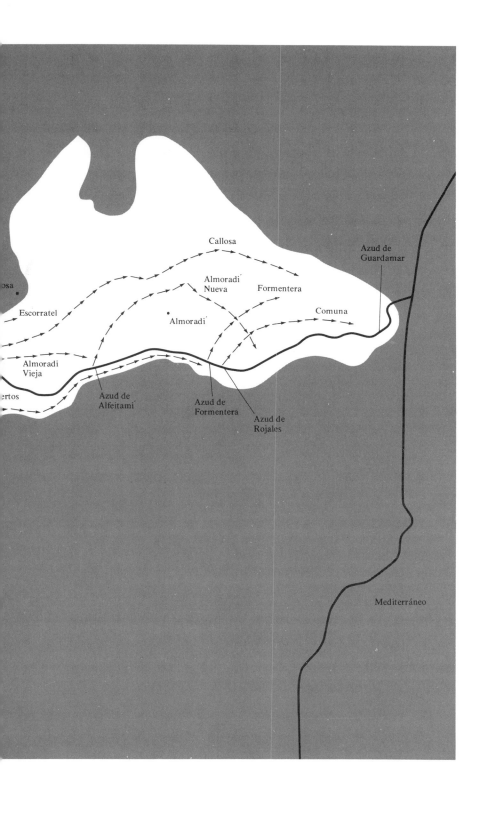

Callosa

Azud de
Guardamar

osa

Almoradí
Nueva

Formentera

Escorratel

Comuna

Almoradí

Almoradí
Vieja

ertos

Azud de
Alfeitamí

Azud de
Formentera

Azud de
Rojales

Mediterráneo

For most of the Orihuela canals there is no special procedure for extraordinary drought that gives preference to certain crops; the farmers adapt to the drought by their own decisions. In Murcia and several principal canals below Orihuela there are extraordinary procedures, however, that differ from Valencia's somewhat in preferred crops and uses and considerably in the timing and methods of their operation. The extraordinary regimes are in each case superimposed on a base representing the operating procedure of ordinary low water, and this base is very different for Valencia and Murcia.

When water is abundant in relation to demands for it, the irrigators of both Murcia-Orihuela and Valencia can largely ignore their basic procedures—the turno or the tanda; their freedom to take water is restricted only to the extent that limited canal capacities necessitate the scheduling of water deliveries. This chapter compares the operating procedures of Murcia-Orihuela and Valencia in terms of the mechanics and administration of the systems as well as the objectives of their irrigation communities. But first we provide a general description of the huertas of Murcia and Orihuela.

The huertas of Murcia and Orihuela constitute the principal irrigated areas of the middle and low valleys, respectively, of the Segura River, although there is no natural boundary, only a political one, separating the two (see figure 3.1).[1] The Segura, which runs from west to east in this region, forms a longitudinal axis of approximately 27 kilometers (km) for the Murcia huerta, dividing it into two equal parts that have an average combined width of 8 km and an area of approximately 215 km^2.

From its Murcia-Orihuela boundary the Segura flows some 50 km to the Mediterranean. The delta lands near its mouth and a good part of those south of the river in the low valley have been considered too marshy for good irrigation, so that the huerta of Orihuela, which covers approximately 250 km^2, has developed largely to the north of the river and upstream from the sea. Near the river's mouth there are several irrigation enterprises that pump from drainage canals large quantities of water that would otherwise waste into the sea. They sell this water in a service area that is largely outside of the Orihuela huerta.

The high valley of the Segura, the area drained by the river above Murcia, includes a number of smaller huertas that have grown rapidly in recent years. The Segura also provides spring and fall seasonal water for cereal culture in the regions of Lorca and Cartagena, but only after needs of the principal huertas have been met. Table 3.1 shows the lands irrigated in the three river zones and their relative growth over more than a century.

The climate of Murcia-Orihuela is mild and the soil of extraordinary fertility so that a large variety of crops is grown and two and sometimes three field crops can be harvested in a year. The main crops, as shown in table 3.2, are fruits, principally citrus (oranges and lemons) and pit fruits (peaches, apricots, and plums) but also apples, pears, quince, and table grapes; vegetables, principally artichokes and potatoes but also lettuce, tomatoes, cauliflower, squash, pepper, eggplant, melons, cucumbers, celery, green peppers, onions, and garlic; and

Table 3.1 Lands irrigated and to be irrigated in Segura River basin, 1835 to 1967, and present water supplies.

	Lands Irrigated (in thousands of ha)					Water for Lands in Column (5) (in Hm³/yr)	
	(1) Circa 1835	(2) Circa 1880	(3) 1933	(4) 1953 and 1967	(5) Future developments based on works under construction in 1967[a]	(6) Allocated by O.M. 1953	(7) "Theoretical" requirement
High valley-above Murcia	2.6	4.8	6.5	11.5	16.0	113	113
Middle valley-Murcia	10.4	10.8	12.2	13.5	18.0	148	217
Low valley-Orihuela and below	20.2	19.0	19.5	21.5	25.0	206	301
Cereal zones and other areas supplied with excess water	No data	No data	No data	34.0[b]	82.0[c]	66, if available	—

Sources: (See note 1, chapter 3, for full citations.) Column (1): For Middle and Low valleys, Mancha, *Memoria sobre;* for High valley, Belando, *El río Segura.* Column (2): For Middle and Low valleys, Llauradó, *Tratado de aguas,* vol. II; for High valley, Belando, *El río Segura.* Column (3): O.M. 25 April 1953. Columns (4) and (5): O.M. 25 April 1953; Ministerio de Obras Públicas, Centro de Estudios Hidrográficos, *Necesidades hídricas de los cultivos en los planes de regadío integrados en la cuenca del Segura* (Madrid, December,1967). Column (6): O.M. 25 April 1953. Column (7): For each valley, estimated annual water consumption in cubic meters per hectare for a typical hectare, assuming certain changes in crop patterns and 60 percent efficiency in water use (derived from *Necesidades hídricas,* pp. 105, 131, 161) multiplied by column (5).

[a]Does not include Tajo-Segura transmountain diversion project. See below.
[b]Consists of the following in hectares: 20,000 near Cartagena, Torrevieja, and the service area of Riegos de Levante; 12,000 near Lorca; 2,000 near Mula.
[c]The entire increase over column (4) of 48,000 ha is estimated for extensive irrigation only.

Table 3.2 Major crops on irrigated land in the huertas of Murcia and Orihuela.

Crop	Percent of land planted
Oranges	25.5
Lemons	18.0
Artichokes	17.0
Corn	8.5
Potatoes	6.5
Peaches	4.5
Alfalfa	4.5
Apricots	3.0
Beans	2.5
Melons	2.0
Tomatoes	1.5
Peppers	1.5
Vineyards	1.5
Other vegetables	3.5

Table 3.3 Size of farms, Murcia and Orihuela.

	Percent and (Number) of Farm Ownerships				
(1)	(2) All	(3) Less than 1 ha	(4) Less than 5 ha	(5) Less than 10 ha	(6) More than 50 ha
Huerta of Murcia	100 (13,302)	83 (11,070)	98 (13,040)	99 (13,196)	— (11)
Huerta of Orihuela– canals under jurisdic- tion of Juzgado Priva- tivo de Aguas de Orihuela	100 (4,831)	64 (3,098)	86 (4,168)	95 (4,589)	— (1)

Source: Ministerio de Obras Públicas, *Catálogo oficial de comunidades de regantes* (Madrid, 1964), pp. 24–25.

Table 3.4 Mean monthly precipitation (1931–1960) (in mm).

	Murcia	Valencia
(1)	(2)	(3)
June	11.7	28.9
July	1.3	7.9
August	6.0	21.3

Source: Tables 2.1 and 3.6.

Table 3.5 Characteristics of major storage dams in Segura River basin.

Name	Talave	Fuensanta	Cenajo	Camarillas
Location	Upper Mundo	Upper Segura	Segura below Fuensanta	Mundo below Talave
Year put into effective operation	1918	1932	1960	1960
Storage capacity (in/Hm^3)	45	238	470	38
Purposes	Flood control, irrigation, electric energy[a]	Flood control, irrigation	Electric power, storage for other purposes	Storage for several purposes

Sources: Various publications of the Ministerio de Obras Públicas and Confederación Hidrográfica del Segura.

[a]Designed initially for flood control only.

cereals, mostly corn, beans, and alfalfa. In the past there have been significant plantings of industrial fibers—hemp, flax, and mulberry trees for silk—but today these are much reduced.

The farms are small, as shown in table 3.3, although they are somewhat larger on the average than those in Valencia. Furthermore, a large percentage of the farmers own their lands. There are no data for the two huertas as such, but for the province that includes Orihuela, 94 percent of farms of 10 hectares (ha) or less are cultivated by their proprietors.

Precipitation in the huertas of Murcia and Orihuela is more scarce than it is in Valencia, so that the Segura farmers are even more dependent on river water than those of the Turia. Compare, for example, the mean monthly rainfall of the cities of Murcia and Valencia for the summer months, shown in table 3.4. At the same time, the flow of the Segura is highly irregular, both seasonally and overyear. Until it was tamed by storage dams it was a torrential stream even in its middle and low valleys, giving rise periodically to devastating floods, while a

Table 3.6 Monthly and annual stream flow entering the huerta of Murcia and monthly precipitation.

	Stream flow entering Murcia, Station 18, Archena, Segura River					
	(1) Means (m³/s)			(2) Standard deviation (m³/s)		
	1916– 1932	1933– 1960	1961– 1965	1916– 1932	1933– 1960	1961- 1965
Jan.	22.8	9.9	4.2	7.88	5.28	0.57
Feb.	33.5	15.3	7.6	18.15	26.10	3.15
Mar.	35.8	20.8	9.5	18.78	27.59	3.72
Apr.	31.4	16.5	9.8	20.29	14.55	1.88
May	23.9	15.2	11.2	11.19	7.17	1.06
June	18.2	12.8	10.6	8.54	3.96	2.56
July	16.0	12.5	12.7	6.73	3.63	3.51
Aug.	15.2	12.5	14.0	6.34	5.28	4.71
Sept.	17.0	13.1	10.3	7.31	6.82	3.79
Oct.	20.6	11.2	8.0	11.19	19.83	2.81
Nov.	26.8	8.7	4.9	19.63	19.31	1.41
Dec.	28.2	9.4	4.4	23.28	5.03	1.14
Annual	23.9	13.1	8.8	—	—	—

Sources: Columns (1)–(3): adapted from Ministerio de Obras Públicas, *Resumen de Aforos,* vol. VII–Cuencas del Segura (1966); and subsequent annual reports. Column (4): Ministerio de Obras Públicas, Centro de Estudios Hidrográficos, *Necesidades hídricas de los cultivos en los planes de regadío integrados en la cuenca del Segura* (Madrid, December 1967).
[a]Drought - mean monthly flow less than 10 m³/s during July and August.

good part of the river channel would be exposed during ordinary low water in summer.

Some dozen reservoirs with a combined storage capacity of 810 million cubic meters (810 Hm³) have been built on the river and its tributaries, providing a substantial degree of regulation for the middle and low valleys, controlling floods and storing water for irrigation and the production of electric energy. Over 97 percent of this storage is in four reservoirs, two on the Segura head-waters and two on the Mundo, the principal tributary. Their main characteristics are given in table 3.5. A reregulating dam will be built below the confluence of the Mundo and Segura to facilitate multiple-purpose operation of the upstream reservoirs. Completion of the Cenajo and Camarillas reservoirs resulted in an estimated 310 to 533 Hm³ increase in the mean annual volume of water available

| (3) | | | Precipitation at Murcia, Station 121 |
| No. of years of drought[a] | | | (4) Means (mm) |
1916– 1932	1933– 1960	1961– 1965	
—	—	—	14.9
—	—	—	17.3
—	—	—	28.7
—	—	—	46.0
—	—	—	34.7
—	—	—	11.7
2	5	1	1.3
3	7	1	6.0
—	—	—	27.7
—	—	—	53.0
—	—	—	16.9
—	—	—	27.7
3	7	1	—

for irrigation below them.[2] It is this increased flow that was allocated to the three valleys in 1953, as shown in column (6) of table 3.1.

For a useful picture of the river water available to the huertas of Murcia and Orihuela each month, both before and after storage became available, see tables 3.6 and 3.7. During the period 1916-1932 there was little storage on the river; between 1933 and 1960 the Talave and Fuensanta dams were in operation, and after 1960 additional storage of 400 Hm³ was provided by Cenajo and Camaril-las dams.

Authority to issue orders for the storage and release of water from the reservoirs is reserved for the regional hydrographic confederation under whose supervision the dams were built. However, irrigation interests in the basin have been able to participate in decisions on seasonal and weekly operations by their representation on a committee on reservoir operations (*junta de desembalses*), similar to the committee described for Valencia. In the early summer of a year when it appears that water storage will be insufficient to meet all needs, the committee seeks agreement on quotas of storage to be released during successive months of

Table 3.7 Monthly and annual stream flow entering the huerta of Orihuela and monthly precipitation.

	Stream flow entering Orihuela, Station 28, Orihuela, Segura River[a]					
	(1) Means (m³/s)			(2) Standard deviation (m³/s)		
	1912–1932	1933–1957	1965–1966	1912–1932	1933–1957 [b]	
Jan.	21.98	11.02	4.2	12.40	7.03	
Feb.	32.88	20.03	6.6	21.62	39.21	
Mar.	33.47	20.42	6.9	21.92	33.19	
Apr.	26.68	18.69	7.3	18.39	25.29	
May	19.9	11.70	7.1	12.88	12.05	
June	15.63	7.8	9.2	10.50	5.15	
July	9.25	5.27	6.6	4.99	3.26	
Aug.	8.0	6.99	8.1	4.77	5.01	
Sept.	13.01	12.11	8.0	7.30	11.02	
Oct.	16.04	13.68	10.8	9.42	18.76	
Nov.	21.73	8.30	6.3	13.90	5.12	
Dec.	24.27	12.99	14.9	16.35	11.49	
Annual	20.0	12.5	8.0	—	—	

Sources: See source note, table 3.6.

[a]This station did not function between October 1957 and September 1964.
[b]There is insufficient data to calculate standard deviations for 1965–66.
[c]Drought - mean monthly flow less than 4 m³/s during July and August.

the season, taking into account monthly water requirements for sanitation, crops, and industry and established priorities of water use in the basin. In subsequent monthly meetings the committee agrees on procedures for releasing the water quotas of each period.

The hydraulic technique used in drought operating procedures is called the big surge (*oleadas*). A monthly quota of water is released in a short period, say fourteen days, rather than uniformly over thirty days. The principal reason for this is to distribute the water among the three valleys with a minimum of administrative regulation. If the water were released uniformly over the month, the irrigators of the high valley would be able to absorb more than their proper share unless regulations were enforced that required them to close down all withdrawals for a certain number of days. Similarly, the middle valley could take advantage of the lower one. If, on the other hand, the month's quota is released in

			Precipitation at Orihuela, Station 164
(3) No. of years of drought[c]			(4) Means (mm)
1912– 1932	1933– 1957	1965– 1966	
—	—	—	19.1
—	—	—	17.8
—	—	—	16.6
—	—	—	40.1
—	—	—	22.9
—	—	—	15.8
4	13	0	2.8
6	10	0	4.5
—	—	—	28.4
—	—	—	45.7
—	—	—	21.4
—	—	—	22.5
6	13	0	—

a shorter period, the high valley will be unable in this limited time to absorb so large a portion of water, more will pass to the middle and low valleys, and less administrative regulation will be required to achieve the distribution desired. If the water is released in too short a period, its flow will be so great that it cannot be used effectively for irrigation; and if the period is too long, the proper distribution among high, middle, and low valleys will not be realized. Above all, the big surge procedure requires a significant quantity of storage and this was achieved on the Segura in the early 1960s.

The largest hydraulic undertaking in Spain's history, which is just getting underway, will transfer between 600 and 1000 Hm^3 of water annually from the Tajo River basin in central Spain to the southeast region, principally to the Segura River basin. This project could possibly add as much as 4500 ha of new irrigation in both the high and middle valleys and 3500 in the lower valley as well as improve the water supply of much of the presently developed area, but competing demands for the water for domestic and sanitary uses make it unlikely that irrigation developments comparable to these figures will be realized. At the time this is written, plans for using the Tajo water are incomplete and this study, therefore, does not take them into account.

To supplement river water, the farmers of the Segura basin have for many years used groundwater, raising it to the surface by means of animal or wind power initially and subsequently by diesel oil and electric energy. In 1870 the first artesian well was dug in Murcia and a number of them can be found in the valley today. In the huertas of Murcia and Orihuela, however, few if any farms depend on groundwater regularly; only during very dry years is the groundwater tapped and relatively few farmers have pumps for this purpose. The areas that rely on groundwater are outside the old huertas, and the productivity of many of them is low due to the high salt content of the water.

DISTRIBUTION OF RIVER WATER TO CANALS

The water distribution network in Murcia-Orihuela is an elaborate double system of channels, one set to carry the river water to farms, another for return flow from the farms to the river in the middle valley and from farms directly to the Mediterranean in the low one. Both huertas are interlaced by watercourses that frequently pass over one another so that the two systems do not mix, although water returned to the river through the drainage channels is used again for irrigation downstream and many farmers irrigate directly from the return flow channels. The supply canals are called *acequias,* the supply laterals, *brazales* or *arrobas.* They deliver what the Segura River farmers call live water (*aguas vivas*). The channels that collect return flow, which is called, despite its frequent reuse, dead water (*aguas muertas*), are named *azarbetas* if they drain three or more farms and *azarbes* if they unite two or more azarbetas. Except for acequia and brazal, none of these terms is commonly used in Valencia.

Among the natural and cultivated features of the Murcia-Orihuela area that give rise to this elaborate double system are the following. The low valley has a very slight slope and therefore poor natural drainage. In fact, the river below the city of Orihuela was diverted over two centuries ago from its natural channel to higher land, the natural channel serving as a large azarbe, and close to 50 percent of the Murcia huerta is poorly adapted to the cultivation of orchards due to the high water table. The subsoil is compact, impeding deep percolation of irrigation water, so that downstream canals receive return flows from upstream irrigations. The canal system was designed, long before river regulation, to make use of torrential flows, that is, to irrigate much land in little time. For this reason canal headgates are larger than they would be otherwise and all canals have drains for excess water. Finally, a shortage of water in relation to demands for it makes it economical to conserve and reuse the return flow.

Water is supplied to the huerta of Murcia by means of a single diversion dam that directs the river's flow into two major distributor canals of equal capacity, one on each side of the river (see figure 3.1). These distributor canals then feed some thirty-two supply canals, and most of the farms of the huerta are served by the supply canals or by drainage canals that receive the return flows. Data on this system are summarized in table 3.8.

There are fifteen canals in the low valley that have service areas of 250 ha or more. Of these, nine receive their water directly from the river with the aid of low diversion dams, five use return flow from the huerta of Orihuela, and one canal is supplied by a Murcia return flow channel. Table 3.9 summarizes the data for this system. We shall be concerned principally with canals under the jurisdiction of the irrigation organizations (*juzgados*) of Orihuela, Callosa, and Almoradí. They were the ancient huerta of Orihuela and they are today the heart of the low valley.

The aliquot portions of the river that are supplied directly to the principal canals of Murcia and Orihuela are controlled by the size of canal intakes. These are always open and their measurements have remained constant over centuries. Local tradition has it that the Moors recorded the dimensions of all principal turnouts on stone tablets and their Christian conquerors reproduced these in bronze. Today the stone and bronze artifacts have disappeared, but the data they carried have been recorded on paper.[3] The farmers and irrigation communities of Murcia–Orihuela attach great importance to maintaining the integrity of these turnouts. For example, they have refused to allow the Ministry of Public

Table 3.8 Canal system of Murcia, service areas in hectares.

Left Bank	
Acequia del Norte (North) or Aljufía	5,860
(13 canals with service areas greater than 50 ha that abstract from Acequia del Norte)	(4,293)
(Lands that irrigate directly from Acequia del Norte or from small canals and laterals that take from same)	(454)
(Lands that irrigate directly from system of return flow channels)	(1,113)
Acequia de Churra Nueva–takes from river upstream from Acequia del Norte	1,082
Right bank	
Acequia del Mediodia (South) or Barreras	5,820
(19 canals with service areas greater than 50 ha that abstract from Acequia del Mediodia)	(3,822)
(Lands that irrigate directly from Acequia del Mediodia or from small canals and laterals that take from same)	(444)
(Lands that irrigate directly from system of return flow channels)	(1,554)
Total	12,762

Source: Records of Junta de Hacendados de la Huerta de Murcia, 1965.

Table 3.9 Canal System of Vega Baja.

| (1) Source of water | (2) Canal | Service area (in ha) | | (5) Jurisdiction of Canal |
		(3) Left Bank	(4) Right Bank	
Return flow from Murcia	Puerta de Murcia	717		Juzgado de Aguas de Orihuela
Diversion dam— Las Norias	Alquibla		1,382	
	Molina		1,031	
	Pando & Moquita			
	Waterwheels	80	178	
Diversion dam— Los Huertos	Huertos		826	
Diversion dam— Almoradí	Old Almoradí	2,166		
	Escorratel & Almoravit	267		
Diversion dam— Callosa	Callosa	5,495		Juzgado de Aguas de Callosa[a]
Return flow from Orihuela	Mundamiento	607		Juzgado de Aguas de Orihuela
Diversion dam— Alfeitamí	New Almoradí	2,641		Juzgado de Aguas de Almoradí
	Río	369		
Return flow from Orihuela	Partición	1,237		Towns of Dolores, S. Fulgencio, S. Felipe Neri (Crevillente)
	Mayayo	784		
	Abanilla	817		
	Reina (or Recibidor)	717		
Diversion dam— Formentera	Small canals	170	85	?
Diversion dam— Rojales	Daya Vieja	308		Juzgado de Aguas de Daya Vieja
	Comuna	1,275		Juzgado de Aguas de Guardamar
	Small canals	65	110	
Diversion dam— Guardamar	Small canal		65	
Total		17,715	3,677	
		21,392		

Sources: Adapted from Justo Llácer Barrachina, "La rentabilidad de las obras de revestimiento . . .de la vega baja del río Segura," Congreso Nacional de Comunidades de Regantes, Segundo Ponencia XXXVIII (Valencia, 1964). Llácer's data are from declarations made to the CHS by the irrigation communities.

[a] Certain sectors of this canal are under jurisdiction of Juzgado of Orihuela and the Sindicatos of Cox and Catral.

Works to rectify or repair the intake structures or the river alignments adjacent to them, insisting on hiring and supervising their own contractors for this purpose.

Today the duty of water and also the rotation intervals vary greatly among the canals of Murcia-Orihuela, as can be seen in table 3.10. The data of this table on water supply and therefore on the duty of water should be considered no more than gross approximations. The 1965 figures for the canals of Murcia represent an actual gauging with relatively high water in the river. The data for the Orihuela canals, however, are theoretical in the sense that they are not actual gaugings but are derived from the size of turnout structures and other physical factors, assuming the same stream flow as for Murcia. The 1815 measurements were of necessity crude.

The uneven distribution of water among the canals is not, as one might expect, due to dissimilar development of canal service areas and water supplies in recent times, for a comparison of data from the early years of the nineteenth century—columns (1)-(4)—with those of today—columns (5)-(8)—shows relative stability and uniformity over this time period. In the middle valley the service areas of the two major canals have grown relatively evenly and no more than 12 to 15 percent over one and a half centuries. In the low valley the service areas of the canals that by location have had the greatest opportunity to expand—Alquiba and Callosa—have grown only 15 and 11 percent respectively and the others about 6 percent on the average. The rotation intervals of the canals have scarcely changed. While the turnout structures have remained immutable, the conditions in the river channel adjacent to them have altered so that the flows into the structures at a given river gauge are not necessarily the same today as they were. On the whole, however, the twentieth-century data are similar to those of the nineteenth and the mid-eighteenth centuries, so that variations among the canals of Murcia and Orihuela in the relation of water to land are of long standing.

There have been numerous efforts since the seventeenth century to redivide the water to achieve greater equality among farmers. Although these reforms have altered the distribution of a canal's water to its laterals and sectors, they have not affected the proportional allocation of river water among the canals themselves, due principally to the invariability of the latter's ungated turnouts.

DISTRIBUTION OF CANAL WATER TO SECTORS AND LATERALS

The *parada,* or canal check, is the principal device for distributing water in the supply canals of Murcia and Orihuela. It is both a hydraulic mechanism, like a demountable diversion dam, for slowing and raising canal water so that it can be delivered to laterals and to farms that take directly from the canal, and the basis for organizing the canal's tanda, or rotation. The rotation begins when the first check is closed (lowered), usually at 0600 hours on the first day. At a given time

Table 3.10 Duty of water in certain canals that abstract from the Segura River in Murcia and the low valley.

	Circa 1815			
	(1) Water diversion (in m³/s)	(2) Lands (in ha)	(3) Duty of water (in ha/m³/s)	(4) Rotation (in days)
Murcia				
Aljufía	9.14	5095	557	Murcia's two dis-
Barreras	8.90	5188	583	tributor canals do not have rota- tions. Supply canals have rota- tions of 7 or 14 days.
Orihuela				
Alquibla	1.66	1197	721	24
Molina	2.71	952	351	17
Huertos	1.98	778	393	15
Old Almoradí	2.20	2047	930	25
Callosa	3.34	4937	1478	24
New Almoradí	5.47	2621	479	15

Sources: See note 1, chapter 3 for full citations. Column (1): Roca de Tagores, *Memoria sobre.* Measurements made in Jan. 1816. Conversion factor used: 50 hilas = 1 m³/s. Column (2): For Murcia, Mancha, *Memoria sobre la población.* Conversion factor used: 9.01 tahullas = 1 ha. For Orihuela, Roca de Tagores, *Memoria sobre.* Conversion factor used: 8.45 tahullas

this check is opened (raised) and the next check downstream is closed, thereby beginning irrigation of the second sector of the canal and its laterals.

Within a canal sector—that is, the length of canal between two checks—farms are supplied either directly through headgates or small laterals along the edge of the canal (*riegos de barba* or *por costeras*) or indirectly by means of larger later-als (arrobas or brazales) that draw their water from the canal sector and distrib-ute it by an internal rotation procedure that may also use checks.

The rotation procedure within a sector typically begins with a given number of hours for the exclusive use of high elevation farms (*altos*). During this period the headgates of the lower lands and the turnouts of the arrobas must remain closed so that the water level in the canal will be high enough to reach the head-gates of the high lands. At a fixed hour the low lands (*hondas*) open their gates, which then remain open until the check immediately downstream from them is opened and canal water proceeds to the next check.

Circa 1965			
(5) Water diversion (in m³/s)	(6) Lands (in ha)	(7) Duty of water (in ha/m³/s)	(8) Rotation (in days)
7.70	5860	761	Murcia's two dis-
8.50	5820	685	tributor canals do not have rotations. Most supply canals have rotations of 14 days.
1.60	1382	862	24
2.00	1031	516	17
1.20	826	688	17.5
3.00	2166	722	25
4.00	5495	1374	24
4.00	2641	660	14

=1 ha. Column (4): Roca de Tagores, *Memoria sobre.* Column (5): "Theoretical Dotations," provided by Confederación Hidrográfica del Segura. Column (6): tables 3.8 and 3.9. Column (8): Records of Juzgados of Orihuela, Callosa, and Almoradí.

The arrobas can be either closed or open. A closed lateral draws water during the same hours as the low lands that take directly from the canal. A typical open lateral begins to irrigate when the canal check immediately below it is opened and continues to draw water during all or a good part of the canal's rotation period (that is, while the lower sectors of the canal are being served). Thus an open lateral enjoys considerably more time than a closed one, but it does not enjoy as high a head of water in the canal from which it takes, since it cannot begin to withdraw until the sector check has been opened. The time available to an open lateral depends on its location along the canal.

The operating procedure of the New Almoradí canal is unique in several ways; but because it demonstrates more clearly than the procedures of most other canals the rationale for water distribution among canal sectors and laterals, we use it for illustration. The canal has two large divisions with variant procedures. For the first seven of the fourteen days of its rotation water is distributed to the division nearest the diversion dam, which is within the municipal district of Almoradí and constitutes the first twelve sectors and checks of the canal. For the last seven rotation days water is distributed to the extended division within the municipal districts of Puebla de Rocamora, Dolores, and Daya Nueva, constituting the last eleven sectors of the main canal. The elevation of farmlands in the first division varies considerably, so they have been placed in three classes: high lands (altos), most of which take their water directly from the canal, and medium-high lands (*segundas costeras*) and low lands (hondas), both of which are served by laterals that draw from the canal. All turnouts in the canal's first division have fixed hours for opening, but once open they need not be closed until the water begins to irrigate the second division (until the beginning of the eighth day). The second division does not have land elevation classes; all its sectors or checks are assigned fixed hours both for opening and closing and all its laterals are closed, that is, they are open only during the hours in which the canal checks immediately downstream from them are closed.

The rotation period begins at 1800 hours on the first day when the first check is lowered for twenty-four hours and the high lands of the first sector begin to irrigate. At 1800 on the second day the first check is opened and the second is closed, also for twenty-four hours. The high lands of the second sector then begin to irrigate along with the medium-high lands of the first. The high lands of the first sector are not required to close their headgates, but since the water will be lower in the canal there once the first sector check is taken down, they are likely to receive water only if it is abundant. At 1800 on the third day the second check is opened and the third closed for twelve hours. The high lands of the third sector then begin to irrigate along with the medium-high lands of the second and the low lands of the first. Again, the headgates of the high elevation farms of the first and second sectors and the turnouts of the laterals that serve the medium-high lands of the first sector remain open, but their ability to draw water is reduced if water is scarce. When at 0600 hours on the fourth day the third check is opened and the fourth closes for twenty-four hours, the high lands of the fourth sector begin to irrigate along with the medium-high lands of the third and the low lands of the second. And so it goes through the first seven days of rotation, after which all headgates and turnouts that take directly from the canal's first division must be closed. At 1800 hours on the eighth day the thirteenth check is closed for nine hours and fifty-three minutes; and when it is opened and the fourteenth check closes, all canal headgates and turnouts of the thirteenth sector must also be closed. The rotation continues in this fashion until 1800 on the fourteenth day, when it begins again in the first division.

On several of the canals the orderly distribution of water by successive canal sectors is interrupted by periods in which water runs unchecked in the canal, free for all to take when and if it reaches them. This water is called *corrible,* and it was provided in rotation procedures originally to ensure that those who used the canal for domestic purposes would not go without water for too long a period, that the canal banks would not dry out, and that the channels would not become health hazards with stagnant pools, but would be flushed out periodically. Nonetheless this water is used frequently for irrigation, and, for example, the farmers of the San Bartolomé lateral, the largest that takes water from the Old Almoradí canal, have carefully allocated whatever water enters their channel during the period of free flow.

In certain other canals and laterals with long rotation intervals the problems of public health, domestic use, and canal maintenance have been met by seating the canal check boards (*tablachones*) a few centimeters above the canal floor so that some water always flows under them when they are closed, or by drilling small-diameter holes (*agujeros* or *marcos*) near the bottom of these boards.

The process of allotting hours and therefore water to canal sectors and laterals is called a *reparto* in Orihuela, *repartimiento* in Murcia, and each canal has had a number of these over its history. The details of allocation are recorded in the canal's official register (*padrón*), which includes also for each sector or lateral a list of the farms that draw from it and for each farm its area, owner, and the drainage canal that receives its runoff.

DISTRIBUTION OF LATERAL WATER TO FARMS

The rotation or tanda is also the model procedure for distributing water to farmers within a canal sector or lateral. Each property has assigned hours for beginning and terminating its irrigation, and these are recorded in the canal communities' registers.[4] Not all sectors and laterals use the model procedure, however, and most canal sectors use two procedures, depending on the season of the year.[5] When water is abundant, farmers must observe the distribution rules only insofar as canal capacities are limiting. To switch from a regime of abundance to one of ordinary low water, the farmers of Murcia-Orihuela use a self-activating procedure called *buscar el agua* (go find the water) that is consistent with their rotation distribution model. On any day that a farmer wants to enforce his right to irrigate at his assigned hour because he fears that water is in short supply, he takes off along the bank of the canal or lateral in search of the water. When he finds it, he informs the farmer who is then irrigating that he is asserting his right, that from experience he knows it will take the water x minutes to travel from its present location to his turnout, and that his neighbor should therefore close his gate and/or open the check at y time. He returns to his farm to await the water and on the way informs all other farmers whose headgates are between the water and his farm that he is asserring his right. If any farmer by his actions interferes with the claimant farmer, the latter can charge him in the community water court. A transgressor must pay both a fine and damages caused to the claimant.[6]

When rotations among canal sectors were established centuries ago for most of the canals in Orihuela and many in Murcia, at a time when irrigation agriculture was less intensive in many parts of these huertas than it is now and when farms were generally larger, each check or sector served one or a few farms. A

rotation by checks approximated a rotation by farms. The one or several landowners who irrigated from a sector were responsible for dividing the water
among their several fields. With more parceling of land and intensification of
agriculture over the years, however, the correspondence between sectors and
farm properties became progressively less. But the sectors, with some exceptions,
were not redefined; the checks were not relocated. To continue the procedure of
rotation among farmers in these circumstances required, then, interior tandas
within a sector. In many cases these were agreed to by the farmers as custom; in
others there was no agreement and all farmers opened their headgates at the
same time. The ordinances authorized those farmers without rotations in a sector to adopt them if they wished and those with customary rotations to convert
these into rotations of record.

Finally, there are two constraints on the supply of water to farmers under
these several procedures. The first prohibits waste. In addition to its normal
meaning that water should not be allowed to run over onto neighboring fields
and roads, waste has been defined in Murcia to mean the use of more water than
necessary to cover plants or to reach the feet of trees or the trunks of palms
(whose roots are frequently up out of the soil). The second general constraint
provides that during a single canal rotation no farmer can take water a second
time until all other farmers have had an opportunity to irrigate once.

SOME SPECIAL PROBLEMS OF A ROTATION PROCEDURE

Although the farmers of Murcia-Orihuela have been ingenious in developing
flexible features such as buscar el agua for their model operating procedure, a
rotation with its fixed hours in the day is inherently more rigid than a turn.
Water not used by a farm or by a sector in its assigned time in rotation becomes
surplus water (*aguas sobras* or *sobrantes*). Within a sector water may frequently
arrive at a farmer's turnout earlier than his assigned hour because farmers ahead
of him have passed up their rights to irrigate in the current rotation or simply
because water is plentiful at the moment. When this happens, the farmer may
take as much of the surplus water as he requires, but he need not take it. He may
let it pass to downchannel farmers and await his assigned hour, by which time he
may be better prepared for irrigation. In any case he cannot take water after his
assigned hour.[7]

Similarly, if the total needs of a canal sector are met without using the full
time and water available to it, the surplus water is passed on to successive sectors. For this purpose the upstream check can be opened partially or fully during
any hours of its assigned time. In several canals where the upstream or older
sectors are better endowed with water than the newer ones and for this reason
have surplus water more frequently than the latter, the downstream sectors have
made a formal distribution of the sobrantes that they receive.

Where water is sufficiently abundant that it reaches a canal terminus before
the full rotation period has ended, regulations of most of the canals provide that

the last check remain closed so that canal water is not wasted to a foreign channel. All farmers from head to foot of the canal are then free to take water as they will until the next rotation begins on schedule.[8] None of these rules for surplus water is necessary where irrigation is conducted by turn, as in Valencia, rather than by rotation.

The combination of water distribution by tanda with the topographical and drainage characteristics of Murcia-Orihuela has resulted in a honeycomb of procedures designed to accommodate the high lands. The principal procedures, some of which we have described already, are these:

1. The pervasive use of canal checks for distributing water in Murcia-Orihuela is in good part a function of the area's topography.
2. Where both high and low lands irrigate from a canal sector, a fixed time has been allotted to the high lands, when turnouts and headgates of the low ones must remain closed.
3. Per unit of area more time is usually allotted to irrigate high than low lands. But why? Once a farm's intake is filled, one should think that the time necessary to run water through it and onto the fields would not vary with the elevation of the farm. There are several reasons why the altos may need more time than lowlands to irrigate. The high lands are less likely to be well leveled. Their surfaces may be so steep that water runs off too quickly for efficient saturation, and they may be irregular. Furthermore, with headgates high on the canal banks, these lands cannot begin to draw water until the canal sector is relatively full; and because they are first to draw, the time needed to fill the sector after the check is closed is charged to them. For this they may receive extra time (*beneficio para encumbrar el agua*). Also the ordinances of Murcia provide that where high lands irrigate first in a sector the sector's canal check can be closed twenty-four hours ahead of time in order to accumulate any surplus water that may be released from the upstream check.[9] Rate of flow into an orifice is a function of the head of water above it, and this is likely to be less for the headgate openings of the high than those of the low lands. Finally, if the altos are so high that they must pump canal water, the rate of abstraction is limited by pump capacity and this could justify giving them extra time for irrigation.
4. Pumps and water wheels (*norias, aceñas*) have been used to draw water from canals for high lands since the earliest days of irrigation, and they have been subjected to special regulations for more than a century.[10] As a general rule any farmer can use a pump if his purpose is simply to distribute to his fields the water to which he is regularly entitled in rotation. If he uses a pump out of rotation, however, the farmer needs special license from the canal community. Where this permission is granted, it is usually because the lands are high and cannot be served adequately in the rotation period. Here too the rules can change according to season.

In a few cases—the Orihuela division of the Callosa canal for example—farmers use their pumps to irrigate fields more than once in a canal rotation.

They have been licensed to irrigate in this way so that they can grow crops that need watering more frequently than the interval between successive turns, which in the case of Callosa is twenty-four days. And to raise water to their farms after the canal check immediately below them has been opened they need to lift it with pumps.

Two canals in the huerta of Orihuela that serve high lands draw their water directly from the Segura River by means of large water wheels that are turned by the river's current, and there are two similar canals in the huerta of Murcia, where the wheels draw one from each of the major distributor canals rather than from the river. These immense and creaking but powerful water wheels are a principal tourist attraction in the area.

The rigidity of the rotation procedure creates problems also for defining the service areas of canals and laterals. Whether farmland is subtracted from, added to, or divided within a service area, the tanda is awkward. To change formally the time allotted to a single property located in the middle of a sector or lateral is likely to require revision of the entire repartimiento, which, being an official document, can be changed only by a procedure that includes approval of the canal community with certain rights of appeal for aggrieved parties. As a consequence, the communities are hesitant to revise the official document frequently, and they allow informal procedures to develop that by long-standing acceptance may then acquire prescriptive justification.

When an irrigated farm goes out of production, the canal communities, rather than revise the whole repartimiento to reallocate the farm's water time, provide that its rotation become surplus water, available to the next irrigator who wants to use it. It is called favor water (*agua de gracia*).[11]

Adding new lands to a service area is not so simple, however. Assume that the new lands are located in the midst of old irrigated farms, that they can receive canal service without any significant changes in the hydraulic distribution system, and that the community wants to give these lands rights that are equivalent to those of older farms. Where water is distributed by turn, as in Valencia, it is a simple matter to add the lands to the canal community's records and then allow the farmer to take whatever he needs when the water reaches him. Under a rotation system like that of Murcia-Orihuela, however, the new lands should be assigned a specific time and doing this is likely to necessitate a full reworking of the repartimiento. An alternative is to improvise, and as we have seen, a number of methods have been practiced (for example, to let several or all headgates within a sector open at the same time).

If, on the other hand, the canal community wants to give the new lands second rather than equivalent rights, that is, rights to surplus water only, then the difference between a turn and a rotation procedure is not so marked. In the former the new lands can take water in order until the canal community proclaims a regimen, of low water, at which time they are cut out. In rotation procedure the new lands can take water so long as the tanda is not in effect; but when it is, they must stop.

If the new lands are located at the tail end of a lateral rather than interspersed within the old lands, and the channel is extended to serve them, then the necessary adjustments in an operating procedure of rotation can be made more easily. The new lands will get water if there is any remaining in the lateral after those with rights have irrigated and during the time when the lateral takes from the canal.

DROUGHT PROCEDURES

When it is unusually dry, the farmers of Murcia modify their model procedures for distributing water. Under a drought regimen (*regimen extraordinario de estiaje*) they follow an order of preferred purposes, make use of special hydraulic measures, and, based on both of these, reorganize their rotations.[12] As one would expect, water for public health and domestic uses has first preference, and in extreme droughts all regulations are designed exclusively to meet these needs. Where water is available for crops, vegetables, alfalfa, and bread grains are preferred; and it is prohibited to irrigate lands not planted to crops or any lands with crops that have received water within the week. Among the preferred crops first priority is given to those that need water each week (tomatoes, string beans, peppers, onions) and second to those that require it less frequently or regularly (corn, potatoes, alfalfa, citrus).

The hydraulic measures may include any or all of the following: restrict mills so water is available for preferred uses. Prohibit all pumps, *rafas,* and any other means that individual farmers might use to obstruct and raise the level of canal water. Shut the tail ends of all laterals and canals so no water wastes from them into the river or drainage channels. Reverse the order in which farmers normally draw water from a lateral so that those at the tail end take first and those at the head take last. Under this procedure any water in excess of the needs of preferred uses can easily be passed on to the next lateral or sector of the canal.

The irrigation organization of each of Murcia's more than thirty supply canals devises a special drought rotation based on the preference criteria; the special hydraulic procedures; and the estimate of water that will be available at the canal intake, which depends in turn on the procedure being used to release water from the mainstem dams and any rotation that may be in effect on the major distributor canals. Normally a canal community's objective is to complete its special rotation within fourteen days so a new one can be devised in the light of current conditions.

It will be recalled that the supply canals of Murcia receive their water from two major distributor canals, one on each side of the river, and that these latter canals do not normally practice rotations. Each runs water through its full reach at all times, and the supply canals that it serves can remain open at all times to withdraw their proportionate shares. Under drought procedure, however, the organization that represents all the farmers of each distributor canal, or alternately the organization that represents the entire huerta of Murcia, devises a rotation among the supply canals using the same criteria used by the supply canal communities for rotations among farmers.

All these actions are triggered by a formal declaration of drought regime issued by the mayor of Murcia in his special capacity as judge, conservator, and distributor of the huerta's water. (The Segura basin watermaster has authority to veto a drought decree, but he has not done so.)

Although it experiences more severe droughts than Murcia because it is downstream, most of the huerta of Orihuela does not have a drought regimen for its farms, apart from any modifications of its rotations that are made necessary by the procedure for releasing water from the river's reservoirs. Irrigators are left to make their own farm adjustments with whatever water supply they receive in these rotations.

The farmers of the New Almoradí canal, however, do practice a special procedure, one that differs in detail from Murcia's, although it is not provided for in their ordinances. If a drought occurs in July and August the canal community can declare a half tanda, that is, each irrigator takes water for half of his regular time. By this means the canal's rotation interval is cut from two weeks to one, with the purpose of providing more opportunities to save crops in danger of drying up. The half tanda is called relief water (*agua de socorro*).

There are certain preferred crops in Almoradí (oranges, lemons, hemp, and artichokes) and if the half tanda does not provide sufficient water for them, a new regime is initiated, a rigorous turn in which farmers take water in order but only for the preferred crops. Other crops are in effect condemned. The four crops are preferred because they are economically significant in the huerta and also because the consequences of their missing one or more irrigations in July and August would be, in the judgment of the community, especially costly. Citrus crops dominate the first and oldest sectors of the Almoradí service area, and water is considered necessary for them in the summer if they are to fructify, especially if they are to produce large fruit. Hemp is harvested in late summer and the last irrigations are necessary to consolidate this crop. And artichokes are planted in August. If at any time during this period the drought becomes so extreme that water requirements of these crops cannot be satisfied, then preference is given to citrus, and if all citrus cannot be irrigated, to plantations of newly grafted trees.

During a field inspection of Almoradí's service area in 1961, an officer of that community commented to Maass that in contrast to Orihuela where there is no drought regime and where, as a consequence, only individual and selfish interests are served, Almoradí has recognized the social interest. After this gentleman had departed, an officer of the Orihuela community who was also on the field trip said with some annoyance that by favoring oranges and lemons in their drought regime, the Almoradí community was favoring the first and older sections of its service area, where these crops were dominant, at the expense of the extended sectors in Puebla de Rocamora, Daya Nueva, and Dolores, where there were few citrus plantations. Almoradí, in his view, promoted group or regional interests whereas Orihuela served only the social good.

GOVERNING INSTITUTIONS

Writing about the huerta of Murcia over a century ago, the French engineer Maurice Aymard said that "administrators and judges all emanate from universal suffrage; and the autonomy of the users is exercised in all of its plenitude." [13] This remains today a good summary of the structures and procedures for decision making in both Murcia and Orihuela.

At the base of their democratic and representative system are communities of property owners who irrigate from each of the supply canals *(heredamientos particulares)*—about thirty communities in Murcia, ten in Orihuela proper, and fewer under the independent jurisdictions of the canals of Callosa, New Almoradí, and others downstream. [14]

A general assembly of all proprietors is held every two years for each community in Murcia and every three for those in Orihuela. In addition a community's chief elective officer can call an extraordinary assembly at any time, and he must call one when five proprietors request it in Murcia—three in Orihuela and in certain other situations that the ordinances specify.

The principal business of a general assembly is to elect canal officers, review the accounts and operations of those currently in office, and vote taxes for ordinary expenses of the canal. Other matters that require action by an assembly of proprietors or are frequently discussed in such meetings, such as special assessments for canal works and maintenance, farmers' requests for licenses to use pumps out of rotation or to use surplus water on dry lands, approval of changes in the repartimientos, and special drought procedures, may be considered in either extraordinary or general assemblies.

In Murcia all community members have one vote in the assembly regardless of the size of their farm and all decisions are made by majority vote. Voting procedures are more intricate in Orihuela. For the election of officers, the names of fifteen proprietors are drawn by lot from the list of those attending a general assembly, and these fifteen then choose the canal's officers by majority vote. For other matters Orihuela has sought "to match a voter's influence in the deliberations with the importance of his property" by allowing each landowner one vote and an additional vote for each 20 *tahullas* (2.4 ha) of land in excess of 20, provided that no owner can accumulate more than twenty votes.

The general assembly of each canal in Murcia elects one or more syndics (*procuradores*) and two or more inspectors (*veedores*). The syndic must be a landowner in the community, but he need not, as in Valencia, be a practicing farmer. He serves without pay, is obligated to accept election, and can be reelected by a two-thirds vote of the assembly. Inspectors are farmers of the area and are paid for the time they put in as canal officers. The syndic and inspectors together constitute the day-to-day government of the community, similar to the syndic and delegates of Valencia. The syndic is in charge of all details of providing water service and of canal cleaning. In the case of an unusual occurrence of grave importance, a flood that damages the canal's intake, for example, the syndic will act immediately to avoid further damage and will subsequently call an extraordinary assembly to decide on a longer term solution. For less serious occurrences the syndic, provided he has agreement of the inspectors, can act on his own judgment. Inspectors hold a considerably more modest office. They carry out the syndic's orders and help him make decisions relating to the maintenance of the distribution system.

The elected officers of Orihuela carry the titles used in Valencia rather than Murcia. Each supply canal has one or more syndics (*sindícos*) and between two and eight delegates (*electos*), and together they constitute the administration of the community. Both classes of officers must be landowners and for the larger canals they should have at least 10 tahullas (1.2 ha). Their duties are similar to those described for the procuradores and veedores of Murcia.

The canal communities of both huertas employ guards who frequently are nominated for their positions by the working farmers of the canal or canal sector where they are to be employed. Their duties combine those performed in Valencia by guards and ditch riders. The guards patrol the canal and report any violations of the ordinances they observe; act as witnesses where one farmer charges another with a violation or themselves bring charges against farmers; and assist in the distribution of water, frequently opening and closing the principal canal checks and the turnout gate of the principal laterals.

A huertawide organization, *heredamiento general,* represents the several canal communities.[15] The Murcia structure, known as the organization of huerta property owners (*Junta de Hacendados de la Huerta de Murcia*), is ruled by a general assembly of the syndics of the canal communities, although interested proprietors may participate with voice and vote. It meets yearly in January or February when the principal business is to elect members of an executive commission and approve the annual budget and taxes. Discussion and action on other policies, for example, how and when to cut off water for canal cleaning, whether and under what conditions Murcia should participate in regional organizations, how to proceed against new upstream abstractors, and amendments to the ordinances, can take place in either the annual or in extraordinary assemblies.

The executive commission, called the *Comisión Representativa de Hacendados,* of the huerta has six members elected by the assembly, three each year for two-year terms. The position is without pay and the man elected is obliged to serve. Canal syndics are normally chosen as commissioners, and among them are representatives from both the upper and lower huerta. The commission is responsible for maintaining the diversion dam in the river and just upstream from it the turnouts of the two distributor canals, making sure that they derive equal quantities of water. (The commission also maintains the turnout of the New Churra canal.) The distributor canals are maintained by the municipal government, although commission members inspect them annually when they are being cleaned of silt. As executive officer of the irrigation organization, the commission approves all expenditures and assesses and collects taxes that have been voted by the assembly. In addition the commission acts as fiscal and records agent of the canal communities, collecting their taxes for maintenance and operation of their distribution systems and maintaining their official registers (padrones) and other accounts. As we have seen, it develops general operating procedures for droughts, based on plans of the canal communities.

Relations between irrigation community and municipal administration in regions like Murcia, where agriculture is the dominant activity, have for centuries been controversial. The Murcian community has never been as autonomous as that in Valencia, and the *ayuntamiento* (city government) in Murcia today has duties and powers in relation to irrigation. The mayor or his delegate issues the call for and presides at all assemblies—those of the organization of property owners for the entire huerta and those of the canal communities. The municipal council is responsible for operating and maintaining the two distributor canals and for providing the money to do so, and as a consequence the city has some say in operating procedures for distributing water to the supply canals. Drought procedures that are prepared by the executive commission, based in turn on plans of the canal communities, are submitted to the city government for approval; and it is the mayor who issues the proclamation that energizes a drought regimen.

In Orihuela the huertawide organization is called the magistracy for water (*Juzgado de Aguas*), and its general assembly consists of the syndics and delegates of the canal communities. Regular meetings of the assembly to elect executive officers are held every three years rather than annually, as in Murcia. For other purposes it meets when the occasion demands on order of its chief elective officer. The assembly elects several officers: a water magistrate (*juez sobrecequiero*), lieutenant magistrate, and solicitor (*síndico procurador general*).

The water magistrate presides at the general assembly of syndics and delegates and also at all assemblies of the several canal communities. The canal communities are responsible for cleaning and maintaining their channels, but the Orihuela magistracy inspects the diversion dams and river banks and in a manner similar to that of the executive commission in Murcia serves the lesser communities, collecting their taxes, providing them with technical services, auditing and approving their accounts, and maintaining their official records.

Relations between irrigation communities and municipal administration have in the past been considerably less agreeable in Orihuela than Murcia, and as a consequence the city government today plays much less of a role.

Each huerta has its own organization and procedures for enforcing its regulations.[16] These are designed to achieve quick and summary justice in cases where a farmer member of any one of the canal communities is charged with violating the ordinances and thereby affecting adversely the common interest of the community, or causing damages to another member. When community interest is affected, the offender can be denounced by the canal's officers and guards or by any community member and if found guilty he pays a fine prescribed by the ordinances. Someone causing damage to another member is charged by the party that claims to have suffered injury and if guilty pays both a fine and damages. The jurisdiction of the water courts of Murcia and Orihuela does not extend to controversies in which a principal party is not a member of one of the participating communities.

The irrigation communities of Murcia-Orihuela depend as much as those of Valencia on farmers' initiative to enforce their rules, and their judicial machinery is especially attuned to adversary proceedings among fellow irrigators. Citizens' suits are relied on more than they might otherwise be because the penalties assessed when canal officers bring an action, namely the fines prescribed in the ordinances, have remained low in relation to the costs of farming, whereas damages, which are assessed frequently when a farmer brings the action, are likely to be considerably more costly to the violator.

It is because they rely heavily on citizens' suits to enforce regulations that Murcia and Orihuela have found it necessary to adopt procedures to discourage farmers from bringing actions for spite, obstruction, or whim. In Orihuela all complaints must be filed within fifteen days of an alleged infraction and the complainant must swear to what he denounces "without hatred or revenge." In Murcia there is no time limit on filing suits except for the charge of stealing water, in which case the complaint must be made in writing within three days of the act. Furthermore, to prove water theft a complainant needs two witnesses to the act of stealing water or three witnesses if the evidence is after the act, namely that the usurper's field has been watered out of turn. In Callosa there are fines for denouncers who, not having been able to prove their claims, are judged to have acted maliciously.

The water court of Murcia, called the Council of Good Men (*Consejo de Hombres Buenos*) was established in the early nineteenth century. It has seven members—five canal syndics and two inspectors—who are chosen by lot to serve one-month terms; no canal officer can serve more frequently than once a year. At the beginning of the year the names of all syndics of the supply canals are placed in one bowl, those of all inspectors in another, and from them names are drawn to constitute the council each month. The mayor of Murcia or his representative presides at council meetings, but he votes only in the unlikely case of a tie. The judges of Murcia's council are thus similar to those of Valencia's court in that they are farm proprietors and operators well versed in the practice of irrigation who have been named by their peers to be canal officers. The syndics of Valencia's seven canals sit permanently on the court; because Murcia has more than thirty canal communities, a rotation has been devised to give their council a similar representative character.

Like that of Valencia's court, proceedings of the Murcia council are oral, public, summary, and cheap. The court meets every Thursday morning and sometimes also on Sunday in city hall. In each case the judges hear the parties, examine any evidence, and give their verdict, which requires an absolute majority vote. A brief abstract of the case and the council's verdict are inscribed in a record book, but formal legal procedures and the use of lawyers are discouraged.

A decision of the Council of Good Men is appealable to the city council if the guilty party considers it legally invalid or notoriously unjust and if he files his appeal within three days of the decision. The city council decides whether or not an appeal is justified; if so, the case is referred back to the Council of Good Men for rehearing. For this purpose the council will be augmented by the seven good men who served in the preceding month. On rehearing, the good men are free to repeat their initial decision or to modify it. Apart from this unique procedure, judgments of the council are unappealable. In fact few cases are appealed, and in only a few of these does the city council order a rehearing. Local custom attaches a stigma to the act of questioning the judgment of the community's good men; and the city council has been "discreet and prudent" in the use of its limited authority over appeals.[17]

Orihuela's water court has only one judge, the *juez sobrecequiero,* and consequently its procedures are different from Murcia's. Any farmer or employee who wants to charge another with violating the ordinances will as a rule make the charge verbally to an officer of the magistracy, who then summons the accused to appear before the magistrate, usually on the following day. If the accused confesses to the infraction with which he has been charged, the magistrate sentences him immediately. If the accused does not confess, the magistrate encourages the parties to come to immediate agreement among themselves and he accepts any accord they reach. A good magistrate is a master at coaxing settlements from farmer adversaries even when, as is frequently the case, their accusations against each other are voiced so raucously that they can be heard some distance down the street from the courtroom. If conciliation fails, the magistrate proceeds at once to hear and decide the case, although he must, if requested to do so, grant a ten-day delay for the preparation of evidence. The magistrate's verdicts can be appealed to the city council of Orihuela within five days, but there is no other appeal except in a case where the accused claims that the verdict is legally invalid. Appeals to the city council are infrequent.

The Murcian historian, Díaz Cassou, concluded in 1887 that the democratic and representative character of the agricultural commune of Murcia had shown a remarkable stability, for a succession of very different national political epochs had offered no serious obstacles to its continued functioning.[18] This conclusion remains valid today after the succession of an additional eighty years and a significantly large number of new and varied national political epochs.

COMMUNITY OBJECTIVES AND COMPARISONS

The stated objectives of the Murcia-Orihuela operating procedures emphasize, like Valencia's, equality, equity, and justice. And like Valencia's, they say little

Table 3.11 Simulation of Murcia-Orihuela using a rotation rule with serious water shortage.

	Farm			
	1	2	3	4
Crop production (q.m.)				
Tomatoes	27.1	0.0	30.0	0.0
Potatoes	15.0	0.0	20.0	80.0
Melons	0.0	17.0	0.0	0.0
Corn	13.6	0.0	12.8	3.8
Pit fruit	0.0	62.0	0.0	94.5
Citrus	0.0	50.0	170.6	300.0
Artichokes	0.0	15.2	0.0	92.4
Vegetables	12.4	0.0	0.0	0.0
Alfalfa	0.0	0.0	0.0	38.8
Water used (m³)	1,591	3,511	5,390	17,418
Crop value (thousands of ptas.)	39.11	85.02	136.17	362.96
Total costs (thousands of ptas.)	24.60	45.00	68.20	186.50
Net value (thousands of ptas.)	14.51	40.02	67.97	176.46

in favor of efficiency, except that water should not be wasted. The irrigators of the middle and low Segura valleys are more explicit than their Turia valley counterparts, however, in propounding as a purpose of their procedures to control conflict and to maintain order. Fearing, for example, that the efficient procedure of separating land and water will promote conflict, they are against it. More basically, these irrigators fear the consequences of allowing farmers to pursue their individual interests without community controls. The following examples of justifications for various operating regulations are taken from the ordinances of the New Almoradí canal: [19]

• "because human frailty frequently incites men to vengeance, and interest to transgression (the more so if the occasion provides the opportunity to do this with indulgence), and because it generally happens that for one or another of these two motives, there are many unnecessary complaints about the stealing of irrigation water" (Ord. XV)

• because "some landowners [are] carried away by interest or by pride, against the principles of equity and of justice" (Ord. III)

5	6	7	8	9	10	Total
26.3	0.0	13.5	27.8	0.0	0.0	124.7
57.8	18.5	0.0	17.0	60.0	18.5	286.8
42.6	0.0	0.0	0.0	16.0	0.0	75.6
34.4	5.2	0.0	7.3	20.0	8.8	105.9
0.0	0.0	19.9	0.0	67.2	33.6	277.2
712.5	22.6	25.0	67.7	564.4	184.0	2,096.8
188.7	0.0	11.8	0.0	120.7	38.0	466.8
11.2	0.0	7.4	8.0	11.2	8.0	58.2
80.5	0.0	0.0	0.0	30.4	0.0	149.7
32,688	1,175	1,937	2,912	23,952	7,974	98,548
692.12	26.40	47.09	73.65	536.91	177.93	2,177.36
392.40	14.60	28.20	40.30	300.80	96.40	1,197.00
299.72	11.80	18.89	33.35	236.11	81.53	980.36

- because "individual interest and cavillation have occasioned almost always doubts and litigation" (Ord. XXVIII)

Equality, when used in connection with the distribution of water, means, as in Valencia, equality in proportion to lands that are irrigated; and the procedures of both regions are similar in the respect that all farmers with rights to water are likely to be affected by water shortages. However in Valencia, where each farmer can take what he needs for his crops when the water reaches him, irrigators suffer shortages roughly in proportion to their normal uses of water; in Murcia-Orihuela, where the quantity of water is measured by time, which is in turn measured basically by land area, water shortages are proportioned according to farm size regardless of the crops grown.

To realize equality for lands that are difficult to irrigate is more complex in Murcia-Orihuela than in Valencia. In the latter the farmer simply keeps his head-gate open until his lands have been fully wetted; in the Segura basin it is necessary formally to allot extra time per unit of area to achieve the same result.

When the Valencians use equality to determine landowners' participation in

Table 3.12 Simulation of Murcia-Orihuela using a turn rule with serious water shortage.

	Farm			
	1	2	3	4
Crop production (q.m.)				
Tomatoes	0.0	0.0	0.0	0.0
Potatoes	13.6	0.0	13.6	64.6
Melons	0.0	13.6	0.0	0.0
Corn	10.2	0.0	10.2	20.5
Pit fruit	0.0	84.0	0.0	89.2
Citrus	0.0	28.8	100.8	216.0
Artichokes	0.0	8.6	0.0	65.6
Vegetables	11.2	0.0	0.0	0.0
Alfalfa	0.0	0.0	0.0	28.8
Water used (m^3)	1,116	3,690	3,358	14,683
Crop value (thousands of ptas.)	21.68	79.25	74.32	289.42
Total costs (thousands of ptas.)	21.60	45.00	65.20	188.90
Net value (thousands of ptas.)	.08	34.25	9.12	100.52

and control over irrigation communities, they use the principle in its absolute rather than proportional form—one man, one vote. The same is true in Murcia and for the election of officers in Orihuela. For other deliberations in Orihuela, however, a voter's influence is matched with the importance of his property, subject to the limits that no community member may have less than one nor more than twenty votes. There are probably two reasons for this. Although 95 percent of its farms are less than 10 ha, there is a greater variance of farm size in Orihuela than in Murcia and Valencia; and this variance was no doubt larger when the rule was written. Also, there is some evidence that, given their skepticism on human nature, the farmers wanted to protect themselves against community actions that might be motivated by vengeance and jealousy—that of small farmers against their somewhat wealthier compatriots. But this should not be overemphasized, for basically, as the ordinances of Orihuela state, "in the communities of property owners all are equal." [20]

Although there is little explicit concern for the objective of efficiency in Murcia-Orihuela's legislation, except for avoiding water waste, efficiency is, none-

5	6	7	8	9	10	Total
21.2	0.0	22.9	22.9	0.0	0.0	67.0
0.0	0.0	0.0	0.0	0.0	13.6	105.4
64.0	0.0	0.0	0.0	13.6	0.0	91.2
64.0	5.4	0.0	5.1	30.7	10.2	156.3
0.0	0.0	16.8	0.0	67.2	42.0	299.2
390.1	13.8	11.6	34.7	274.5	115.2	1,185.5
117.9	0.0	9.7	0.0	92.5	27.6	321.9
16.0	0.0	8.0	8.0	16.0	5.6	64.8
59.8	0.0	0.0	0.0	19.4	0.0	108.0
22,996	700	1,814	1,921	14,434	6,309	71,021
440.48	12.03	40.77	41.40	317.49	131.19	1,448.03
390.90	13.60	29.70	39.30	299.00	96.40	1,189.60
49.58	−1.57	11.07	2.10	18.49	34.79	258.43

theless, an important motive for many procedures. With efficiency as the objective and making numerous simplifying assumptions about cost and benefit functions and operating procedure details, we have compared Valencia's basic procedure, the turn, to the rotation of Murcia-Orihuela by means of our simulation program. The basic data we have used on farm size, crop patterns, yields, costs, and returns can be found in the appendix to this chapter. We assume there is a serious shortage of water late in the season, but not so severe as to call forth procedures for extraordinary drought. The results, displayed in tables 3.11 and 3.12, show that with the same basic water supply, the rotation distribution rule performs far better than the turn in terms of income for the region as a whole and for each of the ten farms and in terms of utilization of irrigation water. For the region, the rotation produces almost four times the net income realized with the turn rule. Under the turn rule some of the short season annual crops are lost due to the long time between successive turns. Yields of tomatoes and potatoes, for example, are significantly less under the turn rule, while the picture for longer season crops is not so clear. Citrus does very poorly under turn; alfalfa

Table 3.13 Simulation of Murcia-Orihuela using a demand rule with serious water shortage.

	Farm			
	1	2	3	4
Crop production (q.m.)				
Tomatoes	0.0	0.0	27.0	0.0
Potatoes	20.0	0.0	20.0	80.0
Melons	0.0	20.0	0.0	0.0
Corn	16.0	0.0	16.0	32.0
Pit fruit	0.0	75.6	0.0	105.0
Citrus	0.0	43.3	170.6	270.0
Artichokes	0.0	14.8	0.0	96.0
Vegetables	16.0	0.0	0.0	0.0
Alfalfa	0.0	0.0	0.0	55.5
Water used (m³)	1,591	3,503	5,330	17,324
Crop value (thousands of ptas.)	32.20	90.15	136.87	381.45
Total costs (thousands of ptas.)	21.60	45.00	68.20	188.90
Net value (thousands of ptas.)	10.60	45.15	68.67	192.55

somewhat less well than under rotation; and corn, apricots, and peaches do slightly better.

Subsequently we compared these two operating procedures with a third one in which farmers can demand water when they want it. Here we assume the quantity of water available for the year is the same as that simulated for the turn and rotation procedures but that there is sufficient storage and canal capacity so that the water to which a farmer is entitled can be made available to him whenever he wants it. Farmers have rights to shares of the water in proportion to the size of their farms, and they know at the beginning of the season how much water will be theirs. As one would expect, this demand procedure is more efficient than either the turn or rotation, disregarding for the moment the costs of storage and of canals, which would need to be enlarged byaabout 15 percent (see table 3.13). For the region as a whole, net income with the demand procedure increases 14 percent over rotation and each farm except the first makes more money. Not all crops produce as high a yield under demand as under rotation, however. This is because the farmers have a choice of ordering water for the

5	6	7	8	9	10	Total
0.0	0.0	0.0	28.5	0.0	0.0	55.5
80.0	20.0	0.0	20.0	60.0	20.0	320.0
80.0	0.0	0.0	0.0	20.0	0.0	120.0
80.0	8.0	0.0	8.0	48.0	16.0	224.0
0.0	0.0	18.9	0.0	75.6	42.0	317.1
675.0	23.1	22.5	69.4	562.5	185.0	2,021.4
213.0	0.0	13.6	0.0	136.0	48.0	521.4
16.0	0.0	8.0	8.0	16.0	8.0	72.0
108.0	0.0	0.0	0.0	40.5	0.0	204.0
32,665	1,158	1,937	2,909	23,913	7,880	98,210
749.50	29.37	39.87	76.97	580.95	196.20	2,313.54
391.90	14.60	26.70	40.30	302.00	96.40	1,195.60
357.60	14.77	13.17	36.67	278.95	99.80	1,117.93

more valuable crops as against those of lower value. As a result tomatoes and potatoes decline in total yield while other crops produce a higher yield. The benefits from a single year's operation of the storage and canal works can be judged
crudely from the demand procedure's greater benefits; and from this and similar
information relating to future years, one can calculate average annual benefits
from building and maintaining such works and then compare these benefits to
costs of the works.

The three procedures will differ importantly in their irrigation return periods.
In the rotation of Murcia-Orihuela it is rigid, every eight or fifteen days, for example; and this has certain advantages over the turn in Valencia, in which the
return period is indefinite, while it is inferior, for the same reasons, to a demand
procedure in which the farmer can obtain water on call. With exact knowledge
of the hour at which water will be available an irrigator can schedule his total
farm operations so that he is prepared to make good use of the water when it
arrives. Also, the turn is potentially the most wasteful of water among the three
procedures. A Valencia farmer is likely to irrigate all his crops in his turn, even

those not quite ready for water, because he has no exact knowledge of when the water will return. And he can do just this because there is no precise time or flow limit on his withdrawal, only the very general constraint that he not waste water. If he and the other farmers were to economize in their use of water, it would return more quickly on the next round; but the individual farmer has no incentive to do this under the procedures of ordinary low water because he has no assurance that other farmers will do the same. In Murcia-Orihuela, on the other hand, when a farmer receives less than he needs in his time period because canal flow is low, he must decide how to use the limited water. He has an incentive to economize.

Finally, in weighing these three procedures for their relative efficiencies, it must be kept in mind that the turn and rotation were developed for rivers on which there was little or no storage, that is, for natural flow conditions. As storage has been added to these systems, the irrigation communities have modified their procedures by the simple expedient of not enforcing them when water is abundant; and this has the approximate result of distributing water on demand.

The huertanos of Murcia-Orihuela have to a remarkable degree retained popular influence and control over their destinies as irrigators. Assemblies of all owners of property served by a canal, along with senior assemblies of representatives of the canal communities of each huerta, are in control of operating procedures. The principal exceptions are those features of canal operations dictated by the storage and release of river water in upstream dams and by requirements of general public health and safety in times of extreme drought; and in these matters the water users are not without a voice. Canal assemblies must approve changes in the ordinances and repartimientos, additions of lands to canal service areas, licenses for the use of excess water on dry lands and of pumps out of rotation. The assemblies control all manner of decisions relating to canal maintenance and repair, including assessments. Furthermore, irrigators can have direct influence over canal employees, apart from their popular assemblies. In Orihuela, for example, any community member can denounce an employee before the popularly elected water magistrate, who can admonish or remove the employee summarily.[21]

For resolving conflicts among the irrigators of each huerta the farmers have developed popular courts that conciliate or judge quickly and summarily. Unlike Valencia, appeals may be had from these courts to the municipal councils of Murcia or Orihuela, but their infrequency may be taken as an indication of the irrigators' satisfaction with their own institutions.

As for relations between a huerta and foreign organizations, the municipal governments of Murcia and Orihuela, especially the former, participate more directly in irrigation affairs than the government of Valencia. At the same time the farmers of the two Segura basin cities have more influence at their city halls than do those of Valencia simply because agriculture is relatively more important in the urban economies of the former.

Like Valencia, the irrigation communities of Murcia-Orihuela have entertained with pervasive suspicion all proposals for basinwide hydraulic organizations, fearful that these will deprive them of their preferred rights to water and of their capacity to control their operating procedures. However, because they have had greater need than the Valencians for outside authorities to police upstream water withdrawals and to construct storage facilities that increase water supply, the communities of Murcia-Orihuela have been more inclined to cooperate with such organizations under certain conditions. The conditions are, first, that the irrigation communities have some say in the larger organizations' decision-making processes and, second, that time of first water use be accepted as the basis for intercommunity conflict resolution.

Segura River water is, like that of all principal rivers in Spain, public water and rights to use it are based, in order of priority, on tradition (the water was used regularly before the national water law was passed in 1866); concession acquired by prescription (twenty years uninterrupted use of the water); or concession granted by the administration. In the first two cases the limits of the rights and obligations of the users are defined by the ways in which the water has been used traditionally. For the third case these limits are defined by the terms of the administrative concession, which can include requirements relating to area of land to which water is applied, capacities of intake structures and pumps, method of return flow, and reduction of diversions in periods of drought.

For over a century the Murcia-Orihuela communities have been opposing applications for administrative concessions to withdraw water in the high valley, and for much longer than that they have been acting to shut down withdrawals they believe derogate their rights. In the former case they have typically presented their evidence to the administrative agency with authority to grant concessions and in the latter, to courts; although, having exhausted administrative appeals, they have gone to court to overrule the granting of concessions, and they have sought ministerial orders to close down specific pumps and turnouts that are abusive. In 1913, for example, the Murcia community initiated action before administrative authorities or courts against eight large and new irrigation pumps in the river channel and three concessions for electric power, and they assembled data preparatory to commencing actions against sixteen new or proposed pumps for irrigation and three concessions for industrial uses of water.

These types of actions in individual cases involved heavy burdens on the Murcia and Orihuela communities. They had to hire guards to inspect the upstream channel, experts to collect the data necessary to bring administrative and judicial actions, and lawyers to present their cases. Thus, as the pressure for upstream withdrawals grew persistently in the early twentieth century, Murcia and Orihuela encouraged the Madrid government to enact general rules and regulations that would accomplish the same purposes and to establish a regional hydrographic organization that would enforce the rules.

The principal technique of general regulation was to tie down or legalize all existing withdrawals. Beginning in 1901 and continuing to the present time, a series of orders and decrees has been issued that call for the identification and recording of all abstractions, including information on the legal basis for each (that is, tradition, prescriptive concession, administrative concession, or without justification) and on the limits and conditions of withdrawal, especially for the administrative concessions. Several of these orders have required also that abstractors without justification proceed immediately to apply for administrative concessions, which, when granted, would state conditions under which water could be withdrawn and used. Any water users who failed to do so would be shut down. But the fact that identical or similar provisions can be found in successive orders—1913, 1935, 1953—constitutes a public confession by the government that its orders have not necessarily been complied with.

For many years the limits attached to new concessions by administrative authorities related primarily to capacities of intake structures and pumps. The irrigators of Murcia and Orihuela argued that this was not enough, that the concessions should state explicitly the lands on which the water could be used. They knew from experience that upstream users frequently altered the capacities of their gates and motors and used the greater quantity of water gained thereby on new lands. It would be considerably easier to catch and stop such adulterators of concessions by detecting newly irrigated lands and prohibiting the use of water on them than by discovering and proving that minor alterations had been made on intake structures. The national government, however, resisted this appeal for greater regulation, arguing for some time that it did not have authority to control the manner in which an irrigator or irrigation community used the water to which it was entitled by administrative concession once the water had left the river.[22]

When, however, the government became involved in allocating storage from its Segura basin reservoirs, it abandoned its reticence to define irrigable zones and went much further than Murcia-Orihuela had wanted, seeking to fix the dotations of traditional as well as concessional water users. But in this the government has succeeded only in part, and this in good part because of the opposition of Murcia-Orihuela. A ministerial order of 1942 called for considerable specificity, fixing for each irrigation turnout on the river its water requirement for each month of the year. The closest the government has come to achieving this regulation is the 1953 order, referred to previously, which allocated among three great zones—high, middle, and low valleys—an annual average flow below the reregulating dam (see table 3.1).

Furthermore, the Murcia-Orihuela communities have to date been even more successful than those of Valencia in opposing the government's efforts to quantify their traditional rights. We have seen that the Ministry of Public Works has finally recorded river abstractions in terms of cubic meters per second for the Valencia canals but that these are not effective because the government has not overridden local opposition to their installing modules that measure and control the water that enters the canal intakes. In Murcia-Orihuela the government has not yet recorded abstractions in quantities of water. The published register says simply that these canal communities have intakes that are always open. Among other problems they have faced, the government's hydrographic officers have been unable to obtain from the irrigation communities the data necessary to fix the withdrawals (that is, the number of hectares with traditional rights in each of the canals' service areas).

Murcia and Orihuela have been zealous in their support of new works that would increase usable water in the middle and low valleys of the river by seasonal and overyear storage. Because, however, basic water law does not assure traditional users a preferred right to "new" water created by dam construction, Murcia and Orihuela have sought to protect and enlarge their advantage by inserting special provisions in the administrative instruments that authorize construction and operation of the dams. In this they have had considerable but not complete success. The orders and decrees enunciate the preference. Thus, for example, the 1953 ministerial order says that traditionally irrigated land will be preferred at all times (*en todo momento*), followed in order by lands then being irrigated on the authority of administrative concessions, areas contiguous to the traditional zones for which new irrigation had been authorized, and finally three concessions for new irrigation in noncontiguous zones of Mula, Lorca, and Cartagena.

In allocating water to the high, middle, and low valleys, the 1953 order shows for each the total area of traditional irrigation, followed by that of irrigation subsequently legalized, and of new irrigation. The order's definition of traditional, however, was not at all to Murcia-Orihuela's liking. The government said that all lands that had used irrigation water in 1933 were traditional and equal in preference. In effect they included in traditional not only uses that preceded the 1866 law but also concessions gained by prescription, which are in a class with the older ones in the particular that they are not burdened with administratively imposed conditions relating to methods of water use and the like. Furthermore, by using the year 1933 in its 1953 order the government gave prescriptive standing to all irrigation enterprises that at the time of its order had enjoyed twenty years' uninterrupted use, even though a great many of them, in not having previously obtained administrative concessions, were in violation of earlier orders and the law. The government could have denied prescriptive rights to these water appropriators, but it apparently felt obliged to include them in the category of prescriptive concessions and traditional users because it had failed to enforce its earlier orders.[23]

In addition to confirmation of their priority in the use of reservoir water, the farmers of Murcia-Orihuela have sought approval of operating procedures for the storage, release, and use of water that give effect to the priority. Because it is difficult to specify in advance and in the language of ministerial orders operating procedures for all situations, Murcia and Orihuela have supported a single administrative authority for the entire Segura basin for this purpose as well as for the purposes of building the dams and of limiting upstream abstractions. It was to be an authority with limited power and with direct representation of users in decision making, both carefully prescribed so that Murcia-Orihuela's superior rights to water would be protected and enhanced. In this, too, they have had considerable, although not full success.

The years 1913 and 1914 were dry ones in which there were great disputes between users of the high, middle, and low valleys. The Murcia and Orihuela irrigation communities petitioned the national government to create a new regional organization, apart from the construction-oriented Segura hydraulic division of the Ministry of Public Works, whose principal purpose would be to exercise police functions over water in the river, preventing the commission of abuses, correcting those that were committed, and aiding irrigators and irrigation communities in all cases they brought against unauthorized water users. This organization was to be governed by an assembly representing all users, while a delegate of the national government was to serve simultaneously as president of the assembly and director of a permanent staff.

The representatives of the middle and low valley communities were explicit in explaining to their farmer constituents that the proposal would not reduce in any respect their rights, uses, ancient customs, or traditional organizations and ordinances. In the words of the Murcian delegates: "We are as enamoured of things Murcian as are all of you and we must defend them always against dangerous innovations. But this being known, what we propose is not a reform; it is a *new organization,* which will perform functions that are distinct from those of our organization and are necessary for the reasons given." [24]

Although the national government approved an organization that was to defend the rights and protect and develop the interests of all irrigators of the basin, it never operated as intended by the Murcia-Orihuela farmers. They may have overestimated their capacity to work collectively with upstream users.[25] But more important, the national government was hesitant to assign police functions to an organization over which it had less direct control than over its regular regional office; and probably most important, the drought ended.

In 1934 the irrigators of Murcia-Orihuela petitioned the national government again to create a new basinwide authority for the Segura, this time a hydrographic confederation. The reader will recall from chapter 2 that autonomous hydrographic confederations were conceived as an administrative means for accomplishing the basic concepts of Spanish hydraulic policy. The first such confederation was established for the Ebro River in 1934. The irrigators of the Segura wrote to Madrid that their river basin, since it was not the first, ought to be the second for which a confederation is established. They wanted a confederation for the reasons that had motivated them twenty years earlier and also to speed the planning and construction of storage reservoirs.

The government complied, establishing the *Confederación Hidrográfica del Segura.* The new organization, however, did not develop as the Murcia-Orihuela farmers hoped it would. To be sure, the Murcia-Orihuela farmers, in contrast to those of Valencia, joined and supported the organization; but they felt their representation in its assembly and other bodies was not sufficient to protect their senior rights against the claims of newcomers.

The new confederation may have advanced the construction of works; it is difficult to say. The national government remained unwilling, however, to give police functions to an organization with a representative assembly. On the same day that it published the decree establishing the Confederación Hidrográfica del Segura, the Ministry of Public Works published a second one assigning responsibilities relating to approval and registration of concessions, enforcement of their conditions, and termination of abusive withdrawals to another new unit, the Office of the Watermaster for the Segura River (*Comisaría de Aguas del Segura*), which was directly under the minister of public works and entirely independent of the confederation. This order contained some important advantages for Murcia-Orihuela. Whereas previously control over concessions had been in the hands of provincial governors or provincial water officers, it was now placed in a single authority for the entire basin. Some of the upstream abstractions to which Murcian farmers had objected most were in the province of Albacete, over whose governor they had little influence; and when Orihuela irrigators had objected to new developments in Murcia, they had to appeal to a foreign governor. Nonetheless, the Murcia-Orihuela communities objected strongly to several provisions of this second decree, including the fact that authority was placed beyond the influence and control of the autonomous confederation and its representative institutions.

Despite these objections, Murcia and Orihuela have on the whole been successful in limiting the authority of national institutions, so that we can reject for these huertas, as we have done for Valencia, theories that predict a radical loss of local control whenever large works are constructed. At the same time, by relying so heavily on priority based on time of settlement, these irrigation communities have placed obstacles in the course of modernization and progress, when these are defined in terms of economic efficiency. This, however, is not inconsistent with their community objectives.

APPENDIX: SIMULATION OF IRRIGATED FARMS IN THE HUERTAS OF MURCIA AND ORIHUELA

Simulation of Procedures

The basic distribution rule used in Murcia-Orihuela is the Rotation, in which each farm, typically in the order of its location on a lateral, begins and terminates irrigation in each irrigation period at assigned hours. When water is abundant, farmers can ignore the rotation schedule and take whatever water they need when it arrives at their headgates. In cases of drought the canals of Murcia and New Almoradí impose special rotation schedules that designate priority crops and provide water for them only. These schedules are specially composed on each occasion in light of the current condition of crops and water supply.

The canals of Orihuela, except for New Almoradí, allow each farmer to make his own adjustments to the limited water supply that he receives in his regular rotation.

Rotation is one of the basic procedures of the irrigation simulation program described in our USDA Technical Bulletin 1431. It can be used in combination with several other procedures, which is the case in Murcia-Orihuela.

In simulation of Rotation procedures water is measured by flow, in Murcia-Orihuela, in cubic meters per second, so that the rotation of a sector, lateral, or farm can be measured by multiplying flow by hours when the unit's turnout is open or its check is down. Flow is considered to be uniform during any one irrigation period, but it may vary from period to period. If in fact the flow is likely to vary significantly during a single rotation, then this rotation can be represented as more than one period.

Each farm is supplied with the flow in the lateral for a fixed period of time based on the rotation schedule. The hours assigned to each farm in the schedule are converted into a percentage of the total hours of the rotation period.

Any water available to a farm in its assigned hour that is surplus to its needs is added to the next farm's water supply.

In the canals of Murcia and New Almoradí water is supplied only to certain crops in extraordinary drought. This is simulated by assigning priorities to the crops and watering all priority crops on all farms before nonpriority crops. In the canals of Orihuela, except for New Almoradí, each farmer makes his own crop adjustments to whatever water he receives in times of drought. This is simulated by the Plan and Replan subroutines, described in Technical Bulletin 1431.

Farmers' use of well water to supplement their entitlements to lateral water is simulated by use of a Demand procedure in combination with the Rotation procedure for lateral water. The farmer can vary his demand for groundwater from one irrigation period to another.

Program designations With reference to table 9, Principal Distribution Rules, of Bulletin 1431, the following programs are used to simulate Murcia-Orihuela operating procedures:

Water Supply	Description of Procedure	Procedure Code
Surface water		
Abundant	Rotation (with excess water available to all)	8
Ordinary low water	Rotation	8
Extraordinary drought (Murcia and Almoradí)	Rotation *subj. to* Crop Priorities	18
Orihuela (except Almoradí)	Rotation	8 (Replan)

Water Supply	Description of Procedure	Procedure Code
Abundant in early season, becomes ordinary low water	Rotation	8
Abundant or ordinary low water becomes extraordinary drought	Rotation; Rotation *subj. to* Crop Priorities	23
Surface water plus well water		
Abundance	Rotation + Demand	9
Ordinary low water	Rotation + Demand	9
Extraordinary drought (Murcia and Almoradí)	Rotation *subj. to* Crop Priorities + Demand	19
Orihuela (except Almoradí)	Rotation + Demand	9 (Replan)

Basic Data

The farm sizes used in the simulation runs are given in table A3.1. The cropping pattern on the farms in the simulation, shown in table A3.2, is approximately that for the huertas given in table 3.2. The yields, costs, and returns used in the simulation are given in table A3.3. These represent the area averages for this region of Spain during the mid-1960s. The allocation through the year of water supplies used in the simulation is shown in table A3.4.

Table A3.1 Farm size used in simulation related to distribution of farm size in huertas of Murcia and Orihuela.

Farm size, irrigated hectares	Actual farms				Simulation farms			
	Murcia		Orihuela					
	Number	%	Number	%	Farm No.	Hectares	% of area	
Less than 1	11,070	83.2	3,098	67.2	1	0.5	>1	60
1–4.9	1,970	14.8	1,070	23.2	2	0.8	1-5	30
5–9.9	156	1.2	421	9.1	3	0.9	5+	10
More than 10	106	.8	25	0.5	4	3.5		
					5	7.2		
					6	0.2		
					7	0.4		
					8	0.6		
					9	5.0		
					10	1.5		
Total	13,302	100.0	4,614	100.0		20.6		100

Table A3.2 Initial crop patterns on simulation farms (in hectares planted).

Crop	Farm										
	1	2	3	4	5	6	7	8	9	10	Total
Tomatoes	0.1	—	0.1	—	0.1	—	0.1	0.1	—	—	0.5
Potatoes	0.1	—	0.1	0.4	0.4	0.1	—	0.1	0.3	0.1	1.6
Melons and peppers	—	0.1	—	—	0.4	—	—	—	0.1	—	0.6
Corn and beans	0.2	—	0.2	0.4	1.0	0.1	—	0.1	0.6	0.2	2.8
Pit fruit (apricots and peaches)	—	0.4	—	0.5	—	—	0.1	—	0.4	0.2	1.6
Oranges and lemons	—	0.2	0.7	1.2	3.0	0.1	0.1	0.3	2.5	0.8	8.9
Artichokes	—	0.1	—	0.6	1.5	—	0.1	—	1.0	0.3	3.6
Other vegetables	0.2	—	—	—	0.2	—	0.1	0.1	0.2	0.1	0.9
Alfalfa	—	—	—	0.4	0.8	—	—	—	0.3	—	1.5

Table A3.3 Yields (in quintals) and costs and returns (in thousands of pesetas) for crops used in simulation of huertas of Murcia-Orihuela.

Crop	Yield	Preharvest cost/ha	Harvest cost/ha	Gross return/ha	Full production, net return/ha
Tomatoes	300	60	30	150	60
Potatoes	200	40	10	100	50
Melons	200	30	5	88	53
Corn	80	18	8	55	29
Pit fruit	210	40	15	125	70
Oranges	250	45	25	150	80
Artichokes	160	45	10	112	57
Other vegetables	80	19	8	56	29
Alfalfa	150	20	15	75	40

Table A3.4 Irrigation water supply used in Murcia-Orihuela simulation.

Irrigation period	1	2	3	4	5	6	7	8	9	10	11	12	13
% of water	1	2	4	7	5	1	5	1	8	7	2	1	8
Irrigation period	14	15	16	17	18	19	20	21	22	23	24	25	26
% of water	3	5	2	8	3	3	3	8	2	3	5	3	0

4 The Huerta of Alicante

As in Valencia and in Murcia-Orihuela, large numbers of users in the Alicante irrigation community are affected by water shortages, for there are no fixed priorities among farms and farmers.[1] But the manner in which the irrigators share water shortages and abundance is very different, due principally to institutions for water transfer from one farmer to another.

Alicantians are sinners in the eyes of Valencians, for they have divorced water from land. The right to water in Alicante is based on the ownership of shares. Some shareholders do not own irrigated lands and most irrigators do not own sufficient shares to supply their farms. Thus in any rotation a significant proportion of shareholders do not use the water to which they are entitled, but sell it to others.

The separation of rights to water and to land occurred in about the middle of the thirteenth century, not long after the Christians had reconquered Alicante from the Moors and distributed the rights to water and land among themselves. The history of the Huerta of Alicante[2] since then has been in some significant degree the history of unsuccessful efforts to reattach land and water.

The Huerta of Alicante includes some 3700 hectares (ha) of irrigated land in a small coastal plain bordering the Mediterranean, about two-thirds of the distance between Valencia and Murcia.[3] It lies just northeast of the city and is defined inland by a series of low mountains and hills and along the coast by the beautiful San Juan beach (see figure 4.1).

The climate is mild, typically Mediterranean. Alicante enjoys 179 cloudless days in an average year, more than either Valencia (138) or Murcia (148). The Huerta's soil is fertile, and it is more a shortage of water than of good land that has limited intensive agricultural development of the region. The cultivated character of this Huerta is unique because of the association of tree and row crops. Some fields have rows of a mixture of fruit and nut trees between which are planted cereals or vegetables or both. The tree crops (almonds, olives, carob for animal feed, figs, dates, and pomegranates) are grown for home consumption; the row crops (principally wheat and beans) are harvested twice a year for the market. Other fields have one or two varieties of trees only, which, along with the interspersed cereal and vegetable crops, are harvested for the market. Trees are not typically grown in association with tomatoes, however, which are a principal crop in the Huerta. The 3700 ha of huerta land are planted roughly as shown in table 4.1.

The farms are small, as shown in table 4.2, although there are a number of good-sized holdings that grow tomatoes for the national and export markets. Some owners of small properties are part-time farmers and others in this class rent additional land, frequently on short-term leases, from those who own 5 ha or more.

Table 4.1 Crops grown on irrigated land in the Huerta of Alicante.

Crop	Percent of land planted
Cereals (mostly wheat)	20.5
Broad beans	10.5
Potatoes	9.0
Peppers	6.5
Melons	6.5
Tomatoes	4.5
Almonds	24.5
Olives	9.5
Other tree crops	1.0
Alfalfa	7.5
Total	100.0

Table 4.2 Farm size, Alicante.

Percent and (number) of farm ownerships

(1) All	(2) Less than 1 ha	(3) Less than 5 ha	(4) Less than 10 ha	(5) 10–50 ha	(6) More than 50 ha
100	63	93	97	3	—
(2,423)	(1,536)	(2,262)	(2,355)	(67)	(1)

Source: Ministerio de Obras Públicas, *Catálogo oficial de comunidades de regantes* (Madrid, 1964), p. 29.

Tibi dam, one of the earliest major hydraulic works in Europe, begun in 1579. Drawing by Cavanilles, 1795.

A canal near the head of the huerta. Olives mixed with field crops on the left.

Maass in regulating reservoir (*pantanet*) during the extreme drought of 1961.

Extraordinary session of the huerta's general assembly during the extreme drought of 1961.

Farmers bidding for one hour of water at the Sunday water auction, 1975.

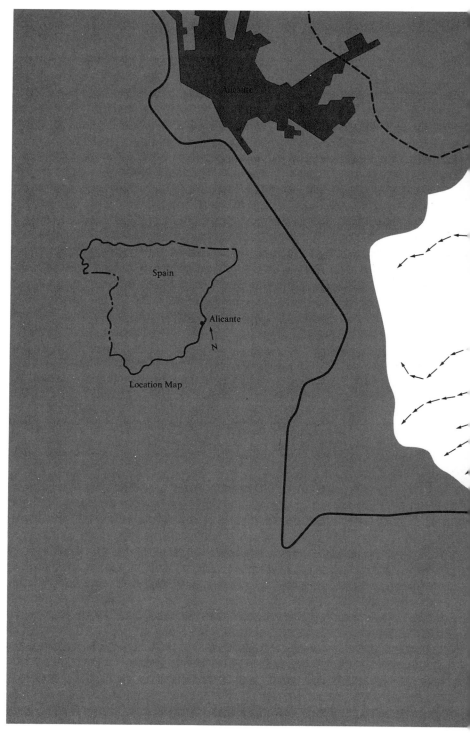

Figure 4.1   The Huerta of Alicante.

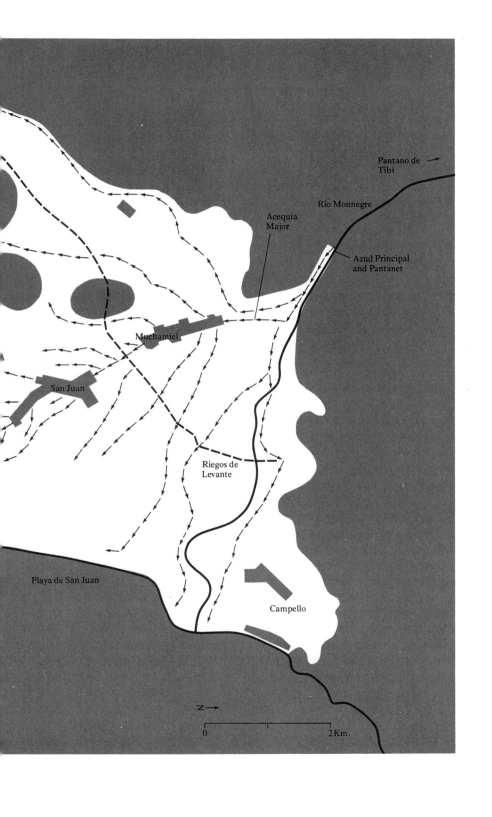

Pantano de
Tibi

Río Monnegre

Acequia
Major

Azud Principal
and Pantanet

Muchamiel

San Juan

Riegos de
Levante

Playa de San Juan

Campello

N→

0   2 Km.

Although precipitation is slightly more abundant in Alicante, especially in the hot summer months, than it is in Murcia-Orihuela (compare tables 4.3 and 3.4), surface and groundwater are markedly less available. The only river is the Monnegre, which, unlike the rivers that supply Murcia-Orihuela and Valencia, rises in mountains close to the sea and is fed by a small drainage area that does not benefit from heavy rains or snow. The natural regimen of the river is highly irregular both seasonally and overyear.

This irregularity led the Alicante farmers in the late sixteenth century to build Tibi Dam, one of the early and most admired major hydraulic works in Europe. Forming a reservoir of 3.7 million cubic meters (Hm^3) capacity, now reduced to approximately 3.2 Hm^3 due to siltation, it remains today the only significant storage facility on the Monnegre, providing seasonal, but little overyear, storage for the exclusive use of the Alicante Huerta. So that they can distribute river water at a constant rate of 150 liters per second (l/s) the irrigation community has built two regulating basins, called *pantanets*, below the dam. The first of these, with a capacity of approximately 10,500 m³ of water, was constructed in 1842 and enlarged to its present size in 1874. The second, which holds about 25,000 m³, was completed in 1954 and provides sufficient regulation so that the farmers have been able to abandon night irrigation, which they detest. In addition to the regulating basins, the distribution system consists of three small diversion dams in the river channel below the reservoir and a principal canal that traverses the entire Huerta and feeds some twenty-two laterals whose service areas vary greatly in size.

There are no reliable hydrologic records of the natural flow of the Monnegre. The only gauging station, located below the dam at the head of the distribution network, was abandoned in 1945. It is estimated, however, that the river with its storage supplies the Huerta with somewhat more than 1.6 Hm^3 in an average year; but this quantity varies considerably from year to year. In a very good water year the irrigation community will be able to deliver sixteen to seventeen rotations of Tibi water, or approximately 4.5 Hm^3, in the average year six to seven rotations. The number of rotations and the estimated water delivered each year for the 55-year period 1914-1968 is given in columns (2) and (3) in table 4.4. These data are primarily a function of river flow, but they reflect also the operation and maintenance of the reservoir, which silts rapidly, and of the distribution system, which in 1940-41, for example, had a major breakdown.

If the 3700 ha of the Huerta were planted to the crops grown typically, the water requirement would be 23.3 Hm^3; yet the Monnegre River supplies in the average year only 1.6 Hm^3. The farmers of Alicante have had to find additional water, and they have in this century developed three supplementary sources. In 1912 the irrigation community entered into a contract with a private company, *Sociedad del Canal de la Huerta,* to deliver water to the Huerta from deep wells near Villena, in the headwaters of the Vinalopo River, some 70 kilometers (km) northwest of Alicante. In 1924 it contracted with another

Table 4.3 Mean monthly precipitation
at Alicante, Station 25 (in millimeters).

Jan.	18.3
Feb.	18.8
Mar.	18.7
Apr.	41.7
May	23.8
June	20.9
July	3.7
Aug.	9.6
Sept.	33.4
Oct.	49.3
Nov.	36.8
Dec.	21.3
Annual	24.7

Source: Ministerio de Obras Públicas, Centro
de Estudios Hidrográficos, *Necesidades hídricas de los cultivos en los planes de regadío en
la cuenca del Júcar* (Madrid, Dec. 1967).

commercial enterprise, *Compañía de Riegos de Levante,* to supply water from
the delta of the Segura River some 50 km away. Methods for distributing to
farmers water from these sources and major events in the history of the relations
between these companies and the community will be studied in a later section
of this chapter. The Huerta receives in an average year 0.85 Hm³ from Villena
and 2.5 Hm³ of Segura River water, although these supplies, especially the
latter, are highly variable.

The final source of water for Alicante is private wells. Groundwater has been
sought in the Huerta for several centuries; but the sinking of large private wells,
some with sufficient production for their owners to market the water, distributing it frequently in the irrigation community's canal networks, is a relatively recent development. Some of the large farms that grow tomatoes rely heavily on
this purchased groundwater. Precise data on the production of these private
wells are not available, but a reliable estimate made in 1960 is that they supply
Huerta lands on the average about 400,000 m³ per year.

Table 4.4 Water delivered in the Alicante Huerta from Monnegre River (Tibi Dam) 1914–1969 and Segura River (Cia. Riegos de Levante) 1949–1969.

| (1) Year | Water from Monnegre River | | Water from Segura River | |
	(2) Rotations delivered (no.)	(3) Est. quantity delivered (Hm³)	(4) Est. quantity available (Hm³)	(5) Quantity delivered (Hm³)
1914	2	0.54		
1915	12	3.23		
1916	7	1.88		
1917	7	1.88		
1918	11	2.96		
1919	11	2.96		
1920	21	5.65		
1921	18	4.84		
1922	11	2.96		
1923	11	2.96		
1924	8	2.15		
1925	5	1.35		
1926	6	1.61		
1927	9	2.42		
1928	4	1.08		
1929	11	2.96		
1930	5	1.35		
1931	2	0.54		
1932	6	1.61		
1933	16	4.30		
1934	9	2.42		
1935	8	2.15		
1936	3	0.81		
1937	2	0.54		
1938	2	0.54		
1939	1	0.27		
1940	6	1.61		
1941	1	0.27		
1942	4	1.08		

Table 4.4 (continued)

(1)	(2)	(3)	(4)	(5)
1943	8	2.15		
1944	7	1.88		
1945	2	0.54		
1946	6	1.61		
1947	11	2.96		
1948	4	1.08		
1949	10	2.69	1.80	3.01
1950	12	3.23	2.41	
1951	10	2.69	2.80	
1952	6	1.61	3.62	
1953	3	0.81	2.30	2.15
1954	5	1.35	2.04	
1955	2	0.54	3.26	
1956	7	1.88	3.26	3.47
1957	4	1.08	2.14	2.49
1958	4	1.08	3.08	
1959	14	3.77	3.13	
1960	16	4.30	4.39	2.85
1961	6	1.61		
1962	5	1.35		
1963	6	1.61		
1964	2	0.54		
1965	4	1.08		
1966	2	0.54		
1967	2	0.54		
1968	2	0.54		
1969	2	0.54		

Sources: Column (2): Archives of Sindicato de Riegos de la Huerta de Alicante. Column (3): Column (2) × 269,000 m^3. A regular rotation consists of 565 hours of water delivered at 540 m^3/hr. (150 l/s) or 305,100 m^3. A summer rotation is two-thirds of the regular rotation, or 203,310 m^3. In a good water year the community will deliver eleven full rotations and six summer rotations, for a total of approximately 4.5 Hm^3, and an average of 269,000 m^3/rotation. Column (4): 0.6 × Q served in entire service area. The quantity served is from archives of Cia. de Riegos de Levante, Elche. Column (5): Archives, Cia. de Riegos de Levante, Elche.

The Huerta's water supply in an average year can be summarized as follows: [4]

Tibi Dam	1.60 Hm³
Compañía de Riegos de Levante	2.50
Sociedad del Canal de la Huerta	0.85
Private wells	0.40
Total	5.35

This is only 23 percent of the water that the area could use.

THE SEARCH FOR MORE WATER—TIBI DAM

The farmers of Alicante have sought to rejoin land and water by regulation, but their principal method has been by increasing the water supply. Water and land were allotted to the thirteenth-century conquerors of the Moors on the basis that the two elements were and would remain united; but almost immediately extralegal practices developed that treated water as private property, separate from land. Due to its relative scarcity, which was due in part to an increase in lands that were plowed and irrigated, water enjoyed a high value. Some proprieters sold the use of their water for varying periods of time to farmers who needed it; others sold or bequeathed their basic water rights to landowners in the Huerta, in some cases to those who did not own land in the area, and especially to churches and church charities. In 1389 John I of Aragon, at the request of Alicante farmers, issued a decree prohibiting the acquisition of water by churches and those who did not own lands in the Huerta and providing that no one could acquire more water than was necessary to irrigate his lands. But this early effort to rejoin water to land failed. It was disregarded, as were subsequent efforts to achieve this result by regulation alone.

Alicante's farmers turned next to increasing their water supply by building Tibi Dam to store flood waters that periodically wasted to the sea. In preparing a new regime for distribution in the Huerta of what was now a regulated water supply, the farmers had in mind two objectives: to rejoin water and land and to honor acquired rights. They combined these noncomplementary goals in the following way. It was assumed that the new dam and reservoir would double the supply of firm, or usable, water. Half of this supply, the "new water" created by the dam, was assigned to all owners of huerta land who had contributed to the cost of the structure. Their irrigable lands totaled about 30,000 *tahullas* (3600 ha), and the new water was divided on the basis of 1 minute per tahulla, or 64 m³/ha, for each twenty-one day rotation. This new water was attached to and was to be inseparable from the land. The other half of the water, the "old water" to which rights had been acquired before the dam was built, was divided among the old rightsholders in proportion to the rights that they owned.

The holders of old water were allowed to continue the practices of selling their basic water rights and of "renting" the use of their water for individual rotations. (It is interesting to note that the Alicantians use the same word, *arrendar,* as the Coloradoans, rent, for this type of transaction. See chapter 6.) Indeed, it was essential that rights to the use of old water continue to be vendible, for the new water alone was insufficient to irrigate the lands to which it was attached. In selling their water, however, old holders were made subject to a rule that it be used only on lands that were entitled to new water. The significance of this geographical constraint is that it prevented any expansion of the Huerta with use of old water and in this way kept down the price that shareholders could demand for their water. There has in fact been remarkably little expansion of the Huerta since the dam was completed. In addition to accepting this limit on the sale of their water, the old holders were required to renounce all claims to the Monnegre's flood waters, for it was these that were captured and distributed as new water.

The very existence of an active market for old water made it difficult to maintain the inalienability of new water, so that the owners of new water soon began to buy and sell rights to its use for individual rotations, even though this was in violation of the operating rules. At the same time, the basic rights to new water remained imprescriptible.

Operating procedures in Alicante today are controlled by this interesting solution to the sixteenth-century community's multiple objectives. Water was not attached to land in the sense that this was so in Valencia and Murcia-Orihuela, but the Huerta was stabilized and, so the farmers believed, provided with an adequate water supply. This turned out not to be the case, however. From the operating procedures adopted in 1594 we can calculate that the farmers expected or hoped to have in a good water year as much as three times the 4.5 Hm^3 that they get today; and so the search for more water has continued. [5] Furthermore, the solution created an antagonism between the owners of old and new water rights that has required continuing adjustments.

Before they found more water Alicante's farmers tried without success to control the price of Tibi's old water and to require the owners of this water to surrender their rights. [6] After repeated petitions by Alicante farmers, the national government in the late eighteenth century issued a directive that set a maximum price for rented water and prohibited the sale of such water to speculators or middlemen, but the order was not enforced. (We shall discuss below why the national government was involved at this time.) Subsequently, in the mid-nineteenth century, farmers petitioned for a regulation that would require the holders of old water to surrender their rights, which would then be distributed to the owners of new water. No such regulation was issued however. Thus of the several regulations proposed to reunite water and land or to reduce the antagonism between the owners of old and new water, only the sixteenth-century one that prohibited old shareholders from renting their water to farmers outside the Huerta appears to have been successful. It fixed the size and shape of today's Huerta.

OPERATING PROCEDURES FOR TIBI WATER

Although the supplementary water supplies that have been developed provide in an average year more than twice the quantity of water that is served from Tibi reservoir, the operating procedures for delivering the new sources are dominated by the procedures that the irrigation community developed centuries earlier for distributing the water behind its own dam.

Alicante's operating procedures are similar to neither the *turno* of Valencia, in which each farmer takes all the water that he needs once it reaches him in a rotation, nor the *tanda* of Murcia-Orihuela, in which each farmer takes whatever is available in the canal during his assigned time period. Unlike both of these systems, Alicante's water is distributed at a fixed rate, 150 1/s, approximately the same quantity of water is delivered in each successive rotation and the proportion of water available to any irrigator varies for each rotation depending on the water shares he acquires on each occasion. Furthermore, there are fewer changes in procedure to accommodate drought and canal officers have less discretionary power than in either of the other two systems.

The normal rotation is now twenty-three and one-half days, derived as follows:

Shares of new water (based on 1 min. for each of 30,660 tahullas)	511 hr.
Shares of old water (based on 1.5 hr. for each of 339 old shares, or 508 hr.; plus 19 hr. of old privileged water)	527
Shares owned by irrigation community (new shares added in 1926 to provide income for irrigation community, which rents them to farmers at each rotation)	92
Total	1130 hr.

The ordinances provide that water should run simultaneously in two continuous streams (*hilas* or *dulas*), each serving one farm at a time and approximately half of the Huerta in a full rotation. Thus forty-eight hours of water are delivered in a day, which, divided into the total shares to be served (1130 hours), gives a rotation period of approximately twenty-three and one-half days. The ordinances provide, further, that when water is short the two hilas are to be combined into one so that twenty-four rather than forty-eight hours are delivered in a day. Concomitantly, the time value of all shares of water is cut in half (a one-hour share is worth thirty minutes) and the rotation interval therefore remains unchanged. This procedure, called "double water," has been in effect constantly during most of this century so that the basic right of each tahulla has been effectively one-half rather than one minute and that of each old share forty-five rather than ninety minutes (although the irrigation syndicate continues to keep its records according to the old norms). Since 1954 when the new regulating basin was completed, water has again been distributed in two hilas, but each of these runs for twelve hours a day (the farmers no longer irrigate at night) so that the time value of individual shares has remained at half and the rotation interval at twenty-three and one-half days.

During the summer, due to heat, evaporation, and the growth stage of crops, farmers prefer water more frequently; it will be used more economically that way. The rotation period and the time value of water shares are both reduced, therefore, by one-third so that a summer rotation takes approximately fifteen and one-half days and an hour of double water is worth forty minutes.

We have said already that an exceptionally good water year will supply seventeen rotations, which are called tandas in Alicante. This consists of eleven full rotations (*tandas de fil* [hilo] or *tandas enteras*) totaling 259 days, and six summer rotations (*tandas de tersos* [*terceras*]) totaling ninety-four days.

When during drought there is insufficient water to follow these procedures, the two daytime hilas are combined into one, which is run alternately for three days in each of the two service areas. Also, a rotation is begun when the small regulating basins fill with water, thereby supplying approximately five days of service. The rotation is then interrupted until the basins refill, at which time service begins at the point in the canal network where it previously terminated. There are no other drought procedures.

When a superabundance of water makes it impractical or inefficient to follow the regular procedures, the community increases, up to doubling, its rate of delivery (from 150 to 300 l/s, the capacity of the canal system and the farmers' headgates). And if this procedure does not distribute the excess, they form additional streams (*hilas extraordinarias*) that run simultaneously with the two principal ones. But periods of superabundant or flood water, called in Alicante *agua de duit*, are short and few. A good water year with fourteen rotations such as 1959 saw only five to seven days of extraordinary hilas and 1960, with sixteen rotations, only three days.

Before each rotation the community posts a notice that announces the date on which the rotation will commence and informs all owners of rights to both old and new water that they should within a certain number of days claim their scrip for this rotation. The scrip, called *albalaes* (*albalás* in Valencian), are printed in twelve denominations (1 hour, and 30, 15, 10, 7-1/2, 5, 4, 3, 2, 1, 2/3, 1/3 minutes) that can be exchanged for one another (for example, a 1-hour albalae can be traded for two worth thirty minutes each). [7] There is no distinction between scrip issued for old and for new water rights and all scrip are exchangeable for Tibi water in any community canal. The actual value of the scrip is one-half its face value, however, because of the now normal procedure of double water. In addition to water time, all albalaes state the year and the number of the rotation for which they are valid, as shown in figure 4.2.

The scrip can be gotten on weekdays within the prescribed period at the syndicate's office in Alicante city, where women frequently claim them for their

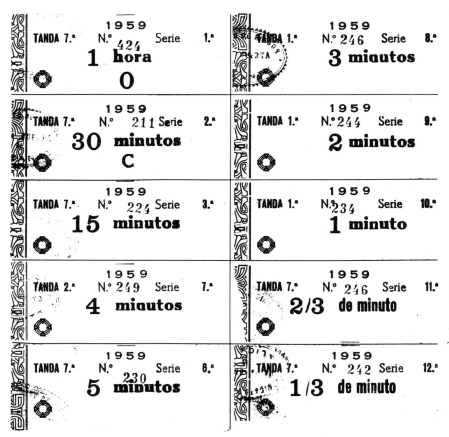

1959 TANDA 7.ª N.° 424 Serie 1.ª **1 hora** **0**	**1959** TANDA 1.ª N.° 246 Serie 8.ª **3 minutos**
1959 TANDA 7.ª N.° 211 Serie 2.ª **30 minutos** **C**	**1959** TANDA 1.ª N.° 244 Serie 9.ª **2 minutos**
1959 TANDA 7.ª N.° 224 Serie 3.ª **15 minutos**	**1959** TANDA 1.ª N.°234 Serie 10.ª **1 minuto**
1959 TANDA 2.ª N.° 249 Serie 7.ª **4 minutos**	**1959** TANDA 7.ª N.° 246 Serie 11.ª **2/3 de minuto**
1959 TANDA 7.ª N.° Serie 6.ª 230 **5 minutos**	**1959** TANDA 7.ª N.° 242 Serie 12.ª **1/3 de minuto**

Figure 4.2   Scrip (albalaes) used for delivery, exchange, and purchase of water
in Alicante.

working husbands, and on Sundays at the town hall in the pueblo of San Juan near the center of the Huerta, where frequently men claim them while their wives attend mass.

Not all farmers will irrigate on every rotation and farmers who do irrigate are likely to water some rather than all of their fields, all depending on their crops. But unless they have old water rights, farmers who irrigate are not likely to have enough scrip to exchange for the water they need; they have by right only four minutes of water at 150 1/s for each hectare they own in the Huerta. They must therefore obtain additional scrip either from nonirrigating farmers, from owners of old water, or from the irrigation community. (Otherwise they must buy water from one of the commercial companies.)

There is an informal market in which farmers can purchase scrip from the first two of these sources and a public auction for buying it from the third. The informal market is conducted principally in San Juan on Sunday mornings when the auction also is held and on Thursdays when, by local custom, farmers come to town for market day. On these occasions the huerta men stand around in small groups outside a tavern talking in subdued voices about all sorts of matters in general and about the price of water in particular. In the process sales are negotiated freely, but it is difficult for an outsider to see precisely when and how. There are no posted prices and no hawking. The prices paid by a farmer for an hour or fraction of one varies over the morning as the supply and demand relations develop in this informal manner. Despite ordinances designed to eliminate middlemen, there are brokers, all of them *huertanos,* who have bought water, principally from old shareholders, and sell it to farmers in need.

There is, however, a monitor on this informal market. It is the public auction of scrip by the community. The irrigation syndicate owns about ninety-two hours of water, most of which was issued to it in 1926 as a means of providing annual income for the community's operations. By voting to increase the total number of rights or hours that need to be served in each rotation the shareholders at that time reduced in effect the value of their individual rights in order to support their community. In addition, the syndicate controls a small number of shares that have been abandoned by their owners. When Huerta lands go out of agricultural production, usually for urban uses, their basic water rights become property of the irrigation community; for the owners of new water cannot transfer or dispose of their rights, which are tied to and inalienable from the land.

Apart from the water rights that it owns, the community sells during each rotation any scrip not claimed within the prescribed period. This frequently amounts to as much as eighty hours, although it may be less when water is in short supply.

The syndicate auctions the ninety-two hours of scrip that represent its own water on the first or first and second Sundays of a rotation, depending on the demand, and the forfeited scrip on the second, third, or if there is one, fourth Sunday, or any combination of these. At precisely 11 A. M. the secretary of the syndicate moves a table from inside the tavern to the covered portico outside, places on it the portfolio in which he has carried from the office in Alicante the albalaes he intends to sell, sits down, and begins the auction. At that moment most private trading ends and the farmers group loosely around the auction table. Water is auctioned in one-hour quantities; and although only irrigators are allowed to bid, the scrip, once purchased, are fully negotiable. Prices vary considerably from one Sunday to the next but are relatively stable on any typical Sunday.

The community makes a genuine effort to provide irrigators with information so they can bid and buy intelligently. The ditch riders are present in San Juan on Sunday and Thursday mornings and can tell a farmer when the water is likely to reach his property. The organization posts on a bulletin board outside the tavern a current report of water storage in the reservoir; a full account of all water delivered in the previous rotation, including the names of irrigators and the amounts of water delivered to each; and a full accounting of all water sold at auction in the previous rotation, including the names of all successful bidders, the number of hours each purchased, and the prices paid.

In Alicante the syndicate's ditch riders open and close all gates—control gates for laterals and headgates for farms, they collect albalaes from farmers in exchange for water they deliver, and at the conclusion of each rotation they render a full accounting to the community's head office of all water released from the regulating basins. A farmer who wants water in any rotation is supposed to give his ditch rider, from whom he can learn the approximate time that the hila will reach his farm, about two days' advance notice of his intention to irrigate; but frequently he gives less warning. According to the ordinances, farmers are to pay for water with albalaes at time of delivery; but this rule has never been enforced, a fact that has had a profound influence on the water market. The ditch riders' detailed reports on each rotation, accompanied by all albalaes they have collected, are due at headquarters three days after the conclusion of a rotation, making it essential that all farmers be paid up by then. But subject to this constraint, local custom has always allowed farmers to pay their ditch riders after they have received water. It is more than likely that the albalaes a farmer purchases in the market or at auction on Sunday are to pay for water already delivered to him rather than for water he intends to order. For this reason the price of water generally is significantly higher on the last Sunday of a rotation than on the first.

To a foreigner who has had an opportunity to study the detailed reports of individual rotations, the close agreement among the hypothetical length of a rotation (determined by the number of rights), the hours and minutes of water actually released from the regulating basins, and the hours and minutes of albalaes collected from farmers is uncanny. Thus shareholders who claim their scrip either use it or sell it—the market is efficient, and scrip that are not claimed are sold at auction by the syndicate. The surprisingly short periods of running water not covered by scrip are almost always accounted for by minor breaks and disruptions in the distribution network and ordinary canal losses.

ORGANIZATION OF ALICANTE'S COMMUNITY OF IRRIGATORS

The very small landowners of Alicante—63 percent of farm ownerships are less than 1 ha—have no direct say in the Huerta's irrigation syndicate. To participate in the community's general assembly, a farmer needs to own fifteen tahullas (1.8 ha) irrigated with water from Tibi reservoir; to vote for the syndicate's executive commission, ten tahullas (1.2 ha); and to be a candidate for election to the commission, thirty tahullas (3.6 ha). By comparison, all landholders are eligible to participate in all three of these activities in Valencia, Murcia, and Orihuela, except that to be an officer in the larger canal communities of Orihuela a farmer must own ten tahullas. On the other hand, each qualified participant in Alicante has one vote and decisions are by majority vote in both general assemblies and elections. Thus very big proprietors do not have a larger voice than others and the owners of large quantities of old water rights are represented only on the basis of their being proprietors of the requisite number or tahullas of huerta land. In Orihuela, for comparison, a landowner has one vote for each twenty tahullas up to a maximum of twenty votes except in election of canal officers, where the rule of one man one vote prevails, while Valencia and Murcia, like Alicante, deny a larger voice to large landholders.

The general assembly meets in February of each year in ordinary session to review and approve the budget and taxes and to consider any other matters submitted by the executive commission or by individual members. Extraordinary sessions can be called at any time by a majority vote of the executive commission or on the petition of twenty qualified proprietors. In the fifteen-year period 1950-1964 nine extraordinary assemblies were held, two in 1952 and one each in 1950, 1954, 1955, and 1961 through 1964. Five of these discussed efforts to bring additional water to the Huerta, two were concerned with "illegal" upstream diversions, and two with lining the huerta's canals.

The community's executive commission consists of twelve delegates, called *síndicos* in Alicante, half of them elected every two years for four-year terms. [8] Unlike Valencia, Murcia, and Orihuela, this commission is not elected by the general assembly because the qualifications of elector are lower than those of assembly member. Instead voters cast their ballots at the syndicate's office in Alicante on the first Sunday and Monday of December of election years. Each elector votes for four candidates and the top six are elected. Service as a delegate is obligatory and without compensation.

The commission elects from its members the principal executive officer of the community, who is called in Alicante *director* rather than síndico. The commission and its director are responsible for executing the operating procedures for water distribution; for regular maintenance and repair of the distribution system, including silt removal; and for naming and supervising the employees. The commission deliberates also on proposed changes in operating procedures, new construction, activities to increase water supply, tax rates and special assessments, the annual budget, and whether to bring or support law suits in the name of the community. But in these matters its recommendations must be approved by the general assembly.

Taxes for annual community expenses are assessed against water rights in the form of pesetas/per minute per trimester (two to three pesetas during the 1960s). Each year three rotations will be designated as *tandas de pago,* and for these community members must pay their taxes when they claim their scrip. The extraordinary costs of new works are financed by special assessments against water rights, and these are collected in the same manner but at different rotations than the ordinary expenses. Old rightsholders, therefore, pay taxes and assessments in proportion to the rights they own, although they are represented in the body that votes these taxes only if they own land in the Huerta and then with no more than one vote each. Similarly, new rightsholders who own less than 15 tahullas pay taxes and assessments on their water rights although they have no voice in the general assembly that has voted the rates; and if they own less than 10 tahullas they have had no voice in selecting the officers who recommend the taxes to the assembly.

The commission employs an executive secretary who runs the office, issues the albalaes, and conducts the auctions on Sundays. Employees who operate the distribution system include ditch riders, called *acequieros* or *martaveros* (from *martava* meaning rotation in Alicante), who deliver the water to each farmer; an inspector, who is responsible for the water from the time it leaves the regulating basins until it is picked up by the ditch riders; a damkeeper or *pantanero*; and guards.

The community's water court is composed of the director and two syndics of the executive commission, the latter rotated monthly. Like the courts in Valencia, Murcia, and Orihuela, it is a customary or private court, concerned only with infractions of the community's ordinances and rules for supply of water. In these matters the court determines the facts and exacts fines. Its proceedings are public, oral, and simple; and its decisions are final—unappealable.

The ordinances specify the offenses and the penalties that the court can assess for each. For the more serious transgressions, such as theft and waste of water, altering or damaging the canals and other works, and formerly for altering the hourglasses that were used to measure delivery time,[9] the penalty is to be as much as twice the damages caused, up to a fixed limit; and if the damages exceed this limit, the penalty can be as much as three times the loss up to a higher limit that is twelve and one-half times the lower one. For less serious offenses the ordinances specify minimum and maximum penalties without relation to damages. In each case the court, if it finds the accused guilty, fixes the fine within the legislative limits and in accord with its "prudent adjudication."

To enforce its regulations, Alicante today depends more on guards and less on adversary proceedings between farmers than either Valencia or Murcia-Orihuela, although this may not have been the case in earlier centuries when the accused typically received one-third of all fines (see table 4.5). In 1950, for example, the

Table 4.5 Enforcement proceedings in the water court of Alicante, 1960-1961.

All actions brought by syndicate employees	1960 (Good water year)	1961 (Poor water year)
For stealing water	3	5
For wasting water	1	—
For damage to canals	—	3
For irrigating without right	—	1

Source: Archives, Sindicato de Riegos de la Huerta de Alicante.

executive commission directed that "for greater effectiveness and as a stimulus to the guards" the latter be given 40 percent of all fines that result from complaints they make and that they be punished with suspension from their jobs for varying periods of time when complaints or knowledge of violations reach the commission from other sources. A farmer who complains about his neighbor will ask the guard to bring charges against him.

On the basis of operating procedures and administrative organization, one can see that Alicante farmers are freer from the discretionary authority of officers and employees of their own irrigation community than those of Valencia and probably of Murcia-Orihuela, also. This is so even though the ditch riders of Alicante open and close farm headgates, for their discretion in this matter is well circumscribed. Unlike their neighbors, farmers of Alicante are subject, however, to the discretion of a water market. How this limits or enlarges their freedom of action will be discussed later. Also, farmers in Alicante are not restricted to the use of water that is supplied by their syndicate; they have limited access to sources from the Segura River and from groundwater near Villena.

At the same time the Alicante community has been less free from the authority of provincial and central governments than the communities of Valencia and Murcia-Orihuela. Its ordinances today provide that the provincial governor can suspend any actions of the executive commission if in his view they are contrary to laws and regulations and that all actions of the director are to be under his "vigilance."[10]

To understand these restrictions, we need to look briefly at the community's history. When near the conclusion of the sixteenth century the landowners of Alicante decided to build Tibi Dam, they appealed to the king for help. Philip the Second responded with protection and limited aid. He gave license to the city of Alicante to build the dam and to borrow money for this purpose. Although he refused to provide capital because the work would in good part benefit existing landowners, he agreed, after obtaining approval from the church, to assign the proceeds of tithes and first fruits from the lands to be benefited (that is, 10 percent of their crops) to the city to amortize the costs of building the dam. He agreed not to take any profits himself from the water; and he provided the services of Spain's most distinguished hydraulic engineer, Juanelo Turriano, to review the plans and supervise the work. Finally, he agreed that authority and responsibility for distributing water from the dam would remain with the city so that the farmers did not lose control over their destinies to any significant degree.

In 1739, however, local control was ended and it was not revived for over a century. Tibi Dam was transferred to the royal patrimony, and a royal agent was appointed to administer the dam and the distribution of its water. Although operating procedures for water distribution remained the same and farmers continued to influence details of carrying them out, administrative and judicial powers were placed firmly in the hands of a royal agent who was known as judge-administrator and conservator of the royal dam works and its water. Among his other duties, this agent annually named the ditch riders.

Large public works, including dams, have typically been appropriated into the royal patrimony of monarchs who have sought to centralize authority. [11] The Bourbon kings, who had gained the throne of Spain at the beginning of the eighteenth century, centralized authority by this means as well as by abolishing many special statutes and privileges and applying the laws and practices of Castile. The irrigators of Valencia and Murcia-Orihuela did not, to the same extent as those of Alicante, lose control over their water distribution systems, the reason being the existence of the dam. There was no large public work to be seized. Also, it may be that the victorious Bourbon monarch was encouraged to exercise his right in Alicante because supporters of Archduke Charles of Austria had been relatively numerous there during the War of Succession.

Local control was reestablished in the nineteenth century, when the royal patrimony was abolished. [12] About 1840 the dam and responsibility for distributing its water were returned to Alicante. They were to be governed by an irrigation syndicate rather than, as before, by the municipal administration; but it was not until 1865 that the farmers won the right to choose and control their syndicate officers, subject to the appeals to the provincial governor mentioned earlier.

Alicante's irrigators lost control over their organization once again between 1936 and 1950. At the beginning of the civil war in 1936 the irrigation syndicate was taken over by workers' groups representing the anarchist *Confederación Nacional de Trabajo* (C.N.T.) and the socialist *Union General de Trabajadores* (U.G.T.). They formed a mixed governing committee that, under various changes in organization and personnel, remained in control until the end of the war in 1939. At that time the civil governor of the province named a commission of persons "disinterested in the politics of the Huerta" to manage the syndicate's affairs; and provincial supervision of the Huerta's administration continued for approximately ten years. As in the early eighteenth century, the farmers of Alicante appear to have paid a heavy price for their region's support of the loser in a civil war.

THE FURTHER SEARCH FOR WATER

In their search for water to supplement Tibi reservoir, and thereby to solve the problems that they could not reach by regulation, the Alicante irrigation community has looked underground within and outside of the Monnegre Valley, and on the surface within the Segura, Júcar, and Tajo River basins.

Monnegre Basin Groundwater

In the mid-nineteenth century the community invested heavily in an effort to gather groundwater in an area below the dam and conduct it to their distribution system by means of underground gravity-flow filtration galleries, similar to the *ganats* or *foggeras* of North Africa and the Near East, but this proved unproductive. Several years later they invested, also without return, in the sinking of artesian wells in the same region; and they have continued off and on to search for artesian sources until this day. As recently as 1957 the community dug a dry hole 210 meters (m) deep at a site named appropriately *Bancal de Mal Añ*. In reporting to the community on the failure of this undertaking, which had been costly, the irrigators' officers displayed a grace in defeat combined with an incorrigible optimism that is typical of Alicante's farmers. They said,

" . . . . All of the calculations of the engineers and geologists failed; similarly the illusion of the Huerta, nourished by 104 years of impatient hope failed. . . . The Huerta has held a utopian illusion for a century.

But as our mission is to find water for our lands, our response to this disillusion is to initiate steps by other ways, or other routes, directed to the attainment of our goal. . . . Today it is premature and perhaps indiscreet to say more, but we want it to be known that we are in a state of vigilance, and we shall not allow any opportunity whatever to escape us." [13]

Villena Water

Groundwater was developed successfully in the early twentieth century in a valley adjacent to the Monnegre, northwest of Alicante. A private company, Sociedad del Canal de la Huerta, produces this water, pumping it from deep wells near Villena, and delivers it to the Alicante Huerta, some 70 km away, and to other irrigable areas that lie between Villena and Alicante. Villena water is delivered to Alicante irrigators through the community's distribution system in canals and laterals that are not at the time receiving Tibi water. Farmers as individuals can buy Villena water by the hour for single rotations from offices of the company in Alicante and San Juan. (The San Juan office has been closed recently.) They will do so if it is available, if they need it, and if the price is right. The price, which is set by management of the Villena company, changes constantly in response to demand; and we shall later compare the cost to farmers of Villena water with that of other sources. Villena company regulations prohibit the sale or delivery of water in quantities of less than one hour, which, because company water is served at 100 rather than 150 l/s, is the equivalent of forty minutes of Tibi water. But the custom in the Huerta of selling small quantities of water is so strong that a farmer who needs only part of an hour that he has purchased can frequently sell the remainder to a neighbor, and the Villena company ditch rider will deliver the water in this way.

The history of contractual relations between the irrigation community and the Villena company are instructive for our purposes. In the original covenant of 1912 the company agreed to supply in perpetuity water that it had available up to 150 l/s constant flow for irrigation of lands that have Tibi rights. If the company had available a larger quantity of water, it could dispose of it in other areas; but it was to offer the water first to the Huerta, giving it "preference equitable in the circumstances." The community gave authority to the company to distribute Villena water through the syndicate's canals without charge.

About 1920 the community complained that the Villena company was not living up to its contract, that the quantity of water delivered to Alicante was less than 150 l/s, even though the company was providing water to lands outside of the Huerta. The company responded that it was impossible to comply with the original agreement because of the company's development as a profit-seeking entity, and it insisted that the agreement be modified. Company officers said frankly that whereas its founders had been altruistically interested in the Huerta, the wide distribution of company shares had changed the character of the organization. The contract required the company to deliver 150 l/s to the Huerta, but neither the irrigation community nor its farmers were obliged to buy any of this water on a permanent, seasonal, or even rotational basis. Farmers bought Villena water for individual rotations when they could not obtain sufficient Tibi water, which was cheaper; but such an arrangement was not the most profitable for the company. As a profit-seeking organization, the company could raise the price of its water if there were competition for it in other communities; but to develop competition the company had to be able to offer to other areas a guaranteed supply—especially since these areas typically did not have as good alternative sources as Tibi. The company's ability to do this was very much restricted by the 1912 contract.

The community agreed reluctantly to negotiations to modify the contract, but at the same time it began bargaining with the Compañía de Riegos de Levante for an alternative source of imported water. In the former negotiations the Villena company proposed that it be obligated to sell to the Huerta 25 percent of the water available at any time; that with respect to the next 35 percent, the Huerta's farmers should have right to the water if they offered a price that was not more than 10 percent below prices offered by those outside of the Huerta, this right to cease when deliveries reached 100 l/s; that the company be at liberty to sell the remaining 40 percent of water in or out of the Huerta. The community's counterproposal was that the company be required to supply to the Huerta 50 percent of its water and in no case less than 50 l/s, or alternatively 75 l/s. The settlement, reached in 1923, required the company to sell to the Huerta 50 percent of the water that it delivers in any year, but in the months April through October this quantity should not be less than 50 percent of what the company sells in one of these months. Also the community agreed that if other commercial enterprises bring new water into the Huerta, the Villena company can call for renegotiation of the contract.

Within a year Alicante announced that it had signed a contract for additional water with Riegos de Levante, whereupon the Sociedad del Canal de la Huerta informed the community that it considered itself relieved of all obligations to sell water to the Huerta. The community threatened to deny the company the use of its canal system; but the threat was ineffective, and to this day no new contract has been negotiated, and the company is free to sell water where it will.

Community officers now admit that they made a mistake in 1923 and 1924 by allowing the two contracts to be broken so easily, that they were at the time overoptimistic about the new contract for Segura River water, and that they could today use all the Villena water. In 1950, as a matter of fact, the community inaugurated a campaign to acquire control of the Villena company, urging farmers to buy shares and purchasing some with community funds. The rationale of this effort, published in a special edition of the syndicate's bulletin, was as follows:

To the Huerta of Alicante:

In the ordinary General Assembly celebrated last March, when the Syndicate disclosed all of its projects for the consideration of landowners, a member of the Syndicate made a concrete and solemn declaration that in the term of a year the water flow that fertilizes our Huerta would be increased. . . .

This promise was not the utopic product of a crazy fantasy. . . ; it is inspired by a tangible reality, with which we can live daily and even so fail to appreciate that only through it can we realize our aspirations of agricultural regeneration: Sociedad del Canal de la Huerta.

This entity, that began its legal life with an unquestionably commercial character, cannot disavow the indubitable and legitimate interests of its namesake, the Huerta of Alicante, by always deferring the Huerta's rights and necessities. . . . At the present time the Canal carries a water volume that is less than half of its capacity, of which almost 99% is distributed through upstream diversions. To completely ignore the Huerta of Alicante, bringing ruin to its farms, is to deny the moral nature of this Alicantían organization, *purely Alicantían,* for this characteristic was the corner stone on which its founders, with the talisman of their indomitable will, fashioned this great enterprise.

The Syndicate, as the genuine representative of the Alicante Huerta and performing a guardian's function, aspires to conciliate in a harmonious unity the interests of all. . . ; it aspires to regain possession for the Huerta of its full rights without injuring in the least the equally respectable interests of those who, motivated by their love of the Huerta, knew in their own time how to give generously of their capital and savings to finance the construction of a work that was the pride of our ancestors and that we, up to now, have not known how to maintain as the sacred legacy that it is. This we must confess. The Canal was built for the Huerta, and the Huerta is least benefited by the advantages that it offers. . . .

The great progressive conquests that improve the conditions of human well being are always the product of work, sacrifice and intelligence. We should not expect ever to get anything free. What, then, will be our rule of conduct in the development of an orderly, free and conscious activity?

The syndicate invites all landowners of the Huerta to invest their savings in the purchase of shares of the Sociedad del Canal, to enable them to control at any time the internal life and activities of the company. No landowner should fail to become a stockholder, with the assurance and guarantee that the invested capital, besides drawing a moderate legal interest, will serve the purpose of making the company by fact and right an Alicante instrument at the service of our agricultural regeneration. The day in which the majority of the capital becomes property of the Huerta will be the day of victory, the Canal will be ours. It was for this purpose that our fathers built this work, representing their tenacity and *alicantinismo*. The ownership of the Dam's water is joined to ownership of land, the two are consubstantial in a unity. . . . In the same way, water in the Canal de la Huerta should be ascribed to shares, and these should be the property of the irrigator. . . .

The Syndicate has established for this purpose an office to expedite the sale and purchase of shares at the current price (875 pesetas each), trying to allocate all of these to the landowners of the Huerta. That is the present road, so that in the near future we shall see turned into a comforting reality and positive work what today is the noblest aspiration of this Syndicate and the Huerta's unanimous desire.

Put aside all doubts and with firmness contribute a mite of your savings. The Huerta should not rest until it can cry out with the hero's conviction: *the Canal is mine. I built it and I have rescued it.* Here is the key to greatness and well being. [14]

But this operation was indeed a *loca fantasía.* There are some twelve thousand shares of the company. In four years the community's syndicate was able to acquire seventy, and although the number of shares purchased by individual farmers is not known, it was presumably few. In 1954 the community terminated the affair by selling its shares.

Segura River Water

Between 1918 and 1922 the Spanish government granted to Riegos de Levante, a new commercial enterprise, concessions to withdraw 7.7 l/s from the Segura River delta to irrigate approximately 10,000 ha in a prescribed service area near Elche, between Alicante and Murcia (see figure 4.1). This water, gathered from the river channel and drainage canals (*azarbes*) would otherwise waste to the sea. The company, with financing from the House of Dreyfus in Paris, built pumping stations to lift water as much as 110 m to the service area, hydroelectric and thermal generating stations to operate the immense pumps, and a distribution system of regulating basins and canals. Almost immediately the company began to expand by supplying more lands than planned initially within the defined service area and by extending service to additional areas.

In 1924 the company contracted to lengthen one of its principal canals about 25 km so that the Segura River water could be delivered to the Huerta of Alicante. The irrigation community provided the capital for the work, raising this by a special assessment of its members and a bank loan. Levante paid the community four pesetas for each hour of water that the company delivered in the Huerta, and the community used this income to pay off the loan. Although the contract, unlike that with the Villena company, did not guarantee delivery of a fixed quantity of water, it did provide that the company was to supply Alicante at all times with a proportion of Levante water to be determined by the size of the Alicante service area in relation to that of all other sectors served by the company. This was made subject, however, to the requirements of any general operating procedures established by the company.

The Levante company sold water directly to farmers at daily public auction, conducted for Alicante's irrigators in San Juan; but auction prices were constrained by minimum and maximum levels that had been imposed as a condition of the government's concession of Segura River water. The minimum price was twenty-seven pesetas per hour of water delivered at 150 l/s—or twenty-seven pesetas for 450 m³. The maximum price during nine months of the year was exactly twice this amount and during the three summer months three times the minimum.

In 1940, after a series of dry years, farmers of the initial service sectors rebelled against what they considered to be company mismanagement and demanded intervention by the national government. They complained that the price of Levante water reached the maximum limit almost every year and that this was too high for their economic well-being and higher than it need or should be for several reasons, principally these: the company had greatly extended its service area beyond the hydraulic possibilities of its water supply. In the authorized zone near Elche it had delivered water to approximately 6500 ha more than the 10,000 initially approved, and it had extended service to approximately 17,000 ha outside of the authorized zone. (The number of hectares to which water was delivered in any one year was, however, considerably less than this total of 33,000.) The company had served water at times and places and by procedures that were most convenient and profitable to itself (to sectors with minimum pumping costs or where the bidding was highest) without regard to the farmers' interests. The company had sold much of its insufficient production of electric energy for industrial uses, relegating irrigation to second place in its operations.

Alicante's farmers were not leaders in the revolt, and this for good reason. Although their supply of Levante water was irregular and less than they had hoped for when they signed the contract with the company, delivery of any water to their zone was unauthorized in the government documents of concession; it was the result of a private contract between the irrigation community and the company.

The government did intervene, and it took seven years to "normalize" the operating procedures of the company, over which time it became a closely regulated public utility. The steps of normalization included careful redefinition of the service area and its several sectors, reform of operating procedures for distributing water to the sectors and to irrigators within each sector, suppressing water sales by auction and in its place fixing uniform prices, organizing a representative irrigation community for the company's full service area and endowing it with some controls over the administration of operating procedures, and minor structural changes in the distribution system.

As a result of the normalization process Alicante was allotted 6 percent of the water supply available to Levante at any time, although the Alicante Huerta constituted 10 percent of the company's service area. [15] This apparent discrepancy was due to several factors, including Alicante's unauthorized status and its rights to an alternative source of water in Tibi Dam. It did not change significantly the actual postiton of the Huerta before reorganization. But this was 6 percent of a highly variable water supply, for the water available to Levante in any year for distribution to all its sectors is a function of flow at the mouth of the Segura River after upstream users have satisfied their requirements and of the availablity of electricity for pumping, which is in turn a function of storage in upstream Segura reservoirs and of electric production in thermal plants.

A rough estimate of Levante water available to Alicante during the eleven-year period 1949–1960, calculated by taking 6 percent of the water delivered by the company to all sectors during these years, is shown in table 4.4, column (4). The water actually delivered to Alicante by Levante in certain illustrative years is shown in column (5). These measures differ for a number of reasons. Irrigators in other sectors of the company's service area may not buy all the water to which they are entitled, in which case more water than the quantity to which they are entitled can be supplied to Alicante. Or Alicante farmers may not purchase the Levante water available to them because they are enjoying a superabundant supply of local water, because a severe drought early in the season has destroyed their crops, or because Levante water is available at the wrong time. (Droughts in the Monnegre and Segura River basins do not necessarily occur simultaneously.) Or there may be maintenance problems in different parts of the company's distribution system that limit water deliveries.

To distribute to each sector its assigned percentage of total supply, the company was directed to use certain procedures, some of them similar to those that had been used before normalization. The company is to deliver water to farmers' headgates at 50 l/s except in Alicante, where to be consistent with the operating procedure for Tibi water, it is delivered at 150 l/s. By delivering water almost simultaneously in several major canals, the company is able to serve 1800 hours of water (at 50 l/s) in a normal day, and at this rate it can reach all zones within three days, which was then fixed as the normal rotation period. With 6 percent of the water, Alicante is entitled to 324 hours in a normal rotation (or 108 hours at 150 l/s), and the normal operating procedure approved for the delivery of this water requires service of 108 hours (36 hours at 150 l/s) each day between the hours of 0600 and 2200. Additional rules, similar in form, were prescribed for periods when water supply is below normal.

These procedures relate to the distribution of the company's total water supply among its principal service sectors and not to its distribution to individual farmers. The fact that Alicante gets x hours of water on a given day or in a rotation does not mean that a farmer who needs water can necessarily get it on that day or in that rotation. According to the procedures adopted in the process of normalization, the right to purchase and use water is limited to property owners whose names are recorded in a census that was taken and is maintained by the new organization that represents the farmers of all of the company's service areas. For Alicante this census is identical to the list of members of the Huerta's syndicate. Each irrigator is given a passbook, called a *carnet*, with his name and the number of tahullas that he irrigates. There are two operating procedures. One, called distribution by carnet, is used when the water available in a sector is persistently insufficient to meet all demands for it; and the other, called unlimited distribution, is used when there is sufficient water. In the former case any irrigator is entitled, by virtue of his carnet, to purchase twenty minutes of water for every ten tahullas (1.2 ha) of land in his farm or fraction thereof. [16] This ration does not represent the amount of water needed for ten tahullas; for on the average an irrigator can wet only two of them with twenty minutes of water at 150 l/s. Nor does it represent the quantity necessary to ensure that each farmer can irrigate on each rotation. It would require a thousand hours of water if every ten tahullas in the Huerta were to receive twenty minutes of water on a single rotation. The formula is simply a means for apportioning a water shortage among irrigators, and it does this in relation to the size of their farms.

As a general rule Levante water is delivered in any rotation to farmers who have purchased it, in the order of their location on distribution laterals, as published in the census. When all farmers who have requested it cannot be served, delivery resumes in the next rotation where it previously terminated until the entire sector has been covered.

Farmers are required to purchase their water at least twelve hours before it is scheduled to run in their laterals, except in Alicante, whose irrigators can buy their water after it has been delivered. Alicante had objected to the general procedure because it was inconsistent with local custom, and the company agreed to follow the methods used for Tibi water.

Water is distributed by carnet in Alicante an average of four or five months during the year. The remainder of the time an unlimited procedure is used. An irrigator's purchase of water is not formally constrained, but this does not mean necessarily that he is able to obtain delivery whenever he wants it.

It is interesting to regard the similarity between the normalization of water distribution for Levante in the 1940s and that for Tibi Dam in the 1590s. In neither case was water attached to land in the sense that this is so in Valencia and Murcia-Orihuela. In both cases a principal result of the process was to stabilize the service area, to stop expansion. And in both cases minimum service was guaranteed to each unit of land—for Tibi one (now ½) minute/tahulla; for Levante, two minutes—while farmers were not required to use this service and were free to transfer it to others. For Tibi water the transfer is made by selling scrip, for Levante, by not purchasing water. As for acquiring more water than the minimum guarantee, a farmer can purchase more Tibi water if he is willing to pay for it; the price system does the rationing. As the price of Levante water is fixed, price is less effective for rationing and regulation is required—a farmer may not purchase more than the minimum as long as demand persistently exceeds supply.

Water From Other River Basins

Finally, Alicante has sought new water in the Júcar and Tajo River basins and in certain coastal rivers northeast of the Monnegre by promoting or supporting large government plans for storage structures on these streams, along with delivery canals and transmountain diversions from them. Thus Alicante has had plans dating back to the seventeenth century to draw water from the Júcar to their Huerta, but when in the 1950s adequate storage came to be provided on that river, the water was diverted northeast to the province of Valencia rather than southwest to Alicante. Similarly, the canal system that was built recently to connect new storage reservoirs on the coastal streams stops just short of the Alicante Huerta.

As mentioned in chapter 3, the national government has recently undertaken a major system of hydraulic works to transfer water from the Tajo to the Segura River basin. Some of this water will be transported as far as Elche for irrigation, but none is expected to reach Alicante.

ANALYSIS OF WATER MARKET

Table 4.6 gives data for twelve auctions attended by Maass in 1960–61. A thirty-minute unit is used because it is the basic unit for sale of Tibi water—one hour of double water. Villena and Levante sell water only by the hour, however, so their data have been converted to the shorter period for purposes of comparison. Also, because Villena water is delivered at 100 rather than 150 l/s, an additional adjustment has been made for it.

Information is incomplete on the informal market for Tibi water—columns

(9) and (10)—and on Villena water—columns (11) and (12). As for the former, one would have to be a local farmer to understand the unstructured negotiations of this marketplace, and then he might not know how to record it. When the Villena company's small office in San Juan was open on Sundays, the price that the company's agent was charging was recorded. If the office was closed on Sunday, as was frequently the case, it probably was closed also on market day, Thursday, meaning that the company was disposing of all of its water in service areas outside of the Alicante Huerta. But this was not necessarily the case, and no first-hand observations were made on Thursdays. The observed Villena data are in this sense incomplete, and the company management was unusually secretive about its operations.

In the last week of December 1960 the community began the sixteenth and last rotation of a very good water year. On Sunday, December 25, the syndicate auctioned approximately half of its own ninety-two half-hours of water; and it is interesting to observe that in rural and Catholic Spain religious imperatives, even those related to Christ's birth, did not preempt local customs and industry—a policy that may itself be very Catholic. The previous Sunday, for which data are not in the table, the syndicate had auctioned the last of its unclaimed scrip for the fifteenth rotation, and the average price had been two hundred fifty pesetas, compared to one hundred seventy-five on Christmas day. The reason is that with the fifteenth rotation drawing to a close, farmers who had taken water service but had not paid for it had little time in which to do so; they had to buy the necessary scrip. Water on the informal market had also averaged two hundred fifty pesetas on the Sunday before Christmas, whereas there was little activity in this arena at the beginning of the new rotation on Christmas day. Consistent with these observations, the data indicate a general rule that the price of water in any rotation increases as the rotation progresses and more and more farmers need to buy albalaes to pay for water already used.

It can be seen also that prices for water at auction and in the market are approximately the same. Since many more hours of water change hands in the market than are sold at auction, it is more likely that the market determines the auction price than the other way around. At the same time, the auction monitors the market and is a more effective regulator of its prices and its operations than have been any legislative efforts.

On Sunday, January 15, the secretary of the irrigation community decided without advance notice not to conduct an auction but to hold the remaining forty-six half-hours of unclaimed scrip for sale on the following Sunday, which would be at the end of the rotation. As a consequence there was fairly heavy trading on the informal market. The secretary has some discretion in deciding whether or not to hold an auction on certain Sundays and how many hours of water to sell on a given Sunday. Thus, for example, on the sixteenth rotation of 1960 and the second of 1961, he divided the syndicate's ninety-two half-hours of water into two lots and sold them on two successive Sundays, whereas he sold them all on the first Sunday for the first rotation of 1961 and did not hold an

Table 4.6 Prices of water from several sources, Huerta of Alicante, 1961.

| | | Tibi Water | | | | | |
| | | Auction | | | | | |
(1) Date	(2) Rotation	(3) Type (S-Syndicate, U-unclaimed scrip)	(4) Hrs. sold	(5) Max. price/ 30 min. (ptas)	(6) Min. price/ 30 min. (ptas)	(7) Av. price/ 30 min. (ptas)	(8) No. buyers
25 Dec. 60	16-1960	S	45	186	167	175	9
1 Jan. 61	16-1960	S	47	190	140	178	9
8 Jan. 61	16-1960	U	35	191	182	187	15
15 Jan. 61	16-1960	—	—	—	—	—	—
22 Jan. 61	16-1960	U	46	215	170	209	10
29 Jan. 61	16-1960	—	—	—	—	—	—
	1-1961	S	92	201	173	198	20
5 Feb. 61	1-1961	—	—	—	—	—	—
12 Feb. 61	1-1961	U	30	251	248	250	15
19 Feb. 61	1-1961	U	30	311	300	305	14
26 Feb. 61	1-1961	U	21	157	153	155	6
	2-1961	S	45	197	191	194	17
5 Mar. 61	1-1961	—	—	—	—	—	—
	2-1961	S	47	212	210	211	10
20 Aug. 61	4T-1961	—	—	—	—	—	—

Source: Observation of Maass while attending auctions.

Notes: Column (2): T = Summer rotation of 20 minutes. Column (12): Villena water is sold in units of one hour at 100 l/s. These have been converted into 30 minutes at 150 l/s. Column (14): Levante water is sold in units of one hour at 50 l/s. These have been converted into 30 minutes at 150 l/s.

		Villena Water		Levante Water	
Informal Market					
(9) Activity (H-high, L-low, N-normal)	(10) Av. price/ 30 min. (ptas)	(11) Selling (O-office open, C-office closed)	(12) Price/30 min. (ptas)	(13) Operating procedure (C-carnet, U-unlimited)	(14) Price/30 min. (ptas)
L	?	O	225	U	120
N	178	O	180	U	120
?	?	C	?	U	120
H	210	C	?	U	120
L	?	C	?	U	120
H	225	—	—	—	—
?	?	O	300	U	120
L	200	C	?	U	120
N	250	C	?	U	120
N	305	C	?	U	120
?	?	—	—	—	—
?	?	C	?	U	120
N	300	—	—	—	—
N	210	C	?	U	120
—	—	C	—	C	120

auction the next week. Similarly, he divided the unclaimed scrip for the last rotation of 1960 into two lots, selling them on January 8 and 22, with no auction on the week in between, while he divided an equal number of unclaimed scrip for the first rotation of 1961 into three lots and held auctions on three successive Sundays. His discretion is controlled, it would appear, by two considerations: first, to obtain a good price for the water; for the higher the price, the greater the income to pay for the community's operating expenses. It may be that by withholding water on January 15 he got more for it on January 22 when the rotation was near its end. Second, to maintain the confidence of his constituents, which means, among other things, that the farmers do not believe or even suspect that he is trying in any way to manipulate prices and that he caters to their convenience. Thus the secretary may have catered to the convenience of farmers and at the same time have reduced speculation in the market when he held the auction at the conclusion of the rotation on January 22 rather than on January 15.

On the last Sunday of January the syndicate sold ninety-two half-hours of water for the first rotation of 1961 at an average price of 198 pesetas; yet water was selling on the open market for 225 pesetas. The reason is that the albalaes being traded on the open market were for the previous rotation. The ditch riders had to balance their books almost immediately, and farmers who had delayed until this very last moment to settle had to pay a premium price.

The price of water rose fifty pesetas per half-hour, or 25 percent, between the first and second auctions of the first rotation of 1961. The reasons are not known precisely, but they include these: Huerta crops were developing rapidly, requiring more water. The rotation was farther along and there had been no auction the previous week, so many farmers needed scrip to pay for water already delivered to them. Most important, whereas 1960 had been a good water year, it began to appear in mid-February that 1961 could be a bad one. January and February had been drier than normal. The posted notices on status of water in Tibi reservoir gave these comparative data (in local units of measurement, whose absolute values need not concern us):

	February 4, 1961	February 18, 1961
Height of water (palmos)	79	70
Side wall exposed (palmos)	32	34
Water entering reservoir in previous 2-week period (hilas)	1	¼
Water released from reservoir in previous 2-week period (hilas)	½	1

Appearances soon became reality. I left Alicante in early March as the second rotation of the year was commencing and returned on Sunday, August 20, when the fourth rotation, for which scrip had been distributed on June 16, was still underway. There was no auction on that day; there was no water. Since July 1 a total of thirty half-hours of water had been delivered.

At the time, there was no equivalent drought in the Segura, and Riegos de Levante was serving water. It was being distributed on carnet at the fixed price of 120 pesetas for the Alicante half-hour. Although it is somewhat inferior in quality to Tibi water, farmers generally prefer Levante water because of this fixed and low price. Few if any irrigators can get all that they need when they need it, however, so they are dependent on both sources. At the same time, the price of Levante water can have an influence on the Tibi product. As a partial explanation for the low price of first rotation water in the February 26 auction a farmer told the author that, expecting to use Tibi water, he had purchased scrip on the previous Sunday but found during the week that Levante water was running well and that it could be delivered to his farm before Tibi water would reach it. He therefore bought Levante water and sold his Tibi scrip on the following Sunday. Because a number of farmers had done the same, the price of Tibi water dropped.

It will be observed that on December 25 and again on January 29 the Villena company was selling water at a price significantly higher than those of the auction and open market. The company agent reported that he had few customers. But why did he have any? Why would a farmer pay such a premium? The reason relates to delivery schedules. The farms of these irrigators may have been one or two weeks away from delivery of Tibi water yet able to receive quick service from the Villena company, and their crops may have needed water. The seasonal water requirements of all crops grown in the Huerta are by no means correlated with the rotation intervals of Tibi water.

The water market, then, is fairly complex. Its prices reflect not only the water requirements of crops that have been seeded, which themselves change in variety from year to year, water available in Tibi reservoir, and rainfall on the Huerta, but also the availability and prices of water from three alternative sources: the Segura River, groundwater of Villena, and local private wells.

Table 4.7 illustrates certain additional characteristics of this market. Prices in the very good water year of 1960, which was the first time in forty years that the dam had overflowed, were generally higher than those of 1950, which had been a fairly good year; and they were markedly higher in the summer months. This was due to a change in crops. The years 1950 and 1960 saw a great expansion in the planting of tomatoes for the European export market. This crop has a high demand for water, and the size and quality of its fruit are sensitive to the water's salt. In the summer months Alicante growers much prefer Tibi to Levante water because of its lower salt content, but in other months of the year they can tolerate water that has been transported from the Segura River.

One might expect the average yearly price of water in a year of severe drought to be higher than that in a year of relative abundance, but the data in table 4.7 demonstrate that this is not the case. The reason is that farmers' demands for water fall precipitously once the drought becomes so severe that they have lost large portions of their crops.

OBJECTIVES AND COMPARISONS

Unite Water and Land

Observers and critics from outside the Huerta, especially those who are partisans of Valencia and Murcia-Orihuela, hold that a principal objective in Alicante is, or if it isn't it should be, to reattach water to land. Alicante's farmers, in recent years at least, have been less persistent about this goal than have been observers from neighboring huertas. One reason for concern about separation of the two resources is fear that sale of water apart from land results necessarily in speculatively high prices for the former. As we have seen and as Alicantians know, this need not be the case.

As for the short-term sale of water for individual rotations, one can argue that this does not involve a basic separation of water from land, that the operating procedures of most communities use some method to transfer water in a given rotation from one farmer to another who has greater need for it, and that Alicante's weekly market and auction are no more than one possible procedure for doing this. Furthermore, although regulations designed to control price speculation have failed, the Alicante operating procedures themselves include certain protections against speculation—the number of potential buyers of water is limited to members of the community who are connected to the distribution system and whose lands are at the moment prepared for irrigation, and there are institutions and procedures that monitor the market, namely the syndicate's auction and the availability of alternative sources of water.

In the long run, regulation for price control has been effective. The sixteenth-century provisions that old water rights can be sold only to those who have new ones and that the latter cannot be sold apart from the lands to which they are attached remain unchanged today.[17] As a consequence the size of the Huerta has been relatively stable for centuries, which has undoubtedly had a profound influence in reducing pressure on water prices. Definition of huerta boundaries is, in other words, an effective method of long-term control. We have seen that it was also used in the normalization of Levante's operations.

A second reason for concern about the marital state of water and land relates to the capacity of farmers to control their own destinies as farmers. Such control requires a strong and coherent community of irrigators that limits the freedom of its members to pursue personal and partial interests that are inconsistent with the community interest and that has the capacity to solve conflicts among its members. A community that is strong in these ways limits the dangers to com-

Table 4.7 Average price of auctioned water in each rotation. Comparison of certain good and poor water years, Tibi reservoir, Alicante (in pesetas per thirty minutes).

Rotation	Two Good Water Years		Two Poor Water Years	
	1950	1960	1953	1961
1	42	144	101	197
2	55	98	105	202
3	32	123	53	229
4	93	186		341 T
5	221 T	152		461 T
6	191 T	180		179
7	200 T	534 T		
8	164 T	959 T		
9	107 T	728 T		
10	152 T	1052 T		
11	79	977 T		
12	102	999 T		
13		432		
14	.	243		
15		166		
16		180		
Annual average	120	447	86	318

Source: Archives, Sindicato de Riegos de la Huerta de Alicante.

Note: T = summer rotation of 20 minutes. Prices have been converted to 30-minute basis.

munity autonomy and interest that are inherent in appeals to higher authorities to settle conflicts and in disorders that result from failing to settle them. The question is whether the separation of land and water rights in Alicante has created antagonistic interests that inhibit forming a highly integrated community. It is doubtful that the short-term sale of water has had such an incapacitating effect. To the contrary, the institutions and procedures for auction and sale of water for individual rotations, including the brotherly Sunday meetings in San Juan where this is done, may have given the community greater strength and integrity. Owing to these institutions, the Alicante farmer may be freer than his compatriots in Valencia and Murcia-Orihuela from operating procedures that greatly restrict his independence, especially those that endow canal officers with considerable arbitrary authority. He is never subjected to an extraordinary drought procedure, as in Valencia, where canal officers allocate water to particular crops and fields. He need not contend with complex rules, like those of Murcia-Orihuela, on the use of "excess" water or with elaborate regulations respecting water waste, service of lands that are difficult to irrigate, and similar matters as in Valencia and Murcia-Orihuela. The market discourages waste and regulates in other respects. And it has done so in a manner that has apparently satisfied its customers, for when foreign sources of water have been imported to the Huerta, the community has required, to the extent that it could, that these be distributed by a procedure analogous to that for Tibi water. Had the farmers been unhappy with Tibi procedures, they might have challenged them by accepting alternative procedures for distributing the new sources.[18]

At the same time, the long-term interests of those who own old water rights without equivalent land and those of farmers who own new water rights that are inadequate for their lands have been sufficiently discordant in the past to create a disruptive environment. To protect against this the community has adopted membership and voting criteria that limit the influence of the interests that are likely to be the most antagonistic: the large holders of old water rights and the proprietors of very small, uneconomic-sized farms.

A third reason for concern over the separation of land and water relates to equity—whether those who contribute neither their capital nor their labor directly to the land should be allowed to profit from it through ownership or control of water, without which the land cannot flower. This particular care for justice is found especially among the outside critics of Alicante's operating procedures. To be sure, the region's land proprietors and farmers have been concerned, witness the petitions in the eighteenth and nineteenth centuries cited earlier for regulations that would require the holders of old rights to surrender them; but Alicantians have typically mitigated their anxieties on this score with concern for the protection of acquired rights. This can be seen in the sixteenth century in the settlement of interests when the dam was built as well as today in a proposal that has been discussed, but not adopted, by the community to retire old rights by purchasing them at full value. The community would borrow money to buy the rights and pay off the debt incurred by renting at auction at each rotation the water appurtenant to them. When by this means enough money had been raised to complete payment, the rights to old water would be distributed to those who own new rights, thereby increasing the irrigators' basic dotation from 1 to 2 minutes per tahulla (actually from one-half to 1 minute).

Equality

As a criterion for the distribution of water, equality is mentioned infrequently in the documentation on Alicante. The 1865 ordinances, for example, say that the syndicate is to decide on any increase or diminution in the quantity of irrigation water "always with the objective of its more equitable and better use," but there is no mention of equality.[19] Regardless, and for purposes of information and comparison, we should determine if the operating procedures in Alicante, like those of Valencia and Murcia-Orihuela, are in fact based on proportional equality, on the concept that basic rights, as well as the shorter term costs and benefits of drought and water abundance respectively, should be distributed among irrigators in proportion to the needs of their crops or the size of their farms.

Operating procedures for drought—doubling water and reducing the number of rotations—affect all land users and all rightsholders. There is no distinction between the scrip issued for old and new water rights, so when the value of scrip is halved or when scrip are not issued for expected rotations, the influence is ubiquitous. Beyond this, however, drought procedures have different impacts on four classes of rightsholders—owners of new and of old rights who use their water on their land and owners of old and of new rights who sell their scrip. Under drought procedures new and old rightsholders who are farming their lands will pay higher prices than normal for additional Tibi water and for Villena and private well water, which will be rationed among them by means of market prices; and they will line up for one-price Levante water, which will be rationed in proportion to the size of their farms. All such rightsholders are equally free to participate in the market and to apply for the rationed water. But the needs of irrigators who own old in addition to new water will be less, obviously, than the needs of those who have new water only, at the same time that the former will likely have greater economic means to meet these needs than the smaller shareholders. The impact of drought procedure on rightsholders who sell their water is clearly different than on farmers who use it, although it is difficult to measure these consequences precisely. On the one hand, the nonusers have less water to sell than in the normal hydrologic situation, fewer scrip and these worth less in water time. On the other, they can usually get a higher price per unit for what they sell.

Operating procedures for flood or superabundant water—doubling the quantity of water delivered in a given time period and forming extra delivery streams —also have differential effects on the several classes of water owners. Rightsholders who do not irrigate do not enjoy the benefits of abundance; they can neither use the water nor sell it since extra scrip are not issued for agua de duit. At the same time, the price that they can command for their scrip in any rotation that is concurrent with flood water is likely to drop, so that superabundance is in this sense especially costly to owners of old rights who do not farm. All who are prepared to irrigate at the time of flood water are likely to share its benefits by either receiving the extra water or, if they are out of reach of this, by paying less on the market for rotation water.

Considering all new water owners as a group, one can argue that there is greater proportional equality for them than there is for irrigators in Valencia and Murcia-Orihuela. Alicante farmers whose lands are momentarily fallow or not in need of water do not lose the benefits of a rotation; they can exchange their basic rights for cash and presumably use this to buy additional water in the future when they need it. The technique of water transfer is much less direct in Valencia and Murcia-Orihuela. It is tempting, then, to treat old Tibi water as simply another external source of supply for which all farmers can compete in a market that is sufficiently monitored to prevent highly speculative prices and to conclude that Alicante's farmers are more equal among themselves than Valencia's. The trouble with such an analysis is that old water is not entirely external to the community of new rights irrigators, because many farmers own both new and old rights. Therefore, the basic distribution of water rights to farms in terms of their size, or to farmers as individuals, however you look at it, is unequal.

Efficiency

The achievement of efficiency, we noted in chapter 1, requires institutions that can maintain a particular balance between flexibility, which is necessary if water is to be transferred from less to more efficient uses, and certainty, needed if farmers are to make the investments of labor and capital that are consistent with efficient use of water. How do we evaluate the Alicante procedures in this context? They rate very high indeed on short-term flexibility. The market works well as a means for transferring water in individual rotations. We have noted the remarkable agreement in the syndicate's records between hours of water available for distribution and hours delivered and used. Shareholders who claim their scrip either use them or sell them and unclaimed scrip are sold at auction by the syndicate. The Alicante procedures are probably less wasteful of water than either the turn of Valencia or the rotation of Murcia-Orihuela, for the incentives to conserve are pervasive. Apart from the market, other procedures such as the delivery of water at a constant rate, made possible by the reservoir and the regulating basins, and the shorter summer rotation are designed for greater efficiency in the use of water and, in part, for convenience as well.

To compare the operating procedures of Alicante, Valencia, Murcia-Orihuela, and a hypothetical community that uses a demand procedure, we have again used the simulation program, which measures efficiency in terms of net increases in regional income rather than the narrower criterion of minimizing water waste. Like the comparisons of the previous chapter, it has been necessary to make many simplifying assumptions about cost and benefit functions and operating procedures. This basic data for the simulation—the percentage of seasonal water supply assumed to be available in each irrigation period, the crops planted and their yields, costs, and returns—are given in the appendix to this chapter. To simulate the market, we assume that all farmers are free to bid for and buy whatever water is available during the irrigation period, whether it is from Tibi Dam, either of the two commercial companies, or wells. Each period the crops with the highest valued use for water outbid lower valued uses, so that crops are watered on a descending basis from highest value to lowest. When there is insufficient water to serve all crops, the low value crops are the first to be left dry; and when there is sufficient water to irrigate a particular crop, we assume that all farmers water the same reduced percentage of that crop.

The results of the simulations are summarized in table 4.8. The first run assumes no water shortage; the second through fourth runs assume a moderate shortage of approximately 15 percent for the season as a whole; and the fifth through eighth runs represent a severe drought, providing only two-thirds of the water needed to achieve full production. To compare Alicante's operating procedures with the basic procedures used in Valencia and Murcia-Orihuela, the Alicante data on water supply and crops are run with the alternative operating rules. Finally the three Spanish procedures are compared under drought conditions to a more generous procedure in which it is assumed that the system provides enough storage so that each farmer can draw his annual entitlement to water on demand and can know before he plants his crops how much water will be available to him for the full season.

With a severe seasonal water shortage, the market procedure used in Alicante produces greater gross and net returns than either the rotation system of Murcia or the turn procedure of Valencia. In Alicante, but not in the others, farmers with the highest value uses for the water are able to outbid others during all periods. Valencian rules attain this result in part by abandoning the basic turn during severe drought and designating priority for certain crops, allowing these to benefit at the expense of others. Even with this radical switch in procedure, which the Valencians hesitate to use these days, the net returns from applying Valencia's drought procedure to Alicante's environment are somewhat less than the result from using Murcia's rotation and considerably less than Alicante's market. Murcia's procedures allow each farmer to make his own decisions on how to use the limited water allocated to him; but that huerta's methods for transferring water among farmers are not as sure as Alicante's, so that some farmers will use water on low value crops while others are short of water for crops with a higher value.

With only a moderate shortage of water the differences between the several procedures narrows, but Alicante's market remains unequivocally the best in both gross and net returns. With a severe drought, Alicante's rules produce 39

Table 4.8 Comparison of operating procedures with Alicante data. Gross and net returns for sample area.

Run	Water Supply	Operating Procedure	Gross Returns (in thousands of ptas.)	Net Returns (in thousands of ptas.)
1	Sufficient	Alicante—market	146.5	83.7
2	Moderate Shortage (15%)	Alicante—market	117.2	54.8
3	(same)	Murcia-Orihuela—rotation	107.8	46.8
4	(same)	Valencia—turn	87.0	26.8
5	Severe drought (30% shortage)	Alicante—market	65.9	7.6
6	(same)	Murcia-Orihuela—rotation	61.5	4.6
7	(same)	Valencia—turn with 5 priority crops	53.7	2.4
8	(same)	Demand-plan crop pattern based on highest return from water in storage	66.4	36.6

percent more in net returns than Murcia's and 68 percent more than Valencia's. With a shortage of only 15 percent in water, Alicante's advantage over Murcia is 14 percent and over Valencia's turn procedure, 49 percent.

Thus Alicante's procedures are well adapted to Alicante's environment. There remains a question of the cost of water, for it has not been subtracted from gross returns. Assuming that 40 percent of water comes from Tibi Dam and 60 percent from Levante, we estimate that the farmers would pay (either by buying water or using water that otherwise they could sell) roughly 10,000 pesetas for the supply available in severe drought and 28,000 pesetas for the larger quantity available when there is a moderate water shortage. Subtracting these costs from net returns of Alicante's market procedure (runs 5 and 2), there results a loss of 2400 pesetas in severe drought and a reduced gain of 26,800 pesetas with a moderate shortage of water. Because water is not sold in Murcia and Valencia, one is tempted to compare these revised results for the market with the original ones for the rotation and turn, in which case Alicante's operating procedures would turn out to be the least well adapted to Alicante's environment. But such a comparison would be faulty for several reasons. The foreign or Levante water would have to be purchased regardless of the procedures used to distribute native water. Income from publicly auctioned Tibi water helps to pay the expenses of the local irrigation organization, which must be paid in any case, and these expenses have not been deducted from gross returns of any of the procedures. Payments for Tibi water that is exchanged among irrigators can be considered as transfer payments that do not affect significantly the income of the area.

As the results of run 8 show, substantially higher returns can be obtained where farmers can order water on demand and select the area of land to be planted, based on forecasts of water supply, before the crop year begins. This requires, however, a large amount of storage, either surface or underground, a condition that is not present in Alicante, Murcia, or Valencia, where the vagaries of the weather during the growing season have a significant effect on the water supply. If physical conditions permitted the development of additional storage, the resulting benefits could be measured by comparing the returns of run 8 to those of the existing situation and these benefits could then be compared to the costs of providing the storage.

As for the long-term stability needed by farmers and others to make efficient investments in the agricultural development of their huerta, it should be recalled that Alicante's irrigators sponsored and financed one of Europe's early great capital works for agriculture, Tibi Dam. Since then investment in the Huerta has faltered when compared to Valencia and Murcia-Orihuela. The intensity of development today is less and Alicante has yet to benefit from large national public works like the Generalísimo Dam on the Turia River and the several Segura River dams. Is this because of instability in the region, which is due in turn to the community's institutions and operating procedures or is it due to physical factors, such as topography and hydrology? Local patriots from the other communities have exaggerated, no doubt, the extent to which the sale of water apart from land is responsible for Alicante's lesser development, and they have underestimated the Huerta's physical problems in reaching good water sources. At the same time it is hard to know if a stronger local organization would have been more successful in capturing and retaining foreign sources of water. Assuming for argument that this is the case, we cannot say with assurance what factors would have made the organization stronger for this purpose. Suppression of the weekly water market would not have done so, for reasons already given. Forced retirement of old water rights with a consequent elimination of conflict between old and new shareholders might have strengthened the organization in centuries past.

Other critics have blamed Alicante's lesser development on investment, rather than lack of it, on the fact that the dam was ever built.[20] The argument runs that the construction of major public works brings in foreign interests to supply capital and expertise; that these interests soon dominate a region, depriving farmers of local control; and that where for some unusual reason they do not do this, the new mercantile interests, who may be agriculturalists, nonetheless create pervasive conflict between themselves and oldtime irrigators. In either case the strength of the old community is sapped and development of the region suffers. This model is a poor fit for Alicante. The dam was financed largely by the local community; new foreign interests did not soon dominate the Huerta. A foreign interest, the king, came to dominate it in the eighteenth century, to be sure, and he would not have achieved such control over irrigation if there had not been a dam to seize for the royal patrimony. But this is not what the model pretends to explain. Finally, the dam did create two interests in conflict, but these perversely defy the model. The new rightsholders who contributed to the dam have not sought to profit from its water except as working farmers. It was the old rightsholders who insisted that, for their shares, basic rights to water and to land continue to be separately negotiable. They were the disruptive influence, although the real picture is more complicated than this because many Alicantians owned both new and old rights.

APPENDIX: SIMULATION OF IRRIGATED FARMS IN THE HUERTA OF ALICANTE

Simulation of Procedures

In Alicante's Huerta the water market, or prices of water, is the major factor in distributing water in the short run. The simulation program therefore focuses on reproducing the market. In our USDA Technical Bulletin 1431 the procedure that reproduces the market is called Turn *plus* Demand *subject to* Crop Priorities.

We have designed a set of farms and fields that represent the variety of farm sizes and combinations of crops typically planted on huerta farms, ensuring at the same time that the combined area planted to each crop on the representative set of farms bears the same relation to the total area of the set as the relation between crops and total areas for the Huerta as a whole.

The distribution of water to this representative service area is made by serving first all fields planted in the highest value crop, and successively fields in other crops in order of their value. Value in this context is determined by loss functions (that is, for each crop the value that is lost if it is not watered, given its current stage in the growth cycle and anticipated future water supplies). The program calculates the marginal value product for water for each crop in each irrigation period. So that all fields planted to one crop will be served before any field in a lower value crop, it is necessary to assume in the simulation that all fields are within a single farm. When the simulation has been completed, the results can be disaggregated into individual farms.

A farm's water supply is assumed to have three sources—the irrigation community's supply in Tibi reservoir, Segura River water delivered by the Levante Company, and well water supplied by the Villena Company. For purposes of simulation the water supplies from the three sources have been combined into a single water quantity available in each irrigation period as seen in table A4.1.

Table A4.1 Irrigation water supply used in Alicante simulation .

Irrigation period	1	2	3	4	5	6	7	8	9	10	11	12	13
% of water	2.2	0.0	5.3	8.2	6.0	5.3	8.6	10.0	2.5	1.2	3.9	1.0	2.3

Irrigation period	14	15	16	17	18	19	20	21	22	23	24	25	26
% of water	5.9	3.7	5.0	4.2	2.0	5.3	5.7	7.0	2.0	1.0	1.7	0.0	0.0

Because of the water market in Alicante, the cost of water must be subtracted from the net returns produced by the simulation. To do this, the total water used is disaggregated into its three sources of supply, since each has its own price. This is done after the program has been run, using the same proportions as were used to calculate the water supply initially.

Additionally, the program can be used to estimate how much farmers would have been willing to pay for Tibi water, given the crop production that they achieved with it.

Program designation   With reference to table 9, Principal Distribution Rules of Bulletin 1431, the following programs are used to simulate Alicante operating procedures:

Water Supply	Description of Procedure	Procedure Code
Tibi plus Segura and Villena, normal and drought	Turn + Demand, with all fields treated as a single farm.	14

Basic Data

The distribution of the water supplies used in the Alicante runs is given in table A4.1. Table A4.2 shows the size distribution of Alicante farms and the sizes of farms used in the simulations of Alicante. The crop pattern of the area is shown in table A4.3, and the crop patterns of the farms simulated, in table A4.4. Yields, costs, and returns used in these runs are shown in table A4.5 and reflect the yields from adequate water supplies and prices of the middle 1960s.

Table A4.2 Farm size used in simulation related to distribution of farm size in Huerta of Alicante.

Actual Farms			Simulation Farms	
Irrigated hectares	Number	%	Farm No.	Hectares
Less than 1	1,536	63	1	.5
1–5	727	30	2	1.5
Over 5	160	7	3	.7
			4	2.0
			5	.8
			6	8.0
			7	.3
			8	.9
			9	5.0
			10	.4
Total		100		20.1

Table A4.3 Typical crop pattern in Huerta of Alicante.

Crop	% of hectarage
Potatoes	9.0
Melons	6.5
Pimiento	6.5
Broad beans	10.6
Tomatoes	4.5
Wheat	20.5
Alfalfa	7.8
Almonds	24.6
Olives	9.4
Other	.6

Table A4.4 Initial crop pattern on simulation farms (in hectares planted).

Crop	Farm										
	1	2	3	4	5	6	7	8	9	10	Total
Potato	0.2	0.2	—	0.2	0.1	0.4	0.3	0.2	0.4	0.2	2.2
Melons	0.2	0.2	0.2	—	0.2	0.5	—	—	0.3	—	1.6
Peppers	0.2	—	—	0.2	—	0.5	—	—	0.2	0.2	1.6
Broad beans	0.1	0.2	0.2	0.3	0.2	1.1	—	0.2	0.2	0.1	2.6
Tomatoes	—	0.3	0.1	0.2	—	0.2	—	0.2	—	0.1	1.1
Wheat	—	0.4	0.2	1.0	0.2	2.0	—	0.2	1.0	—	5.0
Alfalfa	—	0.2	—	0.2	—	0.6	—	—	0.9	—	1.9
Almonds	—	0.5	0.1	1.0	0.2	2.0	—	0.2	2.0	—	6.0
Olives	—	0.2	—	0.3	0.1	0.9	—	0.3	0.5	—	2.3

Table A4.5 Yields (in quintals) and returns (in thousands of pesetas) for crops used in simulation of Alicante.

Crop	Yield	Preharvest cost/ha	Harvest cost/ha	Gross return/ha	Full production net return/ha
Potato	200	40	10.6	100	49.4
Melons	200	30	5	88	53
Peppers	210	40	15	105	50
Broad beans	80	20	6	56	30
Tomatoes	300	60	30	150	60
Wheat	30	2.4	.6	18.5	15.5
Alfalfa	150	20	15	75	40
Almonds	15	10	1.17	40	28.83
Olives	2.52	12	13	65.52	40.52

5 The Kings River Service Area in the Central Valley of California: Land Settlement and Water Distribution to Farms

California is traversed lengthwise by two parallel ranges of mountains, the Sierra Nevada on the east and the Coast Range on the west. These converge at Mount Shasta on the north and are joined by the Tehachapi Mountains on the south to enclose the Central Valley basin. The basin is nearly 500 miles (mi) long, averages 120 mi in width, and includes more than one-third of California. The Sacramento River, which flows southerly, drains the upper one-third of the basin and the San Joaquin River, which flows in a northerly direction, drains the southern two-thirds. The confluence of these two streams is in the Sacramento–San Joaquin delta, from which they find a common outlet to the ocean through San Francisco Bay. The main valley floor, covering nearly one-third of the basin area, is a gently sloping, practically unbroken alluvial area 400 mi long and averaging 45 mi in width. It is America's most productive agricultural region.[1]

The valley floor has warm dry summers with an almost complete absence of rainfall during the midsummer months and mild winters with relatively light rainfall. The surrounding mountains are also generally warm and dry in the summer, but winter temperatures in the Sierra Nevada frequently drop below freezing and precipitation is much heavier than in the valley, with a large portion of it falling as snow. Precipitation in both the mountains and the valley decreases from north to south. For example, the average annual rainfall on the valley floor declines from 23 inches (in) at Red Bluff in the north to 6 in at Bakersfield in the south. On the Sierra Nevada the average varies from about 80 near Chico to 35 in east of Bakersfield. Precipitation in the Central Valley basin also varies widely from year to year, the maximum annual runoff being more than seven times the minimum. The sequence of wet and dry years has been irregular, and not infrequently several wet years or several dry years occur in succession.

The irrigation water supply of the Central Valley is derived chiefly from runoff of the mountains and foothills of the Sierra Nevada. About four-fifths of the annual precipitation occurs between the last of October and the first of April, but snow storage in the high Sierras delays the runoff until April, May, and June, during which months half the normal annual runoff in the valley occurs. By late July the flows of all streams drop to a small fraction of their average discharges, those in the south diminishing to no more than a trickle.

The basin is underlain, but not uniformly, by large natural groundwater reservoirs. On the east side of the upper San Joaquin Valley, which is the basin's most productive region, the greater part of the winter and spring runoff, that not diverted for direct storage or use, becomes groundwater by percolating into the flat alluvial cones of the major streams. The farmers use this water extensively for irrigation by pumping in the summer and fall months.

Water supply and water requirements in the Central Valley basin are unbalanced geographically. As we have seen, available water supplies decrease from north to south. Conversely, the water requirements are greater in the south because of larger irrigable areas, greater population, warmer climate, less rainfall, and greater evaporation. As a result the total runoff into the Sacramento Valley has normally exceeded its water requirements, while in the upper San Joaquin Valley local supplies have been inadequate to meet local demands.

There was little irrigation of significance in California when it was admitted to the Union in 1850. The cattle and stock industries dominated the Central Valley and development of farming awaited the arrival of a railroad. After 1870, when the Southern Pacific extended its route south through the San Joaquin Valley, irrigation agriculture grew at an extraordinarily rapid rate until the turn of the century, and it has continued to expand so that by 1969 there were 6.3 million acres receiving water in the Central Valley (see table 5.1).

As elsewhere in the West, the stockmen fought the development of lands they were using freely for grazing. Their tactics included opposition to state legislation that would aid farming and irrigation and, according to the farmers, bribery of legislators for this purpose; the filing of numerous suits in the courts to enjoin the diversion of stream water for irrigation; and occasionally intimidation and violence against those who were cultivating the land and building the canals. The relative significance of livestock and farming in California in the early years can be detected in the trespass laws. Stock grazing being more

Table 5.1 Acres irrigated in Central Valley and Kings River service area (in thousands of acres).

	1879	1912	1919	1929	1939	1949	1959	1969
Sacramento Valley, including Sacramento–San Joaquin delta	20	231	694[a]	798[a]	1151	1507	1930	2140
San Joaquin Valley	189	1739	2104[a]	2359[a]	2221	3162	3535	4140
Total, Central Valley basin	209	1970	2798	3157	3372	4669	5465	6280
Kings River service area[b]	62	629	553	742	618	695	650	—

Sources: (See note 1, chapter 5 for full citations.) 1879: Calif., Report of State Engineer to Legislature (Sacramento, 1880) Part IV. 1912: U. S. Dept. of Agriculture, Experiment Sta. Bn. 254 (1913). 1919 and 1929: U. S. Census of Irrigation, 1940, Calif. Drainage Basin Table 1. 1939: U. S. Census of Agriculture, 1949, Vol. III, Calif. State Table 1. 1949 and 1959: U. S. Census of Agriculture, 1959, Vol. III, Calif. State Table 1. 1969: U. S. Census of Agriculture, 1969, Vol. IV.

[a] An unidentified portion of the Sacramento–San Joaquin delta is included in the San Joaquin Valley totals for these years.

[b] There are inconsistencies due to differences in the allocation of Tulare Lake lands to the Kings River service area or to the service areas of other rivers that drain into the lake. The 1969 census of agriculture gives no data for the Kings River service area.

Irrigation near Fresno: vineyard (top), plum orchard (left), alfalfa field (right).

Farmers and their wives attend dedication of Pine Flat Dam, 1954.

400,000 ACRES
OF
CALIFORNIA and OREGON
LANDS!
FOR SALE BY
E. B. PERRIN,
584 California Street,
SAN FRANCISCO.

The above lands are adapted for Wheat, Cotton, Vineyard, Fruit, Dairy and Grazing purposes.

Those in California lie in the counties of Shasta, Siskiyou, Mendocino, Tehama, Colusa, Sonoma, Santa Clara, Merced, Fresno, Tulare, Kern, San Luis Obispo and Los Angeles.

SAN JOAQUIN VALLEY LANDS.

Much of this land is well adapted to the cultivation of Grain and Cotton. The irrigating canal from King's river is already constructed so far as to furnish water to farmers within two miles of some of it, and proposals have been submitted to irrigate the entire body.

Dairy and Fruit Lands.

A large portion of the above land is all that can be desired for dairy purposes, with plenty of water ; while a portion is well suited for the Vine and the different varieties of fruit.

Sheep and Cattle Ranches.

To parties in search of Sheep and Cattle Ranches we can offer great bargains.

Much of the above land having been purchased at extremely low prices, will be sold to actual settlers at prices varying from fifty cents to ten dollars per acre.

Also, a large body of MARSH LANDS for sale, situated near the town of Donahue, on San Pablo Bay, at a low price.

E. B. PERRIN,
534 California Street, San Francisco.

WM. S. CHAPMAN,
OWNER AND DEALER IN
Farming, Grazing, Timber,
AND RECLAIMED AND UNRECLAIMED
SWAMP LAND
IN ALL PARTS OF
CALIFORNIA.

RANCHES adapted to SHEEP and CATTLE RAISING OF ANY SIZE REQUIRED.

Special attention given to the location of **COLONIES** on land irrigated and that is adapted to the growth of semi-tropical fruits and other products.

OFFICE OVER THE PACIFIC BANK,
Corner PINE and SANSOME STREETS,
SAN FRANCISCO, CALIFORNIA.

Two of the largest landowners and developers in California and in the Kings River service area advertise their holdings, 1873.

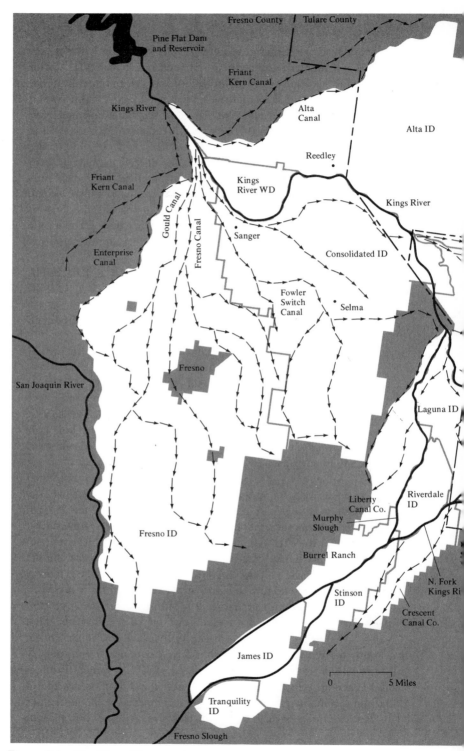

Figure 5.1   The Kings River service area.

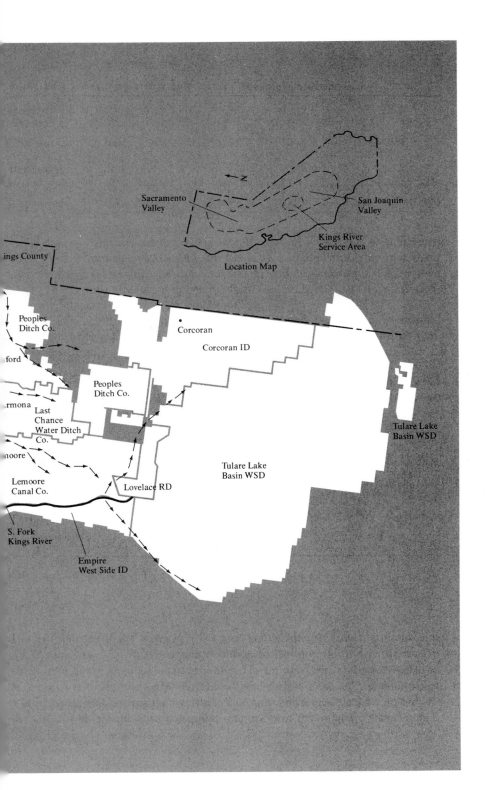

Sacramento
Valley

San Joaquin
Valley

Kings River
Service Area

Location Map

ings County

Peoples
Ditch Co.

Corcoran

Corcoran ID

ford

Peoples
Ditch Co.

rmona

Last
Chance
Water Ditch
Co.

Tulare Lake
Basin WSD

noore

Tulare Lake
Basin WSD

Lemoore
Canal Co.

Lovelace RD

S. Fork
Kings River

Empire
West Side ID

important at the time than cropping, the law of 1852 provided that an owner of crops could claim damages for injury by the stock of others only if he enclosed his cropland by a lawful fence, the cheapest available one being posts and boards. By 1874 farming had begun to dominate stock raising, and the 1852 act was replaced after a bitter legislative struggle by a so-called no-fence law under which the burden was placed on the owner of stock to prevent their damaging crops rather than on the farmer to fence or protect his fields. The stockman had either to fence the land on which his stock grazed or employ enough cowboys to herd his stock night and day, and as a general rule he could do neither. There were not that many cowboys and the cost of fencing was prohibitive since the Glidden barbed wire machine was not available at that time.

The open range in the San Joaquin Valley came to a close; the stockmen could not compete with farmers, who could ship their produce and receive their supplies by rail. The cattle and sheep growers were pushed back, step by step, until the only grazing lands left to them were those less desirable for cultivation and remote from the railroad. But the valley did not turn then into the garden of fruit, vegetable, and field crops that we see today. The range was followed by wheat. As the Central Pacific pushed its rails down the San Joaquin Valley, more and more land was sowed to that crop until by 1874 the entire valley appeared to be one huge wheat field. In 1852 the San Joaquin Valley produced 112,000 bushels (bu) of wheat; by 1874, 7.5 million bu; and in 1876, 12.1 million bu.

The wheat was grown on bonanza farms. One thousand to 3000-acre grain fields were not uncommon, and there were farms covering more than 10,000 acres. Only a small part of the crop was irrigated. It was cultivated by relatively few men using huge gangplows, planters, and combined harvesters, many of them developed and manufactured in the valley. With these methods of cultivation, the land yielded 13 to 20 bu an acre.

Wheat culture reached its zenith in the San Joaquin in 1884 when 18 million bu were harvested from 1.3 million acres. Thereafter the acreage planted to wheat declined steadily, due to the crop's declining price, to reduced yields that resulted from continued use of the cultivation practices of the bonanza farms, and to the instability that resulted from short crops in drought years. By 1895 production had dropped below the 1874 level.

Another important reason for the wane of the bonanza wheat farms was the greater profit that could be made from the land by intensive cultivation of a variety of crops, now that markets were accessible. This required that the land be irrigated and colonized, and these were accomplished in many parts of the valley in an unusual way—by developers and colonies. Developers with considerable capital acquired large blocs of land. They built irrigation canals to provide water to the land. Then they subdivided the land into farms of 20 or 40 acres; built roads and laid out town centers, frequently with community facilities; and finally recruited the farmers, or colonists as they were called, providing them with credit for the purchase of their farms.

Referring to the first colony in the Fresno area, whose "history is only a repetition of the histories of all the others," the author of an 1891 atlas said, "It affords a fair contrast between the wheat growing and horticultural era of the county. Before the colony was settled, wheat was grown on the land now occupied by it, and netted annually not more than $25,000, while only one family lived upon the six sections; now the same land yields an annual cash return of from $500,000 to $700,000, while nearly 200 families have comfortable and happy homes on it. It would be difficult to present a stronger contrast, or one more favorable to the colony system."[2]

As a consequence, in part, of this form of land settlement, the Central Valley's agriculture today is characterized by a great intensity of production and variety of crops. Although livestock is a major source of income on many of the valley's farms, it does not dominate other farm enterprises as in neighboring western states. The region's diversification in field, fruit, and vegetable crops, with local specialization, is exemplified by the orange groves of Tulare County, cotton fields near Bakersfield, vineyards and fig orchards in Fresno County, the fruit lands of the Sierra Nevada foothills north of Sacramento, rice fields along the Sacramento River in Colusa County, and almond groves around Chico to the north. Nearly all the almonds, figs, nectarines, olives, pomegranates, prunes, and walnuts produced in the United States are grown in the Central Valley, as are over 95 percent of the apricots, grapes for raisins, and safflower grain; over 50 percent of the peaches, melons, persimmons, and tomatoes; and between 25 and 50 percent of the asparagus, plums, and pears—all by means of irrigation.

This chapter is concerned specifically with the service area of the Kings River near Fresno, at the geographical center of the San Joaquin Valley (see figure 5.1). The river is formed well up in the Sierra Nevada and is snowfed, since nearly 400 square miles (mi²) of its watershed are above elevation 10,000 feet (ft). The irrigation service area, covering approximately 1 million acres, is a flat alluvial delta with its apex at the point where the river debouches from the mountains. From here the river flows in several channels, generally southwesterly, for about 15 mi through a fertile bottomland district known as the Centerville bottoms. Below the bottoms the river continues in a southerly direction for about 10 mi, at which point several channels branch out to each side of the principal ridge of the old delta. Those that break away to the left, the south fork channels, lead to a landlocked basin that contains Tulare Lake. The north fork channels unite ultimately in Fresno slough, which finds its way into the San Joaquin River.

Rainfall in the irrigated area varies considerably over the year, averaging little more than half an inch per month during May through September and almost 2 in in the winter months of December, January, and February. The climate becomes dryer as one moves south within the service area, even the short distance of 30 mi between Fresno and Hanford (see figure 5.2). Stream flow data for the Kings River just above the irrigated area are given in table 5.2. (These have been calculated to exclude the influence of the principal storage reservoir, which began operating in the 1950s.) Discharges during the high snowmelt period of April

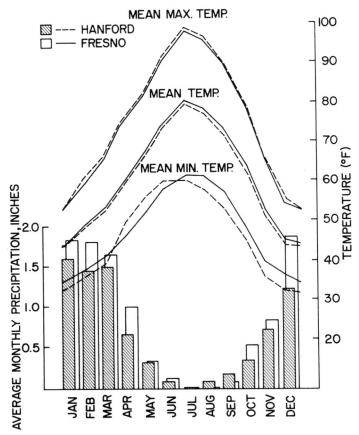

Figure 5.2 Precipitation, temperatures, and growing season, Fresno and Hanford, California.
(Sources: Climatological data: U.S. Weather Bureau. Period Averages: precipitation—Fresno, 30 years, and Hanford, 62 years. Mean temperature: Fresno, 30 years, and Hanford, 60 years. Mean daily maximum temperature: Fresno, 30 years, and Hanford, 58 years. Mean daily minimum temperature: Fresno, 30 years, and Hanford, 57 years).

Table 5.2 Monthly and annual stream flow in the Kings River at Piedra, California, 1895–1966.

Month	Mean flow 1000 acre-feet	Standard deviation
Jan.	63.1	61.45
Feb.	77.9	55.75
Mar.	116.3	67.17
Apr.	221.7	79.93
May	427.4	162.62
June	396.7	217.92
July	165.0	152.78
Aug.	48.8	18.62
Sept.	19.7	11.68
Oct.	20.3	18.03
Nov.	27.2	28.83
Dec.	44.2	57.90
Annual	1628.3	731.10

through June are almost two-thirds of total flow, whereas precipitation during this same period amounts to less than 15 percent of the annual total.

Most of the service area is underlain by material that is adequately porous for groundwater storage, which is used extensively. In good water years the ground water supply is replenished and the water table is raised by the percolation of water applied to the land for irrigation, by running water not needed for crops into the canals and onto certain lands for the specific purpose of recharging the ground, and by general infiltration from upstream areas. In dry years the groundwater is mined, and with a succession of dry years the water table is likely to drop precipitously. Because a significant portion of groundwater supply comes from percolation of the canals and of irrigated lands, the service areas of the large canal systems represent fairly distinct groundwater areas.

The soils of a large part of the Kings River service area have the capacity to use great quantities of irrigation water, fertilizer, labor, and other inputs and to return high yields of fruit, field, and vegetable crops. The numbers of acres irrigated in certain years are given in table 5.1. Within the service area there are four principal irrigating regions: the upper river, surrounding the cities of Fresno, Selma, and Dinuba; the lower southside, sometimes called Mussel slough country, surrounding Hanford and Lemoore; the lower northside, adjoining Fresno slough as it meanders toward Mendota; and the Tulare Lake area, south and southeast of Mussel slough country and including the area around the town of Corcoran (see figure 5.1).

We shall give special attention to the operating procedures of two large irrigation districts that serve the north river area—Fresno and Consolidated irrigation districts—and to those of three mutual water companies that serve the southside—Lemoore Canal and Irrigation Company, Last Chance Water Ditch Company, and Peoples Ditch Company. Both of these regions were planted in bonanza wheat farms in the early 1870s. Crop diversification and the colony movement took hold in Fresno more definitely than in the lower southside, however, so that by the late 1870s farming was developing under different sets of institutions and procedures and the two irrigated areas have remained desynonymous to this day.

Fresno, the principal city of the upper river region, is called the raisin capital of the world, and 36 percent of the irrigated land around the city is planted to grapes. Other crops grown in this part of the Kings River service area include cotton (14 percent of irrigated land), alfalfa (12 percent), figs (7 percent), other fruits (7 percent), nuts (4 percent), grains (7 percent), vegetables, largely melons and tomatoes (3 percent), and pasture (10 percent). The crop pattern changes significantly as one travels south to Lemoore and Hanford, where water is somewhat less abundant and agriculture, less intensive. There barley is the principal crop, grown on approximately 35 percent of the irrigated land, and other small grains occupy an additional 9 percent. Cotton is grown on one-quarter of the land and hay crops, including alfalfa and grass silage, on 22 percent. Corn and sorghums occupy 5 percent, while all fruits, nuts, and vegetables account for no more than 2.5 percent of the land under irrigation.

Farms are somewhat larger in the Lemoore-Hanford area than around Fresno. Data for Fresno and Kings counties show that 81 percent of Fresno farms are less than 100 acres, while only 6 percent of those in Kings County, where Hanford and Lemoore are located, fall in this category. It should be noted, however, that farms in that portion of Fresno county that is within the Kings River service area are somewhat smaller than those elsewhere in the county, so that the county average exaggerates farm size to some extent. Thus, for example, the Fresno Irrigation District, which surrounds the city, serves thirty-six thousand property owners with an average size of less than 6.5 acres. A good number of these are gardens, however, and a typical commercial farm will have 20, 40, or more acres with water service. Only ninety of these properties are larger than a quarter section (160 acres), although these account for 13 percent of the irrigated area within the district. Similarly, the average farm in Mussel slough country is significantly smaller than the average for Kings County, which includes the basin of Tulare Lake where some of the largest farms in America are located.

Finally, it should be noted that these data on farms relate to owners, not to operators. Frequently a single operator will work several farms, in some cases building up sizable operations under a single management.

LAND SETTLEMENT AND WATER DELIVERY TO FARMS NEAR FRESNO, 1870 TO 1968

The Developer Acquires Land

The first colony was established just south of Fresno in 1875. By 1890 there were thirty-four colonies surrounding the town, varying in area from 1 to 14 mi^2 or sections (from 640 to 9000 acres). Land in such large blocs was available to California developers at that time from several sources. First there were the land grants made to individuals by the Mexican government and recognized by the treaty of Guadalupe-Hidalgo that ended the Mexican-American War. Twenty-four such grants, covering approximately 850,000 acres, were wholly or partially within the San Joaquin Valley and one, the Laguna de Tache ranch of almost 50,000 acres, was within the Kings River service area. Although the original grantee of the Laguna ranch, Manuel Castro, did not establish colonies, subsequent owners did so. The ranch was several miles downstream from Fresno, on the lower north side, but, as we shall see, large parts of it were acquired at one time by the Fresno irrigation interests in order to protect their water rights.

A second source of land was the federal government. In the 1860s several million acres of federal land were available for purchase in the Central Valley. Developers could buy these with cash, but they got them for less money by using agricultural college scrip and soldiers' warrants that they had purchased on the open market.

In the Morrill Act of 1862 the federal government undertook to aid all states in establishing colleges at which agricultural sciences and mechanical arts would be taught—the state universities as we know them today. All states were given 30,000 acres of federal land for each representative and senator they had in Congress, and they were to use proceeds from the sale of this land to aid the colleges. States in which there was no federal land or insufficient land were given scrip, which in most cases they sold on the open market to individuals who could then use it to acquire federal land in any state where land was available for purchase. The states that received the scrip were not themselves allowed to use it to acquire land because of jurisdictional problems that would result from one state's owning land in another. A total of 7.8 million acres in scrip was distributed to these states, and more of it was used for entering land in California than in any other state. Whereas developers paid $1.25 or more per acre in cash to the federal government to purchase land, they could buy scrip on the market for a price between $.50 and $1.

The largest user of college scrip in California was William S. Chapman, who on emigrating from Minnesota in the early 1860s had decided to try for a fortune in land rather than gold. He succeeded. Using cash, scrip, and other means to acquire land from the federal and state governments, Chapman within a decade was said to control a million acres.[3] Chapman's partner in land speculation was Isaac Friedlander. Born in Germany in 1823, he came to America as a boy, grew up in South Carolina, and migrated to the California mines in 1849. He soon abandoned them for commerce and speculation in grain and land. At the age of twenty-nine he attracted public attention by cornering the flour market and making a handsome profit. He so dominated the export trade in wheat that he was known as the Grain King, a sobriquet that was reinforced by his appearance—six feet, seven inches tall, weighing three hundred pounds.

In 1868 Chapman and Friedlander organized a syndicate of San Francisco capitalists, mostly of German descent, to purchase agricultural college scrip and locate it on unappropriated federal lands in the San Joaquin Valley. The syndicate acquired 125 sections of land (80,000 acres) in a nearly solid bloc in the area that presently includes the city of Fresno, and it was on this land that the first colony and many of the most successful ones were established. The land patents were issued to Chapman, who then conveyed the whole tract to a trust, the San Joaquin Valley Land Association, in which each investor had a beneficial interest in proportion to the capital he had contributed.

Initially the land was held in trust for the syndicate, but this arrangement proved cumbersome in a fast developing region, especially when the initial holders began to sell portions of their interests to outside purchasers, thereby increasing the number of persons who held beneficial interests in the trust. In 1873 the syndicate was dissolved and the lands were distributed among members in proportion to their beneficial interests. It was these men, either the initial investors or those to whom they had sold their interests, who developed the land in colonies.

A third source for developers was lands that had been donated to the state of California by the federal government. For California as a whole these included 5.5 million acres (two sections in each township) to be sold for the benefit of public schools, 150,000 acres for benefit of the state agricultural college, 500,000 acres to help finance canals and river improvements, and 2.2 million acres of swampland given to the state under the condition that proceeds from their sale or use be applied for reclaiming the lands by means of levees and drains. A significant proportion of the swamplands were in the San Joaquin Valley. Although there was little such land around Fresno, where the colonies flourished, the development of agriculture in the lower north side, along Fresno slough, in the Tulare Lake area, and to a lesser extent, in Mussel slough country was dependent on drainage and irrigation of overflow (swamp) lands.

California's laws governing the disposal of swamplands changed frequently between 1855 and 1875. In essence the lands were sold for a low price, $1 per acre, with only 20 percent down payment. Upon showing proof that he had done work on the land to reclaim it, the purchaser was given title and his payment was refunded. The land that could be bought by a single entryman was limited to 320 acres between 1855 and 1859, to 640 acres between 1859 and 1868, unlimited between 1868 and 1874, and limited again to 540 acres after 1874; but willy-nilly, immense landholdings were accumulated by certain interests who used fake entrymen where necessary. Thus Henry Miller and Charles

Lux acquired 80,000 acres of swampland in the San Joaquin, some of it along Fresno slough in the Kings River service area. James Haggin and Lloyd Tevis acquired 34,000 acres, all of it in Kern County south of the Kings River. In chapter 6 we shall discuss the state supreme court opinion in the case of *Lux* v. *Haggin,* which became the keystone of California water law and had great influence on the development of irrigation in the Kings River service area.

Apart from the state, the railroads in California were given large blocs of federal lands that they sold to defray in part the costs of building the roads and to encourage settlement and the development of traffic along them. The Central Pacific, which was the first road to cross the Kings River area, in 1872, was built, however, without benefit of federal land grants from Stockton to a point southeast of Fresno. The railroad company located Fresno at the center of the then largely undeveloped estate of the German syndicate, purchased the town site from the syndicate, and subdivided it into town lots, which it sold. But the railroad had no farmland to develop or sell in the Fresno area at that time. Subsequently the Southern Pacific Railroad, which was by then allied with the Central Pacific, built additional lines in the Fresno area for some of which public lands were granted. Railroad land grants were important in the development of Mussel slough country.

A final source of land for irrigation developers was the large holdings of bonanza wheat farmers and stockmen, these having been acquired initially by one of the means discussed previously.

The Developer Acquires Water

Having procured land in one or a combination of these ways, the developers next had to bring water to it. In some cases, the 76 Land and Water Company, for example, this was done by the same corporate entity that acquired and sold land, in others by separate companies organized by the land developers. The Fresno Canal and Irrigation Company, an example of the latter category, was incorporated in 1871 by four developers, principally Chapman and Moses J. Church. Chapman was, as we have seen, the largest holder of lands in the German syndicate. With Fresno canal water he developed the first colony, Central California Colony, which served as a model for later ones, in a number of which he also participated.

Church had come to Fresno County in 1868, driving a band of two thousand sheep in search of pasturage. These he soon abandoned to become the father of irrigation in his new home. He planned and built the early ditches that transported water from the river to the plains. Concurrently he acquired large tracts of land and became a developer. In the words of a local chronicler, "by the year 1876, M. J. Church had also for himself developed a valuable property and secured a competency." [4] In 1875 he placed on the market the Church Temperance Colony of one full section that he had acquired from the German syndicate; and after 1877, when he was in sole control of the canal company, Church participated in a number of colonies, sometimes exchanging water rights for land. For example, Thomas Hughes purchased nine and one-half sections from Janssen of the German syndicate in 1880 for $40,000, with the purpose of colonizing it. He needed money to bring water to the land, however, and for this purpose entered into a deal with Church, giving up five sections of the land in return for which Church and the canal company built ditches and supplied water to the remaining four and one-half sections, which became the Fresno colony.

Church and Chapman soon fell into rancorous disagreement; and when Chapman acquired a controlling interest in the company, due to the financial problems of one of the other incorporators, Church disposed of his one-quarter interest to Chapman for $15,000. Soon after, Chapman hypothecated his entire canal interest to the Bank of Nevada in San Francisco because of financial reverses unrelated to the canal company.

The bank took over the canal in May 1877 and hired William Hammond Hall, who was later to be the first California state engineer, as superintendent. After only five months of operating the canal they sold it to Church in return for a long-term note of $28,000. The bank found that there was no profit to be made from the canal alone, only from owning land as well as water. For the investment to have profited them, they would have needed to buy large tracts of land and develop them. Hall, as superintendent, wrote lengthy letters almost daily to the bank officers telling them what needed to be done to make the property profitable. These appear to have convinced the bank that it shouldn't run an irrigation company, although this was not Hall's purpose, for he protested bitterly when the property was sold and he lost his job. With Church again in control of the canal, land development and colonization resumed apace.

In 1887 Church sold out to a group headed by Dr. E. B. Perrin and his brother, Robert, of San Francisco. The Perrin brothers had emigrated to California from Alabama in 1869. They soon acquired immense holdings in land. As early as 1873 Perrin was advertising 400,000 acres of agricultural land for sale in California and Oregon, much of it in the San Joaquin Valley.

In the seventies the Bank of California came to own a large tract—fifty sections or 32,000 acres, northwest of Fresno and of the properties of the German syndicate—through loans and foreclosed investments. Dr. Perrin, with the support of the bank, sought to irrigate these lands by cutting a canal from the left bank of the San Joaquin River, which was the tract's northeast boundary. When the lands were sold after water was available, the bank was to have the first $1.50 per acre, and the balance was to be divided between the bank and Perrin. Perrin expected to make a large sum of money, but the project failed and Perrin turned to the Kings River as a water source. He bought a one-third interest in the Kings River and Fresno Canal Company, which served an area immediately north of the Fresno Canal Company and abstracted its river water through the same headgate as the Fresno canal. But he was unable to water the bank tract from this source either. The distance was great and there was a considerable expanse of dry land between the company's existing service area and the bank's lands, so water intended for the latter would simply disappear in the intervening desert. Of equal importance, Church and the Fresno canal sued the Kings River canal to deny it the right to divert through the common headgate. Church won and so weakened the Kings River company that he was able to buy it at a bargain price, its canal becoming the Gould canal of the Fresno system.

At this point, in 1887, Church offered to sell the Fresno canal to Perrin, telling him that by this means he could irrigate the bank tract. With the assistance of Captain George Cheape, a Scottish capitalist in San Francisco, Perrin made the purchase. Why, it may be asked, did the "father of irrigation" dispose of his offspring? First, Church received a good price for the canal company while retaining his lands and other properties in the area. By 1887 Church had developed a magnificent competency. Also he was exasperated with an ever growing number of court suits entered against the company by others who were diverting water from the Kings River. Many of the suits were of little importance and few of them were pursued in years of good water, but some of them raised questions about the capacity of the company to meet its water delivery obligations. Church claimed that the costs of defending these numerous suits had far exceeded the expense of constructing all of the canals.

All development in the area was in fact arrested soon after the Perrins took over as the result of a series of court decisions that would have limited drastically the water the company could withdraw from the river and would have shut down completely other upper river diverters, including the 76 canal. The Fresno company had claimed the right to between 1000 and 12,000 cubic feet per second (cfs) and the need to withdraw this amount to meet its current and prospective obligations; it was given 100 cfs. The beneficiaries of these court opinions were landowners on downstream canals in Mussel slough country and in the Laguna de Tache grant, whose superior rights were based to a large extent on the fact that their canals' service areas were adjacent, or riparian, to the river rather than removed from the river and out on the plains as were the service areas of the upstream canals. These court orders were not actually enforced, for no judge was willing to dry up the country; but the courts had stopped development of the Fresno region.

To secure an adequate water supply Perrin then entered into negotiations to purchase the riparian and underdeveloped Laguna de Tache grant with the purpose of floating a good part of its water right upstream to the Fresno canal. His friend Captain Cheape owned an interest in the Laguna grant and helped Perrin to get an option on it for $1.15 million in 1891. To finance the deal the canal company mortgaged all its properties and rights, including the 64,000-acre Laguna ranch. The company sold $1 million face value in mortgage bonds to English insurance companies for $850,000 and covered the balance of the purchase price with a mortgage given to the grant proprietors. The Laguna lands were, of course, important to the English as security for their investment.

Since the other upriver canals were at that time under injunctions not to take any water from the river, this move by Perrin put the developers in the service area of the Fresno canal company in a very good spot. "The news soon spread all over the country that the water for the Fresno colonies was the most secure and plentiful in the State, and this created the biggest land boom in Fresno County."[5] Perrin bought large additional tracts of land west and southwest of Fresno and laid out and sold farms in Perrin Colonies 1 through 6. Also, he was able finally to develop the Bank of California tract. Perrin sold to the bank for $150,000 enough water rights to cover the fifty sections, and with the proceeds he began to build the Herndon canal to deliver the water.

The boom ended with a slowdown in agriculture that preceded the national panic and depression of 1893-94. Perrin left for Arizona Territory, where he owned large blocs of grazing land, including a 100,000-acre ranch, the Baca. When he left, interest on the Fresno canal company's bonds had not been paid for several years; so the English companies foreclosed in 1894, acquiring the canal company and the Laguna grant. Subsequently the other canals on the right bank of the upper river—Fowler Switch, Centerville and Kingsburg, and Emigrant—were acquired by the same English interests and combined under the name of Consolidated Canal Company. Thus from about 1890 until 1921, when the properties of both canal companies were sold to public districts—the Fresno and Consolidated irrigation districts—the enterprises that distributed irrigation water to one of America's most productive agricultural regions were financed largely by English capital. From 1895 to 1921 they were owned by English capitalists and managed by an Englishman named L. A. Nares of Liverpool.

The canal companies typically acquired rights to water in the Kings River, installed diversion works in the river, and built the principal canals and channels so they could deliver water at the heads of the laterals from which most farms were to be served. These laterals were then built to the headgates of each farm property by the land developer or by the farmers themselves, who frequently organized cooperatives, called mutual ditch companies, for the purpose. In either case the farmers frequently operated and maintained the laterals once they were built. Thus, for example, the canal network in the service area of the Fresno company by 1920 included 360 mi of main canals and laterals that had been built by the company and were maintained and operated by it and a larger mileage of private laterals or community ditches that had been built by land developers or by farmers and were maintained and operated by the farmers themselves. For the Consolidated Canal Company the figures were 190 mi of main canals and laterals, and again a length greater than this of community ditches.

The basis used by a canal company for supplying water to developers was uniform throughout its service area (with exceptions resulting from the terms by which the company had acquired the water rights or canals of smaller companies). For the Fresno canal company the standard was 1 cfs continuous flow for each 160 acres (quarter-section). On the assumption that it had the right to divert 1000 cfs from the Kings River, the Fresno company agreed to sell 1000 first class rights and no more, which meant that it agreed to limit the area served under such rights to 160,000 acres. If for any reason a quantity less than 1000 cfs was available, each rightholder was limited to a proportional share or one one-thousandth, of the water in the system. If the canals ran more than 1000 cfs, the company reserved the right to supply the excess to holders of second class rights, which, like the first class rights, were based on 1 cfs for 160 acres but entitled the holder to receive water only after all first class rights had been satisfied. The company sold one hundred seventy-five second class rights to the owners of 28,000 acres of land, so its full service area covered 188,000 acres.

For the Consolidated Canal Company the standard was 2 cfs for each quarter-section. The company, assuming that it had the right to divert 1200 cfs from the river, agreed to sell six hundred rights and no more, representing a service area of 94,000 acres. If the canals ran less than this quantity of water, each rightholder was limited to the six-hundredth part of whatever was available. One should not conclude that the Consolidated water right contract, because it was double the quantity of the Fresno contract, was a better one. As we shall see later in this chapter, the Fresno company's right to abstract water from the Kings River was far superior to that of Consolidated, and the individual water right contracts were, of course, subject to the larger rights of the companies on the river.

The water right contracts provided that water was to be appurtenant to land and transferable only with it, and the rightholder agreed that he would not use water on any but the land stipulated in the contract.

The cost to land developers of first class rights rose rapidly in the Fresno canal from $200 ($1.25 per acre), to $800 ($5 per acre), and after 1884 it was fixed at $1600 ($10 per acre). Second class rights were sold for approximately half this price. In addition there was an annual charge of $100 per quarter-section (62.5 cents per acre) for operation and maintenance of the system. Failure to pay this resulted in forfeiture of the land, since the fixed annual rental was made a perpetual lien on the property. The security provided by this feature of the contract was an important consideration for the English insurance companies when they loaned the canal company, under the Perrins, close to $1 million.

The cost of water rights under the Consolidated canal was $400 ($2.50 per acre). This first cost was lower than under the Fresno canal because Consolidated had taken over the Fowler Switch and Centerville and Kingsburg mutual companies, whose farmers had already paid to build a system of supply canals. The annual charge of the Consolidated canal was 75 cents per acre, somewhat higher than that of the Fresno canal.

These provisions can be demonstrated by references to a representative contract between a canal company and a developer. In 1877 Church placed on the market the Nevada Colony of three sections. There were separate but similar contracts for each section between the Fresno canal company and Church as developer. These provided that in consideration for payment by the developer of $3200 ($5 per acre) the canal company would deliver all the water that may be required, not exceeding at any time 4 cfs, for irrigation of the section. The canal company agreed to place a box or gate in the bank of the main canal at the most convenient point for conveyance of water to the land, and the developer was to construct a ditch from this box to the land and any laterals needed to distribute the water over the section. The developer agreed that he would not permit the water to be used on any other land or permit it to run off to contiguous land or run to useless waste, and he agreed to construct ditches to carry any surplus water back into the company's canal. The water was to form an appurtenance to the land and to be transferable only with it. The canal company was not to be held responsible for deficiency of water caused by drought, insufficient water in the river, adverse appropriation, hostile diversion or obstruction, the order or injunction of any court, the destruction of its dams or canals, unauthorized diversion from its canals, or temporary damage by flood. If for these reasons the company's canals fell short of 1000 cfs, the developer was entitled to no more than four-thousandths part of the aggregate quantity. The annual payment to the canal company was to be $400 (62.5 cents per acre).

The Consolidated Canal Company offered an interesting alternative to the normal annual maintenance charge. In the standard contracts, as in those of the Fresno canal, this charge was payable for all land owned and cultivable beginning from the date of the contract. The alternative provided that the payment of 75 cents per acre begin after the year 1910 and that there need be no payments prior to that date except for land actually irrigated, for which half the standard rate was charged. This was advantageous to owners of large tracts of unimproved land. It gave them a water right so that they could develop and sell the land and it gave them sufficient time without water payment to colonize their estates.

The Developer Subdivides

With land and water in hand the developer subdivided his property into farm tracts, built a complete system of laterals and gates to supply irrigation water to each tract, provided certain community facilities, and put his colony on the market. Thus in 1875, six sections of Central, the first colony, were divided into 192 20-acre tracts intended primarily for the production of raisin grapes; and laterals and gates were built to provide water service to each tract.

Twenty acres was the most popular size among colonists, but some developers sold larger tracts and in a number of colonies, particularly where the developer experienced difficulty in recruiting settlers, the portion not marketed in small tracts was sold in farms of a quarter-section or larger. Also on occasion one man would purchase more than one 20-acre tract. Thus the Washington Colony, adjacent to Central, was divided into 20-acre tracts, but one vineyardist bought about 100 acres. The Scandinavian Home Colony of three sections was divided into ninety-six 20-acre lots. In the Nevada Colony only three-quarters of a section was sold, as contemplated, in 20-acre tracts; the remainder was sold in 80-acre farms with some quarter-sections. The Fresno Colony was plotted and sold in 20-acre lots, although one vineyardist bought one section, and another, eight lots. The Easterby Colony was predominantly in 20- and 40-acre farms; but there were several larger tracts, one of 400 acres purchased and cultivated by a group of prominent wine dealers and vineyardists.

Because the new settler would not derive any substantial income from his farm for several years while grapevines matured, the Central Colony developer offered to set out on each 20-acre farm 2 acres of raisin vines and to cultivate them for two years without cost to the purchaser, who during this period could remain at his old occupation away from Fresno. In the first two years such vineyards were planted on one hundred twenty farms. Unfortunately most of them were lost for want of sufficient water, but the developers then allowed the colonists the cost of this planting. Those who wanted to have a larger acreage of raisin vines in place when they settled could enter into contracts with the developer at $15 an acre and about $1 per month per acre for cultivation, and similar arrangements could be made for fruit trees.

To help provide for the first few years, the developer of the Washington Colony built a dairy for the manufacture of butter and cheese on the cooperative plan and imported cows that were sold to the settlers on easy terms, thereby putting an income within reach of all until such time as a profit could be realized from the trees and vines that had been growing in the meantime.

The developer of the Central Colony established a nursery for vines and varieties of fruit and shade trees. At the outset he had sent an agent to Spain to select the best grapes, and this man had returned with thousands of cuttings of muscatel and several kinds of wine grapes. To stimulate orchard planting, the developer of the Nevada Colony donated a quarter-section with water rights for the erection of a fruit dryer by the colonists.

In addition to improvements related directly to farming, developers invested in community facilities. Roads were laid out—23 miles of them in the Central Colony. The relentless summer sun and the absence of trees on the Fresno plains made for easy cultivation and abundant crops, but they made also for hard home life. Shade trees were therefore an important convenience, and the developer typically planted many miles of them along the principal avenues. The developer of the Central Colony planted 36 mi of trees. Cherry Avenue was bordered with nine varieties of cherry, Elm with cork elms, Fig with the White Adriatic variety, Walnut with the English walnut, Fruit with a variety in systematic alternation, East Avenue with Languedoc almonds alternating with red gums, North with Monterey cypress, and Central with Black Mission figs. A considerable amount of this planting was lost for lack of water at the right time, but enough survived to mark the area with distinctive features. In several of the colonies, Washington and Traver, for example, town sites were laid out near the center of the area.

The cost of a 20-acre farm provided with all of these improvements was $1000 or $50 per acre in the Central Colony in 1876. Farmers were given five years in which to pay as follows: $100 down payment, $12.50 per month for five years, $150 at the end of the fifth year, and no interest charges. This installment plan of payment was an important feature of the colony system.

With each tract there was granted a perpetual water right, proportional in amount to the size of the tract. Thus a 20-acre farm in the Central Colony included the right to one-eighth cfs of water from the Fresno canal company. The farmer paid nothing specifically for the right, for this was included in the price of the land; but he did have to pay to the canal company the annual maintenance and operation charges, which for a 20-acre farm was $12.50, and this charge became a lien on his land. Furthermore, the colonist's water right was tied to his land and could not be divorced from it. The form of the water contract the farmer signed was substantially the same, in other words, as the initial contract between the canal company and the developer. It was this transfer of water rights to the owners of small tracts that made the Fresno colonizing efforts successful, and it was a notable departure from the general policy in California of dealing with land only in quarter-sections, thereby excluding the small farmer.

Prices and credit terms varied somewhat from colony to colony depending, among other factors, on the year of settlement, location, soils, and community facilities. Thus a 20-acre farm in Washington Colony sold initially (1878) for $700 plus interest ($150 down payment, thirty-six monthly installments of $12.50, $100 payment at end of three years, and interest at the rate of 10 percent per annum on the unpaid balance). In Fresno Colony (1882) the same size farm sold for $1000 ($300 down payment and the balance bearing interest at the rate of 10 percent). Later in 1891 the Perrins received for their colonies an average price of $75 per acre ($1500 for a 20-acre lot) with liberal credit terms.

The Developer Recruits Colonists

The developers actively recruited colonists, broadcasting posters and pamphlets widely and advertising in San Francisco and in eastern papers and especially in foreign language media. In cooperation with the railroads they organized free excursions from other California cities to Fresno.

The pitch was directed at individuals, but especially at communities and societies desiring to settle in groups. As for the former, the developers promoted the idea that vine and fruit farming would be considerably less arduous than clod busting on the dry plains and that for this reason it was an appropriate occupation for single women, and even for tired businessmen and store clerks, who were sought in the cities as colonists. The first of the quotations below is from promotional material for the Central Colony, the second, from a similar tract for the Washington Colony.

Most of the so-called *light* occupations which are generally assigned to women are remarkable for either a terrible strain on the nervous system, or for one-sided physical exertion. Teaching, stenography, telegraphy, weaving, operating sewing machines, standing all day behind a counter, type-setting and other such employments, are too hard on the system to admit of being followed for life by women of ordinary physical capacity. Besides, such employments generally admit only the earning of monthly or weekly wages, and afford no opportunities for independent business, with a sure living and a possible fortune in the event of extra success.

Fruit culture, the drying of fruit, the manufacture of jellies, canning and preserving berries, tomatoes, etc., gathering nuts, raising poultry and eggs, are employments that offer to women *independent* fields of labor that will neither break down their health nor keep them in perpetual bondage to monthly or weekly wages. We would not like to see American women, or any women in our country, doing rough work in the fields, though riding on a gang-plow is play in comparison with *teaching* or *running a sewing machine.* But all such labor may be done by men hired in the season of it, as all our farmers, big and little, hire help at harvest, while they themselves do little else than supervise.

A woman who is the owner of ten acres of raisin vineyard, five acres of orchard, and devotes five acres more to grass, flowers and poultry will find that all the plowing, cultivating, pruning, wood-sawing and heavy lifting can be done by one man in a *part* of the year; that picking, drying and packing fruit, gathering nuts, making jellies, preserving and canning fruits and vegetables during one season of the year; and milking one or two cows, making butter and raising poultry as a principal business the rest of the year is easier, pleasanter and more healthful than any city employment. Then, when the year's work is done, and no special disaster has interfered with success, two or three thousand dollars clear profit feels much more satisfactory in the pocket than the savings of weekly earnings behind the counter, the case, the desk, or the sewing machine.[6]

Business men who wish to retire from their monotonous toil, can here find change and rest, pleasant surroundings and a better income than they have often realized from their life-long drudgery. People in reduced circumstances who are struggling to keep up appearances in the city, with children unemployed, and with young men and women seeking in vain for employment, should at once seek a good location and direct their energies to the cultivation of vines and fruits. In this way every member of the family can find pleasant and profitable employment, and all can enjoy health and the pleasures of a pleasant and happy home. The thousands of young men who are always seeking clerkships, or "waiting for something to turn up," would do much better to come to the country and go to work, earning money and getting a vineyard and orchard started, that, if well attended to, will make them fortunes for life. Nor should they think that because they have no money their case is hopeless. Every young man of good sense, industry and a will, can easily work his way to a competency if he will determine to be self-reliant and do it.[7]

Under the colony system of settlement the great bugbear of the pioneer—lack of neighbors—was overcome. This was in contrast to the typical American settlement pattern of farm homesteads where each farmer was alone on his quarter-section. Capitalizing on this advantage, developers sought to recruit colonies of hardworking compatible groups to whom community life was especially important, which frequently meant the foreign born. Scandinavians were especially prized as colonists, for although they had had no previous experience with irrigation, they were considered to be "peaceable, industrious, and frugal." Armenians and Syrians were good colonists, for they used their prior knowledge of irrigation to introduce into the Fresno region several of its profitable crops: figs and Persian, Casaba, and other varieties of melon.

When one examines the origins of the colonists of the Fresno region in the years 1880 to 1910 one realizes how successful the developers were in their recruitment efforts. Scandinavians predominated in the Central and Washington colonies. Scandinavian Home Colony was settled initially by a society organized in San Francisco for the purpose. Although no one was barred from buying land because of nationality, none but Scandinavians could join the society, and the original Scandinavian colony was almost exclusively of the stock. A group of Swedish Americans from Ishpeming, Michigan, disenchanted with that area's cold winters, were the original settlers of the Swedish colony at Kingsburg.

A number of Danes, among them several who had settled initially in the Central and Washington colonies, purchased land near Selma. They stimulated interest in their fellow countrymen in eastern states and in Denmark, and Selma became largely Danish in culture. The developers of the so-called Bank Tract near Kerman brought in colonists of Scandinavian and German extraction from Minnesota and the Dakotas.

Mission Colony, across the Kings River from Reedley, was settled by Swedes in 1886. In 1905 a group of Finnish carpenters, longshoremen, and sailors in San Francisco who had joined for the purpose founded a colony near Reedley. About the same time a colony of German Mennonites also settled near Reedley and their favorable reports attracted other Mennonites from Minnesota, Kansas, Germany, and the German colonies in Russia.

Armenians came to Fresno in the years following 1880 from Boston, where they had recently emigrated as refugees from eastern Turkey, and from Turkey directly, mostly from the same region as the Boston Armenians. Although the majority of these colonists belonged to the Armenian Gregorian Church, a considerable number were Congregationalists and Presbyterians, because New England missionaries of these denominations had established schools in Armenia after the civil war. This New England connection had brought the Armenians to Boston in the first place.

There also were significant numbers of Portuguese (from the Azores, many via New England), Swiss, Yugoslav, Chinese, and by the end of the period, Japanese colonists in the Fresno region, which became one of the most cosmopolitan in America.

Nonetheless, native-born colonists outnumbered the foreign born by more than two to one, and certain colonies were almost exclusively old American. Traver Colony, one of the largest, had a population as homogeneous as any older Anglo-American community in the Midwest. American Colony, due west of Washington Colony, was limited initially to native Americans, although the ban on foreign-born citizens was lifted several years after it was founded.

The original colonies were settled around a few towns—Fresno, Selma, Dinuba, Kingsburg, Reedley, Traver—with wide stretches of arid land between them. Further settlement closed the gaps, welded the communities into one solid mass, and obliterated the colony boundaries. Concurrently individual colonies gradually lost their ethnocentricity. But the cosmopolitan nature of the region as a whole remained, although the later influx of emigrants from Oklahoma, Arkansas, and Texas during the Great Depression increased somewhat the percentage of Anglo-American farmers.

The Canal Company and the Farmers Operate the System

For the most part the developers retired as quickly as they could from any responsibility for operating the irrigation systems. This was left to the canal companies, in which, to be sure, the developers frequently held an interest, and to the farmers.

The canal companies, in turn, tried to limit their responsibilities to operating the main canals. They turned into each lateral at its head the water supply necessary to satisfy the contracts that had been made with the developers; and if the canal flow was insufficient to meet the requirements of all laterals, supplies were reduced proportionately, as provided in the contracts. The companies ran water in the laterals in a continuous stream during the full irrigation season. When faced with a severe drought, they could abandon this procedure and rotate the water among the laterals; but the companies were reluctant to use this alternative method since, among other considerations, it required them to exercise more discretion and to employ more operating personnel. When it was practiced, rotation was in the order that the laterals had been built or that contracts had been signed for delivering water to them rather than from the head to the tail of the companies' canals. So delivery could skip from one section of a company's service area to another with attendant waste from canal seepage and evaporation.

More specifically, when the water supply was insufficient to meet demands but there was not a serious drought, water was "prorated" among laterals of more than 200 cfs flow (that is, it was distributed simultaneously and continuously to these laterals in proportion to the acres served by each). On the smaller laterals the water could be "rotated" (distributed discontinuously) but with the objective of providing each irrigator with the same proportion as by prorating. When the drought was serious and water was insufficient to meet 50 percent of the demand, the companies could rotate in all parts of their distribution systems.

Operation and maintenance of the laterals devolved upon the farmers. The water users on many of the larger laterals organized lateral or ditch companies under law. These mutual companies established operating procedures to rotate the water among users, hired ditch tenders to distribute the water, and took responsibility for maintaining the channels. Users were assessed costs in proportion to their acres with water rights and the law could be invoked to make the users pay.

However, the farmers on most of the laterals were organized informally or not at all. Where lateral associations were not incorporated but operated under simple "neighborhood agreements," it was difficult to achieve uniform enforcement of operating procedures and canal maintenance, for there was no practical way to curb recalcitrant farmers who were prepared to disregard the interests of their neighbors. The situation was worst on the unorganized laterals, where in some cases it was the practice for farmers to help themselves to water whenever they wanted it so that a downstream irrigator did not know when his water might be shut off by one above him and once shut off, when it would be available again. Farmers would justify such practices in terms of their water contracts. They had paid for their water rights by the acre and they paid their annual assessments on that basis. Thus so long as they used water on the land to which it was attached, it was nobody's business when they used it or how much they used. And indeed, there was some substance to these claims, for farmers under their contracts were entitled to receive from the canal companies their contract shares of water whenever they wanted them.

The contracts gave the canal companies power to require efficient organizations among water users for distribution and maintenance of the laterals, but the companies found it difficult to enforce this provision and they had relatively little incentive to do so. The annual fee of 62.5 cents per acre that the farmers paid to the company for operation and maintenance did not cover the laterals and the companies found it difficult to collect additional fees for this purpose. Frequently farmers who were receiving poor service would petition the company to take over their lateral, maintain it, control the distribution of water along it, and collect charges to cover the costs of doing so. The company typically resisted these petitions and the assumption of additional duties, arguing that the farmers could and should organize themselves to do these things.

A company might respond that it was prepared to take over a lateral provided it was guaranteed adequate compensation. But this guarantee the complaining farmers, who were usually on unorganized laterals, could not give. Unpaid annual maintenance fees for the principal canals were a lien on the property under the original contracts, but this was not the case for additional fees that the company would need to collect for operating and maintaining the laterals.

Farmers whose water service was insufficient because of poor organization of laterals were not necessarily without water to irrigate, for groundwater was close to the surface and they could install pumps. By 1915 the territory was dotted with hundreds, and by 1925 with thousands, of small pumps that were used typically before and after the season of canal water; but farmers could use them also at any time that surface water was inadequate.

Canal Companies as Public Utilities

California statues of 1862 and 1885 gave power to county boards of supervisors to regulate the maximum rates that could be charged by water companies in the event that a county were petitioned to exercise this power by not less than twenty-five resident taxpayers. But the Fresno, Kings, and Tulare county governments never used this authority over irrigation companies, for several reasons. First, no petitions for action under the statutes were presented to them. Also a question was raised, and it remained unresolved, as to whether water right contracts of the Fresno type, in which landowners paid no water rates, only annual operation and maintenance charges, were subject to the statute.

One of the principal reforms enacted by the California Progressives under the leadership of Governor Hiram Johnson was to invigorate state regulation of railroads. The constitutional amendments and laws adopted from 1911 to 1913 for this purpose covered other utilities as well as railroads, however, so that a much strengthened railroad commission was given jurisdiction over the rates and services of water companies, superseding the authority of the county boards of supervisors. There is no evidence that state authority over irrigation companies was demanded or even supported by the irrigators of the Kings River region or elsewhere in the Central Valley. Public debate on the several measures relating to public utilities focused on the railroads almost exclusively, with occasional references to companies that supplied domestic water.

Nonetheless after 1913 the commission received a number of complaints from water users of the Fresno and Consolidated canal companies, most of them related to poor service on unorganized laterals. The complainants wanted the commission to require the companies to assume responsibility for operation and maintenance of the laterals and to fix a reasonable fee for this purpose. The companies responded that they were willing to manage the laterals but that since many landowners would refuse to pay for this service, they were unwilling to provide it unless they were assured in advance of payment without the necessity of law suits to collect from unwilling landowners. From past experience the companies knew that they had little chance of winning such suits against farmers before local judges and jurors. In an early opinion on this issue involving the Fresno Canal and Irrigation Company the commission said,

... the public interest will be best served by having the irrigation company ultimately operate and maintain all the laterals under its system. It is at times difficult for farmers to induce their neighbors to keep their ditches clean and to permit fair and equitable distribution of the water. . . .

In the present case it appears that a number of landowners do not want the irrigation company to take control of the laterals unless it be done without expense to them, and that they may resist payment. It would be manifestly unfair to direct the irrigation company to perform this work unless there is a reasonable prospect that the company will be paid for it. Hence an order will issue directing the irrigation company to assume control of the laterals and thereafter to maintain and operate them, but only when complainants shall have presented an agreement signed by the owners of 75 per cent of the 1,280 acres of land affected, agreeing to pay the actual cost, not to exceed 85 cents per acre for the first two years, 50 cents during the third and fourth years and 25 cents during each subsequent year, and when the Commission has issued a supplemental order to this effect.

Whatever may be done in the present case, the complainants will have the satisfaction of knowing that they have helped to advance materially the ultimate solution of this problem.[8]

The commission's sense of accomplishment was overreckoned, however, for in the following years relatively few laterals were transferred to the companies for operation and maintenance. One problem was that the commission's orders did not guarantee that farmers would pay the added charges. In subsequent opinions related to the Consolidated Canal Company the commission initially directed the company to continue to maintain a lateral it had operated for one year on a temporary basis and at a loss due to farmers' failure to pay their assessments. The commission also ordered all irrigators to pay all back and future assessments and it authorized the company to refuse to deliver water to any farmer who had not paid. But the commission probably had no authority to order the farmers to pay and certainly it had no way to force them to do so. On rehearing, the commission set aside its first order and provided instead that if the irrigators paid in advance the entire cost of maintaining and operating their private lateral, the commission would then issue an order directing the company to maintain the lateral for the next irrigation season.[9]

After extensive consulting with company management and with certain consumers, the commission issued an identical set of operating rules for the two companies. These for the most part codified the existing practices described in the previous section.

Finally, in a case related as much to water rights as to operation and maintenance, the commission enjoined the Fresno canal company from selling any additional water rights without approval of the regulating agency. Since the company at that time was selling to new farmers only rights released by others, this order was largely grandstanding by the commission; it confirmed the existing situation.

Canal Companies Become Public Irrigation Districts

Railroad commission regulation in the service areas of the Fresno and Consolidated canal companies ended in 1921 when both companies sold their properties to newly organized irrigation districts. Here ended also the role of the developer and of private venture capital in the settlement of land and the delivery of water to farms near Fresno. Developers' profits had come principally from the improvement and sale of land. Once this was completed, they gradually withdrew for there was not much money to be made in operating the irrigation system. The final exit was in 1921 for several more specific reasons.

The original water rights contracts were to expire in 1921. The negotiation of new contracts and new rates was now subject to regulation by the railroad commission, which until then had sought to improve the companies' service but had not interfered with the basic water right contracts. The companies initiated proceedings before the railroad commision to fix new rates. The Fresno canal company requested an annual rate of $3.40 per acre, up from 62.5 cents, to cover operating costs and a reasonable return on the investment, which they valued at approximately $5.7 million.

The anticipation of strong opposition from farmers to a considerable rate increase and of a time-consuming struggle before the railroad commission were important factors encouraging the companies to pursue simultaneously the alternative course of negotiating to sell their distribution systems to public districts, although conditions of such sales would also be subject to railroad commission approval.

At this same time there was growing recognition by farmers and others that the irrigation systems would soon require large infusions of additional capital. In its rate filing before the railroad commission the Fresno canal company included new capital expenditures of $300,000 for the year 1921 for improvements to its distribution system. Much greater capital expenditures were foreseen in future years for the construction of major storage facilities on the Kings River, to be financed cooperatively by Fresno interests and other users of the river.

The canal companies were reluctant to face these obligations. In addition to the reasons given above, the British companies had decided after World War I to retreat from their investments in irrigation canals and agricultural land in the San Joaquin Valley; they were anxious to get their money back. Fortunately, there was available an alternative form of organization that was better adapted than the commercial irrigation company to financing canal improvements and new water supplies in established irrigation communities. It was the irrigation district.

In 1887 the California legislature had passed the Wright Act, authorizing the formation of public irrigation districts, having authority to issue bonds for the purpose of financing their capital expenditures and to impose taxes or assessments for the purpose of meeting their annual costs. Most of the districts organized in the early years failed due to poor planning, insufficient financial supervision, and extensive litigation concerning the law itself. By the turn of the century irrigation district bonds had become unsalable. To meet the many problems that surfaced in these years, the law was amended many times and it was not until 1915 that the public district concept was perfected to the point that it was a viable alternative to commercial water companies for the operation and further development of existing systems.

The outstanding advantage of the irrigation district was its right to issue bonds. These bonds were not backed by the credit of the state, but after 1911 they could be certified by a state bond commission composed of the attorney general, state engineer, and superintendent of banks. When certified, they were legal investments for savings banks, trust companies, trust funds, and insurance companies. Also, the bonds and their income were exempt from state personal property taxes and from federal income tax.

Further, irrigation districts had authority to levy taxes in order to pay interest on the bonds, amortization charges for retiring the bonds when they fell due, and annual costs of operating and maintaining the irrigation systems. The tax power involved several unique advantages not available to commercial companies, principally the right to assess all lands susceptible of irrigation within district boundaries (but not improvements on the land) whether or not the lands were irrigated. Thus, for example, large owners who wanted to irrigate only 40 acres were required to pay taxes on their entire holdings. Also land used for residence or business that was susceptible of receiving water for agricultural or domestic purposes was taxed if it was within district boundaries. In some cases these boundaries were drawn to exclude cities and towns that would otherwise be within the district; in other cases towns were included.

The districts had authority to assess all land uniformly or to establish classes of land with unequal assessments and to impose a uniform tax rate, or to vary the rate by land classification. Finally, the districts were given sufficient authority to collect their taxes, for the lands of delinquents could be sold at public auction to the highest bidder.

The tax and bond powers together were a means for compelling a minority, possibly an otherwise obstructive minority, to contribute to the costs of a system. Commercial irrigation companies, by comparison, were unable to obtain revenue from lands within their service areas that were owned by persons who refused to patronize their enterprises. Put another way, the irrigation district was a means by which a part of the residents of an area could incur indebtedness for which all of the lands in the area were held liable. But how large a part? The law was changed several times in this regard. The provisions in effect when the Fresno and Consolidated districts were formed were these. The first step in forming a district was a petition to the county board of supervisors from landowners and residents within the boundaries of a proposed district. This petition was to be signed by a majority of landowners owning a majority in value of land, or alternatively by five hundred resident voters or landowners, including owners of 20 percent in value of land in the proposed district. Once the petition was approved by the supervisors, after they had received a report from the state engineer, it was put to a vote of all electors residing in the proposed district. Until November 1920, a two-thirds vote was necessary to approve a district. Thereafter, by virtue of an amendment to the law that engendered a bitter legislative controversy, a majority of voters was sufficient.

Bond issues had to be approved by the electors. If the district directors on their own initiative called a bond election, a two-thirds affirmative vote was required. If, on the other hand, a bond election was requested in a petition signed by a majority of landowners owning a majority in value of land or by five hundred voters including the owners of 20 percent in value of land, then a majority vote was sufficient to carry the bonds.

Another advantage of the public irrigation district was that it was authorized to enter into cooperative and contractual arrangements with agencies of the federal and state governments, and the district was considered by these other authorities to be an appropriate instrument for such cooperation. As we shall see, the Fresno district was a leader in the complex negotiations to build Pine Flat Dam.

Finally, irrigation districts were essentially farmer organizations, so that acquisition by a district of a commercial canal company meant in some ways a gain in popular control and perhaps a reduction of antagonisms between farmers and water supplier. This could be especially important in helping to resolve problems of water delivery on informally organized and unorganized laterals. Three or five district directors were to be elected from divisions of a district "as nearly equal in area and population as may be practicable" or elected at large, depending on the provisions of the farmers' initial petition to form the district. An assessor, tax collector, and treasurer were elected also, although two or all of these positions could be combined in one person. The directors were chosen for four-year terms, approximately half of them elected every two years; the other officers had two-year terms.

Seven hundred and eighty-eight landowners in the service area of the Fresno Canal and Irrigation Company, representing nearly one-fourth of the assessed value of land in the area, petitioned the supervisors of Fresno County in March 1920 for the formation of Fresno Irrigation District. The proposed district included an area of approximately 240,000 acres held by more than two thousand landowners. The city of Fresno and the towns of Pinedale, Clovis, Malaga, and Kerman, although they were completely surrounded by the district, were not to be included in it. The population living within the district was approximately fourteen thousand, whereas that of Fresno city was about fifty thousand.

The petition was approved by the state engineer and the county supervisors and was put to election in June 1920, when it was approved by a vote of 1438 to 184. The district began negotiations immediately with the canal company to purchase its properties. The Fresno canal company estimated that its system was worth $5.7 million—$3.4 million for water rights and $2.3 million for the canal system. At the same time it reported that $1 million of company stock and $559,000 of company bonds were outstanding.

The irrigation district questioned whether the company had any property to sell in the water rights, since these had become appurtenant to the farmers' lands under water rights contracts. The company argued that those contracts were for a definite period, which expired in 1921. The legal question here was never settled, for the company soon abandoned its specific claims to payment for water rights and bargained over the value of the canal system. The newly hired engineer and manager of the irrigation district valued the system at $1.7 million and a settlement was reached at $1.75 million.

A special election was held in February 1921 to approve two bond issues, one for $1.75 million to pay the canal company. It was approved by a vote of 1578 to 74. The second bond issue was in the amount of $250,000 for improvements, largely for replacing some five thousand service gates and turnouts. It was approved by a similar vote. Both bond issues were sold at a coupon rate of 6 percent, with maturities ranging from 1923 to 1932, and they were redeemed on schedule.

About a year later than their neighbors farmers in the service area of the Consolidated Canal Company petitioned to form the Consolidated Irrigation District. The proposed district, including approximately 150,000 acres held by 3750 landowners, was approved and company facilities were purchased in a manner similar to Fresno.

Both districts chose to elect their boards of directors by geographic divisions, five in each case. In the Fresno district there have been frequent electoral contests for these positions, but there have been few in Consolidated. Voter turnout in both districts has generally been light, but the men chosen have been dedicated and capable.

With regard to taxation, the basic classification adopted by the directors of the Fresno district separated lands that receive water from the district's system and lands without water service. The latter, it should be noted, are not necessarily without the capacity to irrigate, however, for they can use private pumps for raising groundwater. Until 1927 the district assessed all land at $100 per acre and charged a lower tax rate to the lands without water service. The average tax in 1922 was $1.27 per acre, but in a very short time it almost doubled, reaching $2.40 by 1925. This can be compared with 62.5 cents per acre under the contracts that were to expire in 1921 and to $3.40 proposed by the canal company in its initial filing with the railroad commission, although this latter rate would undoubtedly have been reduced considerably since it included a return on the company's valuation of water rights.

In 1927 the assessment and tax procedures were reversed. A uniform tax rate was used for all land ($2.50 per $100 valuation in 1927) but the value of land without water service was placed at 60 percent of the value of land with service ($60 instead of $100 per acre). The basic assessment of $100 has remained to the present, but the reduction for lands without service was subsequently increased—today the assessment is $40 per acre—due largely to increased costs of pumping as the water table receded. Also the district has introduced a reduced assessment for lands with service that, because of their topography, cannot receive water by gravity flow but must pump it from the district's canals. Such lands are valued at 75 percent of the basic rate.

The land classification adopted by the Consolidated board of directors was somewhat more complex. As in the Fresno district, there was a differentiation between lands with and without water service, but the latter were subdivided into five categories of decreasing valuation.

All petitions for changes in assessment from one category to another must be approved by the district board of directors. In recent years the board has generally refused petitions from landowners to change from water service to nonservice, largely because the rising groundwater level, which has encouraged farmers to use private pumps and to reduce the acres that are served by canals, has been the consequence of district activities and district investments.

Operating Procedures of the Irrigation Districts

The law relating to irrigation districts has provided from the beginning in 1887 that the districts should apportion any water among landowners according to the ratio of the assessed valuation of each tract to the total assessed valuation of the district, with each landowner having the privilege to assign for use within the district his right to the whole or any part of the water apportioned to him. This provision was considered by lawmakers to embody a high order of justice—the United States Supreme Court in passing on the constitutionality of the original Wright Act held that such an apportionment of water coupled with the right of assignment "operates with as near an approach to justice and equality as can be hoped for in such matters"—but in fact the provision has been unworkable in many situations.[10] For example, a town lot within an irrigation district would have a relatively high assessment, entitling it to a good quantity of irrigation water, yet it would need little if any of this. The principal factors that controlled the valuation of agricultural land (not including improvements) at the time were fertility and access to transportation. Therefore a tract of land with poor access but satisfactory soil for irrigation agriculture might have a low valuation, resulting in an apportionment of water that was insufficient to irrigate. Also, the uninhibited right of assignment could disturb the distribution of water in a canal sytem that was built on the principle that water was tied to land.

The law was not repealed, however. In some districts it simply was not followed; in others land assessment procedures that effectively modified the law were used. Significantly, the irrigation districts have insisted on making their own assessment classifications and valuations rather than using those of the county governments; and the elected district boards of directors have devoted a considerable part of their time to questions of property assessment. Also, where a district has taken over a going irrigation company, it usually has acquired it subject to any existing rights of landowners to receive definite quantities or proportionate quantities of water, thereby modifying the principle of the irrigation districts law. Finally, the districts have limited landowners' freedom to assign or transfer their rights, requiring that the board of directors approve assignments between irrigators on different laterals. We shall therefore describe the actuality of distribution to the farmers near Fresno rather than the theory of the water code.

In the Fresno Irrigation District the basic rule is that 10 acres of land on water service are entitled to 1 cfs of water for twenty-four hours on each run. This entitlement is roughly the equivalent of that provided by the water rights contracts of the Fresno canal company (that is, 4 cfs of continuous flow for one section of land or 640 acres).[11]

The amount of water delivered in a crop year depends on the number of runs or rotations as well as the quantity delivered on a single run. The canal water season normally begins in March and before the Pine Flat Dam became operative in the 1950s the season ended on July 30, providing ten runs. Storage supplied by the dam has extended the season through August, providing an additional two runs in a normal year. In addition there is a fig run between December and March and a citrus run in December.

Excluding these special runs, the district can deliver by canal to each acre in a normal year between 2 and 2.5 acre-feet of water (0.20 x 12), yet the average annual irrigation requirement is 4.5 acre-feet. The landowner makes up the difference—both water needed before and after the canal season and additional water needed in the season—by turning on his pumps and extracting the groundwater. Farmers require water until early September for cotton, until about August 25 for the raisin harvest, and many of them need a winter irrigation apart from the special fruit runs.

When water is abundant the district can deliver a larger quantity on any run by increasing the rate of flow in the canals and laterals while keeping the rotation schedule constant. (It may be impractical to increase the time allotted to each irrigator since the normal rotation schedule usually accounts for all days of a month.) Alternatively, the district can increase the number of runs by adding runs before the beginning and after the end of the normal season. Before storage was built on the Kings River the district had to distribute abundant water at the moment it ran in the river channel. Thus unless the large flows occurred before March or after July the only alternatives available were to increase the rate of flow in the distribution system or to let the water pass to downstream users. The Pine Flat Dam, on the other hand, allows the district to store above-normal flows for later use.

The district has adjusted to drought in similar ways. It can reduce the quantity of water delivered on any run by reducing the time allotted to each 10 acres from twenty-four to twelve or even to eight hours while maintaining the normal delivery head. (It is frequently impractical to reduce the delivery head for hydraulic reasons.) Or the district can reduce the number of seasonal runs. Since the storage of Pine Flat reservoir became available, the latter alternative only has been used. Thus in the drought year of 1960–61 the canal water season did not begin until late in April. In 1966–67 the season began in March but was curtailed in April when only one run was delivered.

District laterals have the capacity to run 4-ft heads and the district tries to operate them at this rate twenty-four hours a day and seven days a week. Farmers, on the other hand, may receive water at any flow rate between 1 and 4 cfs, depending on their entitlements, needs, and preferences in relation to those of their neighbors. Thus a 40-acre farm might receive water for twenty-four hours at a 4-ft head or for forty-eight hours at a rate of 2 cfs. In the former case the farm would take the full flow of the lateral, in the latter, half the flow, and the district would schedule other farms simultaneously for the remaining half. In most cases the district delivers water for a consecutive period of twenty-four hours or for multiples of this period.

A rotation schedule for each district lateral is prepared prior to the beginning of the irrigation season. Then at least two weeks before the start of the first run ditch tenders mail or hand to each landowner a card that advises him of his regular rotation days. For the community or private laterals the farmers are responsible for preparing their own rotation schedules.

Table 5.3 is a rotation schedule for the Teilman South lateral. The small properties numbered 5, 6, and 7 that are not on water service are apparently home sites. It will be observed that farm 3 receives water at 2 cfs for two days, whereas farm 4 of the same size has one day at 4 cfs. Farm 4 takes alone on the fifteenth and thirtieth of each month, since it receives the full normal flow of the lateral; while farm 2 shares the lateral with farm 1 on the seventh and twenty-second and with farms 2 and 12 on the eighth and twenty-third of the month. Farms 1, 9, 10, and 14, all 20 acres, receive 2 cfs for one day, but farm 13 of the same size is served 1 cfs for forty-eight hours.

For each run, some three to five days before water is scheduled to be available to a water user the ditch tender contacts the user to remind him of his upcoming rotation and to find out if he plans to use water or to pass on the run. The ditch tender needs this information to determine the proper setting each day for the lateral's control gate and to "order" water for the lateral from the watermaster at district headquarters. The ditch tender then records all deliveries for each run.

To provide some flexibility in the district's operating procedures ditch tenders have been granted authority to approve farmers' requests to transfer water from one property to another. The ditch tenders can do this providing both water users' names appear on the same rotation schedule and the transfer will not interfere with normal deliveries to other water users. Also, if there are a few passes on a run, the ditch tender may use the water thereby saved to make up losses and shortages or to increase the size of heads of other users on the same schedule. Where farmers who want to transfer water are on different rotation schedules, however, their requests must be approved by the irrigation district manager or the board of directors and the transfer must be for the full season.

The ditch tenders set and lock the control structures on the principal canals and at the heads of laterals, checking them or resetting them daily. Normally they leave it to the farmers to open their own turnouts when they are scheduled to receive water and to shut them at the designated times. However the ditch tenders inspect the turnouts that are open to water on each day and they can lock the gate of an irrigator who violates the rotation schedule, thereby assuming full control over its being opened, set, and closed.

The tender with whom Maass rode the ditches of the Fresno district spoke with great urgency and sincerity when he said that he hated to put a lock on a farmer's gate, for this was an insult to the farmer, and the ditch tender's principal job was to get along with water users, not to antagonize them. Fresno ditch tenders, like those in many other irrigated areas of the west, are indoctrinated with this theme by their board of directors: "A poor . . . [ditch tender] , or one whose technical work may be good but who is unable to maintain harmonious relations with the farmers, can keep the board of directors in trouble throughout

Table 5.3 Ditch tender's distribution schedule, Fresno Irrigation District, Teilman South at Cornelia Ditch, 1969–1970, quantity of water (in cfs) to be delivered to each farm in each month of the irrigation season (by days of the month).

No.	Name	Section Township & Range	WS[a]	PFD[b]	NWS[c]
			Acres		
1	W. J. Petersen	15-14-19	20		
2	G. & V. Kirorian		20		
3	C. Envernizzi		40		
4	T. P. Koller		71		
5	T. P. Koller				2.25
6	T. & L. Koller				2.25
7	G. Woods				4.30
8	Peter J. Arriet et al.		60		
9	J. Ostendorf		20		
10	Glenn Koller		20		
11	F. R. & E. J. Andrews et al.	10-14-19	10		10.00
12	E. Kirikorian		10		
13	Peter J. Arriet		20		
14	A. & D. Vanoni	15-14-19	20		
15	Wayne B. Ihde		40		
16	J. J. & M. Quist		160		
Total			511		18.80

[a]Water service.
[b]Pump from ditch.
[c]No water service.

1	2	3	4	5	6	7	8	9	10	11	12	13	14	15
16	17	18	19	20	21	22	23	24	25	26	27	28	29	30
						2								
						2								
							2							
							2							
						2	2							
						2	2							
								3.1	4					
								3.1	4					
										3	3			
										3	3			
												2		
												2		
													2	
													2	
					1									
					1									
							1							
							1							
										1	1			
										1	1			
												2		
												2		
														4
														4
4	4	4	4											
4	4	4	4											

the season. A person to be successful at this work, must be temperamentally adapted to it; it is one of those positions in which personality plays a leading part. The psychological relationship between an irrigation farmer and his water supply is well known throughout the irrigated regions of the West." [12]

Irrigators who have differences with ditch tenders in regard to water delivery or canal maintenance may appeal to the district manager, and if they fail to get satisfaction from him, to the board of directors. When water is running, five to six farmers a week are likely to come into the district office with complaints against other users or ditch tenders. Very few of these farmers, perhaps no more than ten per year, appeal to the board of directors, although others may see the directors who represent their divisions on the board.

Padlocks are used, then, only for chronic offenders and with the approval of the ditch tender's superiors. Also, the district can refuse service to users who waste water willfully, carelessly, on account of defective ditches and structures, or on account of inadequate preparation of their land for irrigation; but this rule is invoked infrequently.

The district has no court like the water courts of Spain to try violaters of its operating rules. It can lock gates or it can charge the offender in the criminal courts, for taking water off the schedule or without permission of a ditch tender is a violation of the penal code. However, Fresno district officers do not recall an instance in which they have had recourse to the courts for this purpose.

To operate and maintain its canal system, the Fresno Irrigation District has a substantial organization, which in 1968 included an operations staff with two watermasters and more than thirty ditch tenders, a maintenance crew, an engineering staff of several professionals, and an office staff.

Consolidated district's operating procedures vary from those of Fresno in several important respects. The basic rule is that 10 acres of land on water service are entitled to 2 cfs of water for twenty-four hours, or 0.4 acre-feet per acre per run. As in the case of the Fresno district this entitlement is roughly the equivalent of that provided by the water rights contracts of the canal company it succeeded.

As we noted earlier, the larger quantity of water in the Consolidated rule does not mean that farmers served by this district have a better water supply than farmers served by the Fresno district, for this depends also on the number of runs and their timing. Due to the inferior water rights in the river of the Consolidated district, it has averaged four to five runs in a season, compared to ten to twelve in Fresno. Also, the water comes and goes more rapidly so that farmers have to apply large quantities of canal water in short periods of time. The storage provided by Pine Flat Dam has enabled the district to smooth out its supply somewhat, but in a typical water year the first canal water run is in mid-May and the last one in mid-July. In the extraordinary drought year of 1960–61 the district was able to complete only one run, in late June and early July, and it had to borrow water from a hydroelectric project of the Pacific Gas and Electric Company in order to do this. The Fresno district was able to abstract in April through August more than 60 percent of its average diversion for the previous ten years.

In a poor water year farmers in the Consolidated district are able to obtain one-quarter or less of their annual water requirement by gravity; the remaining three-quarters must be pumped. With farmers relying so heavily on pumping the district has made special efforts to recharge the subsurface reservoir when water is available. It operates forty ponds, covering 1200 acres, into which it spills above-normal canal flows.

These characteristics of the district's water supply, especially the short season of canal water, have resulted in a distribution procedure for laterals and farms that differs in important respects from that in Fresno. For most canals and laterals there are no rotation schedules such as that shown in table 5.3. The normal procedure is called demand. When a farmer wants water he gets in touch with the ditch tender, who supplies it to him as soon as he can—"first asked, first served, as soon as possible." The ditch tender has discretion to allow an irrigator to take more on an individual run than his entitlement providing this does not prevent another from receiving his entitlement.

The water is normally delivered in twenty-four-hour units, beginning at 0700 hours. The ditch tender keeps records showing for each week the daily deliveries to each farm as well as the cumulative deliveries to the farm for the season. Table 5.4 shows weekly reports of the second and third rotations for a sector of the Selma branch canal in a good water year (1969–70). As deliveries begin and end at 0700 hours, seventeen hours (0700–2400 hours) is the delivery time on the first day that a farmer takes water and seven hours (0000–0700 hours) is the time on the last day.

When water is in short supply the district holds users to their basic entitlements on a single run and applies the rule that no farmer can irrigate twice until all have had an opportunity to take once.

A few laterals in the Consolidated district use rotation schedules. The farmers on these laterals had argued so persistently among themselves under the demand delivery system that the district switched to schedules so that there would be for them the appearance as well as the fact of equity.

To illustrate the effects of irrigation district operating procedures on the production and income of farms near Fresno, we have again used the simulation program. The basic data on farm size, crop patterns, yields, costs, returns, and seasonal distribution of surface water supply are found in tables A5.1–A5.4 of the appendix to this chapter. These data are broadly representative of the Fresno region but are taken more particularly from the service area of the Fresno Irrigation District. We assume three water supply situations—mean seasonal supply of surface or ditch water, 20 percent below the seasonal mean, and 30 percent below the mean. The California simulations differ from those of the other regions because there are no crop losses. If ditch water is insufficient to bring through a farmer's crop, it is assumed that he will pump groundwater to do so. Thus crop production, crop values, and costs of production excluding the

Table 5.4 Composite weekly reports of ditch tender for a sector of the Selma Branch Consolidated Irrigation District, second and third rotations, 1969–70.[a]

Property #	Acres with water service	Name	Crops	Acre-feet to date	May 31	June 1	2	3	4	5	6
3457	31.83	Boyajian	Vineyard	5.42	—	—	—	—	1/17	1/24	1/24
Wildflower Pond[b]					2	8	5	10	5	5	6
3458	70	Carter	Vineyard, alfalfa	20.00	—	—	—	—	—	—	—
3460	20	Munson	Vineyard	8.00	2/24	2/7	—	—	—	—	—
3459	29.07	Barton	Vineyard	24.00	—	2/17	2/24	2/24	2/7	—	—
#20 Lateral-Fannan Nelson											
3463	40	Serimian	Vineyard	16.00	—	—	—	—	—	—	—
3469	40	Singh	Vineyard	16.00	—	—	—	—	—	—	—
3470	20	Jackson	Vineyard	14.42	—	—	—	—	1/17	1/24	1/24
3471	15	Dillon	Alfalfa, cotton, corn	—	—	—	—	—	—	—	—
3462	70	Pimentel	Vineyard	36.00	2/24	2/24	2/24	2/24	2/7	—	—
3464	10	R. Nelson	Alfalfa, corn	4.00	—	—	—	—	—	—	—
3464	70	R. Nelson	Alfalfa, corn	16.00	—	—	—	—	—	—	—
3465, 6, 8A	60	J. Taylor	Vineyard, alfalfa, cotton	16.00	—	—	—	—	—	—	—
Conejo Ave.											
3473	40	T. Taylor	Vineyard	10.83	—	—	—	—	2/17	2/24	2/24
3467	20	Marvin	Vineyard	—	—	—	—	—	—	—	—
4242A	260	G. Rocha et al.	Dairy, rotation crops	197.66	4/24	4/24	4/24	4/24	4/24	4/24	4/24
3499, 3501	80	M. Rocha et al.	Dairy, rotation crops	—	—	—	—	—	—	—	—
3496, 7	160.4	Lamm & Pert	Vineyard, peaches	68.00	—	—	—	—	—	—	—
3498, 3500	80	Panoo	Vineyard	45.00	2.5/24	2.5/24	2.5/24	2.5/24	2.5/24	2.5/24	2.5/7
3504A	60	H. Gruenwald	Vineyard	38.83	2/24	2/24	2/24	2/24	2/24	2/24	2/24
3504C	2.21	L. W. Gruenwald		—	—						
3504D	0.91	Heredia		—	—	—	—	—	—	—	—
3505, 6	40	Fry Bros.	Vineyard, almonds	20.00	—	—	—	—	—	—	—
3504B	40	Horn	Vineyard	30.00	3/17	3/24	3/24	3/24	3/24	3/7	
Wasteway[c]						2		3		2	

[a] Figures above the line are rate of delivery (in cfs); those below the line are duration of delivery (in hr.). The weekly summations for each farm are in acre-feet.

[b] A district pond used to recharge ground water.

[c] Water entering wasteway returns to the river.

Acre-feet to date	June 7	8	9	10	11	12	13
10.00	1/24	1/24	1/7	—	—	—	—
—	5	5	8	10	8	4	4
20.00	—	—	—	—	—	—	—
8.00	—	—	—	—	—	—	—
24.00	—	—	—	—	—	—	—
18.83	—	—	—	—	—	—	2/17
32.00	—	—	2/17	2/24	2/24	2/24	2/7
18.00	1/24	1/7	—	—	—	—	—
—							
36.00	—	—	—	—	—	—	—
8.00	—	2/17	2/7	—	—	—	—
16.00	—	—	—	—	—	—	—
32.00	—	2/17	2/24	2/24	2/24	2/7	—
16.00	2/24	2/7	—	—	—	—	—
—							
255.66	4/24	4/24	4/24	4/24	4/24	4/24	4/24
—							
90.83	—	2/17	2/24	2/24	2/24	2/24	2/24
45.00	—	—	—	—	—	—	—
60.00	2/24	2/24	2/24	2/24	2/24	2/7	—
—							
—							
20.00	—	—	—	—	—	—	—
30.00	—	—	—	—	—	—	—
		2		2			

Acre-feet to date	June 14	15	16	17	18	19	20
10.00	—	—	—	—	—	—	—
—	2	2	0	0	2	2	3
20.00	—	—	—	—	—	—	—
16.00	—	—	—	—	2/17	2/24	2/24
33.42	—	—	1/17	1/24	1/24	1/24	1/24
32.00	2/24	2/24	2/24	2/7	—	—	—
32.00	—	—	—	—	—	—	—
18.00	—	—	—	—	—	—	—
—							
50.83	—	—	—	2/17	2/24	2/24	2/24
8.00	—	—	—	—	—	—	—
16.00	—	—	—	—	—	—	—
32.00	—	—	—	—	—	—	—
22.83	—	—	—	—	—	2/17	2/24
—							
311.66	4/24	4/24	4/24	4/24	4/24	4/24	4/24
—							
118.83	2/24	2/24	2/24	2/24	2/24	2/24	2/24
45.00	—	—	—	—	—	—	—
60.00	—	—	—	—	—	—	—
—							
—							
20.00	—	—	—	—	—	—	—
30.00	—	—	—	—	—	—	—
		2		3		2	

Acre-feet to date	June 21	22	23	24	25	26	27
21.42	—	1/17	1/24	1/24	1/24	1/24	1/24
—	2	7	3	5	5	5	6
34.83	—	—	—	2/17	2/24	2/24	2/24
16.00	—	—	—	—	—	—	—
36.00	1/24	1/7	—	—	—	—	—
32.00	—	—	—	—	—	—	—
32.00	—	—	—	—	—	—	—
25.42	—	—	—	1/17	1/24	1/24	1/24
—							
64.00	2/24	2/7	2/17	2/7	—	—	—
12.00	—	2/17	2/7	—	—	—	—
16.00	—	—	—	—	—	—	—
32.00	—	—	—	—	—	—	—
36.00	2/24	2/24	2/24	2/7	—	—	—
7.42	—	—	—	1/17	1/24	1/24	1/24
367.66	4/24	4/24	4/24	4/24	4/24	4/24	4/24
—							
132.00	2/24	2/24	2/24	2/7	—	—	—
45.00	—	—	—	—	—	—	—
66.83	—	—	—	—	—	2/17	2/24
—							
—							
26.83	—	—	—	—	—	2/17	2/24
48.00	—	—	3/17	3/24	3/24	3/7	—
	2	0	0		1		2

Table 5.5 Water use (in acre-inches) and water costs and net farm returns (in dollars), three surface water supply situations, irrigation district near Fresno, California, late 1960s.

| | | Average Surface Water Supply | | | | | 20% Below | |
| | Total Water Used | Surface Water Available | Surface Water Used | Pump Water | Water Costs | Net Farm Income | Surface Water Available | Surface Water Used |
Farm								
1	474	395	361	113	112.46	2,300.33	317	317
2	2,292	1,975	1,719	573	565.66	6,659.65	1,580	1,529
3	1,736	1,580	1,320	416	434.72	5,811.83	1,264	1,176
4	4,025	3,160	3,077	948	918.16	12,552.18	2,537	2,537
5	2,770	2,370	2,176	594	639.48	7,963.77	1,896	1,883
6	1,654	1,580	1,266	388	422.96	7,966.90	1,264	1,175
7	4,206	3,555	3,229	977	995.34	10,622.86	2,844	2,808
8	9,030	7,110	6,746	2,284	2,129.70	24,318.83	5,688	5,629
9	2,244	1,975	1,724	520	543.40	7,471.70	1,580	1,527
10	1,827	1,580	1,383	444	446.48	7,643.64	1,264	1,229
Total	30,258	25,280	23,001	7,257	7,208.36	93,311.69	20,234	19,810

cost of water remain constant in the several water conditions we assume. The cost of water varies, however, since it is more expensive for the farmer to pump groundwater than to use ditch water; and its variation accounts for all changes in total production costs and in farm incomes as surface water becomes scarcer.

In the simulations ditch water is made available to all acres on an equal basis on each rotation, which approximaates closely the operating procedure of the Fresno district. The seasonal cost of ditch water for each farm is fixed regardless of the quantity it receives and is equal to the annual assessment rate of the irrigation district, $6.50 per acre in the late 1960s, times the number of acres on water service. Also, approximating conditions in the Fresno district, we assume that the service area is underlain with a uniformly productive aquifer so that all farms have the same unit cost for pumped water ($5.04 per acre-foot). The total cost of pumped water, unlike that of ditch water, increases with the quantity used. However its unit cost is constant, whereas the unit cost of ditch water decreases with the quantity used up to the limit allowed to each farm.

The output of the simulations (table 5.5) shows the impact of the variable costs of water on the farm economy. The average cost of ditch and pumped water per irrigated acre for the region as a whole increases 18.7 percent, from $11.26 to $13.36, as the ditch water supply falls to 20 percent below average flow. It increases a total of 31.6 percent, to $14.82 per acre, as the supply is reduced to 30 percent below the average. The cost of water increases from 7.7 percent of net farm income to 9.3 percent and to 10.4 percent when surface water is 30 percent short of the average supply.

Average Surface Water Supply			30% Below Average Surface Water Supply				
Pump Water	Water Costs	Net Farm Income	Surface Water Available	Surface Water Used	Pump Water	Water Costs	Net Farm Income
157	130.94	2,281.55	279	279	195	146.90	2,265.89
763	645.46	6,579.85	1,385	1,385	907	705.94	6,519.37
560	495.20	5,751.35	1,106	1,076	660	537.20	5,709.35
1,488	1,144.96	12,325.38	2,223	2,223	1,802	1,276.84	12,193.50
887	762.54	7,840.71	1,659	1,652	1,118	859.56	7,743.69
479	461.18	7,923.68	1,106	1,079	575	501.50	7,888.36
1,398	1,172.16	10,447.04	2,488	2,486	1,720	1,307.40	10,311.80
3,401	2,598.42	23,850.11	4,977	4,929	4,101	2,892.42	23,556.11
717	626.14	7,388.96	1,383	1,386	858	685.36	7,329.74
598	511.16	7,578.96	1,106	1,089	738	569.96	7,520.16
10,448	8,548.16	91,972.89	17,712	17,584	12,674	9,483.08	91,037.97

It will be observed in table 5.5 that although all farms have to pump water, none of them uses all of the available surface water. This results from the timing of ditch water deliveries. If water is available when the farmer does not need it, due to the combination of crops he has planted, he will let it pass and turn on his pumps at the proper time. Nonetheless the farms together use 91 percent of the available surface water under average conditions, 98 percent when the supply is 20 percent below average, and 99.4 percent when it falls to 30 percent below average.[13]

LAND SETTLEMENT AND WATER DELIVERY TO FARMS NEAR HANFORD, 1870–1968

Farmers Acquire Land

The land developer played much less of a role in Mussel slough country, where farmers claimed the land and cooperatively built the ditches to bring water to it. The first settlers, who were frequently Anglo-Americans in search of homesteads, many of them from the South, came in the early 1870s. Much of the land was owned by the federal government, and the homesteaders were able to acquire it with land scrip purchased on the open market for as little as 45 cents per acre. The cost of scrip rose, of course, as the prospects for successful farming were proved.

The government had reserved a significant part of the land in this area for the Southern Pacific Railroad for a line that was built subsequently from Goshen to Huron, serving Hanford, Armona, and Lemoore. The grant was for every alternate section of land, designated by odd numbered sections, for a distance of 20 mi on each side of the proposed route (or twenty sections—12,800 acres—per mi of road). Early settlers moved on to this land while it was reserved for the railroad but before the road had met the conditions to obtain clear title to it. Later when the land was patented to the railroad, the company offered to sell it to these settlers at a price that reflected the increase in land value due to proximity of the railroad and to the fact that it had by then been irrigated. Since irrigation had been accomplished by the farmers' labor and money with no assist from the railroad, the settlers for the most part refused to pay the quoted prices, whereupon the railroad attempted to sell the land to outsiders and to eject the original occupants. Violence erupted in 1880 in an event known locally as the Mussel slough tragedy. The bitterness engendered, which smouldered for a generation, has been known to many Americans through Frank Norris's novel *The Octopus*. Homesteads established on federal and railroad lands were typically 160 acres, a quarter section.

Some land in Mussel slough country that bordered on the Kings River and on Tulare Lake had been granted to California under the Federal Swampland Act. The state sold this to farmers in large blocs, since portions of the land were under water in wet years, at least until it was reclaimed. By this means John Heinlen, for example, acquired a ranch of about 4400 acres on Kings River near Lemoore.

Farmers Bring Water to the Land

The farmers brought water to the land, laying out and building the canals themselves. For this purpose they incorporated mutual canal companies in which they took shares of stock. These shares were then assessed for the cost of building the canals and subsequently for operating and maintaining them, and a farmer's right to divert and use water from a canal was in proportion to the number of shares he acquired. The share of stock in a mutual irrigation company was therefore distinctive in that it represented not only a proportional part of the ownership of the company, which in the early days had little, if any, value but also a right to receive water and, most important, an obligation to pay a proportion of the costs of building the canal and operating it. Whereas commercial developers and irrigation districts frequently raised capital by borrowing it from lending institutions or from the sale of bonds, mutual companies relied on the water users themselves.

Many of the original settlers paid their assessments not with cash, of which they had little, but with their labor. In some cases the work was divided in sectors and each stockholder was assigned a sector to dig. In others the estimated cost of the work was assessed and stockholders could work off their levies at fixed dollar rates per day. The following description is for a mutual company that was adjacent to the three companies with which we are concerned, but it serves as a good statement of their problems, too.

There was little or no hiring done, as there was no money to pay hired men or horses. Every man did his own part as best he could. The first three miles of excavation were considered of more difficult type of construction than the part further from the river, and it was decided to construct this part as a company project on force account. That is all worked together and received credit for work done according to time worked. Below this first three miles of canal from the head down, the engineer divided the excavation work into sections of equal cubic yardage and these sections were numbered. Duplicate numbers were mixed up in a hat and the numbers were drawn out by the stockholders. The number drawn was the section or "chunk" as they called them, that each respective stockholder had to build. There were as many "chunks" as there were shares of stock. This first drawing was for the main canal from the end of the company work at the lower end of the first three miles to the dividing of the first branch from the main canal, just above Tarn. Then each branch was divided into "chunks" and was built by the men who ran water through that branch. Nearly all men had a "chunk" on the main canal and a "chunk" on the branch canal that passed nearest his farm. . . .

The engineer had staked the ditch width on the ground and had set slope stakes marking his idea of where the outside top of the levee should reach according to the amount of excavation that was necessary. On the center line of the canal he set a stake marked with the amount of cut or fill that was necessary. Before beginning work on his "chunk" each man dug a hole as deep as the cut required and drove a stake in the bottom of the hole with its top as far below the surface as the cut required at that point. He then plowed and scraped out each plowing until he plowed out the grade stake. The canal was then considered finished at that point. . . . All of the work of excavation was done with the small slip or railroad scraper, pulled by two horses. . . .

None had much money and some had none and no credit. When a man was without money and no credit for food or horse feed, he left his work and drove his team and wagon to Visalia, Hanford, Modesto or to some place where he thought he might get employment. He offered to work for anything that he or his team could eat. Hay, wheat, corn, flour, dried beans, dried beef, homemade bacon, potatoes, were all legal tender in his case, and were accepted as wages. He worked as long as he could get employment or needed the supplies and then returned to his "chunk" and finished it. . . . [If any farmer did more work than his chunk the] surplus was paid for by due-bills in this form:

Kingsburg, California, Mar. 15, 1878

$3.50

Due John Smith for one days work with man, team and scraper   Three and 50/100 Dollars.

Centerville and Kingsburg Irrigation Ditch Co.

By James C. Berry, Superintendent.

These due bills [would be used to pay] future assessments on the capital stock. . . . To some extent they circulated as money. They were evidence of value.

Storekeepers at Kingsburg, finding that they were gradually paid off, accepted them in payment for groceries.[14]

Even where the stockholders contributed a large part of the labor of building the canals, they also were assessed periodically for money. The mutual companies needed cash—to pay an engineer or superintendent of works, for example, or to purchase lumber for control structures—and they assessed their stock to raise it.

Many farmers fell behind in their payments, especially where the costs of the canals exceeded original estimates, which was frequently the case. As assessments were a lien on the stock on which they were levied, these farmers had to forfeit their stock, which was then sold at public auction to cover the delinquent assessments. If buyers could not be found, and this was typically the case in the early years, the shares were forfeited to the company. Thus by 1881, eight years after it was incorporated, more than one-third of the stock issued by the Peoples Ditch Company had been forfeited for overdue assessments; and most of it had returned to the comapny, since no one whose lands were covered by the company's canals had money to buy the stock.

California law at the time limited mutual companies in any single assessment to 10 percent of the par value of the stock. As expenses rose beyond initial expectations, the companies had to increase par values in order to be able to assess the shares for the cash that they needed. When the Peoples Ditch Company was incorporated in 1873 it issued one hundred shares of stock at a par value of $100 per share for a capitalization of $10,000. In 1875 the par value was increased to $350 and the capitalization to $35,000. Later the stock was revalued at $1000 and the capitalization rose to $100,000.

The Peoples and the Last Chance ditch companies issued stock on the basis of one share for every section of land (640 acres) that was to be served by the canal, but the shares were distributed in fractions so that a farmer could buy as little as one-six hundred and fortieth of a share to cover 1 acre, although a share would typically be divided among four or more farmers. Thus the forty-five shares of the Last Chance Water Ditch Company were in the hands of approximately 325 stockholders.

The Lower Kings River Canal Company, when it was organized in 1873, issued stock on the basis of one share for every half-section of land (320 acres). One hundred shares were authorized at a par value of $300 for a capitalization of $30,000. Many of the shares were not taken up or were subsequently forfeited, so that fifty-three shares only were outstanding when in 1902 the company was reorganized as the Lemoore Canal and Irrigation Company. Each of the fifty-three shares was then made to apply to 640 acres instead of 320, and the par value of a share was increased from $300 to $2000, providing a capitalization of over $100,000.

Some mutual companies, in order to pay for canal operation and maintenance, charged their shareholders tolls for the actual delivery of water in addition to assessments on the stock. Thus a farmer who used more of the water to which he was entitled paid a greater proportion of canal expenses than one who used less. The three companies in Mussel slough country experimented with tolls briefly before the turn of the century but abandoned them. The Lemoore company, however, supplemented its income by selling "surplus water" to its shareholders. Stockholders were entitled to proportional amounts of the water available but to no more than 1 acre-foot of water for each acre of land represented by stock, or to 640 acre-feet for a full share. With fifty-three shares outstanding this amounted to approximately 34,000 acre-feet. Water in excess of this amount was sold by the acre-foot to shareholders for the irrigation season or for shorter periods of time.

The canal companies did not build or maintain most of the laterals, and on many of these the farmers organized subsidiary mutual companies for which shares were distributed and assessed for both labor and money in a manner similar to that used by the mutual canal companies. Some of these lateral companies took ownership of canal company stock for as much water as was needed to serve their lateral stockholders. They paid the canal companies' periodic assessments on this stock and then added these charges to their operating costs, which were assessed on their own stockholders.

The Jacobs Ranch, 11,000 acres of land along one lateral of the Lemoore system, was held by a large land company that had acquired eight shares of canal company stock to serve it. This company in 1908 sold the land to farmers and organized a mutual water company to operate the lateral and hold the canal company stock. Each farmer received one share of stock in the lateral company for each acre of land he bought. This was his water right and he paid annual assessments on this stock to the lateral company.

By 1918 the service area of the Peoples Ditch Company had 60 mi of main canals, of which the company operated and maintained 33 mi, and 40 mi of main laterals, all maintained by farmers, as well as many miles of small private laterals. The equivalent data for the Last Chance Water Ditch Company were 30, 18, and 60 mi. The Lemoore Canal and Irrigation Company area had about 75 mi of canals and main laterals. Table 5.6 gives data on the stock issues of the three canal companies and the principal lateral companies.

Although each share of stock represented one section or a half-section of land in the mutual company's service area, the stock was not tied to any particular land. It "floated," it was not "located," to use the local expressions; and it could be sold by an owner to any willing buyer. This system had the advantage of flexibility, allowing the water right to be transferred within the company's service area from less to more productive land; but it raised two potential problems that have been of concern to irrigators everywhere: definition or containment of the service area and monopolistic or speculative control over the water resource.

The mutual companies' service areas were not defined by the appurtenance of stock to land or by the companies' articles of incorporation and bylaws, although this could have been done. The only effective limitation was that the land had to be near the canals or it could not be served. But with expanding

Table 5.6 Stock issues of mutual companies near Hanford.

(1) Name of Company	(2) Year Organized	(3) No. of Shares Issued		(4) Par value of shares (in dollars)		(5) Capitalization (in thousands of dollars)	
		Initial	Subsequent	Initial	Subsequent	Initial	Subsequent
People's Ditch	1873	100	—	100.00	350;1,000	10	35;100
Principal lateral companies							
Lucerne Side	1892	—	—	12.50	—	—	—
Melga	1913	—	—	1.00	—	—	—
New Deal	1885	—	—	100.00	—	—	—
Burke	1914	—	—	1.00	—	—	—
Riverside	1894	—	—	100.00	—	—	—
Settlers	1888	—	—	1,000.00	—	—	—
Union	1888	—	—	40.00	—	—	—
Last Chance Water Ditch	1873	30	60	1,000.00	—	30	60
Principal lateral companies							
Blowers Side Ditch	1911	—	—	—	—	—	—
First Side	—	—	—	10.00	—	—	—
Hitchcock	1921	—	—	—	—	—	—
Independent	1883	—	—	500.00	—	—	—
Last Chance Side	1880	—	—	100.00	—	—	—
York Drop	—	—	—	100.00	—	—	—
Lower Kings River Canal becomes Lemoore Canal & Irrigation Company	1873; 1902	100	53	300.00	2,000.00	30	106
Principal lateral companies							
Jacob Rancho	1908	—	—	3.00	—	—	—
Empire Water[a]	1905	—	—	—	—	—	—

Sources: (See note 1, chapter 5 for full citations.) Columns (1), (2), (6), (7): Calif. Dept. of Public Works, Bulletin No. 34 (1930), Table 47. Columns (3), (4), (5), (8): U.S. Geological Survey, Water Supply & Irrigation Papers No. 18 (1898); Calif. Dept. of Engineering, Bulletin No. 7 (1918). Column (9): Calif. Dept. of Public Works, Bulletin No. 36 (1930), Table 37. Column (10): Calif. Dept. of Public Works, Bulletin No. 34 (1930), Table 48.

[a] A contract water company, delivering water for $1 per acre.
[b] Does not include assessments of independent lateral companies.
[c] Includes assessment of mother ditch or canal company.

(6) Approx. No. of Acres per Share	(7) No. of Shares Outstanding Circa 1920	(8) No. of Stock- holders Circa 1920	(9) Approximate Market Value Circa 1920 (in dollars)		(10) Assessments 1923 (in dollars)[c]	
			Per Share	Per Acre	Per Share	Per Acre
640	63.27	(?)	4,400	6.88	480[b]	.75[b]
10	99.67	—	—	—	—	1.47
1	7,997.55	—	—	—	—	1.58
80	77	—	—	—	—	.87
1	1,158	—	—	—	—	1.14
80	71	—	—	—	—	1.37
320	34	—	—	—	—	1.00
10	65	—	—	—	—	.95
640	45	325	1,800	2.81	602[b]	.94[b]
1	—	—	—	—	—	1.24
5	466	—	—	—	—	1.14
1	1,130	—	—	—	—	1.44
320	10.62	—	—	—	—	1.06
160	10	—	—	—	—	1.08
160	16	—	—	—	—	1.13
320; 640	53	305	4,800	7.50	400[b]	.63[b]
1	11,013.50	—	—	—	—	.60
—	—	—	—	—	—	1.00[a]

agricultural development the owners of land adjacent to the original service areas, who could farm if they wished by pumping groundwater, acquired stock, extended laterals to their land, and demanded the delivery of company water. The number of acres entitled to service from a company remained constant, but their location, as a result of this process, became less compact and the distribution system as a whole became less efficient. The costs of this reduced efficiency fell on all stockholders, not simply the new ones whose extra expenses were principally for purchase of the stock and for extending the laterals where this was necessary.

The second potential problem did not develop in Mussel slough country. While it is true that floating stock, unlike stock that is attached to land, can be acquired by speculators who do not own land in the service area or who do not intend ever to use water on their land, such speculation did not occur. There were men who owned several shares of stock, to be sure, but it was they who owned the larger farms, so that any problems that arose between large and small operators were the result of the ownership of land, not of water, the large owners being those who had acquired their farms from the state as swamplands.

Mutual company stock floated not only in the long run (that is, shares could be sold apart from land) but also in the short run. Stockholders could ask for delivery of their water at any point on the distribution system, and they could "rent" their water to others for the season. Such renting was widespread because of the method of irrigation used in this area, which involved saturation of the subsoil rather than spreading the water over the surface of the ground. From the time that water became available in January or February the canals and laterals were kept as full as the supply permitted, as were hollows and ponds and sloughs into which water could be run from the laterals. The water gradually saturated the subsurface strata, and irrigation was considered complete when the water table had risen to within 3 to 4 ft of the ground's surface, where it was within reach of plant life.

The water table in Mussel slough country fluctuated considerably from farm to farm as well as from month to month during the irrigation season and from season to season according to the character of the soil, the distance between canals and laterals, the water supply, the crops planted, and other local conditions. Thus when the water under their farms was near enough to the surface to subirrigate, farmers were likely to rent all or parts of their stock to others who were not so well situated at the moment. In most cases the stock was rented for very little more than the cost of annual assessments.

This method of irrigation was not consistent with rotation schedules, such as those used near Fresno, so that water was delivered on demand. A farmer was entitled to receive a pro rata share of the water currently running in a company's canals, the proportion determined by his control of stock at the moment, and to have it delivered on demand at any location. The company delivered water to the heads of the several laterals in proportion to the amount of stock to be served by each. As many laterals as possible were run simultaneously. When water was plentiful, users could take as much as they needed once they had begun to irrigate. The ditch tender did not measure the water and in some cases he did not inspect the land, leaving it to each farmer's honesty to irrigate no more than his stockholdings justified. As water became scarce, usually in July when demands peaked, the company imposed time limits in order to "hurry things along." For the Lemoore company the limit was usually twenty-four hours for 40 acres.

The unlimited right of shareholders to transfer water from one location to any other at any time in the season caused problems in operating the distribution systems, and for this reason the Lemoore company imposed limits on the right. No stock could be rented after April 1, and all rentals had to run to December 31 of the same year. Those renting stock had to notify the secretary of the company and specify the land to which the water was to be delivered for the irrigation season. The Last Chance company's regulations imposed a deadline of May 1, but this limit was not enforced. There was no effective limit for the Peoples Ditch, where stock could be rented at any time during the season and without previous notice to the company.

Indiscriminate transfers and rentals kept the superintendents of these companies in "hot water" all season, according to an observer of the U.S. Department of Agriculture.[15] They could never be sure that they had cleaned up the irrigation in a section or on a lateral because it was possible for a farmer to call at any time for water to irrigate land formerly not scheduled to receive it, by virtue of his having been able to rent, practically overnight, enough stock to cover it. The Lemoore company's limits on renting were cited favorably by our observer. However it should be pointed out that the Lemoore company had its own source of uncertainty or of flexibility, depending on how one views it; for "surplus" water could be bought by shareholders during the irrigation season. It may be for this reason that Lemoore was stricter than the other companies on water renting.

Farmers in Mussel slough country had considerable livestock, particularly in the service area of the Peoples Ditch Company, whose operating procedures gave preference to stock over crops. To provide stock water, a small stream was run in each lateral all season. As it required somewhat more than 100 cfs to reach the far ends of all laterals, no water was available for crop irrigation when water in the main canal was less than this amount. The agricultural agent complained that this procedure was "prolific of much waste of water," which no doubt it was in a physical sense.[16] Breaking the water up into so many small heads caused large seepage losses in the ditches, although these were no doubt recovered in good part from the groundwater. The water in the main canals and laterals, instead of being allowed to flow freely, was in many cases checked up 1 and 2 ft all season. The resulting sluggishness of the water allowed aquatic vegetation to choke the ditches, adding to the costs of cleaning them. But one cannot condemn this practice without also comparing the return from using water for livestock to the return from using it on crops and placing some value on the farmers' preference for stock to crop farming, neither of which was done by the agricultural agent.

The shareholders of the Last Chance Water Ditch Company, on the other hand, gave preference to crops over stock. They delivered stock water when it could be done without checking up the main canal, but in times of scarcity stock water was not delivered at all.

The shareholders held annual meetings at which they elected boards of directors for one-year terms and considered any proposed amendments to the companies' articles of incorporation and bylaws and any proposed changes in the capital stock, all of which required their approval. They also heard reports from company officers and discussed company problems and policies, such as the preference that should be given to livestock water. Frequently these meetings were sparsely attended and a quorum was achieved only by the use of proxies. When the farmers were excited about their water supply or when they expected an important contest for the position of director, they could and did come, however; so that poor attendance was taken as an indication of satisfaction with current conditions.

Stockholders did not normally vote on the annual assessments, for this was left to the boards of directors. Each board chose from among its members a president, who was vested with general supervision of the company's affairs. The president of the Lemoore company served also as superintendent, supervising two ditch tenders and a gate tender who maintained the diversion dam and headgate. The board of directors of the Peoples company hired a superintendent as well as three ditch tenders who, along with five ditch tenders employed by subsidiary lateral companies, operated the canal system. These employees were local men.

As "cooperative," "democratic" institutions that delivered water at cost to their stockholders only, mutual water companies were exempted from state regulation. A year after the California Railroad Commission assumed jurisdiction over commercial irrigation companies, the legislature passed the Mutual Water Companies Act to make it abundantly clear that the commission would have no jurisdiction over mutual companies unless the companies delivered water for compensation to others than its stockholders.

The Country Develops

With water available, Mussel slough country developed. In 1876–77 the Southern Pacific Railroad built a feeder line from Goshen (southeast of Fresno on the main line that connected the San Francisco Bay area and Bakersfield) west to Huron, traversing Mussel slough country. We have noted that the federal government had reserved land grants for this route many years before, but the company began construction only after the watering of the land by farmers gave promise of increased land values and of rail traffic.

In 1877 the railroad laid out the towns of Hanford and Lemoore 8.5 mi apart and sold town lots, initially at auction. By 1880 the state census showed a population of 1744 for Lemoore township with approximately 500 in the town itself, and Hanford was somewhat larger.

By 1879, 37,000 acres were irrigated in Mussel slough country, including 13,000 each from the Peoples and Last Chance canals, 6000 from the Lower Kings River canal, and 5000 from two small ditch companies. The early crops were wheat; cereal grains, principally barley and corn; and pasture for livestock. As the area developed wheat gave way to these other crops and to tree crops and the newly introduced raisin grape. By 1880 two large wheat warehouses in Hanford had closed. The soil and the water system were particularly adapted to growing alfalfa, and it was so widely planted that the area came to be known as Lucerne valley. The market for hay soon was oversupplied and the farmers took to raising more livestock, thus consuming the surplus product at home. It was claimed that no finer horses or cattle were to be seen than those in the pastures of Lucerne valley.

About 1880 interest grew rapidly in raisins and fruits, especially in the area north of a line drawn between Hanford and Lemoore. This attracted new settlers, many of them from the eastern states. Their farms were typically larger than those in the Fresno area; a good number of them were of 160 acres and some were larger.

Operating Procedures Today

The operating procedures of the mutual irrigation companies today continue to be based on the early procedures, although there are some important differences. To illustrate today's operations, we shall focus on the Lemoore company. There are fifty-three shares of stock, each representing water for 640 acres of land, or in the local terminology each one the equivalent of 640 stock acres, so that the fifty-three shares represent 33,920 stock acres. The area that can be served by the company's canals includes 55,000 irrigable acres; and since the stock floats, the approximately 34,000 acres entitled to water in any season can be located on any of these 55,000 acres.

The 53 shares of stock are owned by approximately five hundred stockholders. Almost all of them own land in the area, but their holdings of stock are not necessarily in proportion to their holdings of land. Except for the Stratford Irrigation District, which owns 8 5/8 shares on behalf of its members, few stockholders own as much as 1 share.

Normally each stock acre is given a basic allotment of 1 acre-foot of water. The company's board of directors can increase or decrease this amount based on the projected water supply, but they must act before the irrigation season begins. In recent times the board has not decreased the allotment, although it has increased it on occasion in flood years.

At the beginning of the irrigation season each shareholder is given a "bank account" of water, normally 1 acre-foot for each stock acre that he controls at the time. He can withdraw from this account, that is, call for the delivery of water, at any time he chooses.

In addition the company announces at the beginning of the season, based on its forecast of water supply, how much surplus water (that is, water in excess of 33,920 acre-feet) is available for purchase and at what price. Farmers can then purchase this water, add it to their bank accounts, and withdraw it as they wish. If water is abundant, the company will place no limits on the amount of surplus water, or "B water," as it is called, that a farmer can buy. If the company estimates that the demand will be greater than the supply, it will ration the B water among shareholders. Typically it will allow shareholders to purchase and deposit in the bank at the beginning of the season .50 acre-foot of B water for every stock acre that they control. If surplus water in this amount is not estimated to be available at the beginning of the season but does show up later, the board will declare the ration at the later date. As the season progresses additional allocations in this amount will be declared if the water becomes available.

Farmers pay cash in advance for B water. In 1968-69 the price was $6 per acre-foot. The annual assessment on stock shares covers the cost of the stock water, or "A water," as it is called. The assessment rate in 1968-69 was $3000 per share or $4.69 per stock acre (and per acre-foot), payable in six installments.

The farmer must plan. He knows from the board of directors when the season will begin—usually the third week in February, although it was late April in the flood year 1968-69—and approximately when it will end—usually in early October. He estimates his water requirements for the season. He knows before the season begins how much A water he will receive and how much, based on the current market, it will cost him to rent additional stock. He knows how much B water, if any, is likely to be available and at what price. He estimates how deep the water table will be at different times in the season and the costs of pumping water if he decides to use this source. He will plan to use his A water unless his pumping costs are less than the price at which he can rent it out to others. Assuming that he uses his A water and needs more, he will either rent stock, purchase B water, or plan to pump, depending on relative costs and on whether B water will be rationed.

Periodically during the season farmers receive statements from the company that show how much water they have consumed and how much remains in the bank. The data on use are taken from ditch tenders' reports, which, because of the banking methods used, need to be more precise in their measurements than is the case in the irrigation districts near Fresno. Figure 5.3 shows the entries that the ditch tender records for a single delivery.

To simulate the mutual company procedures we have used two situations with regard to the ownership or control of surface water, both of which are present in the service area, and have run each of these with three water supply conditions: average surface water supply, 20 percent below average, and 30 percent less than the average supply. As in the Fresno case, farmers do not suffer crop losses when the surface water supply is scarce. To avoid losses they turn on their pumps and mine the groundwater. Thus crop production, crop values, and costs of production excluding the cost of water remain constant for the several assumptions that we make regarding the availability and the control over surface water. The basic data on farm size, crop patterns, yields, costs, and returns are found in the tables of the appendix to this chapter.

Each farmer may have as many as four sources of water at different prices, as follows:

Water Class	Description	Price per Acre-Foot
A	Basic allotment of 1 acre-foot/stock acre	$4.69 (derived from assessment of $3000/share)
A rental	A water rented by one shareholder to another	$7.20
B	Surplus water sold by mutual company	$6.00
P	Pumped water[a]	
	(1) Farms 1–5 are in the northern part of the service area, which overlies a shallow aquifer	$4.92
	(2) Farms 6–10 are in the southern sector, which overlies a deep aquifer	$15.00

[a] Aquifers are sufficiently large that pumping costs do not vary significantly during a single season.

Under the first situation, which we call the basic distribution, the owners of farms 1-5 have only enough shares of stock to supply .50 acre-foot of A water per acre. They do not purchase B water but use their pumps for water needed to supplement their limited A water, at a cost of $4.92 per acre-foot. The owners of farms 6-10 control enough stock to receive 1.28 acre-feet of A water per acre. They buy all the available B water at $6 per acre-foot. This B water varies in quantity with the surface water supply, and whatever is available is rationed to the lower farms, an equal amount for each acre. Farms 6-10 pump groundwater to meet their remaining needs at a cost of $15 per acre-foot. Water use, water costs, and farm net returns that result from these assumptions are reported in tables 5.7 to 5.9.

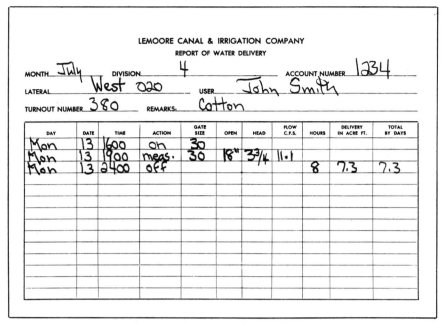

Figure 5.3   Lemoore Canal & Irrigation Company report of water delivery.

Table 5.7 Water use (in acre-inches) and water costs and net farm return (in dollars), basic distribution, with average surface water supply, mutual irrigation company near Hanford, California, late 1960s.

Farm	Acres	Water Use A	B	Pump	Total
1	80	480		3,148	3,628
2	80	480		2,870	3,350
3	160	960		5,566	6,526
4	160	960		6,666	7,626
5	240	1,440		8,360	9,800
6	320	4,920	3,913	4,937	13,770
7	320	4,920	3,913	4,587	13,420
8	560	8,610	6,847	7,643	23,100
9	40	615	489	176	1,280
10	40	615	489	176	1,280
Total	2,000	24,000	15,651	44,129	83,780

Under the second situation, which we call rental distribution, all farms own enough stock to supply 1 acre-foot of A water per acre. Farms 1–5, however, rent half of their A water to farms 6–10 at $7.20 per acre-foot as follows:

Farm 1 rents 20 acre-feet each to farms 9 and 10

Farm 2 rents 40 acre-feet to farm 6

Farm 3 rents 80 acre-feet to farm 7

Farm 4 rents 80 acre-feet to farm 8

Farm 5 rents 120 acre-feet to farm 8

Farms 1–5 supplement the A water they have retained with pump water at $4.92 per acre-foot. Farms 6–10 buy all the available B water at $6 per acre-foot, and this is distributed among them according to their size. They fulfill their remaining water requirements by pumping at $15 per acre-foot. The results are in tables 5.10 to 5.12.

The average cost of water per irrigated acre for the region as a whole under the basic procedure increases 11.9 percent, from $25 to $27.97, as the surface water supply falls to 20 percent below average flow; and it increases a total of

| Water Cost | | | | Net Farm Income |
A	B	Pump	Total	
187.20		1,290.68	1,477.88	6,891.28
187.20		1,176.70	1,363.90	6,750.60
374.40		2,282.06	2,656.46	15,987.56
374.40		2,733.06	3,107.46	15,074.67
561.60		3,427.60	3,989.20	22,556.00
1,918.80	1,956.50	6,171.25	10,046.55	27,961.55
1,918.80	1,956.50	5,733.75	9,609.05	28,678.85
3,357.90	3,423.50	9,553.75	16,335.15	48,628.75
239.85	244.50	220.00	704.35	3,795.25
239.85	244.50	220.00	704.35	3,795.25
9,360.00	7,825.50	32,808.85	49,994.35	180,119.76

Table 5.8 Water use (in acre-inches) and water costs and net farm income (in dollars), basic distribution, with 20 percent below average surface water supply, mutual irrigation company near Hanford, California, late 1960s.

Farm	Acres	Water Use A	B	Pump	Total
1	80	480		3,148.0	3,628
2	80	480		2,870	3,350
3	160	960		5,566	6,526
4	160	960		6,666	7,626
5	240	1,440		8,360	9,800
6	320	4,920	1,929.6	6,920.4	13,770
7	320	4,920	1,929.6	6,570.4	13,420
8	560	8,610	3,376.8	11,113.2	23,100
9	40	615	241.2	423.8	1,280
10	40	615	241.2	423.8	1,280
Total	2,000	24,000	7,718.4	52,061.6	83,780

Table 5.9 Water use (in acre-inches) and water costs and net farm income (in dollars), basic distribution, with 30 percent below average surface water supply, mutual irrigation company near Hanford, California, late 1960s.

Farm	Acres	Water Use A	B	Pump	Total
1	80	480		3,148	3,628
2	80	480		2,870	3,350
3	160	960		5,560	6,520
4	160	960		6,666	7,626
5	240	1,440		8,360	9,800
6	320	4,920	939	7,911	13,770
7	320	4,920	939	7,561	13,420
8	560	8,610	1,642	12,848	23,100
9	40	615	118	547	1,280
10	40	615	118	547	1,280
Total	2,000	24,000	3,756	56,018	83,774

| Water Cost | | | | Net Farm |
A	B	Pump	Total	Income
187.20		1,290.68	1,477.88	6,891.36
187.20		1,176.70	1,363.90	6,750.60
374.40		2,282.06	2,656.46	15,987.56
374.40		2,733.06	3,107.46	15,074.66
561.60		3,427.60	3,989.20	22,556.00
1,918.80	964.80	8,650.50	11,534.10	26,474.00
1,918.80	964.80	8,213.00	11,096.60	27,191.80
3,357.90	1,688.40	13,891.50	18,937.80	46,026.10
239.85	120.60	529.75	890.20	3,609.40
239.85	120.60	529.75	890.20	3,609.40
9,360.00	3,859.20	42,724.60	55,943.80	174,170.88

| Water Cost | | | | Net Farm |
A	B	Pump	Total	Income
187.20		1,290.68	1,477.88	6,891.28
187.20		1,176.70	1,363.90	6,750.60
374.40		2,282.06	2,656.46	15,987.56
374.40		2,733.06	3,107.46	15,074.66
561.60		3,427.60	3,989.20	22,556.00
1,918.80	469.50	9,888.75	12,277.05	25,731.05
1,918.80	469.50	9,451.25	11,839.55	26,448.85
3,357.90	821.00	16,060.00	20,238,90	44,725.00
239.85	59.00	683.75	982.60	3,517.00
239.85	59.00	683.75	982.60	3,517.00
9,360.00	1,878.00	47,677.60	58,915.60	171,199.00

Table 5.10 Water use (in acre-inches) and water costs and net farm income (in dollars), rental distribution, with average surface water supply, mutual irrigation company near Hanford, California, late 1960s.

| Farm | Acres | Water Use | | | | |
		Own A	Use A	B	Pump	Total
1	80	960	480		3,148	3,628
2	80	960	480		2,870	3,350
3	160	1,920	960		5,566	6,526
4	160	1,920	960		6,666	7,626
5	240	2,880	1,440		8,360	9,800
6	320	3,840	4,320	3,913	5,537	13,770
7	320	3,840	4,800	3,913	4,707	13,420
8	560	6,720	9,120	6,847	7,133	23,100
9	40	480	720	489	71	1,280
10	40	480	720	489	71	1,280
Total	2,000	24,000	24,000	15,651	44,129	83,780

Table 5.11 Water use (in acre-inches) and water costs and net farm income (in dollars), rental distribution, with 20 percent below average surface water supply, mutual irrigation company near Hanford, California, late 1960s.

| Farm | Acres | Water Use | | | | |
		Own A	Use A	B	Pump	Total
1	80	960	480		3,148	3,628
2	80	960	480		2,870	3,350
3	160	1,920	960		5,566	6,526
4	160	1,920	960		6,666	7,626
5	240	2,880	1,440		8,360	9,800
6	320	3,840	4,320	1,929.6	7,520.4	13,770
7	320	3,840	4,800	1,929.6	6,690.4	13,420
8	560	6,720	9,120	3,376.8	10,603.2	23,100
9	40	480	720	241.2	318.8	1,280
10	40	480	720	241.2	318.8	1,280
Total	2,000	24,000	24,000	7,718.4	52,061.6	83,780

Water Cost					Net Farm
A	A rental	B	Pump	Total	Income
374.40	− 288		1,290.68	1,377.08	6,992.08
374.40	− 288		1,176.70	1,263.10	6,851.40
748.80	− 576		2,282.06	2,454.86	16,189.16
748.80	− 576		2,733.06	2,905.86	15,276.26
1,123.20	− 864		3,424.60	3,683.80	22,861.40
1,497.60	+ 288	1,956.50	6,921.25	10,663.35	27,344.75
1,497.60	+ 576	1,956.50	5,883.75	9,913.85	28,374.55
2,620.80	+1,440	3,423.50	8,916.25	16,400.55	48,563.35
187.20	+ 144	244.50	88.75	664.45	3,835.15
187.20	+ 144	244.50	88.75	664.45	3,835.15
9,360.00	0	7,825.50	32,805.85	49,991.35	180,123.25

Water Cost					Net Farm
A	A rental	B	Pump	Total	Income
374.40	− 288		1,290.68	1,377.08	6,992.08
374.40	− 288		1,176.70	1,263.10	6,851.40
748.80	− 576		2,282.06	2,454.86	16,189.16
748.80	− 576		2,733.06	2,905.86	15,276.26
1,123.20	− 864		3,427.60	3,686.80	22,858.40
1,497.60	+ 288	964.80	9,400.50	12,150.90	25,857.20
1,497.60	+ 576	964.80	8,363.00	11,401.40	26,887.00
2,620.80	+1,440	1,688.40	13,254.00	19,003.20	45,960.70
187.20	+ 144	120.60	398.50	850.30	3,649.30
187.20	+ 144	120.60	398.50	850.30	3,649.30
9,360.00	0	3,859.20	42,724.60	55,943.80	174,170.80

Table 5.12 Water use (in acre-inches) and water costs and net farm income (in dollars), rental distribution, with 30 percent below average surface water supply, mutual irrigation company near Hanford, California, late 1960s.

Farm	Acres	Water Use Own A	Use A	B	Pump	Total
1	80	960	480		3,148	3,628
2	80	960	480		2,870	3,350
3	160	1,920	960		5,566	6,526
4	160	1,920	960		6,666	7,626
5	240	2,880	1,440		8,360	9,800
6	320	3,840	4,320	937.6	8,512.4	13,770
7	320	3,480	4,800	937.6	7,682.4	13,420
8	560	6,720	9,120	1,640.8	12,339.2	23,100
9	40	480	720	117.2	442.8	1,280
10	40	480	720	117.2	442.8	1,280
Total	2,000	24,000	24,000	3,750.4	56,029.6	83,780

17.8 percent, to $29.46 per acre, as the surface supply falls to 30 percent below the average. The cost of water increases from 27.8 percent of net farm income under average water conditions to 32.1 percent, and to 34.4 percent when surface water is 30 percent short of the norm. Under the rental procedure, data for the region as a whole are almost identical.

Comparing these figures to those for Fresno reveals that water costs more than twice as much per acre and in terms of net farm income is more than three times as costly. The large expense of deep pumping is the most important factor. At the same time, the percentage increase in water costs as surface water becomes more scarce is significantly less in Hanford than in Fresno.

Because farmers can withdraw water from their accounts whenever they need it and can turn on their pumps at will, the company has special problems in operating the system. The monthly variation in water demand is considerable, as seen in table 5.13. Completion of Pine Flat Dam and reservoir in the early 1950s has greatly helped the company meet these uneven demands. All of the Lemoore company's water right in the Kings River is stored in the reservoir and the company has considerable discretion in ordering its release. Based on the delivery demands of its shareholders and calculating thirty hours of travel time for the water from the dam to the Lemoore headgate, the company sends daily water orders to the dam's controllers.

| Water Cost | | | | | | Net Farm |
A	A rental	B	Pump	Total		Income
374.40	− 288		1,290.68	1,377.08		6,992.08
374.40	− 288		1,176.70	1,263.10		6,851.40
748.80	− 576		2,282.06	2,454.86		16,189.16
748.80	− 576		2,733.06	2,905.86		15,276.26
1,123.20	− 864		3,427.60	3,686.80		22,858.40
1,497.60	+ 288	468.75	10,640.50	12,894.85		25,113.30
1,497.60	+ 576	468.75	9,603.00	12,145.35		26,143.05
2,620.80	+1,440	820.40	15,424.00	20,305.20		44,658.70
187.20	+ 144	58.60	553.50	943.30		3,556.30
187.20	+ 144	58.60	553.50	943.30		3,556.30
9,360.00	0	1,875.10	47,684.60	58,919.70		171,194.95

Between 40 and 50 percent of the water diverted into the Lemoore system at its headgate is lost, principally to seepage through unlined canals and laterals during their long irrigation season. Although much of the lost water will be recovered by farmers who pump it from the ground, the company tries to reduce canal losses through its operating procedure, principally by trying to bunch its deliveries to users on each lateral so that it is not required to start up and close down the lateral many times, which is wasteful of water and of ditch tenders' time. Yet this is difficult to achieve in a system where bank accounts and demand withdrawals of water are the order of the day. The Lemoore ditch tenders have trouble getting their shareholders to take water on Sundays, for example. When asked by Maass what he does about this, a ditch tender responded without further explanation that he uses "subtle pressure."

The company's annual income, from which it pays its operating expenses, is derived from two sources: stockholders' assessments, which remain stable so long as the assessment rate is not changed, and income from the sale of B water, which varies from year to year even if the price remains constant. In the year 1967–68 the company received $159,000 from stock assessments (53 shares × $3000 or 33,920 stock acres × $4.69) and $135,000 from the sale of B water (22,400 acre-feet × $6). Its expenses, including assessments for the operation of Pine Flat Dam, were $181,000, leaving a surplus of $118,000.

Table 5.13 Lemoore Canal and Irrigation Company delivery of water to users (percent delivered each month in selected years).

Month	1968–69[a] 52,000 acre-feet delivered	1967–68 51,000 acre-feet delivered	1964–65 49,000 acre-feet delivered	1963–64 46,000 acre-feet delivered
Oct.	b	0	1	0
Nov.	b	0	b	0
Dec.	0	0	b	0
Jan.	0	5	b	2
Feb.	0	5	9	13
Mar.	0	9	16	10
Apr.	2	5	1	5
May.	8	4	6	2
June	15	13	14	13
July	28	16	17	18
Aug.	31	23	21	24
Sept.	15	19	14	12

Source: Records in office of Lemoore Canal and Irrigation Company, Lemoore, California.

[a] Flood year; some farmland under water.
[b] Less than 1 percent.

FRESNO AND HANFORD: COMPARISONS AND OBJECTIVES

Compared to the area near Hanford, the Fresno region is more intensively culti-vated by smaller farms that grow a greater variety of crops. Its towns and farm-ing communities are more thickly populated and more prosperous. An impor-tant reason is that physical conditions, especially those related to groundwater, are different. Whereas the water table is relatively uniform under the Fresno region, it varies greatly from shallow to very deep near Hanford, making it more difficult and more expensive to pump water for irrigation as well as to control the water table and to drain the lands.

In addition the different cultural conditions of early development have had an obvious impact, although this is difficult to measure precisely. The develop-ment of irrigation agriculture by land speculators, using the colony method of settlement, has been more successful in terms of agricultural production and of farmers' living conditions than development by homesteaders, who have formed cooperative organizations for the purpose. Once the farms are well established, however, continual operation of irrigation distribution systems has been more successful when performed by farmers' cooperatives, either irrigation districts or mutual companies, than by commercial enterprises. This latter conclusion results from three related factors. First, since the principal profit is in selling the developed land and not in operating the water distribution systems, the land developers have had little incentive to administer the canals once they have sold the land. Second, operating irrigation systems involves, as we have seen in each huerta we have examined, complex relations among neighbors that can lead to controversy and conflict. To control this conflict farmers need organizations in which they have confidence, and they are likely to have confidence in democratic organizations that they control. This is not to say that commercial companies can under no circumstances operate systems successfully, but the efforts required of them to do so are frequently considered to be not worth the costs. From the beginning in Fresno neither the developers nor the water companies sought to operate the laterals and they opposed all requests by others that they do so. Finally, the state government has provided irrigation districts (but not mutual companies) with authority to assess lands not on water service so that districts have a source of income for system operations not available to commercial companies.

Thus it appears from the California experience that popular control is more essential to operating a system than to developing it in the first instance, or perhaps that the advantages of private development under certain conditions are so substantial for farmers and prospective farmers that they overcome the disadvantages of the absence of popular control.

There remains the question of why private, speculative development has been more successful in the first place than development by farmers' cooperatives. This has resulted from a combination of certain beneficial effects of speculative development and certain untoward consequences of cooperative development.

When the capitalists and speculators first purchased land from the government near Fresno, there were no homesteaders who wanted it. The desert land was unbroken and there seemed to be no prospects for successful cultivation. However some of the land speculators, particularly Chapman, foresaw a possibility of profitable wheat farming, provided very large tracts of land could be assembled under single management and large farm machines were developed for the purpose. Chapman foresaw as a possible subsequent stage the breaking up of bonanza wheat farms into small intensively cultivated tracts, provided capital and labor were available for irrigation. The land speculator, with the support of capitalists in San Francisco and Liverpool, would purchase and assemble the land and subsequently finance the development of irrigation water supplies.

As it turned out, much of area near Fresno did not go through the initial stage of development in bonanza wheat farms; the first crops were irrigated. Land speculators purchased the land and developed it themselves or sold it to developers who acquired water rights in the Kings River and built diversion dams, canals, and a system of laterals and control structures to supply irrigation water to each tract of land. They subdivided the land into small farms, transferred water rights to the purchasers of these farms, and provided liberal credit to their customers. Installment payments were an important feature of the developers' colony system. Besides irrigation water they provided other farm facilities and services at a small additional charge or no charge at all—vine cuttings and nursery stock specially selected for Fresno's climate and soil, education and guidance in irrigation agriculture for colonists who knew little or nothing about it, in some cases planting and cultivating the first crop. The developers frequently provided community facilities for their colonies—roads, land for town sites, shade trees—and bore a substantial share of the local tax burden as their colonies developed. They promoted intensive settlement by advertising their colonies across the nation and in Europe. In all they established a pattern of agriculture and rural life that was much more agreeable to many farmers than was dry land cultivation, which was characterized by social isolation, with no more than four homesteads to the section.

Most of these farm and community facilities and services were not to be had from other institutions. Today's government programs for irrigation, farm credit, extension education, and rural community facilities did not exist and government-sponsored agricultural research was just beginning in California. The federal government was not prepared to provide the means for reclaiming its arid lands (the Reclamation Act was not passed until 1902), and it was a third of a century later before California was prepared to devote any state funds to irrigation.

Furthermore, the fact that these facilities and services were available in combination from a single vendor and at reasonable prices contributed much to the success of the colony movement. The developer's motive was profits, to be sure, but his services were good and his prices were not exorbitant.[17]

At the same time, there should be no question about the nature of the speculation. It was robust, recurrent, cannibalistic. Chapman and Friedlander at one time made a fortune from their landholdings in the Fresno region. So did Church and certain other developers of the early colonies. And after them Perrin and his Scottish friend, Captain Cheape, and subsequently L. A. Nares, the Englishman, and his associate, Charles Laton of San Francisco. An example involving Friedlader, Chapman, and Church will illustrate.

The Bank of California closed its doors on August 26, 1875, for want of cash, causing panic in the streets of San Francisco. The bank had provided liberal "accommodation" to a number of the big speculators with a resulting drain on its reserves that was one cause for the failure. Among those heavily in debt to the bank were Friedlander and Chapman, who had borrowed, without security, $500,000 and $214,000 respectively for various of their speculative ventures. After it closed, the bank demanded security for these loans. Friedlander turned over $100,000 in notes of the Dresbach company, which were backed by crop mortgages on wheat and more than 100,000 acres of land in several California counties. Other borrowers secured their loans in similar fashion, the bank's stockholders put up a guarantee fund, and the California bank opened its doors again within six weeks "amid the din of cannon and the shouts of the multitude." [18] But Friedlander and Chapman found new accommodation at the Bank of Nevada in San Francisco, which loaned them large sums, again without the need for putting up security.

In April 1877, Friedlander "suspended business"—he went broke and had to settle with both banks as well as other creditors. He worked out the following arrangement with the Bank of California: the bank took possession of all the properties he had deposited in 1875 to secure loans except the Dresbach notes, which were returned to Friedlander, who used them to pay some of his debts to the Nevada bank. To compensate the California bank for these notes Friedlander obtained through Chapman and deeded to the bank water rights of the Fresno canal company to irrigate approximately 14,000 acres west of the Central California Colony that were owned by the bank, and he agreed to pay the bank $10,000 in cash and an additional $10,000 in twelve months. Friedlander claimed that the Fresno water rights were worth $10 an acre. As a result of these arrangements Friedlander's obligations to the bank were fully discharged but Chapman's remained in force.

Friedlander deeded the Nevada bank a large number of properties for which the bank cancelled his indebtedness and paid him $30,000, $20,000 of which was to pay his cash obligation to the California bank. The properties included land in San Mateo, Mendocino, and Solano counties; the Dresbach notes, or more properly the crop mortgages in Colusa, Butte, and Tehama counties that supported the notes; margins on 22,500 tons of export wheat that was loaded on board fourteen ships; 10,000 head of meat on Grisley Island in Solano County to be deeded by Chapman; and 4240 shares of the Fresno Canal and Irrigation Company, 3000 owned by Chapman and 1240 by Friedlander.

We do not know how Friedlander settled with Chapman for the water rights, canal stock, livestock, and other properties he used to settle his own debts, but there were abundant opportunities, since they owned jointly a great many speculative investments. Friedlander's creditors, apart from the banks, received $.25 on the dollar.

Returning to the Fresno canal company water rights that Friedlander acquired to irrigate the California bank's lands, Chapman was at the time, April 1877, in full control of the canal company, Church having sold out to him. He signed an indenture with the company, granting himself two hundred water rights (200 cfs) to irrigate 32,000 acres of land he would designate and to which canals were to be built by the company. This deal involved more water rights than had been sold or granted by the company altogether prior to that time.

Chapman was to pay $50,000, or $250 per right. Of this, $45,000 was to liquidate an "obligation" of the canal to him (the nature of this obligation has never been revealed, so far as we can determine), the $5,000 remaining to be paid within one year after the last of the 200 rights had been delivered to its designated land. Also, Chapman was to pay annually for each right, from the date that it was delivered to the land, $50 (31.24 cents per acre) for operation and maintenance, half the fee charged to most developers. On the day after this indenture was signed, Chapman, the Bank of California, and the Fresno canal company entered into an agreement assigning to the bank 85.5 of the water rights, to irrigate 13,680 specified acres owned by the bank. The bank was to pay the operation and maintenance charges on these rights. Chapman therefore retained 114.5 of the 200 rights and the obligation to pay ultimately the $5,000 on the original purchase. When the Bank of Nevada acquired the Fresno canal stock less than a month later, they acquired it subject to the Chapman indentures, but there is no evidence that either Freidlander or Chapman informed the bank about them.

Church regained the canal company from the Nevada bank within five months, it will be recalled, and immediately thereafter the Bank of California gave notice to the company that they wanted canals and laterals built to deliver their water to their land. Church refused, declaring the Chapman contracts to be null and void. "Agreement was made," he said, "and executed by a majority of the company's board of directors in fraud of its rights and in pursuance of a conspiracy and fraudulent agreement to defraud said company." The California bank sued for an injunction to stop Church and the canal company from selling water rights to others so long as the bank's rights were unfulfilled, but they lost in court because they could not prove damage—the canal company had not yet sold the one thousand rights that corresponded to its full water supply. The courts did not reach a decision on whether or not the contracts were fraudulent.[19] Finally in 1883 Church acquired eleven sections of the bank lands, for what price we do not know, irrigated the tract, developed it as the West Park Colony, and made himself a good profit out of it.

The colonists did not necessarily pay the high costs of this gambling. In general, speculators like Friedlander, Chapman, and Perrin made fortunes and lost them several times over. On his death in 1878 the estate of Isaac Friedlander, the Wheat King, was appraised at $350,000. The losers in the Fresno operations appear to have been principally the San Francisco banks and the English insurance companies. There is no direct evidence of the value the Nevada bank placed on the Fresno canal when they took it from Friedlander and Chapman in 1877, but it was in all likelihood considerably higher than the price they got from Church when they gave it up five months later. The California bank didn't do very well with the water rights that Friedlander and Chapman deeded to them. A large percentage of the British investment in the Fresno canal—approximately fifty cents on the dollar—was written off in a 1917 financial reorganization.[20]

The only alternative to using the institutions of land speculation and corporate capital to develop agriculture in the region was to rely on mutual efforts by farm homesteaders. As for building a water supply, the likelihood of success by this means seemed to fall rapidly with distance of the land from the stream bed and delta of the Kings River. As for other factors, we can refer to the experience of the mutual companies in the Mussel slough area. They came to be more concerned with the immediate, short-term interests of their shareholders than with any longer term development of the region. The report quoted previously to describe the farmer-shareholders' grueling work of building a mutual company canal is informative in this regard. Citing the same company a few years after water had been brought to the land the report states, "There was a woeful lack of public spirit or any appreciation of public responsibility for handling the canal system to help the farming population generally. . . . The stockholders looked at all questions of supplying water to the country entirely from their own personal interests." [21] Yet further development of the Hanford region would likely have served the economic interests of the mutual company share-holders as development was serving the somewhat different interests of commercial land companies near Fresno.

The mutual companies, as organizations for agricultural development, appear to have had a shorter time horizon than the type of commercial companies that operated near Fresno. The Fresno and Hanford data lend themselves to a conclusion that concentration of land in the hands of a few individuals, with the prospects of a speculative profit, stimulated economic development and formed a desirable temporary state in a transition from barren public land to intensive agriculture with family farms and healthy rural communities. This conclusion may not hold for other environments, however, and it does not explain why in certain similar environments, in Kern County, for example, immense land holdings acquired by a few individuals were not broken up, why, in other words, there was no transition to the Fresno type of development in such areas. Land speculators, according to the definition used by most economic historians, are those who purchase large acreages of unimproved land intending to sell after land values have risen sufficiently to make the sale profitable and who have no interest in working the land as a personal enterprise or in building up a long-term tenant estate. In these terms the Kern County landowners were not speculators; the Fresno developers were.

Apart from the groundwater situation and the cultural conditions of early development, have the different operating procedures used to distribute water near Fresno and Hanford had an impact on the intensity of development of the two areas? These procedures are based in part on whether water was tied to land or divorced from it. The land speculators and developers of Fresno united the two. They passed water rights to individual farms under the condition that the water not be alienated from the land. The permanent transfer of water rights to small tracts was, as we have seen, an important feature of the colony system and it contributed to the intensive development of the Fresno region. When, however, irrigation systems were transferred from the control of commercial companies to public districts, water was divorced from land in the sense that each landowner was given the right to assign for use within the district the whole or any part of the water apportioned to him. Although the courts considered the right to alienate water from land an important consideration in making the irrigation district law equitable, the district boards of directors found it advisable to limit the statutory right by requiring board approval of alienation in each case.

From the beginning the homesteaders of Hanford divorced water and land.

Table 5.14 Water use (in acre-inches) and water costs and net farm returns (in dollars), Fresno-type distribution with average surface water supply, mutual irrigation company near Hanford, California, late 1960s.

| Farm | Acres | Water Use | | | Total |
		A	B	Pump	
1	80	960	625.6	2,042.4	3,628
2	80	960	625.6	1,764.4	3,350
3	160	1,920	1,251.2	3,354.8	6,526
4	160	1,920	1,251.2	4,454.8	7,626
5	240	2,880	1,876.8	5,043.2	9,800
6	320	3,840	2,502	7,428.0	13,770
7	320	3,840	2,502	7,078.0	13,420
8	560	6,720	4,379.2	12,000.8	23,100
9	40	480	312.8	487.2	1,280
10	40	480	312.8	487.2	1,280
Total	2,000	24,000	15,639.2	44,140.8	83,780

Their stock shares, representing water rights, floated. This did not result in monopolization of water rights as some, Elwood Mead, for example, predicted it would; but it may have contributed to a slow intensification of irrigation agriculture.[22] Those extensions of the service areas of the mutual companies that were encouraged by the floating of stock were frequently uneconomic ones.

Turning to the short-term operating procedures used in the Fresno and Hanford areas, we have compared them by applying an approximation of the Fresno procedure to the physical and economic environment of the Hanford mutual companies. We can do this by allotting to each Hanford farm a uniform quantity of surface water per acre on each rotation and comparing the results of the Fresno-type procedure, given in tables 5.14 to 5.16, to the results of the basic Hanford procedure reported earlier in tables 5.7 to 5.9. In both procedures farmers pump from the ground to meet water requirements that are not satisfied by surface water. If Hanford farmers had used the Fresno-type procedure, their water costs would have been higher and their net farm incomes lower than is the case with their own more complex procedure—for both the region as a whole and for each farm. The comparative average costs of water per irrigated area are the following:

Water Cost				Net Farm Income
A	B	Pump	Total	
374.40	312.80	837.38	1,524.58	6,844.58
374.40	312.80	723.40	1,410.60	6,703.90
748.80	625.60	1,375.47	2,749.87	15,894.15
748.80	625.60	1,826.47	3,200.87	14,981.25
1,123.20	938.40	2,067.71	4,129.31	22,415.89
1,497.60	1,251.00	9,285.00	12,033.60	25,974.50
1,497.60	1,251.00	8,847.50	11,596.10	26,692.30
2,620.80	2,189.50	15,001.00	19,811.30	45,152.60
187.20	156.40	609.00	952.60	3,547.00
187.20	156.40	609.00	952.60	3,547.00
9,360.00	7,819.50	41,181.93	58,361.43	171,753.17

Cost of water per irrigated acre (in dollars)

Procedure	Av. Surface Water	20% Below Av. Surface Water	30% Below Av. Surface Water
Hanford basic	25.00	27.97	29.40
Fresno-type	29.18	30.95	31.84

It will be noted that the cost differential for the two procedures narrows as the supply of surface water decreases. This is to be expected. The difference between the two procedures relates entirely to the distribution of surface water; the costs of pump water are the same for both procedures. Thus as surface water becomes relatively less important and pump water more so, the costs of water in the two distribution procedures converge.

Overall the Hanford short-term procedure appears to be well adapted to the environment in which it is used, better than would be the Fresno procedure. It is more efficient. And it is more convenient in the sense that a farmer can withdraw the water he has in the bank approximately when he wants it; he is not tied to a fixed rotation schedule as in Fresno.

Finally, the forms of cooperative organization—irrigation district and mutual

Table 5.15 Water use (in acre-inches) and water costs and net farm returns (in dollars), Fresno-type distribution with 20 percent below average surface supply, mutual irrigation company near Hanford, California, late 1960s.

Farm	Acres	Water Use A	B	Pump	Total
1	80	960	308.8	2,359.2	3,628
2	80	960	308.8	2,081.2	3,350
3	160	1,920	617.6	3,988.4	6,526
4	160	1,920	617.6	5,088.4	7,626
5	240	2,880	926.4	5,993.6	9,800
6	320	3,840	1,235.2	8,694.8	13,770
7	320	3,840	1,235.2	8,344.8	13,420
8	560	6,720	2,161.6	14,218.4	23,100
9	40	480	154.4	645.6	1,280
10	40	480	154.4	645.6	1,280
Total	2,000	24,000	7,720	52,060	83,780

Table 5.16 Water use (in acre-inches) and water costs and net farm returns (in dollars), Fresno-type distribution with 30 percent below average surface water supply, mutual irrigation company near Hanford, California, late 1960s.

Farm	Acres	Water Use A	B	Pump	Total
1	80	960	150	2,518	3,628
2	80	960	150	2,240	3,350
3	160	1,920	300	4,306	6,526
4	160	1,920	300	5,406	7,626
5	240	2,880	448	6,472	9,800
6	320	3,840	598	9,332	13,770
7	320	3,840	598	8,982	13,420
8	560	6,720	1,047	15,333	23,100
9	40	480	75	725	1,280
10	40	480	75	725	1,280
Total	2,000	24,000	3,741	26,039	83,780

Water Cost				Net Farm Income
A	B	Pump	Total	
374.40	154.40	967.27	1,496.07	6,873.09
374.40	154.40	853.29	1,382.09	6,732.41
748.80	308.80	1,635.24	2,692.84	15,951.18
748.80	308.80	2,086.24	3,143.84	15,038.28
1,123.20	463.20	2,457.38	4,043.78	22,501.42
1,497.60	617.60	10,868.50	12,983.70	25,024.40
1,497.60	617.60	10,431.00	12,546.20	25,742.20
2,620.80	1,080.80	17,773.00	21,474.60	43,489.30
187.20	77.20	807.00	1,071.40	3,428.20
187.20	77.20	807.00	1,071.40	3,428.20
9,360.00	3,860.00	48,685.92	61,905.92	168,208.68

Water Cost				Net Farm Income
A	B	Pump	Total	
374.40	75.00	1,032.38	1,481.78	6,887.38
374.40	75.00	918.40	1,367.80	6,746.70
748.80	150.00	1,765.46	2,664.26	15,979.76
748.80	150.00	2,216.46	3,115.26	15,066.86
1,123.20	224.00	2,653.52	4,000.72	22,544.48
1,497.60	299.00	11,665.00	13,461.60	24,546.50
1,497.60	299.00	11,227.50	13,024.10	25,264.30
2,620.80	523.50	19,166.25	22,310.55	42,653.35
187.20	37.50	906.25	1,130.95	3,368.65
187.20	37.50	906.25	1,130.95	3,368.65
9,360.00	1,870.50	52,457.47	63,687.97	166,426.63

company—under which the Fresno and Hanford regions respectively have operated since the 1920s have had an impact on development. The Fresno cooperatives have benefited from privileges conferred on irrigation districts by state law, principally the right to assess those who do not use the districts' water services, tax exemption for district bonds, eminent domain, and the privilege, as public districts, of using certain county and state facilities. It is true that state regulation has sometimes been a concomitant of these privileges, but the districts appear to have been able to avoid what they consider the most objectionable of these (for example, the requirement that water be apportioned according to assessed valuation). Overall the district has been a more energetic and vibrant organization than the mutual company.

APPENDIX: SIMULATION OF IRRIGATED FARMS IN THE KINGS RIVER SERVICE AREA, CALIFORNIA

Simulation Procedures

Two types of irrigation systems common to this area of California are illustrated in these simulations. The first is an irrigation district that delivers water and assesses the cost of operation on an acreage basis within the district. The second is a mutual irrigation company that delivers water to farmers on the basis of shares owned in the company. Both systems are simulated by use of the Shares distribution rule, which is one of the basic procedures of the irrigation simulation program in our USDA Technical Bulletin 1431. It is used with "demand water," which in this area is groundwater under all farms that can be pumped any time surface supplies are inadequate to meet crop needs.

In the simulation of the irrigation district, surface water is distributed equally to all acres under the system. Crop water needs that exceed surface supplies any time during the season are supplied by pumping from wells on the farms. The irrigation district is underlain with a uniformly productive aquifer so that all farms have roughly the same cost per acre-foot of water pumped and pumping costs do not vary significantly in any one season.

The water supply of the mutual company is divided into two segments. A water is allocated on the basis of one acre-foot of water per acre covered by shares of stock; there are sufficient shares to cover at any time about three-fifths of the service area. An allocation of B water up to one-half acre-foot per acre is given to stockholders desiring additional water. B water is priced at $6 per acre-foot while the original allocation, A water, costs $4.68 per acre-foot.

The mutual company overlies an aquifer that varies greatly in depth; the upper part of the area is over a shallow aquifer while the lower portion must pump from a much deeper one. Pumping costs in the upper part of the service area are about $5 per acre-foot while pumping costs from the deep aquifer are

$15 or more per acre-foot. This means that farms over the shallow aquifer can pump for $1 per acre-foot less than the cost of supplemental surface B water, while over the deep aquifer, surface water charges are substantially less than pumping costs. Given this situation, irrigators over the shallow water aquifer prefer to pump rather than procure supplemental surface water, and they can also rent their A water to farmers with deep wells. Irrigators over the deeper aquifer prefer all the surface water they can get and pump only when additional surface water is not available.

Program Designations With reference to table 9, Principal Distribution Rules, of Bulletin 1431, the following program is used to simulate the California procedures:

Water Supply	Description of Procedure	Procedure Code
All stream flow levels	Shares + Demand	3

Basic Data

The seasonal distribution of surface water used in California simulations is given in table A5.1. Twelve periods are used corresponding to calendar months. Farm sizes used in the two areas are given in table A5.2. Cropping patterns of the areas are shown in table A5.3; yields, costs, and returns of the various crops are given in table A5.4. Costs and returns reflect conditions of the late 1960s.

Table A5.1 Surface water supply used in simulations. Percentage of water available in each month.

	Month											
	1	2	3	4	5	6	7	8	9	10	11	12
% of water available, irrigation district near Fresno	1.0	0	3.0	10.3	17	19.7	21.5	17.2	10.3	0	0	0
% of water available, mutual company near Hanford	1.3	5.4	9.1	5.4	3.5	13.3	16.0	23.0	23.0	0	0	0

Table A5.2 Size of farms used in simulation (in acres).

Farm	Irrigation district near Fresno	Mutual company near Hanford
1	10	80
2	50	80
3	40	160
4	80	160
5	60	240
6	40	320
7	90	320
8	180	560
9	50	40
10	40	40
Total	640	2,000

Table A5.3 Typical crop patterns used in simulations (percentage of acreage planted to each crop in irrigated areas).

Crop	Irrigation district near Fresno	Mutual company near Hanford
Barley	17	35
Beans		4
Cotton	14	25
Alfalfa	12	22
Corn		3
Sorghum		2
Nuts	4	2
Cantaloupe		2
Vineyard	36	5
Decid. fruit	4	
Truck	3	
Citrus	3	
Fig	7	
Total	100	100

Table A5.4 Yields, costs, and returns per acre for crops grown in the simulated irrigation areas.

Crop	Yield	Preharvest cost	Harvest cost	Gross return	Net before water cost
Irrigation district near Fresno, California					
Alfalfa	8.5 T	$ 85.00	$ 68.15	$ 246.50	$ 93.35
Cotton	12 cwt	164.00	93.00	382.00	125.00
Vineyard	6 T	442.00	162.00	750.00	146.00
Decid. fruit	16 T	457.00	246.00	1,280.00	577.00
Truck crop	23 T	292.00	179.00	952.00	481.00
Barley	30 cwt	44.60	11.00	75.60	20.00
Walnuts	1 T	113.43	81.00	420.00	225.57
Citrus	300 Boxes	384.43	250.00	900.00	265.57
Figs	3 T	156.00	259.00	663.00	248.00
Mutual company near Hanford, California					
Vineyard	6 T	$445.00	$162.00	$700.00	$ 93.00
Barley	40 cwt	24.66	14.00	100.00	61.34
Beans	20 cwt	53.86	48.00	220.00	118.14
Cotton	8 cwt	115.46	80.00	364.00	168.54
Alfalfa	8.5 T	40.26	68.60	246.50	137.64
Corn	46 cwt	44.46	33.00	119.60	42.14
Sorghum	50 cwt	80.86	15.00	130.00	34.14
Nuts	20 cwt	95.66	81.00	420.00	243.34
Cantaloupe	160 cwt	162.46	554.00	912.00	195.54

6 The Kings River Service Area in the Central Valley of California: Dividing the River

The land developers of Fresno and the farmers' cooperatives of Hanford staked out their claims to water of the Kings River following the California customs of the time.[1] According to these customs the right to appropriate water was initiated by posting a notice at the place proposed for diverting from the stream stating the appropriator's intent to divert a specified quantity through a ditch heading at that location. The right thus claimed was established by actually diverting the water and applying it to the intended use. Once the appropriation was completed in this way the water right was backdated to the time of the initial posting and from that date it had priority over all subsequent appropriations. The one first in time was first in right.

This procedure was developed originally in the mining camps, and it soon came to be used as the customary method for claiming water for irrigation and other purposes. Not until 1872 did the state enact legislation on the acquisition of water rights and the statute then approved was simply a codification of existing customs. The law required more information on the posted notice than had been included by some appropriators in the past, that a copy of the notice be provided to the county recorder, which had not always been done in the past, and that the work necessary to divert the water be commenced within sixty days of posting of the notice and prosecuted diligently and uninterruptedly to completion unless delayed by rain or snow. But the whole purpose of the statute was to make the customary procedure work better by providing clearer evidence of the dates of appropriations so that respective priorities could be determined more easily by the courts where there were conflicts. Furthermore, appropriators were not required to follow the statutory requirements; they could continue to claim under the less precise customary procedure.

Where there was sufficient water for all appropriators, enforcement of one's right against another was no problem. When the country began to fill up, however, and there was a drought, early appropriators sought to enjoin others from taking water and to do so quickly before a season's crops were lost. Occasionally they took direct action, knocking down upstream diversion structures of those believed to be junior to them in right. Occasionally they made arrangements to acquire by purchase competitors' water rights. Frequently they entered suits in the county courts, and it was in response to such court proceedings that most appropriators were called on for the first time to establish their rights by producing evidence of posted notices and of completed appropriations. When the droughts abated, the suits frequently were not pursued and works that had been destroyed were rebuilt.

The two most noted irrigation engineers of the time, William Hammond Hall, California's first state engineer, and Elwood Mead, expert in charge of irrigation investigations for the U.S. Department of Agriculture, proposed that California abandon its procedures for claiming and perfecting water rights and substitute for them bureaucratic procedures in which the state under its police power would license all diversions from streams. Hall said to the state legislature, "In my opinion the solution of the irrigation problem is in the solution of the water right difficulties, and the solution to the water right troubles is only to be accomplished by a government of the streams and waters on the part of the State, just as there is in every other highly civilized country except the United States. The streams of all European continental countries are in the care of government officers; and no one is permitted to put a permanent structure in the bed, bank, or channel of a stream, or divert its waters from their channel without a permit from the proper authorities." [2]

Mead was even more insistent, the need for reform being the principal motif of his hefty Bulletin No. 100, *Report of Irrigation Investigations in California:*

The system is wrong. It is wrong in principle as well as faulty in procedure. . . . Leaving the ownership of streams to be fought over in the courts and titles to water to be established in ordinary suits at law has never resulted in the creation of satisfactory conditions and never will. As it is now the same issues are tried over and over again. Each decision, instead of being a step toward final settlement, too often creates new issues which in turn have to be litigated. . . . The law affords no means of enforcing a right when once adjudicated except through another law suit. Irrigators cannot live in peace. Litigation and controversy are forced upon them. . . . When the right is insecure and not defined the instinct of self-protection makes an Ishmaelite of every water user. His hand must be against every man, as every man's hand is against him.

. . . . There never was a time when doubtful or controverted policies should have been evaded by the lawmakers and thrust on the courts for settlement. There is as great a need for specially qualified officers to determine the amount of water supply and regulate its distribution as there is to survey the public land. . . . There is as great, if not greater, need of a bureau to supervise the establishment of titles to water as there is for land officers to manage the disposal of public land. . . .

The advantages of public control which would restrict the construction of additional works until it had been demonstrated that there was water for their use and provide for a just division among the works already in existence seemed so obvious that I sought from those directly interested an explanation of why an attempt had not been made to secure it. The reply in every case was practically the same. All classes of water users and water claimants united in saying the State government did not offer any prospect of remedy and that they could not afford to take any chances but preferred to come to an agreement among themselves.

It is not believed that this fear is well founded. It would take remarkably corrupt officials to create evils equal to those now existing. The notion that we must have human nature reformed and all the State machinery perfected before anything is done toward the regulation of streams is certainly erroneous. [3]

The California legislature turned a deaf ear to these pleadings. It fired Hall by abolishing his position of state engineer. Mead, as a federal employee, was beyond their reach. The proposal for an administrative system to license water uses raised questions, as Mead recognized, of the likely competence and integrity of the necessary bureaucracy. Also the proposed reform was unresponsive to the principal legal problem that confronted California water users after 1884, when the state courts recognized riparian rights, thereby confounding the generally accepted procedures for claiming and appropriating water. Not until 1913 did the legislature establish an administrative agency with authority over water rights —the state water commission. Its powers were more circumscribed than those proposed by Hall and Mead. Furthermore, it was required to recognize all vested rights, and by this late date most of the waters of the San Joaquin Valley were in this category. Conflicts among holders of vested rights were settled for the most part not by the commission but, as we shall see in the case of the Kings River, by voluntary agreements and the courts.

THE COMMON LAW OF THE EAST OR THE CUSTOMARY LAW OF THE WEST?

The settlers who moved west into California in the middle of the nineteenth century and into Colorado, Utah, and other arid territories concurrently or soon thereafter took with them the common law, which soon came to be confirmed in the organic and constitutional provisions governing their territorial and state governments. In 1850, the year in which California was admitted to the Union, its legislature passed an act adopting the common law of England, so far as not repugnant to or inconsistent with the Constitution of the United States or the constitution or laws of the state, as the rule of decision in all state courts.[4]

The common law of rivers known to these settlers was the riparian system. Finding this system incompatible with short supplies of water for gold mining on the public lands in California and for irrigating in the valleys of California, Utah, Colorado, and elsewhere, these settlers devised, practiced, and declared a different legal system, that of prior appropriation, even though this new system derogated the generally accepted common law with which they were familiar. Water was one of the very few subjects (mining was another) and the most important one on which the eastern common law was so radically abandoned.

The essential differences between the riparian and appropriative systems of water rights were these: *Location:* Under the riparian system the use of stream flow was limited to the owners of land contiguous to the watercourse, whereas place of use was disregarded in the appropriative system. The riparian limitation was not a serious constraint in the humid East where there were many streams, but if it had been followed in the West, the land developers of Fresno, for example, could not have built their canals and transported Kings River water out onto the arid but fertile plains. *Certainty:* Prior appropriation defined a system of exclusive rights; the prior appropriator had right to a fixed quantity of water to the extent of his priority and could exclude all others. The riparian system, on the other hand, was one of correlative rights; the rights of landowners bordering upon a stream were relative to each other and no one had a right to a fixed quantity of water. The greater certainty provided by the appropriative system was in many cases necessary to attract the capital investments required for works to store and transport water in the arid lands. *Equality versus priority:* The riparian system recognized no priorities in anyone; all riparian owners had equal rights of use and no one was allowed unreasonably to impair the equal use of another. The appropriative system was based on priority; first in time of use was first in right. *Nonuse:* Actual use was the foundation of right by appropriation; thus nonuse caused a loss of the right. Because in the riparian system the right to water depended on the ownership of bankside land, nonuse, per se, did not void a right.[5]

Allocation of limited water supplies on the basis of prior appropriation was practiced, then, in most of the arid West from the time of early settlement. Declaration and confirmation of this practice by law or court decision followed. The courts of some jurisdictions held that because of "necessities growing out of climatic conditions" the riparian common law rule had never obtained in their territories or states, even though some proprietors may have believed it was part and parcel of the generally prevailing common law. As to any conflict between adoption of the common law on the one hand and its abandonment for water on the other, these courts either stated or implied that only so much of the common law as was applicable to the area was in fact adopted.

Thus the Wyoming Supreme Court: "The common law doctrine relating to the rights of a riparian proprietor in the water of a natural stream, and the use thereof, is unsuited to our requirements and necessities, and never obtained in Wyoming. So much only of the common law as may be applicable has been adopted in this jurisdiction. The doctrine involved is inapplicable."[6]

In a leading Colorado case counsel contended that common law riparian principles prevailed in Colorado until 1876 when the doctrine of prior appropriation was first recognized and adopted in the state constitution. In reply the state supreme court held, "But we think the latter [appropriation] doctrine has existed from the date of the earliest appropriations of water within the boundaries of the state. . . . We conclude, then that the common law doctrine . . . is inapplicable to Colorado. Imperative necessity, unknown to the countries which gave it birth, compels the recognition of another doctrine in conflict therewith."[7]

The Idaho Supreme Court said of the new doctrine: "Whether or not this is a beneficent rule, it is the lineal descendant of the law of necessity." And further: "instead of applying the common-law riparian doctrine to which they [the new inhabitants] had been accustomed, they disregarded the traditions of the past, and established as the only rule suitable to their situation that of prior appropriation."[8]

When the California courts were first called upon to settle controversies between water users on the public lands, they recognized the practice of prior appropriation. Less than ten years after the discovery of gold in California the supreme court held that: "The right to appropriate the waters of the streams of this State, for mining and other purposes, has been too long settled to admit of any doubt or discussion at this time."[9] The right was justified by customs and usages and by the peculiar environmental conditions for which there were no precedents. Certain owners of riparian lands in California continued to argue for the common law, however. Most prominent among them were Henry Miller and his associates, who had acquired vast riverbank holdings in the San Joaquin Valley, much of it purchased from the state under the federal Swamplands Act. This land was in varying degrees swampy or arid depending on the season and the year. It was used principally for grazing, and Henry Miller, a German immigrant who began his life in America in 1847 as a butcher boy, had become the Cattle King of the valley. In 1881 Miller and his partner, Charles Lux, brought suit against upstream appropriators on the Kern River, which lies south of the Kings. They lost. The Kern County court followed the prevalent ópinion in California, upholding the upper appropriator against the lower riparian owner on the ground that only those portions of the common law had been adopted that were suitable to California conditions. Miller appealed to the state supreme court, which in a four to three decision overruled the lower court and established the riparian doctrine as fundamental in the water law of California.[10]

The appropriative principle was not rejected; it was limited to appropriations made on the public lands where the federal government had not exercised its underlying riparian rights but instead had acquiesced in diversions of water in accordance with local custom. In its opinion the majority stood fast by the common law:

The act of 1850 adopts the common law of England; not the civil law; nor the *jus commune antiquum,* or Roman "law of nature" of some of the civil-law commentators; nor the Mexican law; nor any hybrid system. And the expression "common law of England" designates the English common law as interpreted as well in the English courts as in the courts of such of the states of the Union as have adopted the English common law. We cannot presume that the members of the legislature, even at that day, were utterly ignorant of the climate and soil of the country in which they lived; and there were included in their number many natives of California, who must be presumed to have represented the intelligence of a race which, for several generations, had been familiar with the natural conditions here existing. . . . Under these circumstances, we must believe that if it had been intended to exclude the common law as to the riparian right, the intention would have been expressed. . . . Whatever the law pre-existing that statute of 1850, it was then and there done away with, except as it agreed with the common law.[11]

Immediately riparian owners throughout the valley brought suits in local courts. By 1887 the development of irrigation around Fresno had come to a stop, as we have seen. There was a great public clamor. The issues were argued in the press. Antiriparian organizations were formed over the state and irrigation conventions were held at Fresno, Riverside, and San Francisco. The articles of association of the Anti-Riparian Organization of the State of California included the following preambulatory paragraphs, which give a sense of the urgency felt by the state's farmers:

Whereas, attempts are now being made to resurrect the English common law doctrine of riparian rights from the grave to which the will of the people long since consigned it, and to impress it upon the jurisprudence of the State; and, Whereas, such attempts if successful, mean the desolation of thousands of homes; means the desert shall invade vineyard, orchard and field; that the grape shall parch upon the vine, the fruit wither on the tree, and the meadow be cursed with drought; means that silence shall fall upon our busy colonies, and their people shall flee from the thirsty and unwatered lands; means that the cities built upon commerce irrigation has created, shall decay, and that in all this region the pillars of civilization shall fall, and the unprofitable flocks and herds shall graze the scant herbiage where once there was a land of corn and wine, flowing with milk and honey, and,

Whereas, if this attempt to forbid the useful appropriation of water is defeated by a righteous public opinion crystallized into law, the homes now planted in midst of fruitful acres will remain the shelter of a happy people, enriched by the productive soil, and irrigation will advance the frontier of verdure and flowers and fruits, until the desert is conquested and has exchanged its hot sands for happy garlands, its vagrant herds for valiant people, and the bleak plains grow purple with the vintage and golden with the harvest, and the pleasures and profits, the peace and plenty that come out of the useful rivers, will make this land the Promised Land to millions of free people.[12]

There were proposals to reorganize the supreme court, to overrule its opinion by legislation or by constitutional amendment, and to authorize irrigators to purchase riparian rights, with compensation to be determined by a public agency on the basis of actual loss or damage.

Governor Stoneman called a special session of the legislature in 1886 to consider remedial action, but a simple solution was not at hand. If the legislators had believed that a statute could have nullified the court's opinion they would have passed it. But once the supreme court had validated riparian rights, it was too late to reject them by statute. Property could be taken only by "due process of law"; and there was little confidence that the proposals before the legislature could meet this test in the supreme court. Chief Justice Shaw represented the view of the court when he said subsequently that once riparian rights became vested, "the much more important public policy of protecting the right of private property became paramount and controlling. This policy is declared in our constitutions, has been adhered to throughout our national history, and it is through it that the remarkable progress and development of the country has been made possible." [13]

There was much debate in the special legislative session and much resoluting, but no significant results. As a symbolic gesture the lawmakers passed a statute repealing a section of the civil code relating to riparian proprietors, but since the issues and opinions in *Lux* v. *Haggin* were mostly independent of that section, the new statute had no impact on the court's ruling.[14]

Failing to reduce the influence of the riparian doctrine by legislative means, the irrigators were forced back into the courts, which on the whole confirmed and emphasized the advantages of riparian lands. In two important respects, however, the courts mitigated the potential damage of their opinion to irrigated agriculture.

First, they gave broad sanction to the acquisition by nonriparians of prescriptive rights to water against riparians.[15] Prescription is a common law doctrine for acquiring title to property by long-continued enjoyment. The elements necessary to establish a prescriptive right were fairly well developed in the law, and in the circumstances the California judges applied these elements liberally to favor farmers who had appropriated water and used it on nonriparian lands. Typically in a case of prescription the claimant was an upstream water user who had acquired an appropriative right, the defendant, a downstream riparian who claimed superior rights under the court's ruling in *Lux* v. *Haggin*. By proving that the riparian user had failed to assert his right or to use the water during the prescriptive period, the appropriator could acquire a prescriptive right that was then superior to the downstream riparian right. The court's development of the doctrine of prescriptive rights to water in California provided a broad avenue for circumventing the barrier that their decision for riparian rights had placed in the way of distributing water widely to nonriparian lands.

The first element of a prescriptive right was that it was hostile and adverse to the right of the owner against whom it was claimed. A use of water was adverse, according to the California courts, if it was actual and open on the part of the claimant and done with the knowledge of the owner of the prior right against whom the adverse claim was asserted. The upstream appropriator, however, was not required to prove that the riparian owner had actual knowledge of his hostile act, only the means for such knowledge. Knowledge could be implied and presumed by the circumstances. Under the doctrine of *Lux* v. *Haggin* every diversion of water to nonriparian lands upstream from the lands of riparian owners was considered an invasion of downstream riparian rights. Under such "circumstances" it was held that the slightest use of water on nonriparian lands by upstream diverters was notice to all lower riparian owners that a hostile right was being asserted and that in consequence a prescriptive right was immediately initiated against the riparians. Furthermore, the notices that appropriators had posted at the place of intended diversion were accepted by the courts as notice of an adverse claim against downstream riparian owners.

Prescription was an effective antidote to riparian rights in California because the time period of continuous adverse use that was necessary to establish the right was only five years. Although prescription was a common law doctrine, the time period had come to be set by statute in many jurisdictions. In England originally the adverse use had to have continued from "beyond the time whereof the memory of man runneth not to the contrary." By the end of the eighteenth century the English courts were interpreting this to mean twenty years, and in 1832 this period was approved by statute. The early American states followed the English standard for the most part, although Connecticut and Vermont adopted a term of fifteen years. Many of the newer states between the Allegheny Mountains and the Mississippi River adopted a fifteen-year term, and some west of the river, a period as short as ten years. The California legislature departed radically from the then common law tradition when in 1850, the same year in which it adopted the common law of England, it passed a five-year statute of limitations. Although we have not found any discussion of the reasons for this remarkably short period, it is doubtless related to the highly unsettled situation with regard to land titles—involving settlers' impatience with the pace of federal activity in settling Mexican grants and disposing of the public domain and the activism of squatters who had organized and rioted in several places. To get conflicting land claims settled quickly was perhaps of paramount importance to the legislators. Whatever the reasons for adopting the five-year period in 1850, it became a great help to the irrigators of California after *Lux* v. *Haggin*.

During the prescriptive period of five years the adverse use had to be continuous and uninterrupted. If the prior owner at any time during this period acted to interrupt the claimant's use of water, this would prevent the acquisition of title by prescription. Acts of interruption could be of various kinds—physical means, court actions, or successfully demanding interruption. The most obvious of these means, the simple act of diverting and using the water, was not available to most riparian owners, however, for they were downstream from the adverse users. Also, large diversions in rivers like the Kings were frequently made near the point of emergence of the streams from the mountains. The riparian lands that would be seriously affected were so far downstream that the diversions frequently provoked no immediate opposition, and sometimes they ripened into prescriptive rights before they were opposed.

As a final element of prescription, claimants were required to have openly asserted their rights to the use of water (that is, the use of water must have been made "under a claim of right"). But the courts held that the actual appropriation of water, followed by open, continuous, and exclusive possession for the prescriptive term, gave the right.

Although the courts paved the way for successful claims to prescriptive rights, titles to such rights in each case were determined only by judicial decrees in actions in which the rights had been established by the adverse claimants. Thus after 1884 irrigation organizations were forever in the courts and a significant part of their operating expenses went for lawyers' fees.

The second way the courts mitigated the impact of the riparian doctrine on irrigators was to give broad sanction to nonriparian owners to purchase water rights from the owners of riparian land and then to transfer the water to wherever they wanted to use it within the watershed—upstream, downstream, or far away from the river bed.[16]

More properly, the courts held that riparian owners could grant or sell their water apart from the land to which it was attached. Severance of the riparian water right from riparian land was contrary to the spirit and the basic characteristics of the riparian doctrine, and severance by grant or sale was considerably more adverse to the doctrine than severance by prescription. Yet the courts sanctioned it so that irrigation could continue, albeit at a cost to the irrigators. On the one hand the court had denied upstream appropriators their water in favor of downstream riparians and on the other hand it allowed them to buy downstream riparian rights and float them upstream.

The riparian doctrine on watercourses did not apply to groundwater; indeed it was scarcely relevant in this context. Under the English common law, then followed in some of the eastern states, the owner of the title to land owned everything under the land, including groundwater. He could extract as much water as he wished without recourse by his neighbor, who could do the same under his own land. When in 1902 basic issues relating to groundwater rights reached the California Supreme Court, in *Katz* v. *Walkinshaw,* the defendants argued that California had adopted the common law in 1850 and that if this included the common law doctrine of riparian rights on surface streams, then presumably it also included the common law doctrine of absolute ownership of groundwater by the owner of overlying land.[17] The plaintiff argued, as had the opponents of riparian rights twenty years earlier, that the common law rule operated simply and equitably in humid areas but that it was highly inequitable in the arid conditions of California. This time the court lent a sympathetic ear to the argument. The absolute ownership doctrine, said the judges, was unsuited to the natural conditions of California, "so radically opposite to those prevailing where the doctrine arose." Public policy, or a regard for the general welfare, did not demand such a doctrine, even though it was a rule of the common law. Hence, "where the differences are so radical as in this case, and would tend to cause so great a subversion of justice, a different rule is imperative."

The rule adopted was one of correlative rights and reasonable use. Each owner of land overlying a common water supply had a right to the reasonable beneficial use of the water on his overlying land, his right being correlative with the similar rights of all other owners of land overlying the same groundwater supply. If the groundwater supply was insufficient for the requirements of all owners, the courts would apportion it. Any surplus in the supply above the reasonable requirements of the overlying lands could be taken to distant, nonoverlying lands; and among distant users the rules of appropriation, including priority of use, were to govern.

This opinion had the effect of limiting the export of groundwater to distant areas, which could have been done without limit under the common law doctrine. However it did not lead to any important judicial determinations of the correlative rights of overlying landowners; for even where considerable depletion of the groundwater occurred the owners generally preferred to leave the outcome to economic competition among themselves, rather than rely on court decrees. As overdrafts lowered the groundwater table, pumping costs increased and the less profitable uses were reduced.

Nonriparian users were learning to live, uneasily to be sure, with a riparian doctrine that was modified by prescription, the right to purchase riparian rights, and the doctrine of correlative rights for groundwater when the California Supreme Court in 1926, possibly concerned about the erosion of the riparian doctrine they had sanctioned, struck another blow for property rights to surface water as they are defined in the common law, in *Herminghaus* v. *Southern California Edison Company*.[18] The Herminghaus lands comprised about 18,000 acres riparian to the San Joaquin River, mainly between the river and Fresno slough. At times of high stages in the river, water overflowed these lands through narrow sloughs and produced pasturage. The lands had been rented for many years at $1 per acre. Herminghaus brought suit to enjoin the power company from interfering in any way with the flow of the river past his lands. The court decided in his favor, upholding the riparian right as against that of an appropriator without regard to the reasonableness or wastefulness of the riparian use. Testimony in the case showed that the water demands of these lands under usual practice would be about 180 cubic feet per second (cfs) but that a river flow of 5000 cfs was required to supply natural inflow at the slough headings. The court decision, in effect, gave the riparian owner, as against an upstream appropriator, a right to the full flow of a river in order to support a natural flow over the riparian lands of only a small fraction of the stream.

The decision aroused as much public clamor as had *Lux* v. *Haggin,* perhaps more. But this time the governor and the legislature were able to devise a constitutional amendment that limited riparian rights but was phrased to discourage the courts from construing it as an attempt to confiscate private property. The amendment limited the riparian right (and appropriative rights as well) to reasonable and beneficial uses of water and to reasonable methods of diverting water from a stream. All water surplus to such reasonable riparian uses was to be subject to legal appropriation.

This amendment declared "that because of the conditions prevailing in this State the general welfare requires that the water resources of the State be put to beneficial use to the fullest extent of which they are capable, and that the waste or unreasonable use . . . of water be prevented."[19] The state in the exercise of its police power had authority to subject all forms of property to reasonable regulation, and the amendment purported only to regulate the use and enjoyment of property rights in water for the public benefit. The proposal was passed by the 1927 legislature and approved at the general election in 1928. Thus California, unlike the other arid western states, continued to recognize both riparian and appropriative rights to surface water, but the conditions under which both could be exercised and the dividing line between the two were now defined, however broadly, in the state constitution.

KINGS RIVER WATER RIGHTS

On the Kings River there were probably more appropriations, more riparian suits, and as many if not more purchases and direct actions than on any other river in the state. Hall reported on the Kings in 1880, focusing on overlapping appropriation claims, and Mead in 1900, on overlapping court decrees.[20] Each expert tells a horror story, as he sees it; and although there was ample reason for concern about the status of Kings River water rights, one needs to read their interpretations with a grain of salt, for both men used the Kings River story to support their reform proposals.

The records of Fresno and Tulare counties that Hall examined showed that eitghty-three claims for water from the Kings River had been filed up to December 1879. Approximately half of these were so imprecise in the amount of water that was claimed—several of them called for all the water in the river—that Hall was unable to calculate the extent of their demand on the river's supply. The remaining claims were stated in a form that was generally used and had been prescribed in the 1872 law, namely, inches of water measured under a 4-inch (in) head. Taking the amount of water discharged through an inch-square opening under a 4-inch pressure as .02 cfs, Hall calculated that the sum of these claims was about 20,000 cfs; and he compared this to the 1879 flow of the Kings River, which had a mean discharge of 1731 cfs, with a maximum of 9030 and a minimum of 210 cfs. Hall's data were from the posted claims, however (that is, from the initial stage of the appropriation process). Most of these claims had not been made good by actual diversion and use of the water. They would have fallen if they had been challenged in court, and they would have been challenged if they had been a threat to users who had rightfully completed their appropriations.

Mead, in addition to updating Hall's survey of appropriation claims (he counted three hundred fifty claims in 1900), made an effort to compile and analyze court decrees relating to water rights on the Kings River. He had no more luck than Hall in arriving at precise results. Seeking to study only the principal cases in which the rights of ditches to divert water from the river had been brought into question, Mead and his associate, C.E. Grunsky, found forty-two cases in the courts of Fresno County, forty-two in Tulare County, and nineteen in Kings County. From these data Mead concluded that even if there were no rights other than those that had been adjudicated in the courts, it would be exceedingly difficult if not impossible for a hypothetical watermaster to divide the river. "He would have no adequate guide for his action . . . . No ordinary mind would be equal to the strain."

Mead compared the situation on the Kings River unfavorably to the settlement of water rights in Wyoming where, under an 1890 law, the state engineer surveyed rivers and subsequently a board, presided over by the state engineer, passed on the claims of appropriators. The comparison rang hollow, however; for Mead was so enthusiastic an advocate of the system in Wyoming, where he had been the first state engineer, that he failed to appreciate that the factor most responsible for the confusion of water rights on the Kings River was not present in Wyoming, namely riparian rights. One of Mead's colleagues subsequently abstracted 137 Kings River cases and found that over two-thirds of them were suits setting up riparian claims.[21] Even if Wyoming's administrative procedures had been superior to California's court procedures for the settlement of conflicting appropriation claims, which is doubtful on several counts, the sister state's legislation was inadequate for the California situation that Mead observed in 1900.

We can take a closer look at cases and actions involving the Kings River irrigation systems of major concern in this study.[22] The Laguna de Tache ranch of approximately 65,000 acres was located on the north side of the Kings River, opposite the Mussel slough mutual companies and some distance downstream from the diversion points of the canals that irrigated the Fresno area. The ranch, situated in low-lying delta lands, was crossed by numerous sloughs, in some of which small diversion structures had been built. But it was watered primarily by flooding from the river rather than by a system of artificial canals. The ranch was devoted principally to stock raising. In 1883–84 the owners of Laguna ranch, claiming superior riparian rights, entered suits in the courts of Tulare County against all major diverters on the river, seeking in each case an injunction to stop the diverter from using river water and to require him to fill in the head of his canal and to destroy all diversion works. Laguna lost its cases against the three mutual companies in Mussel slough country and the small Emigrant Ditch Company on the north side of the river opposite the Peoples Ditch Company, all of which claimed and proved prescriptive rights to water. They had appropriated water from the river between 1871 and 1876 and their appropriations had ripened into prescriptive rights. These companies' victories were limited, however, in the sense that they could not enlarge or extend their canals. Any new appropriations of water for this purpose would fall before Laguna's superior riparian right. And court challenges continued between Laguna and several of the companies over the exact quantity of water that could be withdrawn under the prescriptive right—whether it was the capacity of a canal that had been built in the prescriptive period or the average flow in that canal during the period when flow was less than capacity.

Laguna won its cases against the Centerville and Kingsburg and the Fowler Switch canals (which were later merged to form the Consolidated Canal Company), the 76 canal (except for a small part of its service area that was held to be endowed with riparian rights), and Kings River and Fresno canal (which was just north of the Fresno canal company's service area and received its water through the latter's headgate). The appropriation dates for the first three of these canals were clearly within five years of the filing of suits by Laguna, so they could not claim prescription; and although the last-named canal made such a claim based on an earlier posted notice of appropriation, the court held that it had not met the requisite conditions for prescription. All of the canals were ordered to close

down and to destroy their diversion works. These court orders were not enforced, but they had the effect of stopping all development of the region and of
creating a pervasive uncertainty about the future.

Occasionally the directors of one of these canal companies would be called
into court for running water in company ditches. They would be found in con-
tempt of court and given nominal fines. The superintendent of the Centerville
and Kingsburg canal has described one such instance:

> In the beginning of the water season of 1887 an attempt was made to enforce
> the injunction of the court against the Centerville and Kingsburg Irrigation Ditch
> Co. The water was turned in the canals in February and immediately the com-
> pany was called into court, and the directors were fined for contempt of court.
> After returning from Visalia the directors held a meeting and ordered the super-
> intendent to shut the water out of the ditches and keep it shut off. He shut off
> the water. In about a week the water came down the ditch and the superintend-
> ent went up to see the headgate and shut off the water again. A number of men
> were there armed with rifles and shotguns with bandana handkerchiefs over their
> faces and with their clothes on wrong side out, ordered him to stop and get off
> the gate. He asked who had turned on the water. They did not answer this ques-
> tion direct but told him that the water was turned on and that it was going to
> stay turned on. He started to argue with them and informed them of the court
> order under which the water had been turned off. They simply told him that
> they knew that he had been ordered to close the gate but that they were not
> going to allow him to do so; that they did not want to hurt him but that they
> were going to use such force as might become necessary to keep the gate open
> and ordered him to leave the vicinity of the gate at once and not come back. As
> he had only one man with him and the willows around the gate seemed full of
> men all armed, he withdrew and drove to Kingsburg and informed the canal
> officers of the situation at the gate. At a meeting of the directors held on the
> next day the president of the board of directors in the discussion with the super-
> intendent, intimated that superintendent had not been persistent enough in his
> attempt to close the gate. He at once invited the president to accompany him to
> the gate on the next day. The whole board decided to go along. They were met
> at the South end of the gate and were not allowed to get upon the gate at all.
> The president started to argue with the guards but was curtly told that the
> guards knew what they were there for and that the gate was not to be shut
> down. The directors went home. In a few days the directors were called into the
> Visalia court to answer a charge of contempt of court. The directors and super-
> intendent told of their experience. The court levied a nominal fine.[23]

Laguna's case against the Fresno canal company moved more slowly. When
Church began construction in 1870 he posted a notice of a claim to water "to
be taken from the Kings River at the upper end of Sweem ditch, 20 feet on the
bottom, 30 feet on top, 4 feet deep." A month later he acquired two-thirds interest in Sweem ditch, a small channel then under construction, and he enlarged
it to serve as the head section of Fresno canal. Thus the measure of the appropriation completed in 1871 was the capacity of the enlarged Sweem ditch. In 1875

Church acquired the Centerville ditch, another small canal in the area. He used its channel and acquired its appropriative right of several years' standing. Church paid for both of these ditches by granting their owners free rights to water from his canal. Subsequently the Fresno canal made additional filings on the flow of the Kings River for much larger quantities of water.

Before Laguna's case against the Fresno canal came to trial, the John Heinlen Company, claiming riparian rights, sued in Fresno County court to enjoin the canal from diverting water from the river. The Heinlen ranch, which was in part on swamplands, was supplied by three ditches of the Lemoore Canal Company, in which it held several shares of stock, and by several sloughs. The ranch's principal business was stock raising and its principal crop, alfalfa. The county court granted the injunction. It was subsequently overruled by the supreme court, which held that the lower court had erred by failing to consider Fresno canal's defense of five years' adverse diversion and appropriation, which "its evidence tended to support"; by admitting evidence of damages sustained by Heinlen upon nonriparian lands; and by failing to establish that the ranch was riparian, since there was conflicting evidence on whether a continuous stream ran through the property. The injunction, which had not been enforced, was dissolved.

In the light of this case and of the other Kings River cases it appeared obvious that Fresno canal could prove prescriptive rights for its appropriations through Sweem and Centerville ditches, but there were doubts that it could succeed with such claims for the more than 1000 cfs in later filings. The facts relating to these, including the appropriation dates, were in question. For this reason the canal owners were anxious to prove that the Sweem and Centerville ditches themselves had large capacities. In 1887 Fresno's new owners, the Perrins, asked their canal supervisor and engineer to gauge these ditches, which he found to have a combined capacity of about 100 cfs. What followed is reported in the words of that sober man:

That did not suit Dr. Perrin and he set out to find another engineer that could make more water run through the ditches. He did find one up in the mining districts of California where there were a lot of disputes about water. He also knew that he liked to drink stuff stronger than water.

When he came down to measure the canals it was up to Robert Perrin, a brother of E. B. Perrin, to see that there was plenty of stuff stronger than coffee with the lunch, for it was also up to Robert to see that instead of measuring the two small ditches that he measured the big Fresno canal for one of them. (I was not called upon to come along.) They started out from Fresno with plenty of liquor in the lunch basket and arrived at the canals above Centerville at lunch time. However, they first stopped in Centerville at a saloon to wash down the dust after the 16 mile ride over the dusty road in open spring wagon from Fresno. After lunch the engineer measured water in the big canal and one of the small ditches, according to direction from Robert and not from his own way of doing had he been sober. The results of this measurement was just what Dr. Perrin wanted. [He] then went to trial . . . with the full expectation that he would win the suit and get judgment for over 1000 cubic feet of water. But when the engineer was on the witness stand he was asked about the country road that ran between the two small ditches, he promptly answered there was no such road, which was true. There wasn't any road between the two ditches he measured and he got so tangled up that his testimony was disregarded by the [court].[24]

The Perrins then acted more positively to thwart any further injunctions against the Fresno canal. They purchased the Laguna ranch and floated a good part of its riparian water rights, about 1400 cfs, upstream to the Fresno canal headgate. This transaction we have described previously. It gave Fresno the best right on the river.

Riparian suits caused the principal problems. There were also suits among appropriators, as one would expect, since the California method for resolving conflicting appropriative claims to the use of water was a court trial and decree. The Mussel slough mutual companies challenged Fresno's right to take as much as 1000 cfs upstream from them. After lengthy trials the courts decreed that Fresno was entitled to divert 100 cfs and no more *until* the Lemoore canal (then called Lower Kings River water ditch) was supplied 159 cfs and Last Chance canal, 190 cfs. This was because Fresno's appropriations in Sweem and Centerville ditches, amounting to 100 cfs, were made prior to those of the mutual companies, whereas Fresno's subsequent appropriation of an additional 1000 cfs was later than those of the downstream companies. The Mussel slough companies gained similar limitations on diversions by other upstream appropriators—the Centerville and Kingsburg, the 76, and the Kings River and Fresno canals.

The only diverter upstream from the Fresno company's headgate was the 76 canal and Fresno challenged it, winning a court decree that 76 could take no water until Fresno had received 1000 cfs. Apparently 76's appropriation date of 1882 was held to be subsequent to that of Fresno's large appropriation.

In 1894, when most of these cases had been decided and while other cases were pending in courts, the English interests took over control and management of the Fresno canal company, including its recently acquired Laguna ranch, and they soon procured the Fowler Switch and Centerville and Kingsburg canals, combining them into the Consolidated Canal company. L. A. Nares, the English manager, sought to convince the principal Kings River water users to sign a voluntary allocation agreement that would be based on priorities already determined by the courts. Such an agreement would, he believed, reduce the number of future court cases and some of the uncertainty that pervaded the area and was inhibiting its further development.

In 1897 the Fresno company (for the Fresno canal and the Laguna ranch) and the Peoples, Last Chance, and Lemoore mutual companies signed such an agreement, allocating water between the Fresno canal and the lower diverters collectively; and soon thereafter the three mutual companies signed a supplementary agreement dividing the water among themselves. On petition of the signatories these agreements were incorporated in county court decrees, and they became a milestone on the road to full settlement of Kings River water rights. The agreements contained a diversion schedule that was based on mean daily flows of the river measured at Piedra, a point above all the intakes. The schedule provisions are represented in table 6.1. The agreements also provided for the dismissal of all suits then pending between any of the parties (fifteen principal suits were listed in the agreement between Fresno and the downstream companies).

These arrangements had their defects, to be sure; they included only four of the many units (irrigation systems) that used Kings River water and they allocated only a part of the river flow (up to 1900 cfs). But their form and principles, a schedule based on mean daily flows and dismissal of suits, were to be the basis for future settlements in which additional users were placed on the schedule and the schedule was extended to cover higher flows. The form of the schedule, it should be noted, was different from that frequently found on western streams where each appropriator's full right comes onstream in one lump, its place on the schedule depending on the date of initiation of the appropriation. The Kings River schedule is defined for each 100 cfs of stream flow, and a user's full appropriation can be reached in several steps, depending in part on his actual diversion needs.

PREREQUISITES FOR STORAGE WORKS ON KINGS RIVER

Further progress in dividing up the river among irrigation communities was impelled by a growing realization among the farmers that major storage works were needed for development of the area. There had been talk about building a dam at an upstream site called Pine Flat before the turn of the century, and in 1909 L. A. Nares filed an application with the U.S. Land Office to reserve reservoir lands at that location. The very dry years of 1913 and 1914 prompted mass meetings of farmers to discuss the need for river storage, and several committees of leaders representing the major users of irrigation water were formed to examine the possibilities. It soon became clear, however, that before money could be raised for a dam and reservoir certain prerequisites had to be met, principally a more complete settlement of rights to Kings River water. In addition, agreements had to be reached on the areas to be served by a reservoir, on the allocation of water to be stored in one, and on the organization of a superdistrict to operate the works and the agreements.

Settlement of Water Rights

The water diversion schedules of 1897 needed to be extended, but before this was done the parties wanted more information on monthly river flows and on actual diversions. Although the low flows of the river had been pretty well gauged in connection with the completed water rights cases and agreements, the higher flows were not well documented. Measuring stream flow in a river like the Kings was not a routine operation. As an example, during the spring months there

Table 6.1 Diversion of water (in cubic feet per second) at all Kings River stages up to 1900 cfs—agreements of 1897.

River Stage	Laguna Ranch	Fresno Canal and Irrigation Co.	Lemoore Canal and Irrigation Co.	Peoples Ditch Co.	Last Chance Water Ditch Co.
100	30	70			
200	30	100	70		
300	30	100	85	85	
400	30	100	90	180	
450	30	100	91	183	46
500	30	150	91	183	46
600	30	250	91	183	46
700	30	350	91	183	46
800	30	450	91	183	46
900	30	550	91	183	46
1,000	30	650	91	183	46
1,100	30	750	91	183	46
1,200	30	850	91	183	46
1,300	30	950	91	183	46
1,400	30	1,050	91	183	46
1,500	30	1,150	91	183	46
1,600	30	1,200	93	185	92
1,700	30	1,200	118	235	117
1,800	30	1,250	130	260	130
1,900	30	1,300	143	285	142

Note: If during August or September of any year the river flow is below 600 cfs, Fresno canal may take the first 249 cfs. The other three companies take the next 200 cfs, and Fresno takes all over 449 cfs.

was a large diurnal variation in flow caused by changes in the rate of snow melt, which was due in turn to differences in temperature during day and night. The difference between daily maximum flows, which arrived at Piedra in the morning, and minimum flows, occurring in the late afternoon or evening, could be as high as 50 percent of the minimum for medium stages of the river. To get expert assistance with problems of this type and to get a gauger who was likely to be impartial among water diverters upstream and downstream (recall the Perrins' efforts to misgauge the Sweem and Centerville channels), the water users asked the state water commission (soon to become the division of water rights of the California Department of Public Works) to provide a qualified hydrologist whose expenses they paid.

Gauging the irrigation companies' diversions required their cooperation, which they gave because they agreed on the objective of developing river storage and of taking those preliminary steps necessary for this. The purpose of the measurements was to confront each company with a record of the water it actually was using on its lands so that it would compare this to its adjudicated rights and pending claims. The users attached one important reservation to the gauging operation: that neither the measurements nor other information acquired as a result of the gauging should be used by any of the parties in proceedings or disputes then pending or thereafter to arise in any court or before any commission.

The development of hydrologic data considered adequate to support diversion schedules took longer than expected. The gauges were still being read in 1921 when the region was confronted with the prospect of a new set of riparian suits. The Stinson and Crescent canal companies, which lay downstream from Laguna ranch, had filed riparian suits against Lemoore Canal Company and others. The service areas of the downstream canals had been reclaimed from Fresno swamp and were planted to grain and alfalfa that were irrigated by flooding. The Stinson canal, it should be noted, was controlled by the same interests that controlled the Fresno and Consolidated canals and Laguna ranch; L. A. Nares was its president.

The suits were set for trial in October 1921; and it was apparent to all concerned that if they came to trial, long and expensive litigation would result and progress on the storage project would be stopped. Faced with this danger, a committee was appointed to prepare an agreement that would postpone the litigation by expanding the diversion schedule to include the riparian plaintiffs and others. An agreement was reached and signed on September 27 by interests representing 95 percent of the water used in the Kings River basin.

It provided that all water users submit to the state division of water rights statements of their claims and requirements for water and that the division prepare a temporary schedule that the users bound themselves to accept for the year 1922. Any user could withdraw at the end of the year, but the schedule would continue in force from year to year for those who did not do so. These provisions gave less discretionary authority to the state government than may

Table 6.2 Schedule of right to divert the waters of Kings River for the year 1922.

Kings River at Piedra	Fresno	Consolidated	Alta	Centerville[a]	Kings Cty Canals[b]	Laguna	Murphy Slough	Liberty	Emigrant
Area in Acres	243,900	155,600	129,300	10,000	155,670	37,000	26,700	13,270	4,500
Discharge—cfs									
500	150	—	—	—	320	15	15	—	—
1,000	650	—	—	—	—	—	—	—	—
1,500	1,150	—	—	—	—	—	—	—	—
2,000	1,300	—	—	50	620	—	—	—	—
2,500	1,350	200	200	—	670	—	—	—	—
3,000	1,400	500	300	—	700	25	25	—	—
3,500	1,450	700	550	—	—	—	—	—	—
4,000	—	900	800	—	750	—	—	—	—
4,500	—	1,100	900	—	900	50	50	—	—
5,000	—	—	1,000	—	—	300	200	—	—
5,500	—	1,300	—	100	1,000	350	250	50	—
6,000	—	—	—	—	—	—	—	100	50
6,500	—	1,400	1,100	—	1,100	—	—	—	—
7,000	—	—	—	—	1,200	400	300	—	—
7,500	—	—	—	—	—	—	—	—	—
8,000	—	1,500	1,200	—	1,300	—	400	—	—
8,500	—	—	—	—	—	—	—	—	—
9,000	1,500	—	—	—	—	—	—	—	—
9,500	—	—	—	—	—	—	—	—	—
10,000	1,500	1,500	1,200	100	1,300	400	400	100	50

Source: Calif. Dept. of Public Works, *First Biennial Report*, Part IV, "Report of the Division of Water Rights" (1922), p. 62.

Note: Simplified schedule of the division of the river given in increments of 500 cfs, while the actual schedule uses increments of 100 cfs.

[a] Additional requirements to be supplied by direct diversion of water thereafter generally returning to the river.

[b] Lemoore, Peoples, and Last Chance canals.

appear to be the case, for most major water users had prepared proposed schedules for division of the river that had been discussed and revised over a period of fourteen months prior to the 1922 agreement. These schedules had "no fundamental or radical differences that apparently would justify failure to reach some final conclusion," in the words of the agreement itself, "and it is, therefore, believed that some independent or impartial authority would have no serious difficulty in harmonizing them." [25]

The schedule prepared subsequently by the water rights division is summarized in table 6.2, in which the three Mussel slough mutual companies are combined under the heading of Kings County canals. The schedule followed the basic form of the 1897 agreements, but it covered river stages up to 10,000 cfs, whereas the earlier agreements had included only the first 1900 second feet of flow. Allocations above the 8000 second foot stage were the least firm, and the schedule included a statement that these allotments were not based entirely on

	North Fork						South Fork							
Summit Lake	Crescent	Stinson	Burrel	James	Beta Main	Upper San Jose	Clarks Fork	Heinlen	Empire	Blakeley	Tulare Lake	Corcoran	S.E.Lake
4,080	13,900	14,860	7,500	21,100	15,750	3,300	2,000	6,020	11,040	33,000	50,000	69,000	
—	—	—	—	—	—	—	—	—	—	—	—	—	—
—	—	—	—	—	—	—	—	—	—	—	—	—	—
—	—	—	—	—	—	—	—	—	—	—	—	—	—
—	—	—	—	—	—	—	—	—	—	—	—	—	—
—	—	—	—	—	—	—	—	—	—	—	—	—	—
—	—	—	—	—	—	—	—	—	—	—	—	—	—
—	—	—	—	—	—	—	—	—	—	—	—	—	—
—	—	—	—	—	—	—	—	—	—	—	—	—	—
—	—	—	—	—	—	—	—	—	—	—	—	—	—
—	—	—	—	—	—	—	—	—	—	—	—	—	—
—	—	—	—	—	—	—	—	—	—	—	—	—	—
50	150	150	50	—	—	—	—	—	—	—	—	—	—
—	—	—	—	100	100	—	—	—	—	—	—	—	—
—	175	175	—	—	—	50	30	70	100	—	—	—	—
—	200	200	100	200	200	—	—	—	—	100	100	—	—
—	—	—	—	250	—	—	—	—	150	—	—	—	—
—	225	225	125	275	—	—	—	170	—	200	200	100	—
—	—	250	150	325	250	—	—	—	—	250	300	250	—
—	—	—	—	—	—	—	—	—	—	350	400	350	150
50	225	250	150	325	250	50	30	170	150	400	500	600	300

claims submitted by water users but had been modified as the result of compromise among claimants on the lower river and "the general desire to effect the most advantageous use of water for 1922, without prejudice or effect on their respective rights or claims." This was in part because the sloughs and canals that would be used to carry these high flows were in some cases unmeasured and poorly defined. Another statement on the schedule confirmed Fresno's exceptional low flow allocations in August and September.

If any canal company did not divert for its own use the full amount of water allotted under the schedule, the surplus would be added to the river flow at Piedra and allocated according to the schedule. If there remained a surplus after all allotments on the schedule had been satisfied, water users were permitted to take such additional water as they were able to divert and use.

The agreement provided that the state division of water rights appoint a watermaster for the Kings River to interpret and administer the schedule with provisions for appeal from his actions to the chief of the division. Charles Kaupke, the hydrologist who had been making the record of the river, was named watermaster.

Finally, the agreement provided that the filing of all complaints and the trial of all actions between any of the signers relative to the diversion of water from the river be postponed until January 1, 1923. This postponement was not, however, to affect the legal rights of any of the parties, which were to remain in status quo.

During 1922 the schedule was followed from the beginning of the irrigation season until May 5. From that date until July 1 the river was in flood stage and the flow exceeded the combined requirements of the canals. The schedule was followed again from July 1 until the end of the calendar year. None of the signers withdrew at that time and the 1922 schedule was used each year through 1927.

The 1922 schedule was an important step forward; but it was not sufficient as a prerequisite for planning a major storage facility, for it was temporary (any party could withdraw at the end of a year) and certain rights remained to be defined. Thus the water users in 1925 selected a committee of three engineers to prepare a report on a permanent schedule. Their report was completed in 1926 and agreed to by most of the water users in 1927 after intensive consideration. The only units that did not sign the Water Right Indenture, as it was called, were some small ditch companies in the Centerville bottoms and several canal companies that served reclaimed areas at the tail end of the south fork of the Kings, near Tulare Lake. The indenture provided that the rights of the signatories to divert and use the stream flows allocated in the new schedule "are hereby firmly and finally fixed and settled; and . . . all agreements and judgments in conflict with this schedule are . . . hereby cancelled and annulled . . . and all actions pending between any of the parties . . . are hereby dismissed."[26] The first prerequisite for a dam was met.

The 1927 schedule was more refined than that of 1922, for the engineers used the more extensive hydrologic records that were by then available. As these showed that diversions varied materially from month to month as well as from one river stage to another, separate tables were prepared for each month. The table for December allocated water up to 1000 cfs, that for May, to 9450 cfs, and the remaining months had maximum diversions between these two. The May schedule represented the practical diversion capacities of the canals. For the other months the amounts allocated corresponded closely to the records of actual diversions. For the principal irrigating months of April through July, however, the new monthly tables did not vary much from the simple 1922 schedule.

There was more water in the river at high stages than was allocated by the 1927 agreement; and as the area developed further, various diverters used more and more of this overschedule water. Conflicts arose and to settle these the indenture was amended in 1949 to cover all river flows and to include the missing units near Tulare Lake. The maximum flows allocated on the monthly tables were increased (for example, for December from 1000 cfs to 11,000 cfs and for May from 9450 cfs to 17000 cfs) and any flows in excess of the new maximums

were divided by fixed and uniform percentages among the principal users—
Fresno, 14.5 percent; Consolidated, 26.2 percent; Lemoore, 7.6 percent, Stinson, 2 percent. The 1949 agreement called for the dismissal of three cases pending in Kings and Fresno county courts, and with this action all litigation over
Kings River water rights had been dropped. In the words of watermaster
Kaupke, "there was peace on the river for the first time in eighty years. . . . It
was the largest peaceful settlement of water rights on a major river to be recorded in the history of western irrigation." [27]

Allocation of Storage

With completion of a permanent stream flow diversion schedule, the next prerequisite for a storage project was an agreement on allocation of reservoir capacity—a storage schedule. Some among the water users urged their group to proceed immediately to this task; but since conditions were not favorable in 1927
to raising money for the dam, the majority preferred to delay until they had
gained some experience with the new diversion tables. As a consequence no accord had been negotiated when construction of Pine Flat Dam began in 1947.
By the time the reservoir was ready to operate, however, the water users had
agreed to a storage schedule. The reservoir was operated according to this schedule from the beginning, although a formal contract that incorporated it was not
signed by the parties until 1963.

While studies made before 1920 recommended building a reservoir at Pine
Flat with a capacity of 600,000 acre-feet of storage for irrigation, by the 1930s
engineers had reached agreement that the site should be developed for 1 million
acre-feet and for two principal purposes rather than one. Operating studies had
shown that flood control and irrigation were to a significant degree complementary rather than competitive under the hydrologic conditions that prevailed
in the Kings River watershed.

Floods on the Kings River were of two types: winter floods caused by heavy
rains in the foothills and characterized by high peaks, short duration, and low
volume and spring or early summer floods caused by melting snow in the high
country and marked by low peaks but high volume because of their longer duration. Flood damages resulted principally from the more or less gradual inunda-
tion of lands along the river's several channels, and they were especially great in
the Tulare Lake area.

A dual-purpose reservoir would normally be low at the end of the irrigation
season, so it could catch and hold any winter floods. For this purpose 450,000
acre-feet of reservoir capacity were to be empty from December 1 to March 1,
leaving no more than 550,000 acre-feet of active storage, but spills of water from
the reservoir to maintain the flood capacity would be infrequent and small.

Unlike winter floods, those of spring and early summer were predictable because the snowpack that was their source could be measured. If by March 1 the
snow survey indicated a flood-producing runoff greater than could be controlled

by the 450,000 acre-feet of empty storage, the reservoir would be drawn down further. In certain years of maximum runoff the reservoir might be almost emptied; but whatever the draw down, it would be replaced in short order, for the flood waters would be stored. After the spring floods, if any, had been controlled in this way, water remaining in the reservoir up to its full capacity of 1 million acre-feet would be released as needed over the irrigation season. Also, the flood releases themselves would be used for early irrigation wherever possible.

The reservoir would benefit irrigation in two ways. Part of the water supply that had been diverted to groundwater storage and pumped out by the farmers when they needed it could be stored instead in the reservoir and delivered by gravity. This did not represent an increase in the annual amount of irrigation water but a more efficient use of the existing supply, which could be measured by the reduction in the costs of pumping. A second category of benefits would result from "new" water, stream flow that had not been used but escaped into Fresno slough and Tulare Lake in certain years and seasons of high runoff. This could be stored and, if not spilled for flood control, released for irrigation. Although there was disagreement among engineers on the quantity of new water that would be produced by a reservoir at Pine Flat—most of the estimates were between 20 and 25 percent of average stream flow—there was agreement that it was insufficient for the development of new irrigated areas and should be allotted to existing areas in the basin in order to upgrade the reliability of their water supplies and to reduce further their pumping costs.

The storage space, then, to be allocated among the users was 555,000 acre-feet of so-called primary storage, unrestricted capacity that could be carried over the winter months and from one year to the next, and 450,000 acre-feet of secondary storage that would be available for irrigation when it was not required for flood control purposes.

In working up a storage schedule the water users first agreed to certain principles. Foremost, reservoir operating procedures were not to alter the basic rights of all units to stream flow, as set forth in the diversion schedules. Since, however, these schedules provided water for all units, some more than others, in out-of-season months when they had little direct use for it (although they could run it through their canals to recharge the groundwater), the reservoir procedures were to provide all units with an opportunity to store some of their out-of-season water for use in season. Indeed, this was the major concept of the storage project.

A second principle was that each irrigation unit was to be free to participate in the storage project or not to participate. Each unit that elected to participate would acquire a specified amount of storage space for the regulation of its water supply, the amount to be determined by its own decision-making process subject to the obvious constraint that the sum of all the space subscribed for by all units not exceed the capacity of the reservoir. A participating unit would be able to call for its daily entitlement, as defined in the stream flow diversion schedules, for direct use or it could store the water, provided the quantity stored not exceed the space subscribed for; and at any time it could draw from the reservoir any amount of its stored water. Each unit that did not participate would continue to receive its daily entitlement to direct flow. This water would pass through the reservoir, to be sure, but without benefit of storage or regulation.

These principles, agreed to by the irrigation companies and districts when they began their study of storage allocations, were so well conceived and so strongly supported by the water users that they dominated all later negotiations and were written into the final contracts and agreements among the units themselves and between the local interests and federal and state governments. The basic objectives that underlie the principles for reservoir operation are freedom of individual units to determine their own operating procedures, constrained only by the technological requirements of operating a reservoir, and protection of each unit's water supply from invasion by other units and of the water supplies of all units from invasion by outsiders.

To protect their water supplies from outsiders, the irrigation organizations in addition contracted not to sell or transfer their rights to Kings River water or to Pine Flat storage to any party that would use the water outside the Kings River service area. They also agreed to certain limitations on transfers within the area. Any unit that proposed to sell, rent, or otherwise transfer its water right or its storage right for use within the area was to give notice to all other units so that they could determine if the transfer would affect them adversely by increasing their river channel losses. If there were adverse effects, the unit proposing the transfer was to provide water to compensate for the loss. Until the parties reached agreement on compensation the watermaster was to withhold water needed to effect the transfer. In addition, existing users of the reservoir were to be given first refusal on any storage space that a unit proposed to transfer. To provide stability for all users, storage transfers were to be for a period of not less than three years.

Based on these principles, engineers employed jointly by the several Kings River units made reservoir operating studies to determine the storage space that would be acquired by each unit if all units were to gain an equal percentage improvement in the monthly distribution of their annual water supplies. The results of these studies were presented to the irrigation companies and districts to assist them in making their own decisions on how much storage space to purchase.

In the studies the annual water supply of each unit was taken to be its annual entitlement to stream flow, which was based on the 1927 Water Rights Indenture, as modified to account for overschedule water. Using this base and the daily records of stream flow for the 45-year period 1897–1941, the engineers simulated the water that would have been available to each unit on each day of the 45 years; and from these numbers they calculated an average annual entitlement, or water supply, for each unit.

The engineers defined "equal improvement" in the monthly distribution of the annual water supplies of all units in two alternative ways. One was called

Table 6.3 Allocation of storage (in acre-feet), Pine Flat reservoir.

	Recommended by Engineers for Kings River Water Users–1942			
	Based on Equal Usefulness			
	Primary Storage 550,000	Percent of Storage	Flood Storage 450,000	Total Storage 1,000,000
Main river and North Fork units				
Laguna	27,200	4.9	22,050	49,250
Fresno	58,000	10.5	47,250	105,250
Lemoore	35,700	6.5	29,250	64,950
Peoples	22,100	4.0	18,000	40,100
Last Chance	24,400	4.4	19,800	44,200
Consolidated	122,000	22.2	99,900	221,900
Alta	63,200	11.5	51,750	114,950
Murphy Assn.	22,100	4.0	18,000	40,100
Riverdale				
Liberty Mill and Reed				
Liberty	5,900	1.1	4,950	10,850
Crescent	9,700	1.8	8,100	17,800
Stinson	9,300	1.7	7,650	16,950
Burrel	5,500	1.0	4,500	10,000
James	14,200	2.6	11,700	25,900
Tranquility	8,400	1.5	6,750	15,150
Corcoran	12,300	2.2	9,900	22,200
Kings R. W. D.	—	—	—	—
South Fork units				
Tulare Lake Basin	93,400	17.0	76,500	169,900
Cohn R.D.				
SE Lake				
Tulare Lake W.S.D.				
Tulare Lake Canal				
Stratford	—	—	—	—
Heinlen	6,400	1.2	5,400	11,800
Empire West Side	3,300	0.6	2,700	6,000
Other	6,900	1.3	5,850	12,750

Sources: Recommendations of engineers: Kings River Pine Flat Assoc., *Report on Kings River Project* (Fresno, 1943).
Contracts: U.S. Dept. of the Interior, Bureau of Reclamation, "Kings River Allocation Contract" (Mimeo, Dec. 1963).

				Contracts–1963	
Based on Deficiency in Supply					
Primary Storage 550,000	Percent of Storage	Flood Storage 450,000	Total Storage 1,000,000	Full Storage 1,000,000	Percent of Storage
28,700	5.2	23,400	52,100	44,000	4.4
71,300	13.0	58,500	129,800	119,000	11.9
34,600	6.3	28,350	62,950	100,000	9.9
31,600	5.7	25,650	57,250	107,000	10.6
23,400	4.3	19,350	42,750	64,000	6.4
110,700	20.1	90,450	201,150	120,000	11.9
65,500	11.9	53,550	119,050	100,000	9.9
23,500	4.3	19,350	42,850	(44,000)	(4.4)
				22,000	2.2
				22,000	2.2
6,100	1.1	4,950	11,050	4,000	0.4
10,600	1.9	8,550	19,150	22,500	2.2
9,600	1.7	7,650	17,250	20,000	2.0
5,400	1.0	4,500	9,900	11,000	1.1
11,600	2.1	9,450	21,050	20,000	2.0
6,600	1.2	5,400	12,000	8,000	0.8
14,800	2.7	12,150	26,950	30,000	3.0
—	—	—	—	15,000	1.5
81,200	14.8	66,600	147,800	(133,000)	(13.1)
				40,648	4.0
				18,476	1.8
				33,228	3.3
				40,648	4.0
—	—	—	—	11,000	1.1
6,300	1.1	4,950	11,250	10,000	1.0
2,100	0.4	1,800	3,900	13,000	1.3
6,400	1.2	5,400	11,800	11,000	1.1

equal usefulness, the idea being to allot storage space so that each unit would enjoy an increase in its in-season water supply that was equal, per acre-foot of storage, to the increases of all other units. The second was based on shortages in supplies. Storage space was allotted in proportion to the additional supplies that would be necessary to satisfy each unit's in-season demand, limited by the amount available to each unit from its entitlement. The reservoir space allotted to each unit in all the studies was assumed to include the same percentage of primary and secondary storage.

The results of the operation studies are summarized in the first eight columns of table 6.3. If, under the equal usefulness procedure, each and every unit acquired the storage space recommended for it, all units would be able to increase their in-season water by .76 acre-feet for each acre-foot of capacity acquired.

In presenting these results to the irrigation organizations "as an initial basis for study," the engineers pointed out that "conditions peculiar to each unit" required that each, in the light of its own situation, decide on the amount, if any, of the available storage it would be justified in acquiring. Among conditions peculiar to each unit the engineers subsumed all variations in the yields and costs of production of crops that would be grown. The engineers considered the effects of storage in reducing the needs of units to pump water from the ground, for example, but not the costs that irrigators would save by not having to use their pumps, although these costs would vary considerably from unit to unit. As we have seen in the simulation data, the cost of pumping in Fresno is $5 per acre-foot, while that in the lower portion of the Lemoore service area is $15. As a result, differences among units in the *value* of equal percentage improvements in the seasonal distribution of water supplies were largely ignored by the engineers. Their recommendations for storage allocations were made without regard to the relative worth of an acre-foot of storage space to each unit. The individual units, in other words, were to add their own economic analysis to the engineers' hydrologic studies.

The hydrologic studies themselves omitted several important factors, among them the impact of the proposed reservoir on water losses, due principally to seepage into groundwater basins from the river channel and from the internal distribution networks of the several units. Yet channel and canal losses varied considerably among units and were of sufficient magnitude to influence their storage needs. Lemoore, for example, would lose on the average between 15 and 25 percent of its water in the river and an additional 30 to 40 percent in its own canals, whereas Fresno's river losses were negligible and its canal losses, a little more than half of Lemoore's due to differences in soil permeability, the condition of the canals, and other factors. With no guidance from their engineering consultants, individual units were left on their own to estimate the impact of canal losses on the quantities of water that would be delivered directly to farms from alternative volumes of storage space.

Finally, the engineers' reservoir study results were in terms of mean or average storage usefulness; no consideration was given to variance (standard deviation or any other description). In deciding how much storage to acquire each unit would presumably want to know both the expected (average) result of a given capacity and the certainty (risk) that this result would be achieved. One unit might prefer a high expected value accompanied by high risk, another, a lower expected value with reduced uncertainty, for the intensities and relative frequencies of major shortages affected them differently.

The engineers presented their findings to the irrigation organizations in 1943. By 1953, when the dam was nearing completion, all units had decided to participate, subscribing for storage space in the amounts shown in the last two columns of table 6.3. These amounts vary considerably from those recommended in 1943, especially for the Consolidated district and for the three mutual companies—Lemoore, Peoples, and Last Chance (see table 6.4). To what extent these deviations can be accounted for by one or all of the factors the engineers left to be estimated by each unit is not known, since we have not seen evidence of the decision processes of the several irrigation districts and companies. There seems to be little doubt, however, that the high cost of pumping in Mussel slough country compared to that near Fresno made the substitution of aboveground storage for underground storage especially attractive to the mutual companies.

From data published annually by the Kings River watermaster we have made certain studies of how five units have used the storage they acquired. The results are summarized in table 6.5. The water rights of Fresno were so superior to those of the other units that the district committed itself to storage space for 25 percent of its average annual water supply, the same amount that had been recommended by the engineers. According to our analysis of the nine-year period, this decision provided Fresno with more than enough storage. The space could have held 28.5 percent of the average supply for the period; the district stored on the average 20 percent of its entitlement; and of the surface water that the district used, approximately 20 percent had been stored. Fresno used 80 per-

Table 6.4 Relation of average annual water supply (1897–1941) to storage space recommended by engineers (1942) and acquired by units (1953).

	Fresno	Consolidated	Alta	Peoples	Lemoore	Last Chance
Recommended storage as percent of water supply	25.7	75.9	59.2	28.2	54.1	55.5
Acquired storage as percent of water supply	25.9	42.9	50.6	61.7	85.8	82.6

Sources: Storage space recommended by engineers: average of total storage recommended on basis of equal usefulness and of deficiency in supply—table 6.3. Storage space acquired: Contracts in table 6.3.

Table 6.5 Use of Pine Flat reservoir storage, 1957–1965.

(1) Calendar Year	(2) Stream Flow as % of 70-year period 1895–1965	(3) Used 80% or more space	(4) Total Demand	(5) From Storage	(6) % from Storage	(7) Entitle-ment	(8) Stored	(9) % Stored
			Demand Met from Storage			Entitlement to Natural Flow Stored		
	percent	months	1,000 A.F.		percent	1,000 A.F.		percent

Unit and Storage Space — Fresno Irrigation District—119,000 acre-feet

(1) Calendar Year	(2) Stream Flow as %	(3) Used 80% or more space	(4) Total Demand	(5) From Storage	(6) % from Storage	(7) Entitlement	(8) Stored	(9) % Stored
1957	77.9	6	398.8	99.1	24.8	406.5	98.0	24.1
1958	153.8	5, 6, 7	515.5	80.2	15.6	562.5	104.4	18.6
1959	48.6		352.3	72.7	20.6	354.4	51.6	14.6
1960	45.4		323.6	108.0	33.4	300.7	72.6	24.1
1961	34.0		259.7	93.8	36.1	274.7	95.7	34.8
1962	116.7		489.5	64.6	13.2	485.3	44.5	9.2
1963	124.3	4, 5, 6	440.8	65.1	14.8	512.9	109.2	21.3
1964	60.4		367.8	136.6	37.1	323.8	82.8	25.6
1965	120.7		488.3	41.2	8.4	539.6	69.5	12.9
1957–65	86.9		404.1	84.6	20.9	417.8	80.9	19.4

People's Ditch Company—107,000 acre-feet

(1) Calendar Year	(2) Stream Flow as %	(3) Used 80% or more space	(4) Total Demand	(5) From Storage	(6) % from Storage	(7) Entitlement	(8) Stored	(9) % Stored
1957	77.9	5, 6	161.5	98.1	60.7	143.5	73.4	51.1
1958	153.8	5, 6, 7	171.0	60.8	35.6	214.2	85.0	39.7
1959	48.6	4, 5, 6	146.6	96.6	65.9	108.5	53.1	48.9
1960	45.4		84.8	68.1	80.3	96.4	74.8	77.6
1961	34.0		85.9	68.7	80.0	87.5	63.1	72.1
1962	116.7	5, 6	153.3	59.6	38.9	172.0	72.1	41.9
1963	124.3	5, 6, 7	164.2	68.3	41.6	196.6	91.9	46.7
1964	60.4	5, 6, 7	143.7	88.7	61.7	97.2	41.0	42.2
1965	120.7	5, 6	179.7	63.1	35.1	210.9	79.5	37.7
1957–65	86.9		143.4	74.7	52.1	147.4	70.4	47.8

Last Chance Ditch Company—64,000 acre-feet

(1) Calendar Year	(2) Stream Flow as %	(3) Used 80% or more space	(4) Total Demand	(5) From Storage	(6) % from Storage	(7) Entitlement	(8) Stored	(9) % Stored
1957	77.9		71.7	55.8	77.8	56.7	34.5	60.8
1958	153.8	5, 6, 7, 8	77.2	20.3	26.2	106.0	53.8	50.8
1959	48.6		61.4	46.4*	75.6*	41.5	21.0	50.6
1960	45.4		37.8	34.2	90.5	33.6	26.3	78.3
1961	34.0		31.4	30.5	97.1	25.6	22.3	87.1
1962	116.7		72.7	30.1	41.4	83.6	37.7	45.1
1963	124.3	5, 6, 7	59.7	30.0	50.2	88.5	58.4	66.0
1964	60.4	5, 6	48.6	35.5	73.0	37.2	25.3	68.0
1965	120.7	4, 5, 6	94.5	29.6	31.3	96.8	29.0	30.0
1957–65	86.9		61.7	34.7	56.2	63.3	34.3	54.2

Sources: Kings River Water Association, Watermaster Reports for the years 1957–1965, as follows: Column (2): 1964–65 Report, p. IV-1. Column (3): Monthly summary of storage and diversion operations, for each unit and each year, Column (9). Column (4): Same, Column (5). Column (5): Same, Column (8). Column (7): Same, Column (2) *minus* Column (3) *plus* Column (6). Column (8): Same, sum of positive numbers (only) in Column (7).

+Data for Consolidated Irrigation District include Lone Tree Canal.
*Adjusted to correct for irrelevant data in record.

Consolidated Irrigation District—120,000 acre-feet

(3) Used 80% or more space	(4) Demand Met from Storage	(5)	(6)	(7) Entitlement to Natural Flow Stored	(8)	(9)
	Total Demand	From Storage	% from Storage	Entitle-ment	Stored	% Stored
months	1,000 A.F.		percent	1,000 A.F.		percent
	203.7	85.1	41.8	200.7	70.2	35.0
5, 6	374.0	77.9	20.8	430.0	114.4	26.6
	134.6	74.9	55.6	104.7	45.0	43.0
	114.2	79.4	69.5	106.4	56.6	53.2
	76.3	66.9	87.7	50.5	32.5	64.4
	333.3	63.9	19.2	341.1	59.6	17.5
5, 6	306.0	86.9	28.4	339.2	112.3	33.1
	142.6	88.5	62.1	118.0	62.4	52.9
	300.0	72.2	24.1	319.1	76.6	24.0
	220.5	77.3	35.1	223.3	70.0	31.3

Lemoore Canal and Irrigation Company—100,000 acre-feet

(3)	(4)	(5)	(6)	(7)	(8)	(9)
5, 6	111.8	64.3	57.5	87.8	31.2	35.5
5, 6, 7, 8, 11, 12	98.6	24.7	25.1	154.4	65.9	42.7
1, 2	134.6	85.1	63.2	60.5	3.0	5.0
	52.6	40.4	76.8	53.0	36.5	68.9
	58.7	45.8	78.0	51.6	33.0	64.0
	115.4	47.8	41.4	119.2	44.3	37.2
	137.2	26.1	19.0	136.2	82.6	60.6
	105.4	62.2	59.0	53.5	5.7	10.7
	111.9	41.1	36.7	154.9	71.2	46.0
	102.9	48.6	47.2	96.8	41.5	42.9

Note: With the exception of columns (3) and (8), the data of the table are derived from daily observations for nine years, 1957-1965. Column (3) is based on the amount of water in storage on the last day of each month in this period and for this reason could understate the use of storage space. Similarly, column (8) is derived from monthly positive changes in storage. The numbers would probably be somewhat larger if they were taken from daily positive changes, for in the monthly data daily negative changes have been subtracted. Also it will be observed from column (2) that the average stream flow for the nine-year period was 87 percent of the seventy-year period 1895-1965. We have not worked through the precise distortions that result from use of this nine-year hydrologic record instead of seventy years or the forty-five years used by the engineers in 1942, but we can assume that if stream flow for the nine years had been 100 percent of the longer periods, somewhat more water would have been stored and used from storage. Nonetheless the several indicators in the table give a good view of the use of storage by the units. Finally, the total demand in column (5) does not include the water purchased by Fresno, Consolidated, Alta, and Last Chance in certain years from the Central Valley project. Almost all of this was diverted directly into their distribution systems and not stored.

cent or more of its storage space during three successive months in each of the flood years of 1958 and 1963 and during June 1957, when there was an unusually large runoff, but at no other times.

Consolidate district acquired much less storage space than had been recommended by the engineers but sufficient space, and probably more than enough, to serve its needs. The district stored on the average 31 percent of its entitlement and 35 percent of the surface water that it used. Its storage space was filled to 80 percent of capacity even less frequently than was Fresno's and could have held 53.7 percent of the district's nine-year average entitlement.

Peoples mutual company subscribed for more than twice the space recommended by the engineers and appears to have made use of a good part of it. In the nine-year period of analysis the company stored approximately 50 percent of its entitlement and of the surface water that it used. The space that it reserved was sufficient to hold as much as 62 percent of its long-term average annual entitlement and 73 percent of the average for the nine-year period, to be sure; but the company used 80 percent or more of its capacity during the months of May and June in seven of the nine years, all but the two driest ones.

The Lemoore and Last Chance companies, on the other hand, used considerably less storage than they had reserved. Lemoore acquired space for 86 percent of its long-term average annual entitlement or supply, which amounted to slightly more than 100 percent of the average supply for the nine years 1957–1965. Yet the company stored only 43 percent of its supply and used 80 percent or more of its capacity during three of the nine years. The figures for Last Chance are similar.

Although these data present a good picture of how the several units used reservoir storage, they tell little of the economic benefits derived from it. For this purpose we turn to our earlier simulations of farm operations at Fresno (table 5.5) and Lemoore (tables 5.7–5.9). We assume that if the dam had not been built the several units would have pumped from the ground the quantities of water that they drew from storage in these simulations. Thus the benefits of the project can be approximated by the pumping costs that were saved.

For hydrology we take 1962 to approximate average surface supply; 1957, 20 percent below average; and 1964 to represent 30 percent below average. The percentages of total demands that were drawn from storage in these years, from column (6) of table 6.5, are as follows:

	Fresno	Lemoore
1962 (av. surface water)	13.2	41.4
1957 (20% below av.)	24.8	57.5
1964 (30% below av.)	37.1	59.0

We multiply these percentages by the surface water used in the simulations—for Fresno, derived from the three columns headed "Surface water used" in table 5.5 and for Lemoore from the sum of the columns headed "Water use A" and "Water use B" in tables 5.7 to 5.9—to obtain the additional quantities of water in acre-feet that would have been pumped if there had been no reservoir:

	Fresno	Lemoore
Av. water supply	253	1,371
20% below av.	411	1,520
30% below av.	544	1,365

The costs of pumping near Fresno are assumed to be uniformly $5.04 per acre-foot. For Lemoore we assume that the mutual company sells its stored water for $6 per acre-foot.[28] As all B water under what we have called the basic procedure in Lemoore is purchased by farmers in the lower portion of the service area, where pumping costs are $15 per acre-foot, the increased cost of having to pump would be $9 per acre-foot. Reductions in the costs of crop production that result from using surface storage instead of pumping are shown in table 6.6. These data give a very general indication of the economic value of storage space in the reservoir, excluding its cost.

The cost of storage space for the Fresno district is 44 cents per acre-foot per year, that for Lemoore is not known because the company has not yet signed a contract with the United States. It may turn out to be somewhat higher than Fresno's, but we shall assume the Fresno cost here. No unit would need storage space equivalent to the quantity of stored water used since the space can be filled and emptied many times. It is reasonable to assume for our purposes that a unit will need as much space as the water that it draws from storage in the

Table 6.6 Reduction in costs of pumping due to Pine Flat Dam and reservoir.

Water supply	Dollars per acre-foot		Total dollars for 10 simulated farms		Percent of net farm income	
	Fresno	Lemoore	Fresno	Lemoore	Fresno	Lemoore
Average water supply	5.04	9.00	1,275	12,339	.014	.069
20% below average	5.04	9.00	2,071	13,680	.023	.079
30% below average	5.04	9.00	2,741	12,285	.030	.072

months of July through September following the spring runoff. From the hydrograph used in the simulation (see chapter 5 appendix) this would be 49 percent of the surface water supply for Fresno and 62 percent for Lemoore. We can multiply these percentages by the quantities of water drawn from storage in place of pumping, given above, and by its unit cost of 44 cents to derive an estimate of the cost of storage.

Water Supply	Cost of Storage	
	Fresno	Lemoore
Average	$ 55	$374
20% below average	89	415
30% below average	117	372

These figures can be subtracted from the dollars saved in pumping costs (table 6.6) for a rough estimate of the economic benefits derived from Pine Flat Dam.

In addition to the storage schedule, the Kings River units agreed to provisions for the equitable sharing of water losses due to spills from the reservoir for flood control that were in excess of the normal users' demands, evaporation from the reservoir, and waste from the river channel.

A Superdistrict

The first prerequisite for the construction of storage works on the Kings River was settlement of water rights; the second, allocation of storage; and the third, the creation of a superdistrict representing all participating units to finance and operate the project.

In 1923 the Kings River interests drafted and the California legislature passed an act authorizing such a superdistrict. The legislation was responsive specifically to the objectives and environment of the Kings River irrigators, and for this reason it differed in important respects from other California laws that authorized the formation of water storage districts. The principal objective was to protect the rights and the freedom of action of individual units while promoting construction of a storage project that could serve any or all of them. To this end the superdistrict was to be constituted of existing districts rather than of individual farmers and only areas organized in districts were to be included. The constituent units could be of several types—irrigation districts, reclamation districts, water districts—but they had to be public districts, a requirement that effectively excluded the mutual companies. The farmers of these companies, however, were prepared to organize districts for the purpose of participating in the reservoir. Soon after the law was passed irrigators who were stockholders in the Lemoore company established the Lemoore Irrigation District; those of the Last Chance company, the Lucerne district; and water users on the east side of Tulare Lake, the Lakeside district. But the several districts were not to take over from the mutual companies until the storage project and the superdistrict were set to go. In the meantime the districts were in suspense and in the end they were not activated, for reasons that we shall see.

The law provided that each district was to conduct its own election according to its own voting procedures on whether to participate in the superdistrict, and no unit that voted against participation would be included. Before the superdistrict could be established and before the constituent districts could be called on to decide whether or not to join, the storage capacity of the proposed reservoir and the water to be stored in it were to be apportioned and each district was to be assigned a definite cost. Thus, in voting on organization each unit would have before it the limit of its liability to the superdistrict and the benefits that would be derived from it. Agreement on diversion and storage schedules, in other words, had to precede the superdistrict. Finally, each unit was to issue its own bonds for its share of the costs and was not to be held jointly liable for the costs of any other unit.

By the time the prerequisites to formation of the superdistrict had been met, that is, by the early 1950s when an agreement had been reached on a storage schedule, the institutional situation had changed enough so that the units preferred to seek new legislative authority for a superdistrict rather than to proceed under the 1923 law.

In the meantime the Kings River units had organized without benefit of law to administer their stream diversion schedules, to conduct the engineering studies that were to precede a superdistrict, and to protect and defend their combined rights to the waters of Kings River. At the same time that the units executed the 1927 Water Right Indenture they signed an administrative agreement establishing the Kings River Water Association. The association was to employ a watermaster, who was to be a competent hydraulic engineer nominated by the state division of water rights but approved by the representatives to the association of at least two-thirds of the units. The watermaster was to "patrol the river" and turn into the canal of each unit the quantity of water to which it was entitled under the diversion schedules. He took over all duties performed previously by the state-appointed watermaster, and indeed Charles Kaupke, who had been watermaster since 1918, was reappointed by the association.

The watermaster also was to protect and defend the rights of association members by stopping any parties who were not signatories of the indenture from diverting river water allocated to the members. Similarly the association was to protect the rights of its members by prosecuting or defending actions before courts or regulatory commissions, provided representatives of two-thirds of the units concurred in each case.

The association was governed by a board of directors composed of one representative from each of the irrigation districts and canal companies that had signed the indenture and by an executive committee of five (later six) members chosen to give representation to geographical divisions of the full service area.

Each component unit was to pay a fixed percentage of the association's costs, determined by its relative entitlement to stream flow.

In 1949 the administrative agreement was amended to authorize the association to represent its members in negotiations with the federal government concerning a contract for repayment of costs of the Pine Flat Dam. However, no accord negotiated by the association was to bind a member until that member had ratified its provisions.

NEGOTIATING WITH THE UNITED STATES OF AMERICA

We have seen that the principal objectives of the local interests in developing their diversion and storage schedules were freedom of individual units to determine their own operating procedures, protection of each unit's water supply from invasion by other units, and protection of the combined water supplies of all units from invasion by outsiders. These same objectives dominated the negotiations between the local interests and the U.S. government. While the units were developing their storage schedule, they had begun bargaining with the government over terms for federal financing of the construction of Pine Flat Dam. Initially, federal officials, at least some of them, wanted to reserve new water to be conserved by the dam for the irrigation of new lands that would then be developed in conformity with objectives of federal reclamation policy. More persistently, they sought to integrate the design and operation of Pine Flat Dam with the government's large Central Valley project (CVP), again to advance the objectives of federal reclamation policy—among them to promote widespread ownership of land in family-sized farms; to subsidize the cost of developing irrigation by the production and sale of large blocs of hydroelectric power; and to develop large river basins, like the Central Valley, as integrated, multiple-purpose water resource systems. Finally, whether or not the Kings River was integrated with the Central Valley project, they sought to impose the objective relating to family farms on all irrigated lands in the Kings River service area.

Because these national objectives, when applied to the Kings River, could be achieved only by the imposition of considerable federal control, they were in direct conflict with the objectives of the Fresno and Hanford farmers.

The negotiations were lengthy.[29] In 1937 both the Corps of Engineers and the Bureau of Reclamation began investigations of the Kings River and Pine Flat Dam. In 1940 the two agencies submitted their separate reports to the president and Congress. In December 1944 the plans of the corps were authorized by law; but the president ordered that the repayment contracts be negotiated for the federal government not by the corps but by the Bureau of Reclamation. Periodic meetings between the bureau's agents in California and representatives of the Kings River units were held in 1946 and later, but it was not until January 1950 that the bureau presented its first draft of a contract to the Kings River water users, who rejected it. In the meantime the Corps of Engineers had begun to build the dam. Negotiations continued sporadically between 1950 and 1953, with the bureau presenting at least three additional drafts, none of which was acceptable to the farmers. By this time construction of Pine Flat Dam and reservoir had progressed to the point that water for irrigation could be stored. Lacking a permanent contract, the parties negotiated an interim agreement for the water year 1953–54, which, while reserving the rights and negotiating positions of all parties, provided that the Kings River Water Association should direct the storage and release of water for irrigation according to the units' diversion and storage schedules. The units were to pay $1.50 for each acre-foot of water stored and then released for their benefit. This interim contract was extended for 1954–55 and thereafter for each water year until 1963 when, finally, a more-or-less permanent contract was signed.

The lengthy negotiations were frustrating for both sides and frequently bitter. For example, when the bureau submitted its first draft contract to the water users in January 1950, the association responded that it completely ignored *all* the points they had submitted to the bureau in July 1946 as essential provisions of a contract acceptable to the water users. Further, the association complained that between 1946 and 1950:

the Bureau did not make the slightest effort to negotiate with us, [although] it did continually issue statements to the press to the effect that it was negotiating. It also issued many statements charging the water users with refusal to negotiate. None of these statements was true; they were, besides, seriously prejudicial to the interests of the water users, and they are quite inconsistent with the principles of honor and fair dealing supposedly adhered to by an agency of the Federal Government. . . . The water users demand that . . . negotiations be conducted on a basis of ordinary public decency rather than under continual pressure from the Bureau's propaganda machine, and that the statements given by the Bureau to the press respecting these negotiations contain at least a modicum of truth.

Two months later, by which time the bureau had submitted to the association a second draft contract, the district manager of the bureau in Fresno wrote the association that

while you have not shown us the courtesy of indicating your criticism of this contract by letter or *man-to-man* over the conference table, several articles in the press recently have quoted Kings River spokesmen as asserting that this contract was no more acceptable than the first. . . . Furthermore, as the first of these charges or statements from your group was published only a few days after the contract was submitted, it does not seem to me that your entire board of directors could possibly have had sufficient opportunity to review and concur with the criticism made of the contract in these published statements. . . . The fact, as evidenced by these published statements, that you apparently have chosen to disregard entirely our efforts to spell-out specific guarantees covering major objections long voiced by your group, makes me wonder how I can possibly continue to accept KRWA statements in the press and elsewhere that they are willing to continue negotiations in good faith.

The water users and bureau men in California subsequently learned to live with each other, but further frustration and delay were caused by differences between the negotiating positions of employees of the bureau in California and officials of the office of the secretary of interior in Washington. In April 1957, for example, the principal negotiator for the water users wrote to Secretary of Interior Frederick A. Seaton:

The Kings River Contract was developed over a long period of years. It was pounded out around the council table by sincere men from this District and from the Bureau of Reclamation. It was approved by the Bureau of Reclamation paragraph by paragraph as the long and very trying negotiations were carried on. It is beyond our understanding why it should sit in Washington for sixteen long months without approval, modification or question. . . . [This] has become a source of embarrassment, for the farmers that we represent, as their elected officers do not understand your delay or our inability to secure an execution of the contract or your reasons for not executing it in its present form. . . . This unrest is not just impatience. It is caused by what is becoming to us an intolerable situation.

This confusion between the U.S. government in Fresno and the U.S. government in Washington was caused in turn by differences in Washington between the commissioner of reclamation and the secretary of interior, by several changes in leadership of the department, and by the paralyzing indecision of two of its secretaries. It arose principally over how to apply to the Kings River service area the national policy of limiting the number of acres in any farm that can receive water from a government-financed reclamation project.

During this long period the principal negotiators for the water users, the board of directors of the Kings River Water Association, appear to have had the overwhelming support of farmers in the Kings River service area and very broad support among the voters at large.[30]

In 1948 Cecil White, a Democrat, was elected to the U.S. House of Representatives from the Fresno district, defeating Bertrand Gearhart, a Republican who had represented the district since 1935. In Washington White supported the position of the bureau rather than that of the association, introducing legislation that would have integrated Pine Flat into the Central Valley project and would have authorized the bureau to develop electric energy on the Kings River, to be tied to the CVP distribution network. This became a major issue in the next election. In June 1950, the Kings River Water Association, in a letter charging the bureau with stalling negotiations, said, "We are well aware that the Bureau of Reclamation is now waiting to see what the fate of Congressman Cecil F. White will be in next November's general election." From the bureau's point of view the fate was all bad; White lost his bid for a second term to A. Oakley Hunter. An official of the association said subsequently, "We knocked him flat. The Democrats outnumbered Republicans five to three in the district. And we took a Republican whom nobody in politics ever heard of before, a newcomer, and we swamped Cecil in the last election."[31]

The water users were explicit on their contract demands, most of which were included in two documents issued by the Kings River Water Association: a "statement" of June 1941 and a "resolution" of 1946. We shall examine many of these demands and the relevant contract provisions with a view to determining how successful the farmers were. The demands can be grouped in several categories relating to control over stream flow, the allocation of reservoir space, and reservoir operation; which federal laws and policies were to control construction and operation of the project; applicability of the acreage limitation; future development of hydroelectric power; and the negotiating process and payment terms. We discuss the first three categories.

Negotiating Demands Relating to Control over Stream Flow, the Allocation of Reservoir Space, and Reservoir Operation

All Kings River water should remain within the presently irrigated area. As early as 1941 the bureau stated that "it is not contemplated that any surplus water remains above the needs of the Kings River area"; and in 1946 they were prepared to guarantee that "all Kings River water capable of beneficial use on lands within the Kings River service area now irrigated or which can be irrigated from that stream will remain within the area." Although this meant that water that could be used beneficially within the Kings River watershed would not be transferred to another watershed, it did not define "presently irrigated area" in terms satisfactory to the water users and it left questions as to who would define "beneficial use." Indeed, the bureau, in a project-planning report three years later, said that since regulation by the dam would provide an annual average of 250,000 acre-feet more water than was being diverted in the area, the project would "permit increased development under Reclamation Law of the area through expansion of the irrigated area and by making possible a higher type crop use." [32]

The water users were dissatisfied with this formulation and it was modified several times in succeeding drafts until, by a combination of provisions incorporated in the 1963 contracts, the irrigators had won complete compliance on this point.

The U.S. government should recognize and accept the allocation of Kings River water made by the Water Right Indenture of 1927 as amended (that is, the monthly stream diversion schedules). The bureau agreed to this and the contracts so provide. It will be recalled that these schedules, as amended in 1949, covered all stream flows.

No right or interest in the use of Kings River Water should pass to the U.S. government as a result of the contract. The second draft of the contract in 1950 and succeeding drafts provided assurance that no district or person could be required to deliver or transfer any water or water rights to the government.

The government, however, claimed that it had acquired certain rights to water in Fresno slough at the extremity of the Kings River service area as a result of settlements made in connection with the Central Valley project. To the Kings River water users it was unacceptable that the federal government should own water rights in their service area, however remotely they might be related to the Pine Flat project, for fear that the government might use the rights to exert control over the users. They first demanded that the government renounce the claims, which the water users refused to recognize. When the government responded that it could not do this, the local units negotiated with the bureau to purchase the claims, which they did for $750,000, the cost being allocated among them. The government agreed to convey to the units, as tenants in common, "the Fresno slough claims, and any other claims which the United States may now have or assert to the use of water of Kings River, for irrigation purposes."

Federal control on the Kings River should be limited to jurisdiction over flood control operations at the dam. The bureau determinedly resisted this broad claim, but in the lengthy negotiations its counterclaims were gradually and progressively whittled down, so that in the end the water users had achieved almost all of what they wanted. A combination of provisions in the final contracts, some of which we shall discuss separately, limited federal control in effect to control over flood storage at the dam. However, the water users did not succeed in their desire to acquire physical possession and title to the project works, which remained in the name of the United States.

The Kings River water users should have the entire use of Pine Flat storage, subject only to flood control requirements. The bureau's initial response to this point was that the government was prepared to guarantee that "Kings River interests, present and future, will have the benefit of storage at Pine Flat to the full extent needed for irrigation service, subject only to flood control requirements." The water users were dissatisfied with the generality of this response, and as a result of further negotiations the contracts that they signed in 1963 provided first that "irrigation storage use shall be superior to the use of the project for any other purposes" and second that the contractors "are entitled to use all of the conservation space of the project for irrigation storage use."

Pine Flat reservoir should be operated for irrigation in accordance with instructions of a watermaster appointed by and acting for the irrigation interests. At an early stage of the negotiations the government agreed that water would be released for irrigation purposes "as the watermaster of the Kings River water users requests." This agreement was made progressively more binding in subsequent drafts of the contract. Thus in the second draft of 1950 the government guaranteed to deliver water "as nearly as may be engineeringly feasible" according to a schedule presented annually by the association, such schedule to be changed at any time the association saw fit. And the contracts signed in 1963 provided that "the association shall instruct the Corps of Engineers, from time to time, of the rate at which stored water shall be released for irrigation purposes and shall administer the diversion into storage, storage, regulation and release of such water for irrigation purposes."

The contracts to be negotiated should be repayment contracts for use of storage space in the reservoir. In typical reclamation projects the government agrees to provide water service to irrigation districts. This type of contract was unsatisfactory to the Kings River farmers because, among other things, it gave the government some degree of control over the distribution of water after it was released from the reservoir. A contract for storage space, on the other hand, would deny this control. The bureau's first draft contract used the term "water service." The water users objected. The bureau responded that they had not intended the term to convey the same meaning as in other reclamation contracts and they would not object to "storage space" if that term were adequately and properly defined. The subsequent draft of the contract, however, continued to use water service, although it did provide that the irrigation units would have a "perpetual right" to such service. The term water service was missing from the final contracts of 1963, which vested in each unit "ownership of a percentage share of the perpetual and exclusive irrigation storage use of the project" subject to the unit's repayment obligation. This formulation satisfied the users.

If any unit having rights to Kings River water elects not to participate in the project, it shall be entitled to have any water to which it has a right flow through the reservoir as natural flow without regulation, at no cost, and with no obligation to enter into a contract with the government. There was no disagreement with this demand, which was covered in the contracts by a definition that excluded such natural flows from the term "stored water" to which the contracts applied.

Negotiating Demands Relating to Which Federal Laws, Policies, and Agencies Were to Control Construction and Operation of the Project

The Corps of Engineers should build the project, operate it for flood control, and negotiate repayment contracts with the local interests—all under procedures and policies of flood control law. Immediately following release of the bureau and corps survey reports in 1940 the association appointed an engineering board of review consisting of the chief engineers of the several irrigation districts and canal companies to advise them on the plans proposed. The engineers found that the basic difference between the two plans was not the structures, but the basic water use philosophies of the two agencies. The bureau, as we have seen, viewed improvements on the Kings River as part of a comprehensive plan for the development of the Central Valley basin, with emphasis on water conservation and hydroelectric power. The corps, on the other hand, considered the development of the Kings River in terms of the needs of the local users for flood control and irrigation water.

Based on their study, the engineers recommended that the association approve and support the corps plan, which it did. Representatives of the association traveled to Washington in April 1940 and found overwhelming support in the relevant congressional committees for authorizing the project designed by the corps. The president, however, supported the bureau's plan, and the long struggle over authorization of Pine Flat Dam that followed became largely one between the president and the bureau on the one hand and Congress and the Kings River water users on the other.[33]

The water users won the first round. Even so strong a chief executive as Franklin D. Roosevelt was unable to have his way when the local interests were strongly of the opposite mind. On December 22, 1944, the president signed a flood control act, which, in section 10, authorized construction of Pine Flat Dam in accordance with the corps' plans.

But part of the irrigators' victory was soon snatched away from them by executive actions that in the opinion of the Kings River units violated the intent and language of the 1944 law. The president, then Harry S. Truman, ordered that the repayment contract with the water users be negotiated by the bureau under reclamation law rather than by the corps under flood control law.

Pine Flat project should be a separate entity and not in any way part of the Central Valley project. After they lost the competition for authority to build the dam, the bureau in 1946 responded that the Kings River project and the Central Valley project were "separate legal entities so far as existing authorizations and appropriations are concerned. However, they are located within the same geographical basin and therefore are physically inseparable from the standpoint of water resources development and operations within the basin. Of necessity the operation of Pine Flat reservoir must be coordinated with the operation of other reservoirs in the Central Valley." The Kings River service area would benefit from such coordination, the bureau claimed. This was anathema to the water users. Charles Kaupke, the river's watermaster, responded that "terms like 'integration' are merely gobbledygook for empire building."[34] In the end the bureau was forced to retreat and the government acquired no right to store CVP water in Pine Flat Dam.

Without forfeiting their demand concerning separateness of the two projects, the water users have been able to enjoy some of the advantages of the Central Valley development that the bureau had cited in its argument for integration. The bureau had available in the Friant-Kern division of the CVP a sizable quantity of water that had not been purchased by the districts with which it had negotiated long-term contracts—all of them outside the Kings River service area. To sell this water the bureau made short-term (five year) renewable contracts with any districts or companies that were prepared to take it. The water was called "surplus" or class 2 in the sense that it would be delivered only if available after the needs of the bureau's primary customers had been met; and, indeed, in the water-short years of 1959, 1960, and 1961 no surplus water was available. Surplus water was sold at $1.50 per acre-foot, whereas "firm" or class 1 water was sold to long-term contractors at $3.50.

In the middle and late 1950s several Kings River units signed up for surplus CVP water, among them the Fresno, Consolidated, and Alta irrigation districts and the Last Chance Water Ditch Company. The water was delivered into Kings

River channel *below* the dam and delivered from there to the purchasing units by the association's watermaster. Units buying water could either take it directly or if they had no immediate use for the water they could store it in Pine Flat reservoir by exchange (that is, if a unit had storage space available in the reservoir and if the watermaster had orders for water in excess of the amount of CVP water being purchased, which was almost always the case, a purchaser could request the watermaster to deliver the CVP water to those who had ordered reservoir water and to hold back an equal quantity of reservoir water, crediting it to the purchaser's account). Thereby a form of integration between the Central Valley and Kings River projects was achieved without any of the features of integration that the water users feared.

The two largest buyers of short-term water service from the Central Valley were the Consolidated Irrigation District and the Tulare Lake Basin Water Storage District. In 1963, a wet year, for example, more than 20 percent of the water that Consolidated diverted through its headgate had been purchased from the Central Valley project, all of it delivered directly. For Tulare the figure was 43 percent of its annual diversion, three-quarters of which was delivered directly, the remainder, stored in May and June and released when needed in September and October.

In 1963 when the Kings River contracts were signed those units that elected a forty-year contract (see discussion below) were eligible to conclude long-term contracts for additional water from the Central Valley project. Fresno Irrigation District negotiated a forty-year contract for both class 1 and class 2 water, primarily the latter, in 1965. Since then the district has drawn as much as 18 percent of its headgate diversion from this source.

Negotiating Demand Relating to Acreage Limitation

Acreage limitations should not apply to lands having water rights or rights to water service from the irrigation units. Negotiations over this demand were the most difficult and aggravating of all. To understand them it is necessary to develop more background information than on the other issues. The discussion that follows, however, is not concerned with acreage limitation as a national policy, on which there is an abundant literature.[35] As in the case of each of the other demands discussed, the focus here is on success of the local interests in gaining their goal.

The acreage limitations in reclamation law provide in essence that no water from a federal reclamation project may be delivered to more than 360 acres of land in one ownership (160 acres if the farmer is a bachelor and has no partners). If a landowner wants water for his excess lands, he must sign a recordable contract to sell them at a price that excludes any increase in value that may be due to the building of the project.

In the model federal reclamation project a water supply is developed by the construction of dams and delivered by the construction of canals to arid public land and to interspersed private land, making possible the conversion of these undeveloped lands into farms. Under these circumstances a national policy of acreage limitation governs the size of farm to be sold from the public domain and limits the speculative profit of private owners of undeveloped land who have made little or no capital investments themselves. The situation in most of the Kings River service area and of the service area of the larger Central Valley project was so completely different from that of the model project—the farms were developed; farmers had made large capital investments; individual water rights were vested; a federal project would not provide the basic water supply, but a supplemental one; there was no need to build distribution canals—that it was incredible to the farmers that the policy should apply to them. "The limitation seemed so obviously irrational as not to be real" [36]

The bureau's policy on whether and how to apply the limitation to developed areas appeared to support the views of the Kings River farmers, at least until late in 1943. With regard to the All-American canal in the Imperial Valley of California, the secretary of interior had held in 1933 that the limitation did not apply to lands "now cultivated and having a present water supply." In 1938 the bureau had supported legislation that exempted from the acreage limitation lands served by the Colorado-Big Thompson project because the project would furnish supplemental water to an area long under irrigation and with a developed agricultural economy.

In the early stages of planning for Pine Flat Dam, bureau representatives fairly well assured the irrigators that acreage limitations would not be applied to their lands. If this result could not be achieved by administrative interpretation, then the bureau would support legislation to exempt the project. Thus the bureau's supervising engineer in the region in a 1940 meeting with certain Kings River leaders expressed the opinion that the acreage provisions would not apply to the Pine Flat project if it were constructed by the bureau. The local leaders asked him to obtain confirmation on this point and four days later the engineer reported in a letter to them:

In reply to a telegram I forwarded to our Chief Engineer's office, following our conference, I have received the following reply:
"Procedure in application of 160 acre provision has not been uniform but present trend is to eliminate restriction on projects where water is predominantly supplemental supply or storage and servicing of water previously appropriated as distinguished from projects where entire water supply is furnished to new lands. In our opinion Kings River project would fall under first classification but if any question is raised special legislation could no doubt be secured to remove restriction as was done on Colorado Big Thompson project."

A year and a half later Secretary of Interior Harold Ickes wrote to the president of the Kings River Water Association, enclosing a memorandum of the commissioner of reclamation that Ickes had approved. The memorandum included the following: "[The acreage] limitation is probably unwise for all parts of the

Kings River area. For example, subdivisions and settlement of the Tulare Lake bed would be hazardous, at least until full flood control of all tributary rivers is completed and proven effective. Under these conditions, the law might well be amended to permit the Secretary to determine the proper limitations to be included in the contract to fit the particular circumstances of each portion of the area. If such legislation was presented in a satisfactory form the Department should interpose no objection." Similar promises were made by bureau representatives elsewhere in the Central Valley.

All of this changed in October 1943. Secretary of Interior Ickes sent a message to the annual meeting of the National Reclamation Association saying that the acreage limitation would be applied to "the Central Valley, and the other great land openings of the future." His message and an accompanying letter from President Roosevelt, which was written for the president in the Interior Department, were full of patriotism and the high moral purpose of the national objective of acreage limitation; but they contained no details on how the policy would be applied. "For the sake of our returning sailors and soldiers" this should be done, said the president. ". . . in the great new land openings that will come shortly in the Columbia Basin—in the Central Valley of California and elsewhere —it will now be possible for the Nation to provide opportunities for homes and for honest, valuable work for some of our returning servicemen and demobilized soldiers of industry, under conditions which any working farmer would be proud to bequeath to his own son coming back from battle abroad. They will be the heirs of the wise provisions which were enacted to keep our farmers from becoming victims of Nature and of their fellow men." Secretary Ickes added, "The pioneers among the men who believed in the reclamation of the West fought for conditions under which all of the reclamation farmers could be free and independent. The Reclamation Act is their monument. Its provisions against water and land monopoly and against speculation in improved lands not only protect the farmers today but will protect all of the returning soldiers."

These messages were the result of a review of reclamation policies that was conducted in the office of the secretary of interior in 1943, looking to a revival of the program that had been stopped by the exigencies of the Second World War. The bureau was to be reorganized, a new commissioner and new regional directors appointed, and the direction of government policy on enforcing the acreage limitation was to be reversed.

The bureau admitted that the standard acreage provisions of reclamation law were not well adapted to the California environment, for which special legislation was necessary "to provide for practicable and equitable application of those principles." A draft bill was prepared by the bureau's new command and introduced in Congress, but it turned out to be implausibly insensitive to the California situation. If adopted, the bill would have aggravated rather than mitigated disruption of the developed agricultural economy of the region. Instead of liberalizing the excess land provisions, the bill required more rigorous enforcement than the existing law.

The bill provided that all irrigated farmland served by the Central Valley project in excess of 160 acres in a single ownership (320 acres presumably for a farmer and wife holding community property) had to be disposed of by the owner at a price no greater than one determined by the secretary of interior, or the land would not receive project water. In appraising the land the secretary was to exclude any increment in value attributable to construction of the project. The owners of excess "preproject" land (that is, land irrigated prior to 1937 when the Central Valley project had been authorized by law) were to be given between four and nine years to conform. During this period their excess land could receive an interim water supply, but before the water would be delivered these landowners had to sign recordable contracts to dispose of all their excess land at the end of the extended period; and they would have to pay an annual interest penalty of 3 percent on the construction charges attributable to the water delivered to their excess land. The owners of excess land that had not been irrigated before 1937 were not to be given extra time in which to dispose of their property.

If a landowner were to sell his excess land for a price greater than that approved by the secretary, he would forfeit his right to water not only for the excess land but also for his base farm of 160 or 320 acres.

No water was to be delivered to an irrigation district or company until 75 percent of all owners of excess land within the district had executed recordable contracts to dispose of land. To illustrate, if 90 percent of a district was in holdings of less than 160 (320) acres, the district would be denied water unless three-quarters of the 10 percent comprising excess land was covered by recordable contracts. A decision by a small minority to refuse project water and rely on pumping rather than sell their excess land would thus prevent delivery of water to the entire district.

The U.S. government was to have first option to buy excess land at the appraised price, which the government had set in the first place. Having acquired land in this way, the bureau was authorized to subdivide it into farm units of any size, not exceeding 160 acres, and to sell or lease it to qualified applicants, veterans among them to have preference for twenty years. The U.S. government, in other words, would come to be deeply enwrapped in the region's agriculture and the bureau was given broad discretionary powers in the provisions dealing with management and disposition of privately owned land that had been acquired by the United States. Although the bill referred also to public land, implying that the United States was already involved in the area as landowner, there was no public land to speak of. It had all been disposed of many years before.

This draft bill, titled the Central Valley Soldier Settlement Act, was widely condemned and proved to be a source of acute embarrassment to bureau officials who were familiar with California irrigation. The most that even the new commissioner would say when confronted with sharp questions at a U.S. Senate hearing conducted in Sacramento was that he supported the general principles that lay behind the bill. It made no progress in the Congress.

The messages and the draft legislation spoke of the Central Valley, not of the Kings River specifically, but the Fresno and Hanford water users knew that the new policy was meant equally to apply to them and were doubly concerned that their fate was being tied closely to that of farmers served by the larger project. In this situation they adopted a number of strategies. They intensified their efforts to keep the Kings River project separate from the Central Valley project and to have their project built by the Corps of Engineers under flood control law rather than by the bureau under reclamation law. As a third stragegy, which would be useful in case the first two failed, the irrigation units lent their support to legislation sponsored by water users of the Central Valley project that would exempt the project from the acreage limitation. One such bill passed the House in 1944 but it failed in the Senate, due principally to strong opposition from President Roosevelt.

A final strategy of the water users was to include in the contracts a provision for lump-sum prepayments, on the assumption that any of them who elected to prepay in one lump sum their share of project costs, rather than follow the normal procedure of paying in forty annual interest-free installments, would be free of acreage limitations and other restrictions of reclamation law and policy. In other words, if irrigators were willing to put up the cash, they would be released from federal controls immediately rather than at the end of forty years. Prepayment as a means for avoiding the acreage limitation for other areas had been approved by the department, in a number of actions and opinions dating from 1914.

In 1951 the water users asked the bureau to include a provision for lump-sum payments in the contracts, and the bureau representatives agreed to negotiate on the matter. Because, however, application of the earlier rulings to the Kings River case was clouded by the recent reversal of departmental policy on enforcement of acreage limitation, the bureau's regional director requested guidance from the commissioner in Washington. The commissioner, in turn, wrote to Secretary Oscar Chapman in January 1952, recommending that his bureau follow the lump-sum payout policy but making it clear that the secretary could reverse the earlier departmental decisions if he wished to. The commissioner "solicited" from the secretary "direct departmental policy instruction," saying that in the meantime negotiations would continue under the assumption that lump-sum payments were acceptable.

At the same time the secretary was being implored by a small number of persons who had been involved in the reversal of departmental policy, notably Professor Paul Taylor of the University of California at Berkeley and James Patton, president of the National Farmers' Union, not to allow the Kings River farmers to buy their way out from under federal reclamation policies, thereby encouraging irrigators on other other projects to do the same.

Finally in late December 1952, immediately before Chapman was to leave office because the Republicans had won the presidential election, he instructed the commissioner and officials of the Bureau of Reclamation "to refuse to accept any lump-sum or accelerated payment of construction charges from any individual or organization which would . . . free such individual or the landowners in an area covered by a repayment contract with such organization from the acreage limitations of the reclamation laws. . . . In particular you are instructed not to negotiate a contract with the Kings River Water Association which would provide for or permit repayment of the construction charges allocable to irrigation in less than a pay-out period computed by the methods regularly used by the Bureau of Reclamation."

Chapman's directive was reversed by the new secretary of the interior, Douglas McKay, as Chapman must have known it would be. In November 1943 the department authorized the bureau to reopen negotiations with the Kings River interests on the basis that they would have an option to make lump-sum payments, in which case acreage limitations would be inoperative. Under this policy the assistant secretary wrote to the irrigators' representative, "it is considered permissible for *individuals or organizations* in a part of the Kings River service area to make lump-sum payments of their proportionate shares of the total cost and thus be relieved of the limitations of the excess land laws" [emphasis added].

Negotiations in California were resumed in earnest and two years later, in December 1955, both sides approved the terms of a contract that was forwarded to Washington for review and signature. But the review process went slowly and five months later, before it had been completed, Secretary McKay resigned, returning to Oregon to run for the U.S. Senate.

The new secretary, Frederick Seaton, being of a more liberal persuasion than McKay, undertook to review many of his predecessor's policies and commitments. In July 1957 he rejected the contract on the grounds that the prepayment option, while it could be used by irrigation districts and companies as units, should not be available to individual landowners. "The Department continues to recognize and support the basic concept of Reclamation Law that full and final payment of the obligation of a district to the Federal Government ends the applicability of the acreage limitations. But the overriding issue here is whether this contract which provides for the release of individuals . . . should be approved." Thus, although the department had authorized individual prepayments as a basis for the resumption of negotiations in 1953, Seaton now rejected them.

It was many months before negotiations resumed in California. The pain inflicted by Washington had to wear off first. Thus it was 1960 before the parties in California reached agreement on a contract that would allow lump-sum payments by districts and other units but not by individuals. Under its terms the enforcement of acreage limitations would be deferred for ten years; and if during this time a unit paid its full allocation, the limitation would be cancelled for all time.

On his last day in office, January 19, 1961—the Democrats had won the November election and Kennedy would be inaugurated on the twentieth—Seaton approved the form of the contract but refused to sign it. He said the contract was "in accord with the consistent views of all the chief legal advisors of the Department for nearly a half century" but that because of "conflicting views strongly held by some" he was referring the contract to the attorney general for opinion on the question of whether lump-sum payment by a district could relieve it of the acreage limitation.

Secretary Seaton knew, of course, that Attorney General William Rogers, to whom he referred the contract, would have no time to formulate an opinion since he, too, was leaving office the next day and that the whole matter would be reviewed *de novo* by officers of the new Democratic administration, which, indeed, happened. The new attorney general, Robert Kennedy, returned the contract to the Interior Department where an intensive review of the entire situation was made under the leadership of the department's new solicitor. In late December 1961 the solicitor issued his opinon that the proposed contract was invalid, that no form of prepayment could relieve landowners of the acreage limitation, regardless of past practice. Secretary Stewart Udall announced, accordingly, that he would not sign the contract.

For the Kings River interests at this point the sensible course of action was to remove the matter from the hands of a to-them duplicitous Executive. One alternative was to seek special legislation that would exempt the Kings River project from the acreage limitation provisions of reclamation law, but with a new Democratic administration that would oppose it, the prospects for success seemed dim. A second alternative was to seek general legislation that would amend the reclamation law to make it explicit that prepayment would relieve contractors from the acreage limitation. Kings River leaders discussed this with members of the appropriate congressional committees, but in the end they chose a third alternative—the courts. The solicitor's opinion would be challenged.

At the same time, the water users felt the need for new contractual arrangements with the government to ensure the continued delivery of water during what could be a lengthy litigation. The interim contract, which had been renewed annually since 1954, was becoming a clumsy and expensive instrument. The sum of annual payments for stored water, at $1.50 per acre-foot, was rapidly approaching one-third of the total repayment obligation of the units. Although most of this was to be credited toward the long-term repayment obligation once permanent contracts were signed, it was an uneasy situation for the irrigators. Thus while preparing for a court challenge the Kings River interests went back to the negotiating table with the bureau and concluded a series of contracts that were signed by all parties in December 1963. Under these, each irrigation unit could either sign a forty-year contract with free interest and

Table 6.7 Effect of acreage limitation on land ownership, 1969.

Irrigation district	Service Area		Excess land	
	Irrigated acres	No. of owners	acres	% of total
Fresno	236,340	35,983	16,738	7
Consolidated	150,755	5,807	3,109	2
Alta	102,833	3,245	7,951	8

Source: U. S. Bureau of Reclamation, Summary of Land Ownerships, Kings River, as of Dec. 31, 1969.

[a] Less than 1 percent.

acreage limitation or indicate its preferences for a lump-sum contract, which was drafted and approved in form. The latter would be tested in the courts and both parties agreed to be bound by final judgment in the case. During the litigation the federal government would continue to deliver water to those units that preferred the lump-sum contract at $1.50 per acre-foot of stored water in excess of a unit's daily entitlement. If the court judgment favored the government, so that prepayment would not relieve the landowners from the acreage limitation, then all units were again to be given the option of signing a forty-year contract with free interest. By 1969, the closing date for this study of the Kings River, the U.S. District Court in Fresno had not handed down an opinion in the suit. [In March 1972 the district court held in favor of the Kings River farmers that reclamation laws do not apply to water stored behind the Pine Flat Dam and that if they did apply, pay-out would relieve contractors of the acreage limitation. *U.S.* v. *Tulare Lake Canal Co.,* 340 F. Supp. 1185 (E.D. CA. 1972). The U.S. appealed to the circuit court in San Francisco in May 1972; the appeal was argued in December 1973; and the circuit court overruled the lower court in an opinion of April 1976. 535 F. 2nd. 1093 (9th CCA, 1976). The Canal Company appealed to the U.S. Supreme Court, which denied *certiori* in February 1977.]

As for the forty-year contract, its acreage provisions included an important loophole. If stored water delivered to a district or company reaches the strata underlying excess land and the landowner pumps this water from the underground strata for use on the excess land, the district is not deemed to have delivered water to this land, provided the water reached the strata as a reasonably unavoidable result of the surface delivery of stored water to nonexcess land. In effect, irrigation districts and companies cannot deliver canal water to excess land and they cannot run water through their canals for the specific purpose of replenishing the groundwater table underlying excess land. At the same time,

Owners of excess land		Excess acres receiving project water by direct delivery	Excess acres sold under recordable contracts or to be sold (1963–1969)	No. of new farms created (1963–1969)
no.	% of total			
87	a	0	0	0
24	a	0	0	0
36	1	0	0	0

irrigators are free to pump groundwater for their excess land, although pumped water will be significantly more costly to them than would be surface water if it were available.

Also, the acreage limitation provisions of the forty-year contract are to be considered null if in the future a court of competent jurisdiction rules that the laws of the United States did not prohibit delivery of water to excess land at the time the contract was signed. Thus the outcome of the suit relating to the lump-sum contract could possibly void the acreage limitation of the installment contract, as well as could other court cases.

Twenty-two of the twenty-eight units elected the lump-sum alternative, six, the forty-year installment contract. These six, however, included four of the five largest users of Pine Flat reservoir—Fresno, Consolidated, and Alta irrigation districts and Peoples Ditch Company—and the six together had contracted for 50 percent of the reservoir's storage space and served about 50 percent of the irrigated lands. Final results are not in on the irrigators' efforts to escape federal control over the size of their farms. But to date no unit has been forced to comply with the acreage limitation in return for water from Pine Flat Dam. Twenty-two units with 50 percent of the water supply have been delivering stored water directly to excess lands for sixteen years (1953 to 1969). Six units representing the other 50 percent have agreed voluntarily to contracts with the limitation, but this has had little or no effect on land ownership in their service areas. Table 6.7 shows the impact of the acreage limitation, as modified, on farm ownership in three irrigation districts. No excess land has been sold, no new farms created.

In the end, units with rights to 50 percent of the storage space, the largest of them dominated by small farms as they had been since the early days of colonization, signed contracts that contained the acreage limitation. Why, then, had they stood shoulder to shoulder with the other units, especially with the owners of gigantic farms in the Tulare Lake basin, during the lengthy period of frustrating negotiations with the United States? In somewhat different terms, 75 percent of the area irrigated by Kings River water was held by nonexcess landhold-ers having rights to divert more than 85 percent of the average annual natural flow of the river. The 260,000 acres of excess land were owned by approxi-mately 230 owners. Of this excess acreage 144,000 or 55 percent was in the Tulare Lake basin, where there were several corporations owning between 10,000 and 20,000 acres each—although only portions of farms in the lake bed could be cropped in years of high water. Why did the great preponderance of family farmers agree to suffer so long and so much in order to pull out of the fire the chestnuts of these big landlords—to enable them to have water for their large farms?

This question had perplexed supporters of the national policy. The principal reason they have given is that there was a conspiracy by the big landowners—the monopolists—to control the negotiations and to mislead the small farmers. The representatives of the Tulare Lake farms were aggressive and hard hitting, to be sure; but the argument that they duped the vast majority of farmers or that they gained control of the negotiating machinery by undemocratic and conspiratorial means does not withstand the evidence. Between 1940 and 1963, whenever association officers testified before congressional committees against the limita-tion, members of the boards of directors of the Fresno, Consolidated, or Alta districts testified separately to the same purpose or sent communications to the committees; and these men were elected by district farmers, very few of whom owned excess lands. Furthermore, the leaders of the association in the long fight against the limitation, Philip Gordon and William Boone, were elected board members of the Fresno and Alta districts respectively and represented these dis-tricts in the association. Even after they had signed contracts that included the acreage limitation, the Fresno, Consolidated, and Alta districts and two other units jointly filed with the U.S. District Court, in the big test case, an *amici curiae* brief supporting the lump-sum contract.

Another reason offered by the supporters of acreage limitation was that the voices of the farmers who would benefit from breaking up the large estates were not heard in the local negotiations. This is true, for the new farms would not be given to farmers in the area who already had family farms, but to prospective farmers from outside the area who might be returning veterans, men on skid row in San Francisco, or others. Support for them was more likely to come from statewide organizations or national interest groups in Washington than from Fresno and Hanford. Although this argument explains in part why there was so little support for national policy in the area, it does not explain why the up-stream family farmers supported the downstream corporation farms, when frequently in the past these interests had been at cross purposes.

Basically the supporters of national policy have asked the wrong question because of their single-minded preoccupation with acreage limitation. If the question is put properly it can be answered authoritatively. Why were the inter-ests of units representing family farms and units representing big landlords har-monious in negotiations with the United States? The answer is local control. The small and large farmers were equally concerned about maintaining the local control of their irrigation systems that they had achieved. Acreage limitation was simply one of many issues involving local control. The government's conduct of negotiations on acreage limitation intensified the irrigators' fear of the dangers of federal control. Indeed it is difficult to imagine how the bureau and department could have performed so as to induce greater fear. The big landlords had no need to manipulate the family farmers, assuming that they could have done so, which is highly unlikely.

Apart from the dominating influence of the objective of local control on the negotiations concerning acreage limitation, certain other factors may have helped to join the irrigators of small and large farms. The family farmers were doing well and had good reason to feel secure in their relative prosperity. Thus they were neither as envious nor as fearful of the large landowner as the reformers believed them to be.[37] Many of them no doubt wanted freedom themselves to buy additional land in the future.

Nor in all likelihood were the small farmers as fearful of speculation as the reformers believed them to be or thought they should be. After all, their successful family farms had been developed by land speculators. With a firmer water supply, additional flood protection, and as a result the possibility of more intensive irrigation agriculture, the immense lakeland estates would probably be broken up in the future in any event. The question was whether this should be done by elaborate government regulation and control or by the play of entrepreneurial forces.

Finally, disagreement in the ranks of the federal government about the objective of acreage limitation when it is applied to developed agricultural regions led the government to speak in conflicting tongues that exasperated all water users, small and large. The more idealistic and reform-minded federals believed the objective should be straightforwatd land redistribution—break up large estates into family farms before supplying them with water. For others the immediate objective was to disallow federal subsidies in developing irrigation water for excess lands—for example, the subsidy of free interest in the forty-year repayment contracts—on the basis that the general taxpayer should not be asked to subsidize the large landholder. This approach would have resulted in a two-price system for water—one for small and another for large irrigators—that would have encouraged the breakup of large estates, but only gradually and indirectly. The Kings River water users were prepared to accept the second interpretation in the form of a prepayment contract. Many bureau employees favored the second concept, as did Secretary McKay and Commissioner Straus. But Secretaries Ickes, Krug, and Udall appeared to favor land distribution, although none of them was consistent on the issue; and Secretaries Chapman and Seaton couldn't make up their minds.

In conclusion, there is no need to recapitulate the many elements of the water users' success in dealing with the United States—from an agreement that all "new" water would be given to existing units rather than to new areas to the definition that a unit has not supplied water to excess lands if landowners pump that water from the ground to their excess lands. But it is worthwhile pointing out how unified local interests can use or manipulate governmental institutions to achieve their purposes. And irrigation communities are likely to be unified because of the natural, hydrologic necessities of the common life of their members.

Their success was not without cost, however—nineteen years between authorization of the project in 1944 and the signing of conditional contracts in 1963 (plus an additional twelve to fifteen years before permanent contracts are likely to be signed for most of the units). More than nineteen years of negotiating expenses, frustration, and uncertainty. At the same time, the farmers did not have to wait this long for water.

When the president in 1944 delegated to the bureau the authority to negotiate the repayment contracts, the bureau said that the contracts would have to be signed before construction could begin. The water users demanded that construction begin at once; and they were supported by the Corps of Engineers, the construction agency, and the Congress, which appropriated money to begin the work. The president, supporting the bureau, impounded the funds, making their release subject to the satisfaction of two conditions: agreement on an allocation of costs between the purposes of irrigation, flood control, and hydroelectric power and "the making of the necessary repayment arrangements." He released the funds almost a year later, and construction began although neither condition had been met. The cost allocation was imprecise and the parties were no closer to signing a contract.

When the dam was finished and contracts remained unsigned, the bureau proposed that the reservoir be operated for flood control only, passing on to the irrigation units their daily preproject entitlements to stream flow but denying them any benefits of conservation storage until they had agreed to repayment contracts. Obviously the water users objected and the bureau backed down in signing the interim contracts. In a technical sense, it would have been simple for the bureau to carry out its preferred policy by opening and closing the dam outlets, allowing the conservation storage water to flow into waste channels and Tulare Lake unused; but it is doubtful that any bureau in the federal government in similar circumstances could have enforced such an inefficient and, to their constituents, dictatorial course of action as was proposed in this instance by the Bureau of Reclamation.

7 Irrigation Systems in Northeastern Colorado

While modern irrigation in Colorado was first introduced along the Rio Grande in the southern portion of the state by Spanish settlers coming up from what is now New Mexico, the most extensive irrigation development was located in the river valleys of the eastern plains by settlers from the humid areas of the East. Development in the plains began during the Colorado gold rush and expanded rapidly after the close of the Civil War. By early 1900 most of the land currently irrigated by surface sources in eastern Colorado was under a ditch.

Distribution of irrigation water in Colorado is dominated by the prior appropriation doctrine of water rights. First in time, first in right spells out the basic rule for distributing water. This rough and ready rule of the Old West still holds for the most part; junior appropriators are cut off from irrigating with stream flow in order to supply water to senior appropriators. In order to avoid disastrous water shortages that are bound to occur with strict application of prior appropriation, many adjustments have been developed to meet water deficiencies of junior appropriators. This chapter will discuss the various adaptations that irrigation organizations have made to adjust to the time priority rule in developing dependable water supplies.

The region of Colorado discussed in this chapter is the middle portion of the South Platte basin located immediately east of the Rocky Mountains in Boulder, Larimer, and Weld counties, extending along the South Platte River and its major tributaries, Boulder Creek and the Big Thompson and Cache La Poudre rivers (see figure 7.1). There are 3,200,000 acres in farms in this area, of which 830,000 are in cropland and 560,000 are irrigated.

The summer climate in northern Colorado is characterized by warm, sunny days with cool nights. Afternoon temperatures during July and August are frequently in the 90 degree F. range with extremely low humidity. Average annual precipitation for the year is around 15 inches (in), although occasionally the annual total falls to less than 7 in (see figure 7.2). Rainfall is sparse after early spring and much of the summer precipitation comes as afternoon thundershowers, which often do not deliver enough moisture to be useful for agriculture. The heavier thundershowers frequently contain hail, which makes them more damaging than beneficial. The frost-free season extends from May into September.

The hydrology of mountain streams used for irrigation follows a fairly uniform cycle. Figure 7.3 shows hydrographs of the Cache La Poudre River just above the major irrigation diversion works. Stream flow is typically low early in the spring; as temperatures rise, snow melt increases and stream flow increases rapidly until mid-June, when the crest occurs. Then stream flow declines rapidly throughout the remainder of the irrigation season. Occasionally a rain early in the season will cause the low-lying snowpack to melt rapidly, creating an early rise in stream flow, such as shown in the 1962 hydrograph. The June crest then will be lower than normal. Heavy rains accompanied by snow melt lead to flood

Combined offices of ditch company and reservoir company in Greeley. The building was constructed by the ditch company in 1890.

Water rental and sales board, North Poudre Irrigation Company, Wellington, with two retired irrigators. There was no activity in the rental market.

Anderson at outlet that feeds Larimer and Weld Reservoir Company water into canal system of Larimer and Weld Irrigation Company. Reservoir embankment and building for control works at top right.

Irrigated farmland, mostly alfalfa and small grains, in Cache La Poudre Valley.

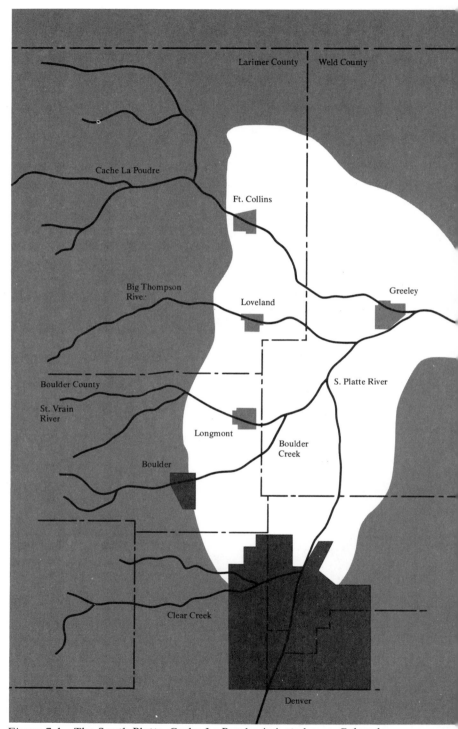

Figure 7.1   The South Platte–Cache La Poudre irrigated area, Colorado.

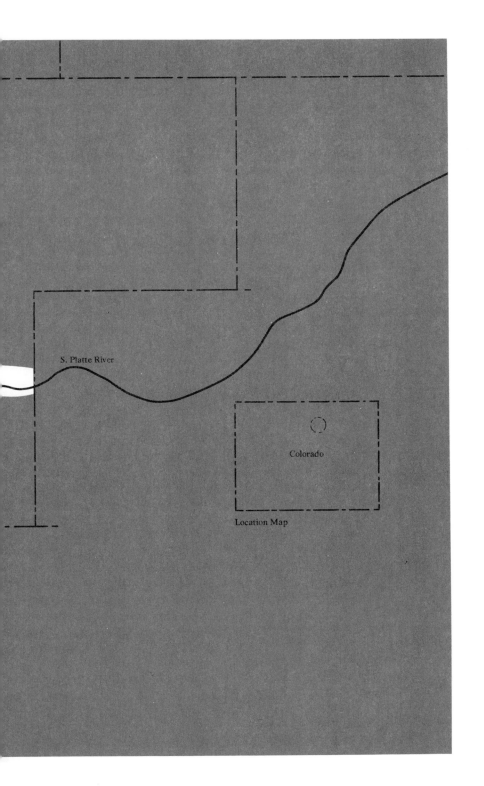

S. Platte River

Colorado

Location Map

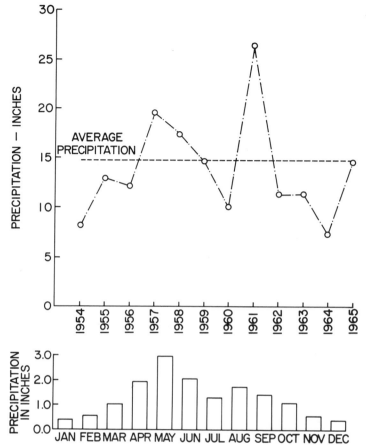

Figure 7.2 Yearly and monthly precipitation for Fort Collins, Colorado, 1954–1965.

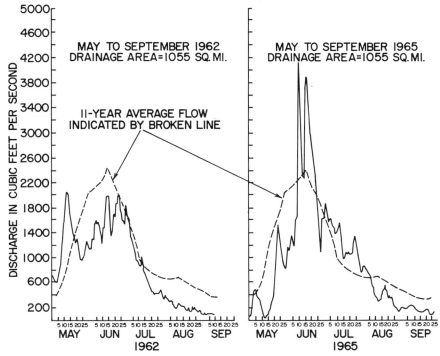

Figure 7.3   Two hydrographs for the Cache La Poudre River at Fort Collins, Colorado.

crests, as shown in the 1965 hydrograph. Rain in the mountains late in the summer will occasionally strengthen the stream flow. However, the river will seldom rise over 1200 cubic feet per second (cfs) after mid-July while water rights on the Cache La Poudre have been decreed in excess of 4000 cfs, making it apparent that much of the irrigated land must rely on a water supply other than direct diversion from summer flows of the river. These sources are primarily reservoirs built by the irrigation companies, wells on individual farms, and the Colorado-Big Thompson (C–BT) project, which diverts water from the west to the east side of the continental divide and stores it for supplemental irrigation use.

During the 1960s irrigated lands were used to grow the following crops: alfalfa, 27 percent of irrigated area; corn, 25 percent; sugar beets, 16 percent; small grains (barley, wheat, oats), 19 percent; dry beans, 9 percent; potatoes, 3 percent; and a small acreage of vegetables. Only 17.5 percent of the land in farms is irrigated. The remaining dry farmlands are used mostly for grazing, but there are some dryland crops, such as wheat and other small grains.

The number of irrigated farms decreased by 42 percent in the two decades of the 1950s and 1960s; as a result the remaining farms increased in size from an average of 95 irrigated acres per farm to 168 irrigated acres. Average farm size,

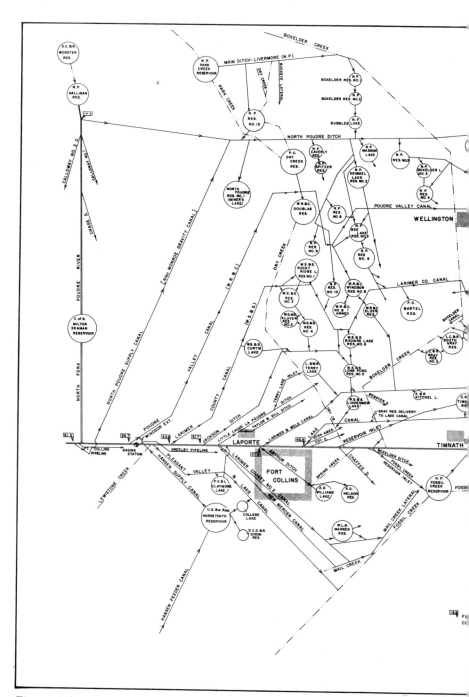

Figure 7.4 Schematic diagram of the irrigation canals and reservoirs in the Cache La Poudre Valley. (Source: Prepared for NCWCD by Morton W. Bittinger & Associates, Fort Collins, Colorado, 1967.)

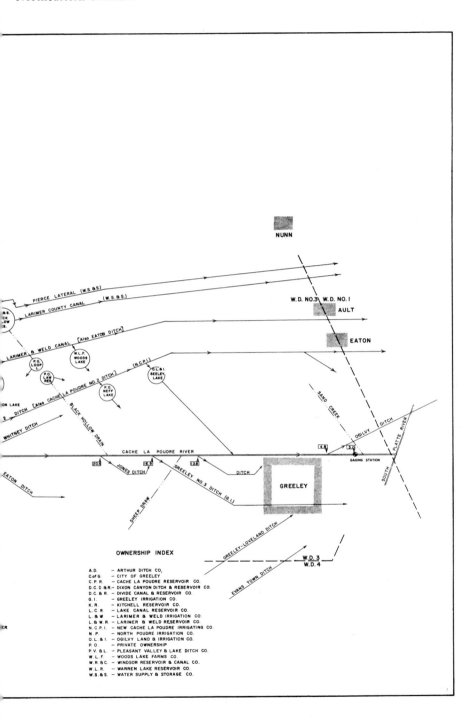

NUNN

PIERCE LATERAL (W.S.8S.)

LARIMER COUNTY CANAL   (W.S.8S.)

W.D. NO.3 W.D. NO. I

AULT

LARIMER & WELD CANAL [Also EATON DITCH]

EATON

W.L.F. WOODS LAKE

(N.C.P.I.)

O.L.8 I. SEELEY LAKE

P.O. LOOP

P.O. LAW RES.

LARIMER 8 CACHE LA POUDRE NO. 2 DITCH

P.O. NEFF LAKE

SAND CREEK

ON LAKE

2 DITCH [AINS

BLACK HOLLOW DRAIN

WHITNEY DITCH

OGILVY DITCH

SOUTH PLATTE RIVER

CACHE LA POUDRE RIVER

GAGING STATION

EATON DITCH

JONES DITCH

GREELEY NO. 3 DITCH (G.I.)

DITCH

GREELEY

SHEEP DRAW

GREELEY-LOVELAND DITCH

W.D. 3
W.D. 4

EVANS TOWN DITCH

OWNERSHIP INDEX

A.D.   — ARTHUR DITCH CO.
C.of G.   — CITY OF GREELEY
C.P R.   — CACHE LA POUDRE RESERVOIR CO.
D.C.D.&R.—   DIXON CANYON DITCH & RESERVOIR CO.
D.C. & R.   — DIVIDE CANAL & RESERVOIR CO.
G.I.   — GREELEY IRRIGATION CO.
K.R.   — KITCHELL RESERVOIR CO.
L.C.R   — LAKE CANAL RESERVOIR CO.
L.& W   — LARIMER & WELD IRRIGATION CO.
L.& W.R.   — LARIMER & WELD RESERVOIR CO.
N.C.P.I.   — NEW CACHE LA POUDRE IRRIGATING CO.
N.P.   — NORTH POUDRE IRRIGATION CO.
O.L.& I.   — OGILVY LAND & IRRIGATION CO.
P.O.   — PRIVATE OWNERSHIP
P.V.& L.   — PLEASANT VALLEY & LAKE DITCH CO.
W.L.F.   — WOODS LAKE FARMS CO.
W.R.& C.   — WINDSOR RESERVOIR & CANAL CO.
W.L.R.   — WARREN LAKE RESERVOIR CO.
W.S.& S.   — WATER SUPPLY & STORAGE CO.

including irrigated and dry lands, increased from 296 acres to 454 acres.[1] These average figures are somewhat misleading, however, for it is mainly on the fringes of the long irrigated valleys that irrigated farms have large acreages of nonirrigated lands.

Over one hundred irrigation organizations serve more than 500,000 acres of irrigated lands in the South Platte–Cache La Poudre area. To illustrate the density and complexity of the irrigation canal system, a schematic diagram of the canals and reservoirs in the valley is shown in figure 7.4. The other river valleys have similarly intertwined systems. Most of the irrigation systems are organized as mutual irrigation companies, although a few are irrigation districts. Three types of companies operate in the region: canal and reservoir companies supplying both direct flow and storage water to farmers under their ditches, canal or ditch companies supplying only direct flow water, and reservoir companies supplying only storage water. These several types frequently deliver water in the same canals and some canals carry water of more than one reservoir company.

In Colorado water is not necessarily attached to any particular parcel of land. Irrigation organizations typically hold the water rights and are the appropriators of water from the streams. This water can be used anywhere within the company's service area. Farmers gain the right to use water through ownership of capital stock in the irrigation company. Water deliveries to farmers are based on the number of shares of stock owned, and these have no necessary relationship to the amount of land irrigated. Figure 7.5 shows variations in company-supplied water, using as a sample farms sold between 1954 and 1960. As a consequence, a seasonal variation in water supply has quite different effects on water users within a system, depending upon their relative holdings of shares of canal and reservoir stock.

During their developmental periods some irrigation systems sold or granted a specific number of shares or rights to each quarter-section (160 acres) of irrigated land. Others sold shares for cash to finance the project or issued them to those who did construction work in proportion to work done by each.[2] Stock shares, however they were distributed initially, could be transferred freely, so that the distribution of stock within most companies has shifted over time.

Maintenance and operation expenses are usually met by levying annual assessments upon capital stock. Thus a farmer's operating costs and his water deliveries are both figured on the same basis—the shares of stock that he owns.

CHARACTERISTICS OF IRRIGATION ORGANIZATIONS

The service areas of individual canal and ditch companies in the South Platte–Cache La Poudre area range from 140 acres to over 50,000 acres. About 60 percent of the companies serve fewer than 5000 acres each and they cover only 13 percent of the total irrigated area. Somewhat more than one-third of the enterprises serve areas ranging from 5000 to 40,000 acres and cover about 63 percent

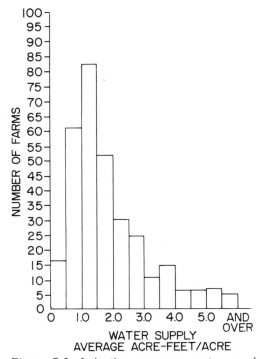

Figure 7.5 Irrigation company water supply on farms sold in South Platte-Cache La Poudre area, Colorado, 1954–1960. [Source: L. M. Hartman and R. L. Anderson, *Estimating Irrigation Water Values* (Tech. Bulletin 81, Colorado State University Agriculture Experiment Station, 1963) p. 13]

Table 7.1 Service areas of eighty-six canal and ditch companies, by size of enterprise, South Platte-Cache La Poudre, Colorado, 1960.

Size of enterprise (service area) (in acres)	Enterprises		Area served	
	Number	Percent	Acres	Percent
Under 500	8	9.3	2,735	0.4
500–999	6	7.0	4,973	0.7
1,000–2,999	26	30.2	45,347	6.3
3,000–4,999	12	14.0	45,096	6.3
5,000–9,999	10	11.6	68,630	9.5
10,000–19,999	15	17.4	206,922	28.7
20,000–39,999	6	7.0	177,325	24.6
40,000 and over	3	3.5	169,525	23.5
Total	86	100.0	720,553	100.0

Table 7.2 Shares of irrigation stock outstanding, 101 mutual canal and reservoir companies, South Platte–Cache La Poudre, Colorado, 1960.

Shares of stock	Number of companies
1–99	24
100–499	36
500–999	16
1,000–4,999	20
5,000 and up	5
Total	101

Table 7.3 Water allocation per share of stock, nineteen reservoir companies, South Platte–Cache La Poudre area, Colorado, 1960.

Acre-feet of water allocated per share	Reservoir companies	
	Number	Percentage
Under 5	8	42.1
5–9.9	5	26.3
10–19.9	5	26.3
Over 20	1	5.3
Total	19	100.0

of the area. The largest enterprises, with service areas over 40,000 acres, constitute 3.5 percent of the companies but serve 23.5 percent of the area (table 7.1).

Stock outstanding in 101 of the companies ranges from eight shares to over ten thousand shares (table 7.2). The number of shares of stock issued by any company depends on complex financial and operating requirements, including, of course, the size of the irrigated area that it services.

Water deliveries by mutual canal companies can be expressed in two ways: by the number of acre-feet delivered per share or by the average number of acre-feet delivered per acre under the system. Since shares of stock are generally not evenly distributed over the service area, the number of acre-feet delivered per share and the number of shares of stock owned by the farmer combine to determine the irrigation water supply available to a farm.

Each year companies allocate a quantity of water per share of stock. This can be as little as 0.4 acre-foot per share or as much as 400 to 600 acre-feet per share. Figure 7.6 indicates that in 1960 about 75 percent of the companies allocated under 60 acre-feet per share and 25 percent allocated over 60 acre-feet. Only 7.4 percent of the companies allocated over 200 acre-feet per share. The allocation of small quantities per share of stock has the advantage of allowing greater flexibility in ownership of shares and in the delivery of water.

On a per-acre-served basis, water deliveries by canal and ditch companies vary from an average of 0.4 foot (ft) to 6.6 ft per acre. About 38.5 percent of the organizations deliver up to 1.5 ft of water per acre, and they serve slightly over 62 percent of the land area (figure 7.7). Forty percent of the area receives from 1 to 1.5 ft per acre. Over 39 percent of the irrigation enterprises supply between 1.5 and 3 ft of water per acre and cover 30 percent of the irrigated land.

Reservoir companies supply part of the water to most of the larger irrigation systems in the area. Only farms that receive water from canal companies with the earliest water decrees on the stream can irrigate successfully through most seasons without resorting to reservoir water. For data on deliveries by reservoir companies see table 7.3.

In addition to the more than one hundred ditch and reservoir companies

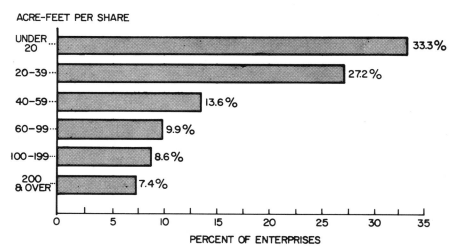

Figure 7.6   Acre-feet of water delivered per share of stock by canal and ditch companies in South Platte–Cache La Poudre area, Colorado, 1960. (Source: U.S. Department of Agriculture, *Irrigation Enterprises in Northeastern Colorado,* ERS117, 1963)

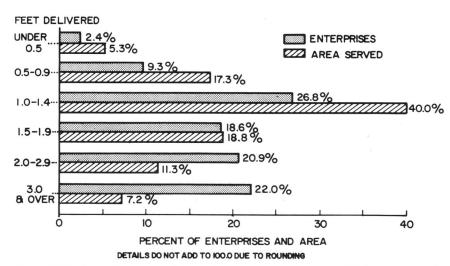

Figure 7.7   Irrigation water delivered per acre by canal and ditch companies in South Platte–Cache La Poudre area, Colorado, 1960. (Source: U.S. Department of Agriculture, *Irrigation Enterprises in Northeastern Colorado,* ERS117, 1963)

there are numerous lateral companies that carry water from the main canals of the larger system to farms. They regulate water delivery in the laterals and maintain the lateral canals but do not own any water rights. Farmers typically own lateral company stock in addition to canal company and reservoir company stock.

Canal, reservoir, and lateral companies in the South Platte–Cache La Poudre are mostly irrigator-owned cooperatives. As in the Kings River of California, the term mutual company is used in this area instead of cooperative. Management of the organizations is conducted by boards of directors elected normally for one-year terms at annual mid-winter meetings of stockholders. Voting is on the basis of one vote per share of stock. No single stockholder has enough stock to control the board of directors or even individual directorships, although it should be observed that large stockholders tend to be elected to a disproportionate share of the directorships in the companies examined. Attendance at the annual meeting ranges from good to sparse depending on the problems confronting the company. Voting on directors is fairly high, but most of the votes cast at the meeting are by proxy.

The directors choose a president and also hire a secretary, superintendent, and other personnel needed to operate the organization. Where there are separate canal and reservoir companies operating on a system, it is common practice for the same individuals to serve as director, secretary, and superintendent of two or more associated organizations. At the same time, separate stock, water, and operating accounts are maintained.

The directors establish operating rules and regulations and modify these as the occasion warrants; for the most part the rules are rarely changed. The major issues handled by the directors are financial, having to do with adjusting water assessments and arranging for funds to cover costs of system operation, maintenance, and improvement. Most directors serve for several consecutive terms. One canal company secretary observed that one of his directors inherited the post. Daily operations of the system are conducted by the superintendent, his gate keeper, and the ditch riders. Their principal function is to deliver the water orders as given to them by the secretary. The secretary is the nerve center of the operation, taking orders from farmers and passing these on to the superintendent and ditch riders. Water is normally run in the canals for several days each week when demand is sufficient, and a farmer can order water only at a constant rate for one or more twenty-four-hour periods.

HISTORY OF WATER RESOURCES DEVELOPMENT

Encountering extremely dry summers and frequent droughts, the first settlers found it necessary to bring stream water to the crops. As individuals or in small groups they built small ditches to irrigate narrow areas on the floodplains of the streams, some distance from the mountains.

The second stage of development was accomplished through community effort. Larger canals were built by groups, such as the Union Colony at Greeley and the Fort Collins Colony on the Cache La Poudre River, to convey water away from the river to uplands and to serve large areas that previously had been considered infertile and valueless. These enterprises required ingenuity, community spirit, and considerable fortitude to accomplish an extremely difficult task.[3]

The Union Colony was formed by a group of businessmen from New York under the auspices of Horace Greeley and was heavily publicized in his paper, the *Tribune*. Greeley had traveled through the area in 1859 and was of the opinion that the higher lands could be adapted to cultivation. The colonists, under the leadership of N. C. Meeker, arrived at the lower end of the Cache La Poudre Valley in the spring of 1870. They immediately began constructing a small canal to irrigate the town site, which was named Greeley in honor of their chief sponsor. Four major canals were envisioned by the colony, three to draw water from the Cache La Poudre and the fourth to draw from the Big Thompson River. The canal serving the town site was designated No. 3 canal, with two larger canals to be constructed upstream on the Poudre. The No. 2 canal, a short distance upstream on the north side of the river, was started in 1870 and, after some difficulties in delivering irrigation water during its initial irrigation season, was improved and extended to become the first large canal in Colorado. The colony never built the other two canals that it had proposed, and these were soon built by other groups.[4]

The Fort Collins Colony was patterned after the Union Colony and, building its canals upstream from the Greeley area, became an arch rival for the limited stream flow in the Cache La Poudre River. It was a conflict between the Union Colony and the later organized Fort Collins Colony that led to the adoption in the constitution of Colorado of the doctrine of prior appropriation, although several years earlier the territorial legislature and the Colorado Supreme Court had sanctioned the abandonment of the common law or riparian doctrine of water rights. When in 1874 the Fort Collins Colony began diverting water upstream, the Union Colony's water supply was greatly reduced and cut off entirely during the latter part of the summer. David Boyd has described the situation as follows:

As a consequence, in the latter part of the year 1874, a time of unusual scarcity, the river was dry at the head of the canal that supplied the town, and there was great danger that trees, small fruits, and lawns would be ruined. A meeting was called,about 40 delegates representing the various irrigation interests being present. A proposition was offered to appoint a disinterested person to divide the water according to the necessities of the users, disregarding, for the present, priority of appropriation—a doctrine which was generally recognized, but which under the conditions then existing was found impracticable.

The men upstream would not listen to compromise, relying upon their advantage of position, nor would most of the Greeley people accept it, as they were afraid that the concession would be used as a precedent, and that they would thereby lose an undoubted right. Debate ran high. Threats of appeal to arms were freely exchanged. But at last the men above agreed to let down some water to save the most valued trees and shrubs in the town. The promise was not kept, and violence would have been resorted to but for a timely heavy rain, which both raised the river and moistened the parched gardens and lawns of the town and the fields in the country. From that day forth the people of Union Colony set their hearts upon having a law enacted to enable them to have the water of the river distributed according to the vested rights of all concerned.[5]

The Fort Collins group became supporters of this idea when construction of another large canal was started upstream from their diversion point. These conflicts led to incorporation in the first state constitution (1876) of a provision that "the right to divert the unappropriated waters of any natural stream to beneficial use shall never be denied. Priority of appropriation shall give the better right as between those using water for the same purpose."[6] This constitutional article goes on to list preferences for uses when unappropriated water is limited, giving domestic use preference over agriculture, which in turn has preference over manufacturing.

A third stage of development in the 1870s and 1880s was carried on by out-of-state corporations, some British, which had sufficient capital to build still larger canal systems for reclaiming extensive areas of bench lands and to enlarge some of the existing canals. Most of these ventures failed financially within a few years with considerable loss to the investors. Practically all of the systems that failed at this stage of development were reorganized by farmer-water users as mutual irrigation companies. The North Poudre Irrigation Company near Fort Collins is an example.

During this period canal development came to exceed the capacity of the natural stream flow to provide adequate irrigation water. Failure of the stream led to a period (late 1880s to 1910) of extensive development of relatively small reservoirs to store winter and flood flows. Some of the reservoirs were incorporated under existing ditch companies and others were developed as separate mutual companies. When these reservoirs proved inadequate for local demands, a few companies developed ditches and reservoirs high in the mountains to bring water from adjacent watersheds.

The amounts of water added by reservoirs and transmountain diversions did not supply adequate irrigation water to the area, however, so after World War I the farmers began to drill irrigation wells where the underlying aquifers were sufficiently productive, and this activity has continued apace to this day. Maps of well locations in the area show 911 wells in 1940 and 2533 wells in 1967. Most wells are used to supplement existing water sources with no extensive areas in the South Platte-Cache La Poudre basin being supplied entirely by pump irrigation. Many of the wells are located on river bottom lands and draw from groundwater that is closely associated with river flow.

After the available local stream flow in the South Platte-Cache La Poudre irrigation area was fully developed and utilized, farmers remained chronically short of irrigation water, about half an acre-foot per acre on an areawide basis. Local stream flow and reservoir storage provided on the average about a foot and a half of irrigation water per acre, but it takes about 2 acre-feet of water on the average to irrigate crops in the area successfully.[7] The recurring shortages meant that either the area irrigated would have to be permanently reduced or additional supplies of water would have to be located and brought into the area.

The search for additional water supplies led to the grandiose idea of a transmountain diversion to bring surplus water from the western slope of the continental divide to the water-short eastern slope. It was apparent that none of the independent irrigation systems in the South Platte-Cache La Poudre area had sufficient financial or technical resources to develop such a project. As a result the local companies formed an organization to promote and develop the project. However, they soon found that even the combined resources of all of the companies were insufficient to develop a project of the magnitude and cost that would be necessary to provide adequate supplemental water to the area.

At this stage irrigators on the eastern slope began looking to the national government—to the Bureau of Reclamation, U.S. Department of the Interior—for aid. Reclamation had skill, experience, and access to the necessary resources to build such a project. The result of this effort led to passage by the Colorado legislature of the Colorado Water Conservancy Act in 1937, formation of the Northern Colorado Water Conservancy District (NCWCD), and the building by the reclamation bureau of the Colorado–Big Thompson transmountain water diversion project.[8]

The C-BT project, which began full operations for irrigation in 1957, consists of a series of collection reservoirs on Colorado River tributaries on the western slope of the continental divide. The water is transported under the 13,000-ft divide by means of a 13-mile (mi) tunnel. On the eastern side of the divide the water is carried through a series of power plants to the foot of the mountains where it is stored in two large reservoirs before being delivered to farmers and other water users. This water is used as supplemental irrigation water on irrigated lands and increasingly for municipal supply within the boundaries of the Northern Colorado Water Conservancy District.

The NCWCD is a governmental body whose boundaries overlie most of the irrigation enterprises within the area. The district's principal responsibility is distribution of C-BT water. The district issued 310,000 water allotments, each valued at 1 acre-foot, to farmers and others who needed additional water and were willing to assume a tax lien on their properties as security for payment of annual fees for water service. Water is available to these allotment holders on demand any time during the irrigation season. Allotments for supplemental irrigation water are held by over 2500 farmers and by five irrigation companies. In addition, nine municipalities, seventeen rural domestic water systems, and a number of subdivisions and corporations own units of C-BT water for domestic or other purposes. Water deliveries by the district range from 180,000 to 310,000 acre-feet annually and averaged 236,000 acre-feet during the first ten years of operation. When the water yield is less than 310,000 acre-feet, the value of each unit is reduced proportionately. Since water yield on the western slope has been less than estimated when the project was planned, it has been impossible for the C–BT system to deliver a full acre-foot per unit allotment each year.

In addition to distributing the annual supply of water the district controls the release of water from the eastern slope reservoirs and maintains and operates the canals that deliver C–BT water to area streams. The district collects water service fees and an *ad valorem* tax on all real property in the district in order to repay the district's share of the project's construction cost to the federal government.

The NCWCD is governed by a twelve-member board of directors appointed for two-year terms by the presiding judges of the district courts in the region, sitting *en banc*. Directors can be reappointed and usually serve several terms. Three directors are appointed from each of the three principal counties within the district and one director from each of three outlying counties. The directors choose one of their members as chairman of the board and president of the district and select a secretary of the board and of the district, who may or may not be a member of the board. The board also hires the staff to operate the system's works.

General policies for operating the system and rules and regulations for delivering water, transferring allotments, and adjusting water rates are determined by the board and are discussed at open meeting that can be attended by interested water users and taxpayers. Completion of the C–BT project brought to a close almost a century of irrigation water development in the area.

ADMINISTRATION OF WATER RIGHTS IN COLORADO

The first irrigation law was passed by the territorial legislature in 1861; it gave the owners of land along streams the right to appropriate water for irrigation. The Colorado constitution of 1876 adopted the principle of prior appropriation, as we have seen, largely in response to agreements that had been reached in the South Platte–Cache La Poudre. But it was the irrigation acts of 1879 and 1881 that provided for the procedure of adjudicating streams that is used in Colorado to this day. In the discussions that preceded these acts, most of the farmers of northeastern Colorado favored the determination of rights by a special tribunal composed of practical men who were personally familiar with the conditions and methods of irrigation. But the farmers yielded to the lawyers, who insisted that the final determination of titles to streams was a judicial function that should be performed by the courts. At the same time, the judges appoint referees, who are practical men with knowledge of the stream, to prepare the draft decrees.[9]

Under the acts of 1879 and 1881 anyone with a legitimate interest can petition the district court for the adjudication of rights on a stream. The court typically appoints a referee to ascertain, by examination of witnesses and documents, the relative priorities among the several ditches and the volume of water lawfully appropriated by each. The district court issues a decree based on the referee's findings specifying the name of each water right holder, the priority date, priority number, and stream flow allocation in cubic feet per second. The decree also fixes the point of diversion. If in the future any user wants to increase his diversion, believing that there remains unappropriated water in the stream, or to change his point of diversion, he must petition the court, which will approve the proposed change only if it will not, in the court's opinion, affect adversely any other decree holders on the stream.

The state engineer is charged with administering the distribution of the water in accordance with the decrees. For this purpose the state has been divided into seven water divisions composed of seventy-four water districts corresponding roughly to individual streams or segments of the larger streams. There is a water commissioner for each district and he controls the actual diversion of the stream flow to water right holders in order of priority. Water commissioners were originally nominated by county commissioners. Although they were appointed by the governor, they were essentially independent of the state engineer's control on their respective streams. Since then, these positions, as well as those of division engineer and state engineer, have been covered into state civil service, where competitive examinations are used to select incumbents for these positions; and there have been efforts to subject the commissioners to greater authority and control of the state engineer. However, local irrigation officials continue to influence who is chosen to be their water commissioner by insisting that the man have adequate knowledge of the stream he is to supervise, and they exercise considerable influence over his conduct as commissioner. Furthermore, water commissioners usually have served a number of years as deputy commissioners on the stream and are well acquainted with it and with the ditch companies.

The water commissioner measures the flow at specified locations along a stream and notifies water right holders when there is sufficient stream flow for them to exercise their entitlements to divert water for irrigation. The commissioner sees that no water right holder is deprived of water by another appropriator who holds a junior right. Should the water users be dissatisfied with the activities of a water commissioner, they can appeal to the division engineer to correct the situation. Likewise the water commissioner, if he has difficulties with decree holders, can call on the division engineer for help in resolving problems. In particularly difficult situations the state engineer may be called in, but this is rare.

During the irrigation season water in all streams is distributed to the holders of water right decrees, starting with the earliest and proceeding down the priority list until all stream flow is exhausted or all water rights on a stream are served. As a stream rises in the spring, as many water rights are allowed to divert as can be served by the stream flow. When the stream flow declines, the most junior rights diverting water at the time are cut out of the river. Each day during the irrigation season commissioners oversee the canal companies that draw water. Companies holding junior rights are forbidden to divert water whenever the demands of earlier right holders are unfulfilled. As many water rights as necessary are prohibited from diverting in order that full water delivery can be made to the earlier rights. As the stream rises and falls, larger or smaller numbers of rights are allowed to divert water. Table 7.4 shows the priority numbers of water right decrees and the dates and amounts of appropriation for several irrigation companies on the Cache La Poudre River. It will be noted that the companies have many decrees rather than a single water right. These decrees were filed as the canals were enlarged and extended during the early development period. As the river flow declines, some of the later rights of a company may be cut off while earlier rights are still effective. Depending on the relative size of each water right held by a particular company, much or little water might be available. As can be seen in table 7.4, when all priorities above No. 85 are cut off, the Larimer and Weld canal and the Larimer County canal lose their major appropriations while the other two canals are not affected.

There are frequent periods during the irrigation season when senior right holders do not draw water because their crops have been sufficiently irrigated. When this happens the commissioner informs junior right holders of the amounts that they can divert from the stream. When the senior rights call for water or the river flow declines, junior rights are again cut out of the stream. The water commissioners make weekly reports to the division engineer on the flow of water in their streams, the water rights entitled to water, and those actually drawing water.

In addition to his other duties the water commissioner keeps track of water brought into an area by transmountain diversions and sees that it is diverted to the proper owners. Foreign water is not subject to appropriation after it has been introduced into a stream; rather it is the personal property of the company that has brought it into the river. The diverters of foreign water are subject, of course, to the decrees in force on the streams of origin. Colorado–Big Thompson project water is handled in this manner also.

As noted earlier, water diversions per acre for the small systems are typically high compared to those for the large irrigation systems. There are two reasons for this. The small canals are typically early ones that claimed and received large amounts relative to land area because very little was known about the amount of water needed to irrigate successfully when they filed their claims and there were no regulations on the amount of water a canal builder could claim for a proposed irrigated area. They made large claims to be on the safe side. For fear of losing their rights by nonuse, most of these ditches divert as much water as possible, more than they need. Nonetheless, many small companies have not been able to draw their full decrees because their canals are not large enough to carry this quantity of water (see table 7.5). Also, these canals are typically short and a large part of the water they divert quickly returns to the stream through

Table 7.4 Water rights of selected canals of the Cache La Poudre Valley, water district 3, Colorado.

Canal	Priority no.	Priority date	Amount of appropriation (cfs)	cfs flow needed to fill appropriation[a]
Larimer County Canal	5	3-1-1862	10.77	38.35
	12	9-15-1864	13.89	237.90
	28	3-15-1868	4.66	401.25
	56	3-20-1873	4.00	1,398.31
	84	4-1-1878	7.23	2,172.12
	100	4-25-1881	463.00	3,360.36
Total			503.55	
Arthur Ditch Company	2	6-1-1861	0.72	4.22
	19	7-1-1866	2.16	335.13
	29	6-1-1868	2.16	403.41
	32	6-1-1869	1.67	481.25
	38	4-1-1871	31.67	693.51
	52	7-20-1872	18.33	1,183.18
	66	9-1-1873	52.28	1,682.77
Total			108.99	
Larimer and Weld Canal	10	6-1-1864	3.00	194.38
	21	4-1-1867	16.67	353.96
	45	9-20-1871	75.00	998.51
	73	1-15-1875	54.33	1,990.39
	88	9–1878	571.00	2,758.45
Total			720.00	
Greeley Canal No. 2	37	10-25-1870	110.00	661.84
	44	9-15-1871	170.00	923.51
	72	11-10-1874	184.00	1,936.04
	83	9-15-1877	121.00	2,164.89
Total			585.00	

[a]Gauging station is located upstream from canal intakes.

Table 7.5 Comparison of water rights and capacities of selected canals, Cache La Poudre River, Colorado, 1921.

Canal name and company	Total water rights (cfs)	Maximum water canal can carry (cfs)	Canal capacity as a percentage of water rights
B.H. Eaton Ditch [a]	42	23	55
Arthur Ditch [a]	109	51	47
Boyd and Freeman [a]	99	24	24
Coy Ditch [a]	32	18	56
Larimer County Canal (Water Supply and Storage Co.)	504	597	118
Larimer and Weld Irrigation Co.	720	754	105
Greeley Canal No. 2 (New Cache La Poudre Irrigating Co.)	585	558	95

Source: R. G. Hemphill, *Irrigatión in Northern Colorado,* U. S. Dept. of Agric. Bul. 1026, May 1922, p. 16.

[a] Ditches with early decrees.

wasteways or underground flow. Thus, although the diversions made by some of the small systems seem excessive, relatively little more irrigation water is actually consumed by them than by other systems.

Some of the companies with late water rights can irrigate their lands for only a short time each year with direct stream flow; and most of the companies are not able to draw enough water during the latter part of the season, when stream flow is typically low, to irrigate effectively. Companies, except those with the earliest rights, are largely dependent upon storage water from the reservoir companies or C–BT for water supply after mid-season.

Rights to store water in reservoirs are separate from rights to divert water for direct use. They are effective only during the nonirrigation season from late fall through early spring and during flood flows and are recorded in acre-feet rather than cubic feet per second. Storage rights are based on priority of appropriation and are fixed by court decrees in the same manner as direct flow rights. Irrigation systems with poor direct flow rights generally have compensated by acquiring storage rights. See especially the water supplies of the North Poudre Irrigation Company, Larimer and Weld Irrigation Company, and the New Cache La Poudre Irrigation Company as shown in table 7.6. The Water Supply and Storage Company relies on transmountain diversion from both the Colorado River and the North Platte drainage for a substantial part of its water supply.

The development of reservoirs has allowed the canal companies greater flexibility in the distribution of water supplies. For example, the earliest stream rights are frequently located on the lower reaches of a stream, with later rights

Table 7.6 Water supply used by selected irrigation companies (in acre-feet), Cache La Poudre Valley, Colorado, 1951–1970.

Company	Service area (in acres)	River	Reservoirs
North Poudre Irrigation Company	30,800	11,626	28,921
Arthur Ditch	2,400	5,573	90
Water Supply and Storage Company (Larimer County Canal)	46,800	19,236	3,858
Larimer and Weld Irrigation Company and affiliated reservoir companies (Larimer and Weld Canal)	55,725	31,284	44,845
New Cache La Poudre Irrigation Co. and affiliated reservoir company (Greeley No. 2 Canal)	36,900	42,756	26,278

Source: Robert G. Evans, *Hydrologic Budget of the Poudre Valley,* Appendix D. Environmental Resources Center, Colo. State Univ., Sept. 1971.

on the upper portion. Strict adherence to the list of water decrees would require that canals on the upper reaches allow direct stream flow to run down to the earlier decree holders, depriving the upper systems of water and causing large channel losses due to seepage and evaporation. To enhance their water supplies and to avoid this type of loss, the canal companies with late decrees have built reservoirs to store off-season and high flows, which they subsequently exchange for stream flow that is decreed to the lower ditches.

The major systems frequently developed reservoir sites that lay below the level of their main canals. This was done to save the expense of building a canal to fill the reservoir and to use a good reservoir site that was under the company's control. Placing a reservoir below the main canal meant that most of the company's service area could not receive water from the reservoir, while the service areas of downstream companies could do so, and this has led to exchanges of water between companies. It might appear more rational for the irrigation companies to trade or sell the reservoirs rather than exchange water, in which case each company would operate its entire water system. But differences in reservoir water rights and operating costs have so far precluded major realignments of the

Foreign water	Colorado–Big Thompson	Total surface	Wells	Total per acre
—	19,472	72,297		2.34
			17,783	.57
				2.91
—	754	6,417		2.67
			0	0
				2.67
25,860	21,615	70,569		1.50
			46,765	1.00
				2.50
—	29,603	105,732		1.89
			35,988	.64
				2.53
—	1,434	70,468		1.91
			29,420	.80
				2.72

ownership of ditches and reservoirs. As long as the exchange process works reasonably well, the companies seem to be satisfied with the security and cost of their water supplies.

As the conservancy district cancels all C–BT allotments not called for by water users before October 31, allotment holders or their companies try to draw their entitlements before that time. Companies that have not used all their C–BT water during the season run it into company reservoirs for use in the next season.

PLANNING CROPS ON THE BASIS OF SEASON WATER FORECASTS

Irrigation farmers in Colorado enjoy the advantage of advance knowledge of the water supply that they will have available to grow crops during the coming season. This preseason knowledge enables them to choose crops that can be brought to maturity with the greatest return from the anticipated supply. Since most of the usable water supply originates as mountain snowfall, it is possible for irrigation officials to estimate the amount and, to some extent, timing of runoff well in advance of its occurrence. Other factors taken into account are soil moisture conditions in the mountains and in the irrigated area, reservoir storage at the time of forecast, and the water rights held by the irrigation organization. With this information at hand, each company notifies water users of the water supply they can expect during the season. For instance, a ditch company may estimate 30 acre-feet of water per share, most of which would be available before mid-July. An associated reservoir company might declare 5 acre-feet of water per share of stock, available on demand. The conservancy district also announces early in the spring the quota that it intends to deliver. Farmers' C-BT allotments are based on units of 1 acre-foot and each year the district delivers a quota of this, for example 70 percent, depending on the quantity of water held in its reservoirs, expected runoff in the Colorado River drainage on the western side of the divide, and the status of local water supplies. Since the C-BT system supplies supplemental irrigation water, the officials try to vary deliveries to match the seasonal condition. If local reservoir storage is short or the snowpack is likely to yield a light runoff, the district will deliver as much water as it can. But if local supplies are good, the district will declare a low quota with the aim of holding water to meet possible shortages the following year.

After receiving information about water supply from the various sources, farmers can calculate total expected supply and the seasonal availability of the water. With water supply information at hand and knowing the general water requirements of crops, farmers can plan to plant the acreages of crops that will maximize income.

OPERATING PROCEDURES FOR DELIVERING WATER TO FARMS

The major irrigation systems have formal rules and regulations for distributing irrigation water to farmers within their service areas. Water often is delivered to a large number of users from a variety of sources under several different kinds of canal and reservoir company stock, making it necessary to keep close control of water in the system and precise records of deliveries to water users.

Most of the larger companies deliver water weekly during the season for periods of three to five days and, if demands are unusually high, for the full week. In order to coordinate deliveries on a canal, the ditch officials must know in advance how much water the farmers will want during a particular run. They need to know also the expected flow in the river in order to judge how much water will be available from that source, so that reservoir releases can be planned to supplement direct diversions should the river diversion be inadequate to meet the needs of the farmers. In cases where exchanges of reservoir water for river water are to be made, all companies involved in the exchange must know the timing and amounts of water to be released and the exchange must be cleared with the river commissioner.

Each Saturday the officials of the major irrigation systems and the water commissioner have a conference to determine water deliveries for the coming week based on anticipated river flow, reservoir releases, and C-BT releases. Any evening during the week irrigation officials and the river commissioner can confer by phone to make adjustments necessitated by changes in river flow.

So that company officers will have advance knowledge of the weekly water requirements of their constituent farmers, delivery rules specify typically that farmers desiring to irrigate on a run that begins on Monday must call the company office by noon on the previous Saturday to place their orders for water. And there may be other requirements. According to the rules of the Larimer and Weld Irrigation Company, for example, each water user who wants to receive water during the week must place an order for the first day of the run, along with any additional days that he may need. This is done so that the company can be sure that there is sufficient demand to start the canal and to spread out the delivery over a three-to five-day period. Later in the season when the company must rely on reservoir water and there are not enough orders to reach two hundred fifty rights of reservoir water (180 cfs), the secretary declares an insufficient demand and no water is run that week. Whenever undelivered orders fall below two hundred rights, the run is stopped until orders for more than two hundred fifty rights are again effective. This procedure saves labor and also saves water that would be lost from running a low head of water in the canal.

If a farmer does not want to irrigate early in the week, he can order the smallest quantity the company will deliver on the first day, have the water shut off for one or two days, and then have water delivered again late in the run for one, two, or more days. Alternatively, he may arrange with a neighbor to take his full first day's run, and the neighbor will repay him later in the week or in the next week.

Some companies place time quotas on the water deliveries. They specify, for instance, that 30 percent of each farmer's water allotment must be run by July 1, 50 percent by August 1, and 70 percent by September 1. All accounts are reduced to these levels at specified dates so that a water user who used less than 50 percent by August 1 would nonetheless have only 50 percent remaining after that date. Time quotas are placed on deliveries in order to use stream flow as it becomes available and to prevent water users from placing too heavy a demand on the ditch system late in the season. Quotas make better utilization of both direct and reservoir water when they are allocated on the same stock. They also prevent those who rent out water from profiteering on late season shortages.

The irrigation company's secretary keeps a record of water used by farmers. Each day water is run the quantities delivered are deducted from the farmers' accounts. Most farmers inquire frequently as to the status of their water accounts so they can plan future orders for water in relation to the needs of their crops.

The operating rules of the companies in the area do not specify any special procedures to be followed in the case of drought or of water-short years. The reason is that each farmer has a water allotment that reflects the seasonal status of water supply and he can use this as he wishes, subject only to regulations needed to operate the canal in hydraulic terms. In this way the use of water in times of shortage is left to the discretion of the water users.

As for the hydraulic rules, the canal companies have special procedures when water demands exceed canal capacities, which is likely to occur when water supply is plentiful and water use is high because of high temperatures and rapid growth of crops. For the Larimer and Weld company this rule is designed to give canal stockholders preferential treatment and to make those farmers who own mostly reservoir water wait until canal stockholders have been served. Postponement of water delivery normally lasts for only a few days, however; and if deliveries get very far behind demand, the company can run water for seven days a week rather than three or five. Irrigators who do not own canal stock may have to irrigate on weekends during periods of high demand. During periods of short water supply company officials may, for hydraulic reasons, schedule fewer runs, aggregating the smaller supplies in order to maintain an effective delivery.

The larger canals run by divisions. A run is started at a specified time when water deliveries are begun in the canal's upper division. Enough water is turned into the canal to serve the division and to begin filling the second division and so on until eventually all divisions are delivering water to farmers at the same time. At the end of a run the upper division is shut down first, then the second, on down to the last division, which may finish deliveries a day or so after the first division has shut down. There may be one or more large check dams in the canals of each division to maintain the water level necessary to make deliveries. Since the main canals on large systems are 25 to 30 ft wide and may be 10 ft deep, these check dams are major structures. The canal superintendent adjusts the major canal checks to assure that each division and major laterals receive adequate water each day during a run.

Most companies deliver the same quantity of water per share to all water users regardless of their location on the canal. A few of the companies, however, deliver different quantities to different divisions of the system. For example, a company may deliver 30 in per share on the upper division, 25 in per share on the middle division, and 20 in per share on the lower division. On the face of it, this policy may seem to penalize water users at the lower end of the system; however, in systems using this type of rule the lower division lands pick up runoff from the canals of companies that serve lands at a higher elevation. Frequently this runoff will allow as great or greater deliveries per share at the lower end of the canal as at the upper end.

Each division has a ditch rider who measures the water at the head of his division to determine that there is enough inflow to supply the farmers who have placed orders. He also opens and closes or adjusts headgates to make sure that the water is delivered to the proper users. On most systems the ditch riders lock all headgates to keep farmers from adjusting them during a run, thereby upsetting the ordered deliveries of water. Locking of headgates is practiced for two reasons: to keep any user from getting more water than that to which he is entitled and to keep farmers from closing headgates and flooding the canals lower down on the system.

The small companies—those with service areas less than 5000 acres, constituting about 60 percent of the companies in this area—generally deliver water to farmers on an informal basis. One man functioning as superintendent, record keeper, and ditch rider handles water distribution problems as he travels up and down the ditch setting headgates to deliver water to the farmers. He knows how many shares each water user has and how much water each is entitled to receive, and he can adjust deliveries to make the most effective use of water available in the canal. When demands get too great for the water available, the superintendent sets up specific delivery times for farmers or he institutes rotations or other means of rationing water to meet demands. Most farmers will be served within a few days of when they order water. The small systems allow for greater flexibility in water delivery, and generally these systems have more water per acre to deliver to farmers so that any delays in water delivery will not have serious consequences.

IRRIGATION WATER RENTAL

An unusual feature of the irrigation communities in the South Platte basin is their water rental markets, which have developed in response to continuing small imbalances of water supply among farmers.[10] These imbalances are always present, due to perpetual changes within the irrigated area, such as new crop patterns, development of irrigation wells, development of additional land for irrigation, and transfers of water stock for any of several reasons. To help adjust the resulting deficiencies and excesses of water supply without revamping the whole distribution system, water rentals have developed widely in the area.

Under the strict appropriation doctrine water is attached to the lands for which it was initially appropriated. If an appropriator uses water on lands located elsewhere or if he grants or sells it to others for this purpose or does not use the water, the basic water right can be lost. However, in the South Platte–Cache La Poudre water rights are typically owned by the canal companies and not by individuals. The significance of company ownership of water rights is that the water is attached to the company's service area as a whole and not to any specific farm. Thus water users own stock in the company rather than water rights, and water dividends or allotments are declared on the basis of stock ownership rather than land owned in the service area. These stocks—and the water allotments—are treated as personal property that can be bought, sold, or rented for the season or a shorter period at will, although such transactions are normally possible only within the confines of the service area of the company that owns the rights.

Stock and water allotments of the reservoir companies are also treated as the personal property of individual owners, who are free to sell or rent them. Reservoir water is more amenable to renting than direct flow because it is normally delivered on a demand basis and in many cases it can be delivered in more than one canal system.

The greatest flexibility in water use by means of renting is achieved with Colorado–Big Thompson water. C–BT allotments owned by farmers or other users can be transferred (rented) for the season to any water user within the NCWCD. The allotment holders make arrangements for transfers with other water users and then inform their ditch company officials of the amount of water to be transferred and to whom. If a rental agreement is made between C–BT allotment holders under different systems, a water transfer order is sent by the ditch company office to the conservancy district office so that the water accounts can be adjusted and the water turned to the renter's ditch on the day desired. Municipalities frequently rent their unused allotments of C–BT water to farmers throughout the area.

Water rental practices vary by irrigation companies according to their size, historical development, and other factors. Rental procedures for representative companies in the Cache La Poudre–South Platte area are presented in table 7.7. The small companies typically keep no record of transfers. Any exchange of water is arranged between individuals, with the ditch rider adjusting water deliveries.

The major irrigation companies, with several hundred water users, usually maintain a rental service in the company office. The stockholders who have excess water list it with the secretary and those needing additional water contact the secretary to obtain it.

In some companies the rental price is set by the board of directors and everyone who buys or sells water does so at the established price. Other companies post the asking price along with the quantity of water being offered. Users who need additional water take the lowest price posted or bargain with the sellers for lower prices. If the season turns hot and dry, the shares available for rent are quickly taken up and the price rises in the process. If it rises sufficiently, more shares will appear on the market because farmers with low-return uses for the water, such as pasture or hayland irrigation, will find it more profitable to rent water to farmers who wish to use it on high-value crops such as corn or sugar beets. All three types of water are involved in this process and the prices are generally the same.

Water rentals during the 1959 irrigation season are used to illustrate the operation of the water rental market. Records of five ditch and subsidiary reservoir companies and the Northern Colorado Water Conservancy District were examined to determine the nature of water rentals during the year. In the five companies 645 transfers of irrigation water took place, which shifted the use of 16,353 acre-feet of water. In the conservancy district 376 transfers were made totaling 73,967 acre-feet of water. Water rentals occurred from March through October, with the greatest activity occurring in July, August, and September (table 7.8).

Most rentals involve relatively small quantities of water, indicating the marginal values of this water. According to the 1959 study, about 88 percent of the transfers within the irrigation companies were for less than 50 acre-feet of water per transaction and almost 75 percent were for less than 30 acre-feet. Conservancy district records show that about 80 percent of the transfers were for less than 80 acre-feet and 72 percent, for less than 60 acre-feet. At the same time, conservancy district rentals tend to be larger than those involving company water. These larger transfers involve municipally-owned C–BT water that the

Table 7.7 Representative water rental procedures in the South Platte basin.

Company	Method of renting	Method of pricing	Kind of water rented
Larimer and Weld Ditches, Eaton, Colo.	Available water is listed in company office. Secretary allocates to those wanting additional water.	Board of Directors sets price for season.	Reservoir water rented by day's run.
New Cache La Poudre Irrigating Co., Greeley, Colo.	Available water is listed in company office. Buyers contact secretary for water.	Secretary and board of directors set price for season.	Reservoir water rented by day's run. Few shares of direct-flow water rented each season.
Water Supply and Storage Co., Ft. Collins, Colo.	Shares of seasonal water are rented from the office. Small daily transfers are traded between farmers. No office record is kept.	Farmers set the price of both seasonal and daily rentals.	Both direct-decree water and reservoir water are rented by the day and the share.
North Poudre Irrigation Co., Ft. Collins, Colo.	Water for rent is listed on a board in office. Farmers who need water contact one of those listing water.	Asking price quoted along with number of shares each individual has for rent.	Shares of stock including both direct-decree and reservoir water are rented.
Greeley and Loveland Irrigation Co., Greeley, Colo.	Lists water only if requested. Most rentals are between farmers.	Farmers set price.	Mostly Colorado–Big Thompson water is transferred.
Bijou Irrigation District and Riverside Irrigation Co., Ft. Morgan, Colo.	Farmers arrange for transfers. Transfer orders are recorded in office.	Farmers negotiate price when arranging transfer.	Mostly reservoir water by the share, but some direct-decree water when farmer has well.
Farmers Reservoir and Irrigation Co., Denver, Colo.	Most water rented between farmers. Must submit water transfer order to company office to effect transfer.	Farmers set price.	Rent stock or acre-feet. Most rentals are reservoir water.

Table 7.8 Water rentals by months for five irrigation companies and the Northern Colorado Water Conservancy District, 1959.

Month	Five irrigation companies			N. C. W. C. D.		
	Transactions		Amount of water	Transactions		Amount of water
	No.	%	Acre-feet	No.	%	Acre-feet
Mar.	3	0.5	69	2	0.5	228
Apr.	8	1.2	476	11	2.9	3,659
May	20	3.1	1,064	14	3.7	9,180
June	45	7.0	1,877	22	5.8	11,975
July	149	23.0	4,115	105	28.0	14,777
Aug.	220	34.1	4,391	131	34.9	22,745
Sept.	196	30.4	4,332	88	23.4	9,166
Oct.	4	.7	29	3	.8	2,237
Total	645	100.0	16,353	376	100.0	73,967

Table 7.9 Variable cost and rental price of water (in dollars per acre-foot), representative irrigation companies, 1959.

Company	Cost[a]	Rental price	
		Early season	Late season
North Poudre Irrigation Co.	2.50	2.50	4.20
New Cache La Poudre Irrigation Co.	2.50	3.25 all season	
Greeley and Loveland Irrigation Co.	2.87	3.00	5.00
Water Supply and Storage Co.	1.92	5.00	8.00
Farmers Reservoir and Irrigation Co.	4.04	4.60	6.00
Larimer and Weld Irrigation Co. and Windsor Reservoir Co.	1.03 3.72	2.70 all season	

[a] Annual stock assessment divided by water delivered per share.

cities do not yet need and rent to irrigation companies. The cities can return this water to their own uses whenever they desire, and in the interim period they are able to hold the rights to the water at no cost.

The rental rates for water generally reflect the yearly stock assessment plus an interest charge on the market value of the stock. Beyond this the rates will vary with the status of the area's water supply. When the area supply is short, the higher marginal value of the water will be reflected in higher prices. Rental prices for the 1959 season are shown in table 7.9. In dry years the rental price is reported to have risen to $30 per acre-foot, and both irrigation officials and farmers believe that this is too high a price to pay. Community pressure against one farmer's taking advantage of natural catastrophes to profit at the expense of others does not allow the market price to reach the level that farmers short of water would be willing to pay. As a result of this social restraint, the quantity of water available for transfer during some dry years is probably less than it would be otherwise.

The rental market, while dealing only in a relatively small amount of water, makes possible a better adjustment of the land-water relationship than is found in many western irrigated areas. Considerable losses in crop production can be avoided.

SIMULATION OF AN IRRIGATION SYSTEM IN THE
SOUTH PLATTE–CACHE LA POUDRE AREA

A series of simulation runs was made to illustrate irrigation water distribution in the South Platte–Cache La Poudre area. The system simulated represents a lateral canal of a large irrigation company. The lateral serves six farms that collectively irrigate 1000 acres. Under the basic rule for distributing water, designated shares in the simulation program, each farmer receives water in each irrigation period in proportion to the amount of stock owned in the irrigation company. Water deliveries may include a mix of stream flow and reservoir water, although some systems have supplementary reservoir water that is delivered to crops as needed, independently of the basic shares. Basic data relating to seasonal distribution of water supply, farm size, and crop patterns, yields, costs, and returns can be found in the appendix to this chapter.

Twelve simulation runs are summarized in table 7.10. The shares rule is used, except in run 4, where surplus water in any period is rented to farms that are short of supply, and runs 6 and 7, where the turn rule is used to illustrate the effect of a different method of distributing water.

Run 1 shows the production attainable on these farms with typical crop patterns and abundant irrigation water. All farms make a profit and net return to the system is $48,392. In run 2 the crop pattern has been selected to achieve the highest possible returns, given an abundant water supply and certain constraints on crop acreages planted on each farm. (The simulation program will select the optimum crop pattern when instructed to do so.) Net returns increase on all farms and system net return rises to $62,434. In runs 3 through 7 seasonal water

Table 7.10 Results of simulation of an irrigation system with various water supplies and distribution rules, South Platte–Cache La Poudre area.

Run	Water supply	Procedure	Gross return	Net return
1	Ample	Shares–typical crop pattern.	$148,174	$ 48,392
2	Ample	Shares–crop acreage planned with knowledge of ample water supply.	191,450	62,434
3	15% seasonal shortage	Shares–typical crop pattern.	113,014	13,426
4	Same	Shares–excess water rented to farmers who are short of supply.	120,921	21,139
5	Same	Shares–crop acreage planned with knowledge of water shortage.	146,759	47,734
6	Same	Turn–typical crop pattern.	76,914	−19,217
7	Same	Turn–typical crop pattern. Beans and potatoes as priority crops.	85,724	−10,543
8	Same, with additional storage water–2 acre-inches/acre.	Shares–typical crop pattern	132,414	32,632
9	Same, with additional storage water–4 acre-inches/acre.	Shares–typical crop pattern	139,815	40,033
10	23% shortage occurring late in season.	Shares–typical crop pattern.	80,485	−14,047
11	23% shortage occurring late in season.	Shares–water application schedules modified when shortage occurs.	105,905	11,769
12	37% shortage beginning mid-season	Shares–water application schedules modified when shortage occurs.	88,133	− 2,079

supply is 15 percent below the abundant supply used in runs 1 and 2. In run 3, with the typical crop pattern, system net return falls to $13,426. In run 4 excess water on any farm can be rented to farms that have shortages during the period. When better use is made of the water in this manner, all farms show a profit and net return to the system rises to $21,139. In run 5 the crop pattern is planned with knowledge that water supply will be 15 percent short over the season. In this case net returns to all farms rise substantially because most of the water is used on crops with higher value, the acreages planted to low-value crops having been reduced. The net return to the system rises to $47,734.

For comparison with another distribution rule, the turn procedure, typical of Valencia, Spain, is used in run 6, with the same water supply and crop patterns as run 3. The turn distribution rule, it will be recalled, requires that each farm receive all of the water that it needs during any period before the next farm is served. No farm will receive water again until all other farms have been fully watered. This rule, when it is applied rigorously to the typical crop pattern in northeastern Colorado, proves disastrous. The first two farms make a small net return, but all others lose heavily. The system net loss it $19, 217. Run 7 is similar to run 6 except that beans and potatoes are designated priority crops that must be watered on all farms before other crops can be irrigated. As a result beans and potatoes yield full production; however, all farms except number 1 lose money and system net return is $10,543 below production costs.

In runs 8 and 9 additional reservoir water is added to the seasonal water supply, which was 15 percent short. Run 8 adds storage water of 2 acre-inches per acre to each farm's supply to be used as needed, while in run 9, 4 acre-inches of storage water per acre are available. With 2 acre-inches, system net return rises to $32,632, and with 4 per acre, to $40,033.

Runs 10 to 12 show the results of unanticipated late- and mid-season water shortages. In run 10 the crop acreages remain fixed in the face of the water shortage and net returns drop to a system loss of $14,046. Run 11 simulates the situation in which irrigators replan the irrigation sequence on their farms when they encounter a late season shortage in an attempt to use the limited water in the most productive manner. As a result the net return of the system rises from -$14,046 to $11,679. Run 12 introduces a water shortage in mid-season. The longer duration of the shortage results in a system loss of $2,079 even with changes in crop irrigations. If certain crops could not have been abandoned, however, and irrigation schedules changed, losses would have been much greater.

OBJECTIVES OF THE OPERATING PROCEDURES
FOR DISTRIBUTING WATER

When irrigation company officials were asked to name the objectives of their organization in distributing water, they responded that their companies operate to supply irrigation water. Most of them speak of day-to-day operations. If the organizations are looked at carefully, however, several objectives emerge in the operating procedures of the systems and in the ways company policies are established and maintained, and the company officials might have responded in these terms had the question been put to them more explicitly.

Efficiency

Prior appropriation is an efficiency-oriented doctrine in the sense that the earlier appropriators of water presumably selected the farmland that could be irrigated most efficiently and subsequent settlers who progressively acquired lands that were more costly to irrigate were given lower priority in water use. At the same time, the doctrine has certain inflexible characteristics that militate against efficiency, so that giving first right in water use to the one who was first in time does not guarantee that water will be put to the highest value use. Efficiency in irrigation agriculture, as we have noted, requires a significant degree of flexibility in operating procedures. Irrigation companies in the South Platte-Cache La Poudre have succeeded to a remarkable degree in introducing flexible features into their dominantly appropriation-type environment, principally by procedures for transferring water among companies and farmers. These procedures are possible because the users have developed three water sources, each with certain distribution requirements that are unique and others that are common. The renting of shares, exchanges of direct flow and reservoir water, exchanges of reservoir water among companies, and flexibility in the ownership and use of C–BT water are examples. In the latter case, the possibilities for exchange are so general that the situation approximates a market for water.

But this very flexibility of use of CB–T allotments has in recent years proved to be a problem for irrigation farmers needing supplemental water. The highest value uses are no longer found in irrigation but in municipalities, industries, and domestic water systems where the operators are increasing their water supplies to meet expanding demands. These organizations are removing water from the irrigation community, thereby cutting down the total water available for crop production. The ability to transfer water to areas where it can create the greatest economic contribution is causing transfers not anticipated by irrigation organizations at the time the conservancy district was formed. An examination of changes in ownership of C-BT allotments from 1957 to 1969 shows that over twenty-six thousand units have been transferred out of irrigation use to municipalities, rural-domestic water systems, and industries (see table 7.11). Approximately 24 percent of the C–BT supply is now held by nonirrigation users. The twenty-six thousand units of C–BT water that were transferred out of irrigation have the potential of supplying supplemental water for 50,000 to 53,000 acres at about half an acre-foot per acre. The companies that have sustained an appreciable reduction in the amount of C–BT water available to their systems are beginning to develop water shortages that would not have occurred had the C–BT water not been transferred to nonirrigation uses.

Apart from water transfers, the mutual companies have promoted efficiency in certain of their operating procedures for distributing water to farms. For ex-

Table 7.11 Ownership of Colorado–Big Thompson water allotments (in acre-feet) indicating changes in ownerships in major use groups, 1957–1969.

	1957	1969	Change
Individual irrigation allotments (Class "D")	197,340	170,744	−26,596
Municipal (Class "B")	44,950	56,265	+11,315
Irrigation Districts (Class "C")	6,000	6,000	0
Corporation contracts (Section 25)			
a. Rural domestic water systems	—	13,442	+13,442
b. Irrigation companies	57,330	56,728	−602
c. Multi-purpose, subdivisions, and miscellaneous	4,380	6,821	+ 2,441
Total	310,000	310,000	0

ample, company rules typically specify the number of orders necessary before starting the canal and the number necessary to continue a run; thus runs of water are made only when there is sufficient demand to justify operating the canal, saving both water and labor. Headgates are locked and controlled by company officials in order to maintain efficient deliveries. No water user can take more or less water than ordered, so little water is lost down the canal and wasteways. The relative freedom of farmers to order the delivery of their annual entitlements when they want and need the water contributes to the efficiency of farm operations. They can order sufficient heads of water to irrigate their fields efficiently. Water loss through deep percolation and field runoff are reduced and labor is saved by not having to handle small streams of water.

Equality

While the appropriation doctrine is basically an efficient one, it is antagonistic to equality in the diversion of stream flow to water users. The first priorities are always served first regardless of the effect on later rightsholders or on the use of water. The Colorado irrigation companies have mitigated the harshest consequences of the doctrine by their storage of outseason and high-flow stream water, which they then deliver with less strict adherence to the appropriation priorities, and by their irrigators' purchase of C–BT water. To illustrate this, we have derived from table 7.6 the water per acre available to selected irrigation companies from their stream flow decrees and the total water available to them when reservoir, C–BT, and well water are added to stream flow.

Company	Water from River Decrees	Total Water Supply
	(Acre-feet/acre)	
North Poudre Irrigation Company	.40	2.91
Arthur Ditch	2.30	2.67
Water Supply and Storage Company (Larimer County Canal)	.41	2.50
Larimer and Weld Irrigation Company and affiliated reservoir companies	.56	2.53
New Cache La Poudre Irrigation Company and affiliated reservoir companies	1.16	2.71

Using median deviation as a measure of inequality in the availability of water to irrigation companies, this has been reduced from .52 to .12 by the acquisition of additional water supplies. The new supplies were not costless, of course, so that the reduction in inequality when measured in terms of the net income of the companies' service areas is somewhat less. But the objective of equality needs to be defined more carefully in the South Platte context. It has been to provide each company and all farmers with an adequate irrigation water supply. When C–BT water was allotted to individual farmers as supplemental water, each farmer could claim as much as was needed to bring his average surface supply to approximately 2 acre-feet per acre. As the above data indicate, the equality objective when measured in these terms has been fairly well realized.

Most irrigation companies are guided by the principle of equality in their operating procedures for the delivery of water. Many companies deliver the same amount of water to each share of stock, regardless of the water user's location on the canal. In these cases the company spreads the water loss in transmission (shrinkage) uniformly over the system. The canal superintendent knows generally the amount of water lost along the canal and releases sufficient water to ensure a full delivery to all water users. The companies that deliver varying quantities to shareholders on different sections of the canal deliver water uniformly in each section so that all users in a section are treated equally. As discussed earlier, unequal water releases per share to various sections of the main canal may not mean unequal deliveries to water users due to return water from irrigated lands above the canal.

Contrary to the principles practiced in farmers' cooperatives of one man, one vote, the mutual companies have adopted the corporate system of control where each share of stock has one vote. The extent to which this principle varies from individual equality and from equality based on size of farms depends on how water stock is distributed in the service area of a company. Table 7.12 shows the distribution of stock holdings by individuals in three of the larger companies in the Cache La Poudre area. The service areas of these companies range from 30,000 to 46,000 acres and they have issued from six hundred to ten thousand shares of stock. The number of stockholders ranges from 256 to 318. Since water deliveries are based on shares held, the number of shares owned is a fairly good indicator of the size of the stockholder's farm. Assuming about 2 acre-feet of water per irrigated acre, the stock holdings tend to group around the amount of stock needed to irrigate farms of 100, 160, and 320 acres. From examining the amount of stock held by various categories of stockholders it can be seen that no small group of large stockholders controls enough stock to be able to dictate company policy, although 13 percent of the stock of Company A is held by its two largest stockholders. Companies A and C report a small amount of stock held by two or three nonfarm organizations, including a city, a rural water district, and a manufacturing company. Costs of operation and maintenance are assessed uniformly on all shares.

Popular Participation and Control

Since most of the units are organized as farmer-owned mutual irrigation companies, operating procedures and related matters are controlled by the water users through their boards of directors. Most of the operating policies have been in effect for decades and appear to satisfy the water users, for there has been in recent years relatively little debate on them in elections or board meetings. The principal issues today relate to the handling of special supplemental water supplies such as municipally owned C–BT water that the companies sometimes rent for irrigation use or to financial management of the company. Questions relating to employees' wages and expenditures for system maintenance and improvement are likely to draw the attention of stockholders, insofar as these issues directly affect the cost of water.

We observed earlier that the larger landowners (and consequently stockholders) hold a relatively large number of the positions on the boards of directors. At the same time the small stockholders have sufficient voting power to control company policy (see table 7.12), and they are apparently not dissatisfied with management, for we could uncover no recent instances of stockholder reversal of policies established by the directors. One company secretary commented that some years it is difficult to get stockholders to attend the annual meeting in sufficient numbers to get the quorum necessary to conduct business.

Local control of irrigation company affairs has long been a jealously guarded objective of all irrigation companies. They submit to the authority of the state-appointed water commissioner because he is in a sense the cop on the beat who keeps the peace and maintains order by dividing the stream flow according to established decrees. At the same time, the irrigation companies have strenuously opposed any efforts by the state to readjudicate water rights in the light of abandonments and other changes; they have made their own adjustments to these factors.

Table 7.12 Distribution of stock holdings in three irrigation companies, Cache La Poudre Valley, 1971.

Company A			Company B		
Shares	No. of stock-holders	Shares owned	Shares	No. of stock-holders	Shares owned
Less than 1	11	5.5	Less than .5	8	2.08
1– 4.9	99	182.45	.5– .9	31	18.517
5– 9.9	30	200.0	1.0–1.49	46	46.75
10– 14.9	25	283.25	1.5–1.99	17	25.667
15– 19.9	15	242.5	2.0–2.49	63	126.75
20– 29.9	47	1,127.5	2.5–2.99	26	65.5
30– 39.9	20	684.5	3.0–3.9	38	120.25
40– 59.9	34	1,663.0	4.0–4.9	15	62.58
60– 79.9	13	883.05	5.0–5.9	6	30.75
80– 99.9	8	807.0	6.0–6.9	4	25.5
100–149.9	6	696.0	7.0–7.9	4	30.15
150–499.9	8	1,870.0	8.0–8.9	3	24.75
500 and over	2	1,355.25	9.0 and over	2	18.5
Total	318	10,000.00		263	597.744
Irrigated area (in acres)		30,000			46,000
Av. water delivered/share (in acre-feet)		7.2			82

When it became necessary to obtain outside aid to develop supplemental water supplies by means of the Colorado–Big Thompson system, the local irrigation organizations were careful at each stage of the negotiations and development of the project to retain control of local operations and to remain free from control by a federal agency. This was not an easy task, because entrance of the U.S. Bureau of Reclamation into the development of the project led to serious problems from the standpoint of local control. We shall discuss three of them, principally from the farmers' point of view: (1) How to minimize interference by the federal government in the allocation and distribution of the water to be provided by the project. (2) Specifically, how to avoid the provision of federal law that water from a project financed by the federal government cannot be delivered to any farms greater than 160 acres in size. (3) How to minimize the amount that the farmers need repay the federal government for its investment.

Minimizing Federal Role in Water Distribution   Development and execution of a

Company C		
Shares	No. of stock-holders	Shares owned
1– 3.9	11	24.0
4– 7.9	87	398.66
8–11.9	93	773.0
12–15.9	28	343.5
16–19.9	21	347.5
20–29.9	8	205.5
30–39.9	3	99.5
40–59.9	3	128.0
60 and over	2	180.0
	256	2,499.66
		36,000
		20

repayment contract with the United States presented special problems because the water was to be distributed to many different organizations operating under a variety of conditions. To make each organization a party to the contract would have been cumbersome and impractical. After considerable searching, the promoters of the project settled upon the idea of forming a superdistrict under state law that could contract with the United States for repayment, handle the distribution of water to the various allotment holders, and collect the yearly water fees and *ad valorem* taxes to be levied. Such a district would act as an intermediary organization between the irrigation companies and the federal agency. To establish it required an act of the Colorado legislature and, according to the provisions of this act, a favorable vote by the people within the proposed district. The legislative act, the popular vote, and a contract between the new district and the federal government were concluded in short order.

It was agreed at an early stage that C–BT water was to supplement existing irrigation supplies—no new lands were to be brought under irrigation as a result of the project. Because C-BT was to provide supplemental water, a strong case was made, and made successfully, for giving the users almost full discretion in operating procedures for delivering it. The conservancy district takes charge of the water once it is delivered to the eastern slope reservoirs and the district delivers it, in turn, to irrigators on their orders and through their respective ditch companies. Thus the district decides when water is to be released from the eastern slope reservoirs, basing its decision on consumers' demands; maintains the distribution works; makes the required payments to the federal government; and negotiates with the Bureau of Reclamation over any problems that arise. The bureau does not interfere with the individual companies; they are free to follow their traditional operating procedures.

Formation of the superdistrict and definition of the relations between it and the federal government did not solve all problems. Many of the irrigation companies remained reluctant to commit themselves to repayment contracts, fearing that to do so might lead to interference in their operating procedures and financial management by the conservancy district or by the Bureau of Reclamation. Also, stockholders with adequate water supplies did not want to enter into agreements that would increase their water costs or restrict their freedom in system operation. As a result most of the companies declined to apply as companies for water from the C-BT project. They preferred that those of their farmer members who needed supplemental water obtain individual allotments from the Colorado-Big Thompson and that this water be delivered to the farms by means of the companies' canal systems. The North Poudre, Platte Valley, and Bijou Irrigation companies and the Riverside Irrigation District were exceptions; they were prepared to contract for C-BT water.

A plan was devised to grant individual allotments to farmers. The conservancy district would accept applications for supplemental water and grant allotments sufficient to meet a farmer's normal water needs. In return the farmer would accept a yearly tax lien on his farm of $1.50 for each unit of C-BT water allotted, which was necessary in order to meet repayment security requirements of the federal reclamation law. The irrigation companies would agree to carry the C-BT water to water users under their systems for a company-determined running charge.

The arrangement to carry C-BT water in company canals has generally worked to the benefit of both the individual allotment holders and the irrigation companies. When C-BT water became available, however, a small number of irrigation companies made unreasonable demands on C-BT allotment holders for running charges and canal shrinkage during delivery. In these cases the farmers sold off their allotments to farmers under other systems or to other users such as municipalities or rural-domestic water organizations. Thus the companies that made larger than normal charges for carrying C-BT water reduced the total water that would otherwise have been available to their systems.

Allotments are attached to specific tracts of land or to specific organizations. Should an allotment holder desire to transfer all or part of his allotment to someone else, he can do so by obtaining the consent of the board of directors of the district, who will order the allotment, along with the tax lien, transferred to another user. It is interesting to note that today officials of the companies that originally rejected C-BT water by imposing high charges for delivering it complain regularly when C-BT water allotments are transferred out of their systems. Apart from the transfer of his basic allotment, an allotment holder can transfer (rent) his annual water supply to other users simply by informing the conservancy district of the transaction, as described earlier. The district makes the appropriate debits and credits in its water accounts and informs the affected irrigation companies of additions to or subtractions from the C-BT supplies they are to deliver. Thus while water allotments are formally attached to specific lands, allotments can be moved easily within the district boundaries and uses can be changed from irrigation to municipal or industrial supplies.

The NCWCD reserves the right to deliver less than a full supply (that is, less than 1 acre-foot) for each allotment unit, and this has been the source of some friction among allotment holders, the companies, and the district. However, all shortages are shared equally among users in the sense that each allotment unit is reduced by the same amount; and the district's operating procedures are designed to provide as much supplemental water as possible during the drier years and to store water when local supplies are more plentiful.

As a consequence of the way in which the repayment contract was negotiated and of the resulting relationships among individual farmers, their ditch companies, the conservancy district, and the Bureau of Reclamation, the NCWCD performs as a buffer between the local farmers and irrigation companies on the one hand and the national government on the other. The irrigation enterprises have maintained their operational independence intact while arranging to have supplemental water delivered to their service areas by a large, federally financed project.

Avoiding the 160-Acre Law   The acreage limitation provision of federal reclamation laws was unacceptable to most promoters of the project. Many farms in the area were larger than 160 acres and few of these farmers were prepared to sell their "excess" lands in order to obtain a supplemental water supply. They could make other, more economic adjustments to the existing water supply. The U.S. statute of 1937 that appropriated money for the Colorado-Big Thompson project provided that construction could not begin until a repayment contract had been signed by the conservancy district, but the farmers in the district were unwilling to sign such a contract until they were assured that the 160-acre provision would not apply to them.

They argued that the excess lands provision of the federal law was intended to apply to the opening of new lands to reclamation and settlement, not to providing supplemental water to existing farms, and they sold their view to the federal government. A bill to exempt the Colorado-Big Thompson project from this provision of reclamation law was introduced in Congress early in 1938 with the support of the reclamation bureau and it passed almost immediately and without opposition. The farmers of northeastern Colorado had won their point: "That the excess-land provisions of Federal reclamation laws shall not be applicable to lands which now have an irrigation water supply from sources other than a Federal reclamation project and which will receive a supplemental supply from the Colorado–Big Thompson project" (Act of 16 June 1938, Public Law 665, 75th Congress).

Minimizing Farmers' Payments for the Project   Reflecting the generally depressed conditions of agriculture during the great economic depression of the 1930s and the effects of a drought that gripped the Great Plains at the same time, the promoters of the Colorado–Big Thompson project were intent on making the repayment obligation to farmer-irrigators as light as possible. Water charges had to be kept low to encourage the hard-pressed farmers to obligate themselves to long-term contracts for repayment of the project. Early promotional material describing repayment provisions for the project stated that water would be delivered for not less than $1.50 per acre-foot in order to pay for the project. As time went on the documents came to read that water charges would not exceed $1.50 per acre-foot. What started out to be a floor under water charges became a ceiling over them, and to this day the charge to most users is $1.50 per acre-foot. However, the district has been able to raise the assessments where the original water contracts have been altered. This includes water transferred from farmers to municipalities and to rural-domestic districts as well as that transferred among irrigators. Domestic users currently pay an assessment of $5.00 per acre-foot while irrigators pay around $2 for transferred water allotments. Water allocated to the Boulder division, which was added after the district was formed, costs $2.

The C–BT promoters realized that a project of this magnitude would generate considerable benefits for the general business community through increased prosperity created from an expanded and stabilized irrigated agriculture. To capture some of these indirect benefits, the NCWCD was authorized to levy an *ad valorem* tax on all real and personal property within the district. The millage rate was set at .5 mill during the construction period and 1 mill after the project began operation. Should the NCWCD default on payment to the United States, however, the millage rate can be raised an additional .5 mill to help meet the obligation. This provision for taxing all real and personal property within the area of an irrigation project as a means for paying project costs was an innovation. Prior to this time the practice had been to assess all costs to the direct beneficiaries of project development.

The *ad valorem* tax has proved to be the most lucrative source of revenue to the district. In 1937 assessed valuation of the district stood a $120 million, it was $280 million in 1958, and by 1970 the assessed valuation of the district had reached $656 million and was rising at a rate of about $35 million per year. In 1970 water revenues amounted to $608,000 while *ad valorem* tax revenue brought in $645,000.

The original repayment contract between the district and the Bureau of Reclamation, which was signed on July 5, 1938, provided that the district pay for
the irrigation facilities, which were then estimated to cost half the total cost of
the multiple-purpose C–BT project, or half of $44 million. The district's obliga-
tion was limited, however, to $25 million should costs rise beyond the estimates.
The district was taking no chances of being stuck with large cost overruns.

Payments to the United States were to be made over a forty-year period
without interest beginning the year following completion of the project. Annual
payments were to be $475,000 the first twenty years, $500,000 the third ten
years, and $1,100,000 the final ten years. Water and tax revenues anticipated at
the time the contract was drawn would not have been sufficient to meet the payments of the final ten years. But since the last payments were due fifty to sixty
years after signing the contract, well beyond the lifetime of most of those who
drew it up, the negotiators decided to let someone else worry about completing
the contract.[11] Increased revenues from higher rates on transferred water and
from the rapid rise in property valuations is creating surpluses that now appear
to be sufficient to meet the ballooned payments at the end of the contract. The
fact that the irrigators are not charged for interest during this long repayment
period means that they are obligated to pay less than half of the full costs of the
irrigation features of the project, even assuming a low rate of interest.

Work on the project was in its early stages when the United States became involved in World War II, which greatly slowed construction. Along with the war
came a rapid rise in the prices of labor and material. The district became concerned over the resulting increase in construction costs and was at first unwilling
to accept the wage contracts agreed to by the Bureau of Reclamation. The
bureau prevailed upon the district to accept its settlements, however, so that
construction could move forward. The district decided as a "matter of policy"
that it would not interfere in matters of construction costs and would instead
rely on the $25 million limit to its obligation as provided in the repayment con-
tract.[12]

While construction was near a standstill during the war, the bureau elaborated
some features of the project, notably increasing the power-generating facilities.
The combined effects of higher construction costs and expanded facilities increased the total costs of the project from the original estimate of $44 million to
approximately $160 million. Faced with these costs, the bureau sought, with the
strong backing of the Appropriations Committee of the House of Representatives and others in Congress, to renegotiate the repayment contract; but the
board of directors of the conservancy district steadfastly refused to sit down to
any such negotiations. It would not forfeit its $25 million payment limit. Why
should it?

At the same time the reclamation law, under which the bureau was building
this project, required that costs of irrigation and power facilities be repaid by the
beneficiaries, the former without interest, the latter with interest. To satisfy the
law, constrained as they were by the 1938 contract with the irrigation benefi-

ciaries, the bureau has resorted to several strategems. Power revenues are to be used to pay off all costs of power facilities and all costs of irrigation features in excess of the $25 million that the irrigators will pay. To obtain so much money from power revenues, reclamation has increased the power-generating capacity of the project and has extended the repayment period beyond forty years. Although the irrigators will pay off their $25 million obligation in the forty-year period provided in their contract, it will take approximately forty-seven years to pay off the remaining irrigation costs with power revenues. Not only have the local interests maintained their operational independence when confronted with a heavy investment of federal funds, they have arranged to pay back only a small part of the funds.

Conflict Control

During the formative years of irrigation development in Colorado, conflicts arose between established irrigation companies and developing companies. The Union Colony-Fort Collins Colony conflict was typical of disputes on most streams. In some of these the parties resorted to armed conflict and destruction of irrigation works, but most disputes were carried to the courts. The territorial courts first struggled with the problems, and later district courts of the newly established state government resolved the disputes. But these courts were not without legislative guidance, for Colorado was the first state to enact a code of laws for the administration of streams.

Removal of the water rights struggle from the hands of the irrigators to the courts and the state engineer had a salutary effect on conflict resolution. Farmers have been willing to make their cases before the district court and its referee and to abide by the court's decrees. And the nature of these decrees—the absolute priorities among all parties that they fix—has removed most causes for future conflict. Also, the transfer of water conflicts to the courts has had a dampening effect on the enthusiasm of disputants for the reason that legal services are expensive and sometimes the only notable winners are the attorneys on either side.

Conflicts have arisen, however, when appropriators have wanted to sell all or parts of their water rights to other users at different locations on a stream. These transfers have been fought consistently on the basis that a change of the point of diversion will upset the rights and established regimen of downstream appropriators. By now enough court decisions have been handed down to establish the futility of trying to change a point of diversion and rarely is such a change attempted today.

Within irrigation companies internal disputes are handled by the ditch superintendent, the company secretary, or ultimately the board of directors if the employees are not able to satisfy the complaining water users. Grievances over internal company operations are carried to the courts infrequently. By establishing uniform delivery of water per share and having hired employees make all water deliveries through set and locked headgates, most companies have eliminated disputes over misappropriation of water. Water users tend to view water supply as they do a bank account. The size of the water account and the increments that will be added to it are established in the spring, and farmers draw on it as needed within the limitations imposed by the system. When a farmer's share is exhausted, he knows that he will get no more unless he can secure additional water from another stockholder. This approach tends to eliminate the type of charges of unfair treatment that one finds in systems that use other forms of water rationing, where there is more need for administrative discretion.

APPENDIX: SIMULATION OF IRRIGATED FARMS IN THE SOUTH PLATTE-CACHE LA POUDRE AREA, COLORADO

Simulation Procedures

In northeastern Colorado each farmer receives water in proportion to the number of shares of stock owned in the canal and reservoir companies that serve his farm. The procedure of the irrigation simulation program, described in our USDA Technical Bulletin 1431, that reproduces this distribution rule is called Shares *plus* Demand.

When the irrigation system runs stream flow, each farm receives its proportionate share of the available water. Farms are served in order and the amount of water allocated to each is based on the shares owned by the farmer. There are two options available in the program for handling unused water. In the first the farm either uses its share of water or it is wasted away. In the second water not used by a farm in any run remains in the system and is used by the next farm that has an inadequate supply during that run. This simulates the rental procedure.

As the stream flow proves to be inadequate, reservoir (demand) water, if any is called upon to meet the deficiencies during the period. When the irrigation system runs reservoir water, each farm receives the quantity of water it has ordered. After each irrigation period the amount of reservoir water used by each farm is deducted from the farm's reservoir account.

When it is apparent that the reservoir water will be inadequate to supplement deficiencies in stream flow for the entire season, the Replan subroutine can be activated to obtain the highest possible return given the limited stream and reservoir supplies.

Program Designations   With reference to table 9, Principal Distribution Rules, of Technical Bulletin 1431, the following programs are used to simulate the Colorado operating procedures.

Water Supply	Description of Procedures	Procedure Code
Surface water	Shares	1
Surface water plus reservoir (demand) water		
Ordinary supplies	Shares + Demand	3
Drought	Shares + Demand	3 (Replan)

Basic Data

Irrigation water is distributed over fourteen two-week periods during the growing season. Table A7.1 shows the mean percentage of water supply available by periods for the season and the percentage of water available during a year with mid-season drought. A frequency distribution of farm sizes in the area and farm sizes selected for the simulation, along with the assigned shares of the water supply, is given in table A7.2. The typical crop pattern in the area is shown in table A7.3. Table A7.4 shows the initial acreages of crops assumed on the simulated farms. These acreages closely approximate the area crop patterns for the sizes of farms that were selected. Yield, cost, and return data used in the Colorado simulation are given in table A7.5. Crop prices and costs are those current in Colorado in the late 1960s.

Table A7.1 Irrigation water supply used in South Platte–Cache La Poudre simulation (percentage of seasonal water).

Irrigation Period	1	2	3	4	5	6	7	8	9	10	11	12	13	14
Average seasonal supply	6	7	7	9	10	12	10	8	7	6	5	4	4	4
Mid-season shortage	6	7	7	9	10	12	5	5	4	4	4	4	4	4

Table A7.2 Farm sizes and water shares owned by farms.

Farm size, irrigated acres	Farms		Simulation Farms		
	Number	%	Farm No.	Acres	% of system water owned
1– 49	796	18	1	80	8
50– 99	1,054	23	2	140	16
100–199	1,761	40	3	140	12
200–499	746	17	4	220	22
500+	89	2	5	260	26
			6	160	16
Total	4,446	100		1,000	100

Table A7.3 Average acreages of crops grown on farms in the area, 1959.

Crop	% of crop acres
Sugar beets	16
Corn	26
Beans	11
Alfalfa	26
Wheat	18
Potatoes	3
Total	100

Table A7.4 Initial crop pattern on simulation farms (in acres planted).

Crop	Farm						Total
	1	2	3	4	5	6	
Sugar beets	12.80	22.40	22.40	35.20	41.60	25.60	160.00
Corn	20.80	36.40	36.40	57.20	67.60	41.60	260.00
Dry beans	8.80	15.40	15.40	24.20	28.60	17.60	110.00
Alfalfa	20.80	36.40	36.40	57.20	67.20	41.60	259.60
Small grain	14.40	25.20	25.20	39.20	46.80	28.80	179.60
Potatoes	2.40	4.20	4.20	6.60	7.80	4.80	30.00

Table A7.5 Crop yields, costs, and returns per acre for crops used in the simulation of the South Platte–Cache La Poudre area, Colorado.

Crop	Yield	Preharvest cost[a]	Harvest cost[a]	Gross return	Full production, net return
Sugar beets	21.6 ton	$127.00	$ 56.16	$286.20	$103.40
Corn	57.0 cwt	65.17	30.15	142.50	47.18
Dry beans	16.15 cwt	53.00	35.85	137.00	48.15
Alfalfa	5.0 ton	51.53	25.00	110.00	33.47
Small grain	60.0 bu	40.50	10.26	72.00	21.24
Potatoes	225.0 cwt	118.80	112.40	292.50	61.30

[a]Preharvest and harvest costs include labor; machinery; materials such as seed, fertilizer, pesticides, and herbicides; real estate taxes; water; and interest on cash and land investment.

8 Utah Valley

The irrigation systems in Utah are perhaps the oldest continuous operations in the West outside of the areas of Spanish influence.[1] The Mormon pioneers began to irrigate after they entered the Great Salt Lake Valley in 1847. These were Anglo-Saxon people whose background, customs, and experience were rooted in a civilization that had no experience in irrigation. They were the first agriculturalists from the humid eastern United States to face the problem of developing an intensive cultivated agriculture in a desert region.

It was obvious to the Utah settlers that the riparian doctrine of the English common law used in the eastern United States, which gave water rights only to lands adjacent to the streams, was not suited to irrigation farming and it was promptly discarded. Water had to be taken from the streams and carried to the land if agriculture was to be successful and the new settlements were to survive. At the same time, because all settlers were members of the same religious order that had come to establish new cooperative communities, the Mormons could agree that no user or groups of users should be allowed to enjoy exclusive rights to water to the disadvantage of other users in similar circumstances. Thus, while the Utahans adopted a system of appropriation in place of riparian rights, they deemphasized absolute priority of use, which is a typical characteristic of the appropriation doctrine, and proportionate sharing became an important principle for appropriating and allocating water. Water law as it developed in Utah included an additional important feature that was foreign to the riparian doctrine and in some ways to the appropriation doctrine as it was then being developed in Colorado and other western states. Beneficial use was declared to be the basis, the measure, and the limit of a water right. Brigham Young is reported to have said, "No man has the right to waste one drop of water that another man can turn into bread."[2] The principle was laid down that the water belonged to the people, "all the people," and no man could gain a right to more than he could use in a beneficial manner.[3]

Determining what constitutes beneficial use of water proved to be a difficult task. But in the Utah irrigation communities the acceptance of standards of water use by irrigators was eased by the fact that they all subscribed to the same religious faith and they respected and obeyed the decisions of the church "courts," which in the early days settled these community matters.

Utah, then, provides a revealing case study of the development and operation of a system of water-related institutions by agriculturalists who had had no previous experience with irrigation. To see how these institutions distribute irrigation water today, a hundred years after their beginning, we shall study the irrigation systems in the Utah Valley. The valley remained predominantly agricultural from the 1860s and 1870s, when it was settled by Mormon colonies, until World War II. Since then industrialization has provided more employment and

Utah Valley looking north from Spanish Fork toward Wasatch front.

Orem residences and Geneva plant of U.S. Steel encroach on irrigated agriculture
in Utah Valley. Utah Lake at top; Provo Reservoir canal in mid picture.

```
        1976 WATER SCHEDULE COMPUTED AND PRINTED BY DATAMAX
                P.O. BOX 367 OREM, UTAH 84057


   11 24 WELLMAN BISHOP                           CREM, UTAH
   SHARES     1.00          KNIGHT DITCH CO.
   TURN =  3 HRS AND 21 MIN,  0 MIN RUN TIME INCLUDED.


   BEG    MAY  9   8.33 PM    MAY 17   4.33 AM    MAY 24 12.33 PM
   END    MAY  9  11.54 PM    MAY 17   7.54 AM    MAY 24  3.54 PM

   BEG    MAY 31   8.33 PM    JUN  8   4.33 AM    JUN 15 12.33 PM
   END    MAY 31  11.54 PM    JUN  8   7.54 AM    JUN 15  3.54 PM

   BEG    JUN 22   8.33 PM    JUN 30   4.33 AM    JUL  7 12.33 PM
   END    JUN 22  11.54 PM    JUN 30   7.54 AM    JUL  7  3.54 PM

   BEG    JUL 14   8.33 PM    JUL 22   4.33 AM    JUL 29 12.33 PM
   END    JUL 14  11.54 PM    JUL 22   7.54 AM    JUL 29  3.54 PM

   BEG    AUG  5   8.33 PM    AUG 13   4.33 AM    AUG 20 12.33 PM
   END    AUG  5  11.54 PM    AUG 13   7.54 AM    AUG 20  3.54 PM

   BEG    AUG 27   8.33 PM    SEP  4   4.33 AM    SEP 11 12.33 PM
   END    AUG 27  11.54 PM    SEP  4   7.54 AM    SEP 11  3.54 PM

   BEG    SEP 18   8.33 PM    SEP 26   4.33 AM    OCT  3 12.33 PM
   END    SEP 18  11.54 PM    SEP 26   7.54 AM    OCT  3  3.54 PM

   BEG    OCT 10   8.33 PM    OCT 18   4.33 AM    OCT 25 12.33 PM
   END    OCT 10  11.54 PM    OCT 18   7.54 AM    OCT 25  3.54 PM


   1.ALL CHANGES MUST BE MADE BY APRIL 1ST.
   2.USE JUNE AND JULY FOR NEXT APRIL AND MAY.
   3.EACH STOCKHOLDER IS RESPONSIBLE FOR HIS OWN WATER.
```

A "water ticket," typical of those mailed by canal companies at the beginning of each irrigation season to farmer-shareholders informing them when they can take their turns. In this example Wellman Bishop of Orem owns one share of stock, representing a "turn" (rotation in our terminology) of 3 hrs and 21 min in Knight Ditch company. Note that the intervals between each three successive rotations are not uniform, but 8, 7, and 7 days, so that Bishop does not have to irrigate at night in each rotation, nor on the same day of the week throughout the season. Note 3 at bottom of ticket means that the company ditchrider turns water into Bishop's lateral, and thereafter farmers distribute it. For example, at 8:33 P.M. on the first rotation Bishop will close the gate of the preceding irrigator and open his own, and at 11:54 P.M. the farmer below Bishop will close Bishop's gate and open his. We know that Bishop's headgate is close by that of the preceding irrigator, for his schedule includes zero minutes of "run time."

urbanization has been growing out into the irrigated areas. Professor James L. Hudson has studied extensively the irrigation organizations and practices of the Utah Valley. His book, *Irrigation Water Use in the Utah Valley, Utah,* is a major source of the data used in this chapter.[4]

Utah Valley is located 22 miles (mi) south of Salt Lake City. It is a sharply defined irrigated valley with the Wasatch Mountains rising abruptly 5500 to 7500 feet (ft) above the valley floor on the east. Hills and low mountains form barriers on the other three sides. The valley itself is 35 mi long and about 12 mi wide. Utah Lake covers most of the western half of the valley floor. This is a shallow fresh-water lake of about 150 square miles (mi²) draining northward into the Great Salt Lake. The irrigated area occupies about 250 mi² along the valley's eastern edge.

The climate of the area is arid. The winters range from moderate to cold and the summers are hot and dry. Precipitation averages around 14 inches (in) a year, with only 1.6 in falling from July to September and about 3 in in April, May, and June. Length of the frost-free season ranges from 120 days to 190 days, with an average of about 145 days.

Most of the stream flow into the valley is derived from melting snowpack and results in high flows early in the growing season. Occasional summer thundershowers cause streams to rise for short periods during the irrigation season. The Provo River, Spanish Fork River, American Fork River, and a number of lesser streams provide irrigation water in the area and feed Utah Lake. Figure 8.1, based on thirty years of data (1931-1960) on the American Fork River, shows probabilities of various levels of natural stream flow during the irrigation season in Utah Valley. Reservoir releases are not included in these figures.

During the period 1949-1959 the annual flow of streams into Utah Valley averaged 501,000 acre-feet. Average flow during the irrigation season was 344,000 acre-feet; of this 261,000 came in April, May, and June and only 83,000 came during July, August, and September. In the northern valley stream flows average 174,000 acre-feet in April, May, and June but only 61,000 acre-feet of flow, including reservoir releases, is available during the high irrigation water demand period of July, August, and September. Water distribution over the season is even poorer in the southern valley. There during an average year 87,000 acre-feet of flow, including reservoir releases, occurs during July, August, and September for a much larger irrigated area.

Water derived from wells contributes around 30,000 to 38,000 acre-feet to irrigation supplies in northern Utah Valley and about 6000 to 12,000 acre-feet in southern Utah Valley.[5] The irrigation census shows that irrigated lands in the northern valley receive an average water delivery of 3 acre-feet/acre and the southern valley 1.9 acre-feet/acre.[6]

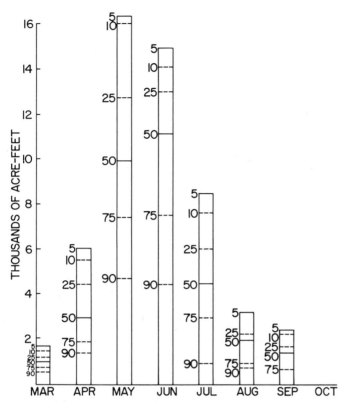

Figure 8.1   Probability hydrograph, American Fork River, Utah, 1931–1960.
[Source: *Hydrologic Atlas of Utah* (Logan, Utah: Utah Water Research Laboratory), p. 94]

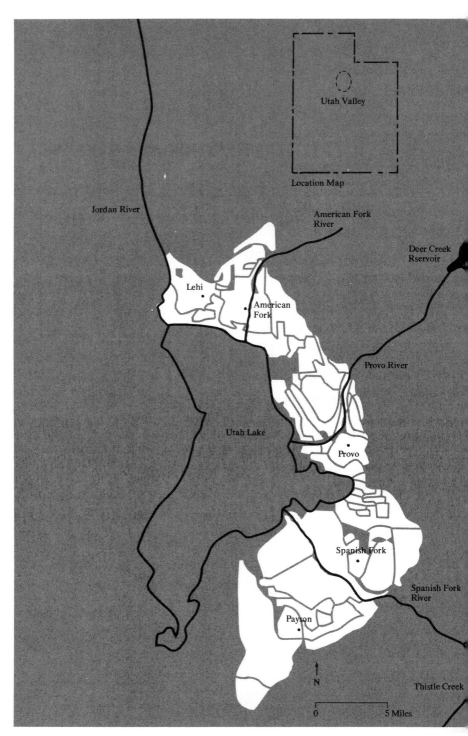

Figure 8.2 Irrigation companies in Utah Valley. [Source: James Hudson, *Irrigation Water Use in the Utah Valley* (Chicago: University of Chicago Press, 1962)]

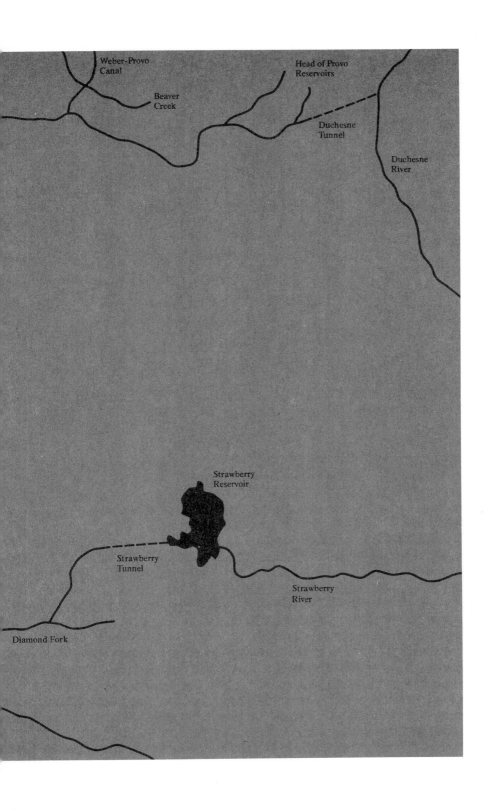

IRRIGATION COMPANIES

Irrigation water is provided to 94,000 acres of land by more than fifty irrigation companies in Utah Valley (see figure 8.2). Some irrigated areas are served by private ditches, springs, and wells, but most of the area is served by the companies. For the size of these companies in terms of their service areas and for the number of stockholders, see tables 8.1 and 8.2.

Compared to irrigation companies elsewhere in the West, those in the Utah Valley tend to be small. One reason for this is broken topography; there are not many large areas that can be irrigated easily from a single canal. But this alone does not account for the small areas served by many companies; these were fixed by the manner of their settlement. The Mormons, when colonizing the Utah Valley, as in the rest of the state, formed villages rather than farmsteads scattered on the land, which was the common practice in most areas of the United States. As each village was established it developed its own irrigation system just large enough to serve the lands to be farmed by its villagers. These lands were allotted to settlers in parcels of 10 or 20 or more acres, depending on family size. Where land quality was poor, irrigators were sometimes given two or more small tracts to equalize their opportunities for farming. Farms in Utah Valley today reflect the pattern set during the settlement period. In 1964, 30 percent had fewer than 10 irrigated acres and 73 percent had fewer than 50 irrigated acres. Only a little over 10 percent of the farms had more than 100 irrigated acres (table 8.3).

One reason for this development pattern was the need to build irrigation systems quickly to provide food for the settlements. New villages had very little capital to invest in canal construction or other purposes and they had to become

Table 8.1 Number of irrigation companies and acres irrigated in each size group, Utah Valley, Utah, 1959–1960.

Type	Number of companies	Acres irrigated directly	Acres in group
No acreage	3	None	—
Minute	2	1–99	119
Small	27	100–999	12,639
Medium	5	1,000–2,999	8,746
Moderately large	12	3,000–6,600	58,101
Large	1	Over 6,600	15,000
Total	50		94,605

Source: James Hudson, *Irrigation Water Use in the Utah Valley, Utah* (Chicago: University of Chicago Press, 1962) tables 39 and 40.

Table 8.2 Irrigation companies, Utah Valley, by stockholders and number of companies.

Number stockholders for Israelsen survey or no. of farms for Census Survey	Number of Companies Reported	
	1940 Israelsen Survey	1950 Census of Irrigation
None	3	1
1–3	—	4
4–9	2	12
10–29	12	21
Subtotal	17	38
30–99	8	11
100–299	11	13
300–999	5	2
Subtotal	24	26
Total given	41	64
Not given	4	—
Total	45	64

Source: James Hudson, *Irrigation Water Use in the Utah Valley, Utah* (Chicago: University of Chicago Press, 1962) p. 117.

Table 8.3 Size of farms by number of acres irrigated, Utah County, 1964.

Acres irrigated	Number of farms	Percentage
1–9	640	30.5
10–49	896	42.7
50–99	325	15.5
100–199	169	8.0
200 +	68	3.3
Total	2,098	100.0

Source: *U. S. Census of Agriculture,* 1964, table 2, p. 207.

self-sufficient almost immediately so that they would not be a drain on the limited resources of the older villages. In building the irrigation systems, the settlers had little more than their own labor to rely on. Horse power was scarce and heavy equipment almost entirely lacking. If, with their meager resources, the early settlers had attempted to build systems that would irrigate large tracts of land, they would have failed to keep their small villages alive.

Irrigation systems in Utah are organized typically as mutual irrigation companies. Originally the irrigation systems were voluntary cooperative ventures run principally by the village officials, who were almost always functionaries in the local ward of the Mormon church. Following the developmental period most irrigation systems reorganized as mutual irrigation stock companies, with stock being issued to water users.

Today the Utah Valley irrigation companies can be divided into two major classes. The most numerous are formal, original companies. They are formal in the sense that they are incorporated mutual companies with capital stock, boards of directors, and company officers. They are original because they were established in the early days as part of village development. More than two-thirds of the companies fall in this class.

A second category, the informal, original companies, are unincorporated mutuals. Although these companies were founded under circumstances similar to the formal companies, their small service areas have made formal organization unnecessary. These mutuals make up a little over a quarter of the companies in this area.

Irrigation companies in Utah Valley are farmer-owned and controlled. Stock in the companies is typically held by water users in the companies' service areas. Thus a water user's voice in the affairs of the company, the amount of water he receives, and, usually, the amount of money he pays the company depend upon the amount of stock that he holds.

Elected officers direct operations and determine the policies of the typical mutual irrigation company. Normally, an annual meeting is held at which officers are elected, assessments are proposed and agreed upon, and water supply prospects for the coming season are discussed. The typical company has a president and a board of directors of four or more water users. The directors are usually elected for one- or two-year terms, with the directors selecting the company president. In most companies directors can be reelected and many serve for long periods. The officers of the company hire a secretary or secretary-treasurer, a watermaster, and any necessary assistants. As a rule all stockholders, officers, and employees are farmers served by the system.

The most important person in the operation of an irrigation company is the watermaster. He administers the allocation of water to the water users throughout the season. The duties of a watermaster in Utah correspond roughly to those of the superintendent in many Colorado companies, except that in the Utah Valley's typically small companies the watermaster usually performs the duties of a ditch rider as well. If he has assistants, they are the true equivalents of ditch riders. The watermaster is usually a farmer and a shareholder.

Water Resources of Irrigation Companies

The first irrigation systems depended entirely on natural stream flow for water supply. In time small springs, wells, and return flows were captured and used for irrigation. By the turn of the century the natural and return flows of the valley's streams had been almost fully appropriated and the irrigators, besides increasing their pumping of groundwater, turned to engineering works by which they could modify these flows. About 1910 several interests, including a Utah Valley mutual company, the city of Provo, and irrigation companies located in the upper Valley, built fifteen small reservoirs at the headwaters of the Provo River with a combined storage of approximately 10,000 acre-feet. Although each reservoir is separately owned, they are operated as a unit. In the spring the reservoirs are filled by snow melt. When during the irrigation season a company calls for some of its water, this is not released necessarily from the reservoir that it owns, but from the one that is being drawn down at the time.

The Wasatch Range separates the headeaters of Spanish Fork in the southern Utah Valley from the Strawberry River, which is a tributary of the Duchesne River in the Colorado River basin. The diversion of Strawberry River into the Spanish Fork was first investigated in 1902 by a local irrigation company. This investigation indicated that the project was too large an undertaking for the company or for the water users of the valley, who then turned to the new United States Reclamation Service. Twelve hundred citizens owning more than 26,000 acres of land in the vicinity of Spanish Fork petitioned reclamation to study the project and to construct it—if it were found to be feasible. The engineers' reports were favorable and Strawberry Valley came to be one of the first irrigation projects built by the federal government.

Construction began in 1906, and irrigation features were completed substantially by 1916. Water of the Strawberry River is stored in a reservoir with a capacity of 270,000 acre-feet. It is transported from there to the Spanish Fork through a 3.8-mi tunnel that pierces the Wasatch Mountains. Average annual diversion is 61,000 acre-feet, which is supplied largely as supplemental water to 42,000 acres of land.

For lands that could be served by the canals of mutual companies, the Reclamation Service initially delivered water in bulk to the canal headgates and the companies, in return for a reasonable carrying charge, assumed responsibility for delivering it to farmers who had contracted with the service to purchase water. To serve an area of approximately 25,000 acres of higher lands, the greater part of which had not previously been irrigated, the Reclamation Service built the Highline canal, which on completion was turned over to the water users, who formed a mutual company for the purpose of operating and maintaining it. In

1926 the United States government withdrew completely from operating the project, turning it over to an inclusive organization of beneficiaries, incorporated as a supermutual company—the Strawberry Water Users Association.

A second federal project that supplements the irrigation water supply of Utah Valley has been built on the Provo River at the north end of the valley. The natural flows of the Provo and most of its flood flows were fully appropriated before the turn of the century, so that they are rarely available for storage, but the water users saw an opportunity to divert into the Provo River unused water from two adjacent rivers: the Weber to the north and the Duchesne in the Colorado basin to the east. In the early 1920s they interested the Reclamation Service in investigating such a project, but it was not until an extraordinary drought in the early 1930s threatened the municipal water supply of Salt Lake City that plans began to move. In 1938 construction was started on a multipurpose project to provide domestic water supplies for Salt Lake City, Provo, and four other communities in the Utah Valley and irrigation water for farms in the northern Utah Valley and across the Jordan narrows in the southern Jordan Valley.

Water is brought into the Provo from Weber River by means of a 9-mi canal with a capacity of 1000 cubic feet per second (cfs), and from Duchesne River through a 6-mi tunnel with a capacity of 600 cfs. Deer Creek reservoir, with a capacity of 150,000 acre-feet, was built on the Provo to store this foreign water, and a power plant with 5000 kilowatt (kw) capacity was built at the dam. The irrigation water is distributed to farms through company canals, one of which was enlarged for the purpose; and Salt Lake City's municipal water moves through a 42-mi aqueduct from Deer Creek reservoir to the city.

The users of Deer Creek reservoir organized the Provo River Water Users Association, a supermutual company whose stock was issued to subscribers on the basis of one share for each acre-foot of stored water. The Metropolitan Water District of Salt Lake has purchased 61 percent of the stock and the water; the other cities and towns, 12 percent; and the several irrigation companies, the remaining 27 percent, although not all of this was purchased by Utah Valley groups. Only a few of the original Utah Valley mutual companies subscribed for stock. Conservative voices in the others successfully raised questions concerning costs and the need for water. In the service area of one of the mutual companies the farmers desiring water from the reservoir formed a new company to purchase it. The officers of several of the companies, interviewed by Hudson after a summer drought in 1959, regretted that their companies had not purchased Deer Creek water or had not purchased a greater supply of it.[7] At the same time, the cities and towns have rented some of their water to irrigators—they have not yet used all of it for domestic purposes, so that approximately 29,000 acre-feet of storage in Deer Creek reservoir are presently used to irrigate Utah Valley farms.

In the late 1960s the Bureau of Reclamation began construction of a long-range multistructure and multiple-purpose water resource development in central Utah. Its principal purpose is to capture flows in the headwaters of the Duchesne River and certain other streams that are tributary to the Colorado River and divert them through the Wasatch Mountains for domestic and irrigation uses in the drainage basins of Utah Lake, Jordan River, Sevier River, and Great Salt Lake. Some of the water is to be brought into the Provo River, where a new storage reservoir will be built upstream from Deer Creek Dam, but little of this water will be supplied to Utah Valley farms. Farms in the southern portion of the valley are to benefit, however, from greater diversions into Spanish Fork from across the divide. Mean annual flows into Spanish Fork are to be increased from 61,000 to 195,000 acre-feet, and for this purpose Strawberry reservoir is being enlarged from a storage capacity of 270,000 acre-feet to 700,000 acre-feet. Most of this increased water supply will be used for irrigation in southern Utah Valley and in the Goshen, Northern Juab, and Sevier valleys to the south. The increased supply in the Utah Valley will be used largely as supplemental water for presently irrigated lands, while in the other areas irrigated acreage will be increased substantially.[8]

From among the several water sources available, those utilized by any company depend on the age and size of the enterprise. They range from companies that rely completely on one source, such as a stream, a spring, or reservoir, to companies that obtain water from up to four different sources. The larger the service area of a company and the more recent its founding, the more likely it is to secure water from several sources. Stream flow was largely appropriated by the earlier companies, so the later ones found it necessary to develop wells, springs, and return flow to secure an adequate water supply. The last irrigation companies to be developed in the valley are dependent primarily upon reservoirs. They do not have effective water rights to stream flow during the irrigation season and secure their supplies mainly by water that they store off-season and by flood flows.

The water available today in the Utah Valley does not match irrigation requirements. A detailed study of irrigation needs using current irrigation practices and efficiencies shows that most areas within Utah Valley suffer from inadequate irrigation supplies during the later part of the irrigation season. Figure 8.3 shows the actual water supply by months in relation to a full irrigation supply for Utah Valley. Only an average for the valley is shown; individual companies will have greater or lesser water supplies, depending upon their water rights and sources of water.

ALLOCATION OF WATER RIGHTS ON STREAMS

We observed in the first paragraphs of this chapter that the Colorado doctrine of absolute priorities was not followed in Utah to the extent that the Mormons gave greater weight to proportionate sharing of water shortages and to beneficial use of the resource. When the rights to water on a river were settled or adjudicated in Colorado, each claimant was given a fixed quantity in cubic feet per second of flow and a fixed priority. Thus an irrigator or a mutual irrigation company with rights that are junior may not use any water at all at any time until

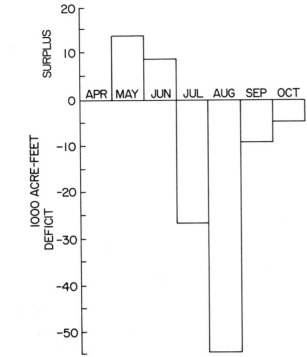

Figure 8.3 Monthly water supply surplus and deficit at present irrigation efficiencies, Utah Valley. (Source: Adapted from figure 14, Hiro Mizue, *Irrigation
Demand in Utah Lake Drainage Area,* unpublished M.S. thesis, Utah State University, 1968, p. 108)

the senior users have received their full entitlements or any parts of them that they want to use. Under this practice holders of early rights who, when they established their fixed priorities, were using the water for only a short period each year, could later extend the time period of their withdrawals, thereby injuring those who, coming later, found plenty of unused water when they established their junior rights. Senior appropriators must use their water beneficially, to be sure; but the measure of "beneficial" in Colorado is unrigorous.

When rights to Utah Valley streams were apportioned each claimant canal was assigned shares or percentages of flow. The shares assigned to each canal were based on priority of appropriation—the canals that had first diverted water and put it to use in irrigation were given preference over later canals, but this principle was far from absolute, as it was in Colorado. Time priority was modified considerably by several factors, first among them being the actual use of water at the time an allocation was made. When a stream came to be apportioned among canals—and this happened only when abstractions began to exceed the stream's capacity—the then actual uses of water by each canal would be measured; and these measures became an important factor in the apportionment, more so than specific dates of first claims to water. To the extent that apportionment was based on actual use and to the extent that all canals were using water with equal efficiency at the time of apportionment (a not unreasonable assumption, since up to that time, presumably, none of the canals had suffered great injury because of the use of water by others), the Utah Valley agreements allotted water to each canal according to the amount of land that was then dependent on it for water supply. This service area was not necessarily limited to the lands being cultivated by the first villagers; by the time streams were apportioned in the Utah Valley, new settlers had been admitted to most of the communities.

The Utahans used fractional parts of a variable water supply rather than fixed quantities of water as their technique of allocation, and by this means they spread the costs of drought over a larger number of water users than was the case in Colorado. This was their second modificaiton of time priority.

Where water supplies are prorated, as in Utah, some technique is required to prevent the proliferation of farms and ditches beyond the point where water can be used effectively. In Valencia this was done by defining a canal's service area, allowing no delivery of water beyond it, and placing land within a service area in two categories—fields with old rights and fields that were settled later, with secondary rights (*extremales*). The latter were denied service in periods of ordinary low water and of drought. Similar techniques were used in Utah, where the ditches were considered to have either primary or secondary rights. The first class included all ditches that had acquired rights to use of a stream up to the time that the sum of the rights was equal to the ordinary low-water flow of the stream. Ditches that acquired rights to water after the low-water flow had been exhausted or that received service during periods of high water only had secondary rights. All holders of primary rights were considered equal in the sense that they received their fixed proportion of water regardless of whether the stream in any year had an insufficient, a normal, or an abundant water supply. Analogously, all second-class rights were equal with respect to abundant water.

Since the streams of Utah Valley were first apportioned among canals at a time when abstractions had just begun to exceed ordinary low flow, most claimants were then in the first class. Second-class canals were frequently those that began to use water beneficially during the period between the initial, and frequently informal, apportionments and later modifications of these. Thus the water supply of the Provo River was adequate for all from 1849 to 1880. In 1880, however, the supply failed partially; and the amount of water furnished by the river barely satisifed the needs of the canal interests, who thereupon sought to work out an apportionment agreement. In January 1884 such an agreement was reached in which all canals that had used water beneficially prior to 1880 were conceded to have primary rights. Among them, each canal's fraction of supply was a factor of its service area and the length of time it had used water.[9]

The division of water rights into classes was peculiar to Utah in the western United States and was, as we have seen, Utah's method for achieving a higher degree of sharing of the costs of drought than was possible in systems that used absolute time priorities, while protecting water users against an increase in their numbers so great as to destroy the utility of water to them all. In the Colorado system it makes no difference how many users are added to the bottom of the priority list. They get no water until the needs of all senior users have been met.

The rigors of the doctrine of prior appropriation were further mitigated in Utah by defining canal rights so that they varied over the irrigation season. The shares that each canal received typically varied with either the time of year or the flow in the stream. The Provo River is an example of the former, where the percentages of flow assigned to each canal change on specified dates throughout the season. Table 8.4 illustrates this with regard to those canals that have primary rights. When the actual flows in any period exceed the "assumed natural flow" shown on the table, canals with secondary rights can draw water. Assuming natural flows, Canal D receives 16 cfs from May to June and 10 cfs from September to May. These quantities approximate, no doubt, those that the canal was using when an early apportionment was made. By using a time-variable method of apportionment, the water users of the Provo River have guaranteed to other canals the use of water that would have been D's from September to May if D had been granted a fixed right of 16 cfs from September to May or alternatively a fixed percentage of flow, which in this case would have been approximately 14 cfs. If the Colorado system had been used on the Provo River, in other words, these other canals would have been forever at the mercy of Canal D, which at any time could have increased its use of water in the winter months.

On the Spanish Fork the shares assigned to each canal change with the river flow rather than on fixed dates. Figure 8.4, in which each company's shares have been converted into flows, illustrates this technique. It will be observed that the changes in canal abstractions can be substantial, as at the flow rate of 148.5 cfs.

Table 8.4 Water rights on the Provo River, Utah Valley.

	Percent of assumed natural flow			
Canal	May 10 to June 20	June 20 to July 20	July 20 to September 1	September 1 to May 10
A	40.7	39.2	38.2	39.2[a]
B	20.2	20.5	21.0	20.2
C	10.9	10.4	10.2	10.3
D	5.2	4.9	4.8	3.9
E	4.9	4.7	4.6	4.7
F	4.6	4.4	4.2	4.3[a]
G	3.2	3.2	3.1	3.0
H	2.2	3.8	5.4	5.7[a]
All others	8.0	8.8	8.5	8.1
Total	100	100	100	100
Assumed natural flow (cfs)	308.9	290.0	268.0	260.2

Source: James Hudson, *Irrigation Water Use in the Utah Valley, Utah* (Chicago: University of Chicago Press, 1962) table 36, p. 89. Taken from the Commissioner's Report, Provo River, 1959, pp. 16, 18.

[a] Absolute amount remains the same; in all other cases for major companies absolute amount also changes.

The current legislation in Utah requires that water rights be stated in second-feet of flow or acre-feet of storage rather than fractional parts of the whole supply, and it no longer recognizes the use of classes of rightsholders. But before these provisions were enacted the rights of irrigation canals in the Utah Valley and in most other farming areas had been apportioned under the earlier customs and legislation, and these remain in force (although some of them have been translated into modern terms).[10]

A fourth restriction on the appropriation doctrine resulted from the early development in Utah of a more rigorous concept of beneficial use than evolved in Colorado and certain other western states. This concept was used when the Utah Valley streams were initially apportioned, that is, when the actual uses of water by each canal were measured as a basis for apportionment, only those uses that were considered beneficial and economic were counted.

In northeastern Colorado we have seen that renting and sale of water are important practices for mitigating the rigidities of prior appropriation. They are used, although less extensively, for the same purpose in Utah. The right to the use of water in Utah is independent of the right to land and water rights may be

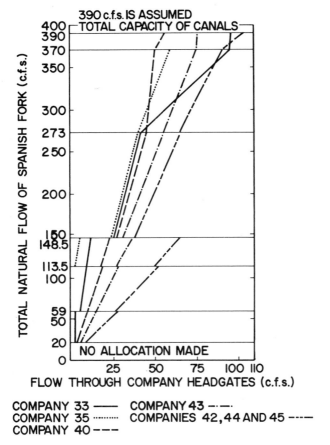

Figure 8.4 Allocation of water from the Spanish Fork, Utah Valley. [Source: James Hudson, *Irrigation Water Use in the Utah Valley, Utah* (Chicago: University of Chicago Press, 1962) figure g, p. 95]

sold separately from the land. But such a reading of Utah legislation and court opinions, although it is formally correct, is highly misleading as a description of the relation between land and water in the Utah Valley.

The irrigation practices encouraged by the Mormons were based on the principle that water rights should be inseparable from the land. From the beginning there was, to be sure, some buying and selling of water rights, but this was limited in amount. These sales were not prohibited by law, but neither were they based on any explicit legal right or established custom. In 1880 the territorial legislature provided for the first time that waters when appropriated became private property that need not be appurtenant to land. But this legislation did not have as great an impact on irrigation practices as one might expect.

There were few farmers in the Utah Valley who owned water rights. When the first settlers diverted streams for irrigation, the water they abstracted was considered the property of the community of farmers that built the ditches or of the larger municipality. Individual rights were not recognized as such, each settler's interest being considered part of the community right. When these informal ditch communities became mutual companies, their water rights passed to the companies, as did those of any individual farmer who, claiming separate water rights, joined a company. The informal mutual companies then issued certification to farmers for the use of water on stated numbers of acres of land; the formal ones issued stocks or shares to farmers in proportion to their traditional uses of water.

Under the current law mutual companies can sell their rights to water apart from the land, but they will do this only where increasing urbanization or industrialization have reduced the demand for irrigation water and never to place their shareholders in a position where outside interests can control farmers' water supplies.

As for the farmers themselves, the water rights represented by each irrigator's shares in a formal mutual company may be severed from the land on which the water has been used and transferred to other land by transfer of the stock. In short, farmers can sell their shares apart from their land. But the number of such sales in the Utah Valley has been small, principally to transfer water from one farm to another under the same ditch or in recent years to accommodate increasing urbanization in areas where it is overtaking agriculture. Furthermore, the sales prices have been below those one would expect in a market situation. As Hudson reports, the farmers believe in a "fair price" and socially proscribe "water profiteering." [11]

There remains the question of short-term flexibility in a water distribution system based on the principle of prior appropriation. A farmer who has a right to more water than he plans to use in a given season or in a given rotation may rent his rights to a farmer who needs it, as in Colorado. Arrangements for such transactions are quite informal, less elaborate even than those in the South Platte-Cache La Poudre. Prices are usually modest and, as in the case of the sale of mutual company shares, do not seem to reflect prices that would be determined in a truly competitive market. "The farmer with excess water thinks it not right to charge all the traffic will bear, and the farmer with the water need thinks it wrong to pay such a fee."[12]

WATER DELIVERY WITHIN COMPANIES

In Utah Valley most of the irrigation companies use a rotation system to distribute water to farmers. This system was developed in the early days as a more economical and convenient method than continuous flows, which would have resulted in streams that were too small to be usable in many cases and in each farmer's having the nuisance of constant water management. Under the rotation delivery system a farmer (or small group of farmers) receives water for a certain length of time during each run, which is the term used for one complete rotation of water to all farmers on a ditch. The quantity of water delivered to a farmer during a run depends upon the length of time water is available to him and the amount of flow in the canal during this period.

The time period that water is available to a farmer in any run is determined by the number of shares he owns in the company and the number of days required for a complete rotation. The length of a rotation varies by company; some use one week, others ten days, some two weeks or longer. Some companies vary the length of rotation during the season, depending upon level of stream flow and needs of crops. When stream flow is high, a short rotation may serve all water users adequately. When it is low, not all lands can be watered during an average run and either the rotation period is lengthened, the time that water is delivered per share of stock is reduced, or both changes are made. The rotation period will not be lengthened beyond the point where the resulting interval between successive rotations causes more damage to crops than results from reducing the time, and therefore the quantity, of water delivered in a single run. The rotation period usually includes a fraction of a day so that a farmer's successive turns will occur at different times of day and no farmer will have to irrigate at night on every rotation. By the same token, many companies have avoided a rotation interval of seven days or multiples of seven so that farmers' turns do not fall on the same day of the week throughout the season.

Some companies, when they have sufficient water, operate two "streams" instead of one. If, as the natural flow decreases during the summer months, there is insufficient water to operate two streams effectively, they will be combined into one, and the farmer's time will be cut in half while the rotation length is maintained. In a few companies, however, the farmer will continue to receive water for the same number of hours and the rotation interval will be doubled.

The length of rotation in hours is divided by the number of shares in the company to determine the time entitlement of each share, and the water time available to each farmer is then figured by multiplying this quotient by the number of shares he holds.

The quantity of flow in a ditch during the time a farmer is being served depends principally on the season of the year, but also on the farmer's location on the ditch and on the hour of day or night when his turn comes. Canal flows vary considerably over the year, as we have seen. They will typically be high in the early part of the season and diminish as the snowpack runoff from the mountains declines in mid-season, coinciding with the period when water needs of crops are increasing because of rapid growth and high temperatures.

A water user's location on the ditch may have an important effect on the amount of water he receives during a rotation. If stream flow is high and not all water users take their complete turn, those at the lower end of a ditch may get the excess water released by users above them. On the other hand, if stream flow is low, farmers at the lower end may get less water per time period per share because of greater conveyance losses through the full length of the canal. This effect will vary in significance depending on the length and condition of the canal; but in most cases where the canals are not lined, farmers on the lower end are hurt at a critical time of crop growth (July and especially August).

Streams fed by snow melt have diurnal variations in runoff. During the snow melt period the American Fork River, for example, peaks between 11 P.M. and midnight and reaches a low flow during daylight hours.[13] Thus the quantity of water a farmer receives on any run depends in part on the time of day assigned to him in the rotation schedule. A schedule in which each farmer receives water at the same time of day on all runs may be inequitable in the sense that some farmers will regularly receive more, and some less, water per time and share. To avoid this inequality, as well as for reasons mentioned above, some Utah Valley companies use rotations that include a fraction of a day.

In the spring, prior to the beginning of scheduled deliveries, the watermaster sends out water "tickets" that inform each farmer of the hours he is to take his turns. In most companies, the procedure is for the watermaster to deliver the water to the headgate of a lateral or of the first farm on the lateral and thereafter for the farmers to take responsibility for distribution. When the first farmer's turn is finished, the next farmer in order closes the first farmer's gate and turns the water through his own headgate and so on to the last farm on the lateral. In other companies the watermaster turns the water into a lateral, follows it down to the end, making sure that all gates are closed, and begins delivery with the last farm. Thereafter the farmers take over, as in the previous example.

Both of these procedures place heavy reliance on water users for enforcement. For farmers who violate the procedures, the watermaster serves as a "court of first instance." He will lecture a misfeasor, and if this does not succeed he will consult the president of the company, who may call together the board of directors to consider the problem. The president or the board will then either talk to the farmer—by phone or by visiting his farm—or write him a letter, threatening to close and lock his headgate if the farmer persists in his misconduct. If he does persist, the president will direct the watermaster to lock the offender's headgate for some fixed period of time. There is usually no need to take disputes to higher authority—the civil courts—for social pressures against such litigiousness are considerable. In a few companies, however, the farmers' discretion in water distribution is much less. The watermaster supervises deliveries closely, opening and closing all gates himself.

As noted earlier, a number of companies deliver reservoir water as well as natural flow water. Where, as in the case of the Provo project, the mutual companies own the reservoir water, they combine it with natural flows in calculating a uniform seasonal entitlement for each share of company stock. At any time the companies will have good estimates of the quantities of their stored water, which the company watermasters will plan to withdraw as needed to supplement natural flows that cannot be stored. Providing there is capacity available in Deer Creek reservoir, a company can hold over to the next season any water not used in the current crop cycle.

In the case of the Strawberry project and to a large extent of the Provo Reservoir Company, the reservoir water belongs to the farmers individually rather than to the mutual companies; and in modifying their operating procedures to deliver both sources the companies have sought to give each farmer some freedom in deciding when and in what quantities to use his reservoir water. Most of the companies that deliver both types of water use a rotation procedure for natural flow water that varies over the year. During the late season, when natural flow has decreased, the amount of time per share of stock is reduced. If then a farmer wants more water on a run than he would get with the reduced time, he can draw on his reservoir water, which will be delivered along with the natural flow to which he is entitled. The reservoir water he receives on any run is deducted from his water account. From the point of view of the company as a whole, however, the watermaster cannot be guided simply by the sum of individual farmers' orders for water where they would result in large daily variations in the stream flowing in the company's ditches. For reasons of efficiency he will want to keep a steady stream, and this criterion will help determine the reservoir releases that he calls for.

One company that pools reservoir and stream flow water as the basis for determining the amount of time per share of stock that water may be delivered during the season uses a demand procedure rather than rotation or variable rotation. Each farmer can order water on demand, as he needs it, within the limitation of the hours credited to him for the year. The water user informs the company of the number of hours he wants on each irrigation run.

From among this variety of operating procedures, those practiced today by any company are the results of trial and error over a number of years in reaching an adjustment that has proved to be satisfactory to the company's farmer shareholders.

All these procedures have been criticized for being inefficient in the production of crops because of both the inflexibility of the irrigation return period and the variability of flow for all farms.[14] Thus it is argued that a farmer whose crops are in need of water cannot obtain it until his turn in the rotation, whereas under a demand system of delivery he could choose the times when he uses the water to which he is entitled over the season. As a consequence, he is limited in the type of crops that he can grow; and he may be encouraged to waste water, for he will irrigate when his turn comes even if his crops are not yet in need of water. If he were not to do so, he might suffer great crop losses before his turn on the next run comes around. This is true, of course, but a demand system, providing greater flexibility, would require the construction of reservoirs with large storage capacity. A comparison by use of the simulation of a set of typical irrigated farms in central Utah Valley suggests that if reservoir storage could be developed to capture one-third of the present water supply available and redistribute it on demand, the gross value of crop production using current crop patterns could be increased by about 10 percent or a little over $10 per acre. If the expectations of a firm water supply created by storage led to changes in crop patterns from low-valued grain production to larger acreages of orchards or other high-return crops, the value of the storage water would be even greater, particularly for farms now forced to grow early maturing crops because of late season water shortages. Whether it would be economical to build such storage is not clear. It would depend, of course, on availability of reservoir sites, the cost of reservoir construction, and the interest rate charged on the investments.

Proportional sharing of water shortages by all farmers is said to be less efficient than would be an operating procedure based on absolute priorities, in which high-priority farms received sufficient water to bring through their crops without losses and low-priority ones suffered the full impact of drought. Assuming that an absolute priority system can be devised in which high-priority farms do not waste water and all farms are equally productive, this argument is true. But the Utahans' objectives of equality and equity have constrained so purposeful a pursuit of efficiency; they have mitigated the Colorado system.

IRRIGATION INSTITUTIONS

The practice and the law of water use have developed differently in the Utah Valley than in northeastern Colorado for several reasons. One is that the Utah area is more arid during the growing season than Colorado. (Summer precipitation averages less than 5 in from April through September.) But this explanation can be carried only so far, for similarly arid areas in other states of the West use their water according to practices that are closer to those of Colorado than are Utah's. The Colorado doctrine of absolute priority was incompatible with the cooperative community approach to agricultural development used by the Mormon church in colonizing the irrigated valleys of Utah. There the idea of proportioning limited flows was a natural outgrowth of the common community interest. The church could not allow some settlers to have a full supply of water while others were denied access to it.

To negotiate the Utah type apportionments and to administer a system of water distribution in which the automatic features of the doctrine of prior appropriation were modified as significantly as they were in Utah has required different institutions than those developed in Colorado. These institutions were derived, in part, from the Mormon experience in community life. In part they were pure invention. For the Mormons, with no prior knowledge or experience of irrigated agriculture, "the path was new and unbeaten and common sense was the only guide." [15] In brief, the construction, operation, and maintenance of irrigation distribution systems was put largely in the hands of laymen—or more properly, of the farmers themselves. Disputes were usually settled by arbitration, encouraged by church officials; if arbitration failed, the church officers would make binding decisions.

When it was decided to colonize a new locality, such as Provo, American Fork, or Spanish Fork, the Mormon church authorities called up the desired number of colonists and chose their leaders—a bishop and two councilors. These men were selected not only for their religious zeal but also for their ability to solve the practical problems connected with the establishment of new settlements, of which irrigation was an important one.

To construct the irrigation system, the villagers chose a committee to which the bishop himself was frequently elected. Once the canal was built, this committee was discharged and the irrigators as a group elected one of their own to be watermaster in charge of operating and maintaining the system. His term was one year and he was paid by the farmers for those days when he worked for the community. The watermaster drew up rotation schedules and distributed the water, and he was in charge of the annual canal cleaning and repairing.

Each year in March or April he called together an assembly of all irrigators. This meeting, in addition to other matters of business, ordinarily appointed a committee of three to estimate the cost per irrigated acre of annual canal maintenance and the value of a day's work by a farmer or by the farmer and his team of horses. Each farmer was then assigned a number of days' work, depending on the acres that he irrigated, and the watermaster organized and supervised the whole job. Alternatively, the committee would divide the canal into sections, called "stints" of different lengths, and assign a stint to each farmers, depending on the size of his farm.

When disputes arose, typically between canals drawing water from the same stream, the bishops urged and provided facilities for voluntary agreements and arbitration. Where arbitration failed, however, recourse was had to the bishop or, where the controversy involved several wards (that is, the jurisdiction of several bishops), to the high council of the stake, whose decisions were accepted as final. These institutions controlled the construction, operation, and maintenance of the new settlements' irrigation systems and the adjudication of disputes over their water rights until civil authorities were ready and willing to take over, and where this did not happen, until mutual companies were organized for operating and maintaining the canals.

After the territorial government was established by Congress in 1851, its legislature, in granting charters of incorporation to the cities and towns, included in almost all of them control over waters. As the city limits in most cases included the adjacent farmlands, this meant control over irrigation as well as domestic supplies. The cities had jurisdiction over areas that were significantly larger than those of the wards over which the bishops presided, and one reason for taking irrigation matters out of the hands of the several bishops was to provide a central and uniform system for operating canals that were closely related hydrologically.

Only a few towns ever exercised this authority, however, and of these only two, Provo and American Fork, both in the Utah Valley, continued to do so for some years. One reason for this was that the farmers in most places feared that with increasing migrations to their towns—much of it by Gentiles (non-Mormons)—they might lose control over their water supplies by losing control over their municipal councils; but this was not the case in Provo and American Fork. There the city councils, with farmers in control, operated and maintained and extended the canal systems, allocated the water, and settled disputes.

The territorial legislature in 1865 and 1866 provided for an alternative to municipal administration of irrigation, namely special-purpose irrigation districts. Whenever a majority of the citizens of a county (the successor for civil government functions of the Mormon stake) or a part thereof petitioned the county court, the court was authorized, subject to a further popular referendum, to organize the entire county or a part of it into an irrigation district. There were provisions for popular election of district officers and popular control over their affairs. Initially there was much activity in establishing districts, but few were organized successfully and fewer survived, none in the Utah Valley. This was due in part to deficiencies in the statute, many of them relating to taxation.

Thus, efforts to turn over to civil authorities the responsibility for irrigation canals failed in good part. Yet the original system, involving active participation by church authorities, became progressively less viable as population increased, turning all the time less homogeneous, and as demands for water rose rapidly. Instead of civil authority, the administrative machinery that evolved was one of voluntary farmer cooperatives—the mutual irrigation companies. These were in effect the farmer assemblies of the first years, but without the bishops and with certain more formal features. Some of the companies were incorporated, and a law of 1880 encouraged this. Others, as we have seen, have remained unincorporated to this day. The city canals, too, became mutual companies for the most part.

But this method of administering individual canals did not provide a means for apportioning water among companies that used the same source or for adjudicating disputes among them. The territorial legislature in 1852, about the same time that it authorized the cities to act on water matters, gave broad authority to the county courts to apportion water according to the principle of beneficial use, to see that the apportionments were carried out, and to settle disputes. In doing this the legislature was not removing authority entirely from farmers who knew the practice of irrigation and giving it to litigious lawyers, for the new county courts consisted of a probate judge and three selectmen. Three-quarters of the membership of a court, in other words, was made up of practical men who were likely to understand the problems of irrigation and to use simple and direct procedures.

The law was changed in 1880, when jurisdiction was removed from the county courts and given to county boards of selectmen who became *ex officio* the water commissioners of the counties. County water commissioners inherited the courts' authority to apportion water and to settle disputes, and the courts' wide discretion that derived from authority to initiate actions on their own and to apply the concept of beneficial use in their actions was narrowed somewhat.

Neither of these arrangements had an important impact on the apportionment of streams in the Utah Valley, however. The courts asserted their jurisdiction in few counties and the Utah County Court did not do so with respect to the Utah Valley. The county commissioners' law, like its predecessor, was enforced in only a few counties, although there was some activity in Utah Valley. But the acts of the commissioners were generally believed worthless, as the law was considered to be void for the reason that it granted judicial power to a body not named in the section of the Organic Law that created the courts of the territory. [The territorial supreme court was never called upon to pass on the question, however.]

The county courts and the county boards of selectmen dealt with water problems mainly as administrative bodies. Questions of law could be raised in the regular district courts, but in fact very few cases found their way to the civil courts until just before the turn of the century. When they did, it was usually to confirm—to put a stamp of approval on—agreements that had been reached elsewhere.

Thus, as in the case of operating the canals, efforts to turn over to civil authorities responsibility for apportioning water among canals and settling their disputes largely failed; and in a manner similar to canal operations, the solution was a continuation of informal or nonstatutory procedures, but with less direct participation by the Mormon church.

Take the case of the Provo River in Utah Valley, for example. The first court decree for this river was given in 1902, but it was the outcome of a series of informal arbitrations and voluntary agreements between 1884 and 1902. Each agreement had narrowed the areas of dispute until by 1902 there was practically no controversy remaining and then the civil court stamped "approved" in a decree to which all parties agreed.

After the turn of the century the Utah State Legislature enacted several laws that have governed since then the state's activities in apportioning water. These laws made no important change in the jurisdiction of the civil courts; they simply codified existing laws and procedures that related to the courts' adjudication of water rights. The office of the state engineer was established to perform some of the functions previously fulfilled by the county courts and county water commissioners—principally the collection of data to serve as the basis for apportioning streams, the administration and enforcement of apportionment agreements, and the approval of applications for the use of unappropriated waters. After consulting the water users the engineer appoints a water commissioner for each important drainage area and supervises the commissioner's work in distributing among mutual companies and others the waters of the drainage in accordance with apportionment agreements in effect. Thus the commissioner of the Provo River is appointed by the engineer upon the recommendation of a board consisting of five representatives of water users in the Utah Valley and four users in the upper basin, and the commissioner of the Spanish Fork, by a board of eight members from the Utah Valley and one from irrigated areas in the mountains.

When the Utah Valley farmers were first called on to form organizations larger than their original mutual companies in order to participate in federal reclamation projects, they did not, as in many areas of the West, create governmental units, that is, irrigation districts. Instead, they set up water users' associations that were simply supermutual companies. [The need to assess all property, rather than simply irrigated lands, in order to help pay for the latest and largest of the federal projects, the Central Utah project, has required them to abandon this preference, however, and to organize a conservancy district.]

Although the water institutions of Utah have at times been wanting in what some believe to be a necessary centralization of authority, they have from the beginning been endowed with officers who possess a detailed knowledge of the local water supply and of local irrigation practices and with a high level of farmers' satisfaction with the control that they, the farmers, exercise over the institutions.

UTAH VALLEY FARMERS AND THE UNITED STATES

The long history of relations between Utah Valley farmers and the federal government on the Strawberry Valley and Provo projects illustrates the impacts of foreign capital on local control in the Utah Valley. In its 1905 annual report the Reclamation Service announced that the Strawberry Valley Water Users' Association had been formed to unify all the water interests of the Spanish Fork Valley, to merge into one association the old water rights of the valley and the new water supply to be developed by the project, and to take over control of all existing canals. Each farmer was to purchase stock in the new association covering his total irrigable area, whether this was entirely without water or partially or entirely supplied from presently available sources. In other words, his lands and existing water rights were to be merged into the association. To this end each farmer was to turn over to the new association his mutual company stock certificates, which represented his old water rights, and each canal company was to be dissolved by court order. These two actions were to be taken at the time that the Reclamation Service was ready to deliver water from the project to the lands involved.

With respect to these arrangements, the Reclamation Service reported, "Of course the surrender of old water rights was a serious matter and really the only question in this organization that caused any apprehension. Finally, in order to secure entire unity of effort and to prevent possibility of question in any case, the association entered in [an] agreement with each subscriber owning water in Spanish Fork Valley" to the effect that the rights represented by his forfeited stock certificates "shall retain priority and right of use," so that should the supply of water from the Strawberry Valley project fail in any year, any farmer's priority of right "shall be protected and preserved for [his] use and benefit." [16]

The association entered into a contract with the Reclamation Service in 1906, issued stock, and signed contracts with the owners of approximately 50,000 acres of land. But these actions turned out to be largely symbolic, for the unity that was sought among the farmers and between the water users and the federal government did not develop. Farmers in the old canal systems could not reach agreement with those in the area that was to be newly irrigated on the division of water to be stored in Strawberry reservoir, and without such an agreement the former group were unwilling to forfeit their mutual company stock, representing their water rights. The Reclamation Service sided with the dryland farmers for whom they were to build a distribution canal. Furthermore, the irrigators along the old canals objected to being assessed for construction of the canal that was to serve the new area.

As a consequence of these differences the Strawberry Valley association first split into two associations, one representing the existing and one the to-be-irrigated areas; but this accomplished little and the whole organization expired when the Reclamation Service in 1914 abrogated the contract with it. As an investigating committee reported subsequently: "It is practically impossible to mingle control of the rights of the private canals and the Government project." [17]

The old mutual companies, then, did not fade away, as they were supposed to in the initial grand plan, and an additional mutual company was organized to maintain and operate the new Highline canal. The Reclamation Service then contracted with these mutual companies to deliver through their canal systems water that the service sold from the Strawberry Valley project. This water was delivered in bulk at the heads of the several canals, and the canal companies delivered it at a reasonable running charge to the farmers. The farmers, on the other hand, applied to reclamation directly for water, according to their different needs. They could purchase 1 acre-foot of water/acre, or 1.5 or 2 acre-feet, but they were not to be supplied with an amount that would exceed 2 acre-feet/acre from all of their sources. Depending on the amount of water they needed, the farmers were assessed a construction charge to be paid to the service in twenty annual installments—each of the first four installments being 2 percent of the total charge, the next two, 4 percent, and the remaining fourteen installments, 6 percent each—and an annual operation and maintenance charge. (In addition the farmers paid their canal companies a charge for delivering the water.)

In the process of working out these arrangements, so different from the original plans and so unsatisfactory as they turned out to be, relations between the water users and the federal government became highly antagonistic. In March 1913 the government issued an ultimatum giving the association sixty days to comply with the terms of the 1906 contract. The farmers ignored this. Later the same year the government issued a new ultimatum, giving the water users sixty days to comply with one of two alternative solutions proposed. The farmers ignored this. In March 1914 the government abrogated the 1906 contract.

Such relations between the government and water users were not unique to the Strawberry Valley, however. Similar antagonisms and problems on most projects led the secretary of the interior in 1923 to set up a committee of special advisors, otherwise known as fact finders, to suggest "radical reforms or improvements" in this, the early reclamation program. The fact finders found that water users' associations had been formed for all reclamation projects and most of them had signed contracts with the government; but, with two exceptions, none of these associations had functioned in any significant respect.

It is difficult, after these many years, to understand why the water users' organizations . . . were not made to function from the very beginning, and to take upon themselves their share of responsibility for the work of reclamation. . . . Unquestionably on most of the projects there would have been a very different feeling toward the whole Federal reclamation program had the water users themselves been responsible from year to year for the management of the projects. . . . The water users' associations should be awakened, and should be required, where conditions are proper, under satisfactory contracts, to take over the management of the projects, and to carry the full responsibility for operaton and maintenance. . . . A fundamental principle of success in the handling of reclamation projects is to place the management of the project in the hands of the water users, just as soon as the project is in a suitable condition for such transfer.[18]

Specifically with respect to Strawberry Valley, the fact finders recommended that management and operation of the project "should be taken over at once by the water users."[19]

The fact finders' conclusions and recommendations were accepted by the Executive and Congress, and there followed feverish efforts to reactivate the water users' organizations. For Strawberry Valley, a new organization, the Strawberry Water Users' Association, was created, embracing all users who had purchased project water. In 1926 this association signed a contract with the Reclamation Service under which they took over operation of all project facilities.

A key to the water users' signing a new Strawberry Valley contract, as was the case in most other projects, was the government's willingness to renegotiate their repayment obligations. When the Strawberry project was initiated in 1906, reclamation policy required that water users on all projects repay project costs within ten years in equal annual installments and without interest charges; but the early projections of the government that farmers would be able to repay costs within this short period proved without exception to be wrong. The Reclamation Act was amended in 1914 to allow twenty years for repayment, again without interest, but in annual graduated payments; and it was under this provision that the Strawberry Valley farmers signed the previously mentioned individual contracts. This relaxed obligation also proved to be beyond the financial capacity of the irrigators. They fell behind in their payments—by 1926, 29 percent of the construction charges that were due were uncollected as were 15 percent of the charges for operation and maintenance—and in the early 1920s the farmers, along with their colleagues on other projects, requested of Congress and were granted moratoria or deferrals of payment on several occasions. The Reclamation Service was unhappy over these moratoria. "The purpose of Congress," said the service, "was commendable, but there is no question that these acts have worked injustice on the debt paying water user, and have demoralized reclamation finances. . . . A strong local sentiment exists in some projects in favor of keeping the money at home rather than paying it to the Government and taking it from the community." [20]

The repayment problem was a principal reason for the appointment of the fact finders, who concluded, "Neither time nor arbitrary fixed percentage of cost is a sound basis for determining annual payments. . . . Construction cost can only be paid out of the produce of the lands; hence productivity is the only safe and fair basis for fixing annual payments. . . . The principle of a definite period of repayment . . . [should] be replaced by the principle of a varying period of repayment, depending upon the base cost . . . and the productive capacity of the land." [21]

The Executive and Congress accepted in good part the proposal of the fact finders that repayment be related to land productivity; any reservations they had were due largely to the obvious problem, apparently overlooked by the expert advisers, that any extension of the repayment period would be costly to the government and would involve a larger subsidy to the farmers because repayments for irrigation are made without interest.

As for the Strawberry Valley project, the 1926 contract gave the water users the financial benefits of the so-called fact finders' laws in return for their agreement to organize an association that would act as fiscal agent between the water users and the United States government and guarantee the payment obligations of the individual farmers as well as maintain and operate the project. With respect to the financial advantages, the farmers were permitted to fund most of their delinquencies in payments for construction, operation, and maintenance, totaling more than a quarter of a million dollars. All project lands were classified and farmers could convert their individual contracts into new ones based on land productivity, thereby cutting drastically their annual payments while increasing from twenty to forty or more years the time they had to repay their obligations. For example, a Spanish Fork farmer who received a full water supply of 2 acre-feet/acre from the project was paying annually $7.50 per acre under his old contract, regardless of the productivity of his land. Under a new contract he would pay approximately $3.75 if he had first-class land, $2.50 for land of the second class, and $1.15 for the third. In the end he would pay the same total construction obligation, but his annual charge was based on his ability to pay, which was derived in turn from the productivity of his land.

Construction charges were again deferred during the depression years of 1931 through 1936 as a result of annual moratorium acts, and it was not until the late 1960s that the farmers had paid off their debts that began to run when they first received water between 1915 and 1925. Nonetheless, by paying all costs of the project within this extended period, without interest charges, the Utah Valley farmers in fact have paid a larger percentage of real costs than will the farmers who receive water from the Colorado–Big Thompson and Kings River projects and a larger percentage than they themselves will pay for the Provo project, the second federal undertaking to provide them with supplemental irrigation water. Furthermore, it would be wrong to conclude that the Strawberry project was unjustified because of repayment problems. The project created a variety of benefits for others than the farmers in the region, yet the water users alone were required to repay all of the costs, as was the case in all of the early reclamation projects.

By the time the Deer Creek project on the Provo River was begun, reclamation's policies and procedures on relations between water users and the federal government stated clearly that the government would contract only with organizations of water users, never with individual farmers. Thus the prospective users of the water to be stored in Deer Creek reservoir formed in 1935 the Provo River Water Users' Association, a supermutual company with a capital stock of one hundred thousand shares, which were subscribed to by the municipal water districts of Salt Lake City and of five Utah Valley cities and by irrigation companies and districts, mostly in the Utah Valley, in the proportions given earlier in this chapter. The association signed a contract with reclamation in 1936 obligating itself to pay $7.6 million, the then estimated cost of the Deer Creek project, in forty annual installments without interest payments. (In addition, the Metropolitan Water District of Salt Lake City contracted to repay the cost of the aqueduct from Deer Creek to the city, $5.5 million, in forty annual installments.) The companies and districts that subscribed to stock in the association made only a nominal down payment—$.05 per share. The purchase price, $76 per share ($7.6 million divided by one hundred thousand shares) was to be paid over a forty-year period without interest, one-fortieth part to be paid each year after completion of the reservoir. If there were to be any variations in the repayment schedules of different farms or canal companies due to differences in the productivity of their lands, these would have to be negotiated between the association and its stockholders. In addition, the association could from time to time levy assessments against its stock to pay its operating expenses and for deficiencies that resulted from failure of any subscribers to pay their annual indebtedness, but the contracts between the association and its stockholders included limits on such assessments.

Shortages of labor, materials, and capital brought on by the Second World War and other factors delayed construction, resulting in sharply rising costs that characterized the immediate postwar period. Thus with a substantial portion of the project unconstructed, reclamation and the water users were faced with the prospect of total costs greatly exceeding the original estimates that were used in establishing the irrigators' repayment obligation. In 1946 the association and reclamation met this problem by increasing the contract obligation by 50 percent, from $7.6 to $11.4 million, to be paid in the same forty-year period. (Thus the price of a share rose from $76 to $114 and the annual payment from $1.90 to $2.85). But construction costs continued to rise, and by 1948 estimated costs were approximately $1 million in excess of the 1946 contract. A new solution was sought, found, and enacted into law in 1948, which had the effect of maintaining the annual payment at the rate agreed to in 1946 but extending the years for repayment to a sufficient number beyond forty to recover costs.[22] When this solution was adopted, reclamation estimated that it would take approximately six additional years to pay out. However, by the time the project was completed several years later, costs had risen to $23 million. It will take thirty-five years to pay off the costs in excess of those contracted for in 1946 and, therefore, seventy-five years to retire all costs.

By 1952 all irrigation works except Deer Creek Dam had been turned over to the association for operation and maintenance, and Deer Creek Dam was placed in their hands in 1958, so that the water users then had full control over this largely supplemental water supply that they were paying for at an annual rate considered well within their financial capabilities.

Extension of the repayment period from forty to seventy-five years grants a large additional federal subsidy when one calculates interest payments that the users need not make over this longer period. Nonetheless, and excluding interest, the Utah Valley farmers are paying the full cost of irrigation water from Deer Creek, whereas those in the South Platte–Cache La Poudre region of Colorado are defraying a much smaller percentage of the cost of their water, and a good part of this is paid for by the nonfarm population in the form of *ad valorem* taxes and power rates.

The Bonneville project, part of which is currently under construction by the Bureau of Reclamation, will benefit Utah Valley farmers, among others. This project is a unit of the Central Utah project, which is in turn a "participating project" in reclamation's immense Upper Colorado River Storage project. Given the early stage of development of this complex undertaking, the relative insignificance of Utah Valley's benefits in the total picture, and the uncertainty of the evolving contractual arrangements between Utah Valley farmers and the federal government, we have not discussed the project in any detail.

Because we have been concerned principally in this section with contractual relations between water users and the United States, we have focused on water users' repayment of costs rather than on economic justification of the several projects. As stated previously with regard to the Strawberry project, it would be wrong to conclude necessarily that any of these projects is unjustified because of repayment problems. Economic justification of a reclamation project involves identifying the objectives for which the project was proposed and measuring benefits and costs in terms of these objectives, an analysis we do not undertake here. In this context, repayment policies have an important impact on some objectives but very little impact on others, and in any case repayment of the costs of a project and its economic justification are different matters. (If income redistribution is the objective of a project, for example, a requirement that beneficiaries repay project costs has the effect of reducing project benefits. On the other hand, beneficiary repayment has no direct relation to the objective of national economic growth.)

OBJECTIVES OF OPERATING PROCEDURES

Those who have studied carefully the development of Utah irrigation in the early years are one in emphasizing that the Mormon community's objectives were stated explicitly in terms of enhancing the welfare or interests of the public rather than that of the individual, unless these interests happened to coincide.[23] By public welfare the Mormons meant the development of self-sufficient communities of small farmers. For this purpose no settler was to own more land than he, with the labor of his family, could cultivate intensively; and given the labor requirements of irrigation farming, this meant small farms. When new communities were colonized by the church in the early 1850s, for example, a bachelor farmer received 10 acres, a married man with one wife and a small family, 20 to 30 acres, while a polygamist with several grown sons was given a 60-acre tract.[24]

Equality and Equity

The operating procedures the Mormons devised for distributing water were consistent with the enhancement of the public interest thus defined. Basically water was allocated in relation to size of land holdings and since these were based on the Mormon concept of equality, this objective, along with that of equity—fairness or equality in the treatment of all members of the community in the same situation—dominated their water distribution procedures.

We have seen that the Anglo-Saxon colonizers of Utah, like those of Colorado, abandoned the riparian system of water rights because they found it inapplicable to the aridity of their new lands and adopted in its place a system of prior appropriation. But the Mormon version of this time-priority system was modified in many ways to emphasize "equality" in the allocation of water and in the sharing of the costs of drought. Thus decrees that divided stream flow among canals gave more credit to actual and beneficial uses of water and less credit to time priority of claims than would have been the case under a pure appropriation system. Furthermore, their operating procedures accommodated newcomers rather than simply protecting priority claims of the original colonizers. The spirit that made the early settlement of Utah successful, according to one observer, was that of live and let live—not how much water could be used in crop production, but how much could be spared to the new settler so that he could produce a crop.[25]

Also, the Mormons shared the costs of seasonal drought among a larger number of water users than would otherwise have been the case by their practices of using as a metric of allocation fractional parts of a variable water supply rather than fixed quantities of water, by defining canal rights so that they varied over the irrigation season, and by dividing water rights into classes. For greater equity they arranged their rotation schedules so that no farmer would have to irrigate at night or on Sunday on every rotation and so that the benefits and costs of diurnal variations in stream runoff would be shared broadly.

The Utah Valley irrigation communities of today are no longer as homogeneous as they were in the nineteenth century. Nor are the unifying authority of the Mormon church and its goal of self-sufficient communities as pervasive as they were. Nonetheless the objectives of equality and equity have continued to influence the procedures by which irrigation water is used. This is due in part to the continuing influence of the doctrines of the early Mormon church; in part to inertia—that is, the continuing influence of the procedures themselves that were adopted in the early years; and in part to the facts that the farms have remained uniformly small in comparison to those of northeastern Colorado and the Central Valley of California, for example, and that control over procedures has to this point remained in the hands of the farmers themselves. The puissance today of equality and equity is illustrated in farmers' attitudes toward selling their mutual company shares and renting their water. These exchanges are made typically below what would be market prices because the farmers think it not right to charge all that the traffic will bear; they believe in a "fair price" and they are against "water profiteering."

At the same time, the inability of the new Highland canal and the old Spanish Fork interests to work together in the early days of the Strawberry project, and to a lesser extent the conservatism demonstrated by some of the old mutual companies when they failed to sign up for Provo project water, raise questions about the continuing influence of the early spirit, the special togetherness of the Utahans. It may be that entry of the federal government, even though it was by invitation of the irrigation communities, introduced an element so foreign to their normal operations that it became an antagonistic influence, making it more difficult for them to settle their problems on the basis of equality and equity. Reclamation, for example, appears to have favored the Highland canal interests over those of the older companies. It may be true also that the old spirit waned to some degree with the declining authority of the church.

Conflict Resolution

The special affinity between water and community conflict is now familiar—it was presented in the introductory chapter of this book and has been discussed subsequently. If the Mormons were to succeed in establishing self-sufficient communities of small farms in a short time, they needed to make sure that conflicts and potential conflicts over water were resolved promptly. The operating procedures they initiated in Utah satisfied this objective admirably. In the early years the authority of the doctrine and hierarchy of the Mormon church was important in this regard, but the capacity of the irrigation communities to prevent and to settle disputes has survived the decline of this authority by means already described. After observing that the distribution system today does not encourage the most economic use of water or great flexibility in the use of resources, Hudson says, with some exaggeration, perhaps: "But the function of the system is none of these; it is, rather, to divide the water peaceably; in that it succeeds." [26] Here, too, the Strawberry project experience calls for a reservation.

Popular Participation and Control

Water users in the Utah Valley own, manage, and operate their systems. Popular participation and control is an objective they have achieved in high degree. A farmer's voice in the affairs of an irrigation community and the amount of water he receives from it depend primarily on the shares of stock he owns in his mutual company. As a rule, all stockholders are farmers served by the system, and the number of shares a farmer owns is related principally to the acres he irrigates. Since farms are small, as is the variation in their sizes, the resulting community participation is broad and general. The elected officers of the companies are farmers in almost all cases; and the watermaster and other employees, if there are any, are frequently farmers and shareholders.

The water users rely primarily on themselves for enforcement of their operating procedures, and any disputes that arise are settled by the watermaster or by the president and board of directors of the company. The only regular outside control comes from the river commissioners who administer the decrees that divide river water among several companies and canals; and the commissioners are selected with the advice of the farmers.

In the early years of settlement broad popular participation proved to be consistent with the objective of developing self-sufficient communities of small farms. To be sure, a highly centralized Mormon church directed the whole colonizing movement. No activity, economic or social, was beyond the church's reach. For each community the church selected the initial settlers and their bishops. But these men had no previous knowledge of irrigation practice, and the church could provide neither technicians to help and direct them in this activity nor any significant amount of capital. In this situation common sense and current experience were the only guides to action and the labor of the farmer and of his wives and sons, the principal resource. This meant that the water users themselves played the dominant role in building, operating, and maintaining their irrigation systems.

Furthermore, when the natural water supply in the Utah Valley was almost fully allocated and the lands under the several irrigation canals fully occupied and cultivated, the church turned its attention to developing colonies in other areas of Utah and in Idaho, Nevada, and Wyoming. As a consequence, any control of irrigation that the church, as a strong central power, might have exercised in the valley was forfeited to the water users, even though they continued in many cases to elect officials of their church wards to be officers of their canal communities. The church withdrew, leaving behind diffusion rather than centralization.

We have seen that efforts to transfer to institutions of civil government the authority over irrigation matters that the church had held were largely unsuccessful. The administrative machinery that evolved was one of farmer cooperatives—the mutual companies. And the machinery for adjudicating water rights, although it came to terminate in court decrees, was based on informal and voluntary agreements.

The Church of Jesus Christ of Latter-Day Saints had no capital to invest in irrigation. The federal government has invested a great deal. Yet the Utah Valley irrigators have forfeited little of their objective of local control to the central government. Like their compatriots in northeastern Colorado and the Central Valley of California, they have been given the federal projects at bargain rates while avoiding significant federal controls. The acreage limitation provision of federal law has been no issue in the Utah Valley because the farms are small; but the Utahans have challenged successfully other perceived threats to self-determination. The history of the Central Utah project remains to be written, to be sure, but it will be recalled that the federal fact finders' principal complaint about the users of the Strawberry Valley project was that they failed to take full control away from the central government when they had the opportunity to do so. The early Utah experience involving the church and the subsequent experience with the federal government both raise questions for Wittfogel's analysis of hydraulic societies, questions to which we return in the concluding chapter.

Efficiency

The continued and persistent emphasis that the Utah Valley farmers have placed on popular participation, conflict resolution, and equality in their operating procedures has meant that today their irrigation agriculture is less efficient than otherwise it would be. Utah Valley lands would yield more crops if there were less emphasis on proportionality in the sharing of seasonal shortages. The invariability of irrigation return periods and the variability of water controls, including the absence of modern measuring devices, are inefficient, as are variations among the individual companies in their operating procedures, even though these are not large. Merging some of the companies would be more efficient.

Most of these now inefficient procedures were relatively more efficient when they were adopted. Since then environmental factors have changed; but the companies, reflecting the desires of their farmers, have been conservative institutions. They have been less aggressive than their counterparts in northeastern Colorado and the Central Valley of California, for example, in acquiring new supplies and in adopting new operating methods. This inertia has had a greater adverse effect on the objective of economic efficiency than on those of popular participation, conflict resolution, and equality, and this no doubt helps to explain it. If, in response to new technology and a desire for greater productivity for the Utah Valley as a whole, the farmers were to change the allocation of water and procedures for distributing it, they would forfeit some of their internal democracy. At least they see it that way. Hudson reports that mergers are blocked "by the fear of farmers of being . . . dominated by outside groups of farmers, and of losing the advantages of present informal personal relationships with officials, such as watermasters."[27] Other and related reasons for conservatism are the small size and fragmentation of farms, the increasing number of part-time farmers, and the advanced age of many of them.

Utah Valley farmers, in sum, do not pursue efficiency as aggressively as many agricultural economists think they should. This can be seen no place better than in their attitude toward water itself, which is to them more than simply an economic good. They believe in "fair" prices, not market prices, for their irrigation water.

APPENDIX: SIMULATION OF IRRIGATED FARMS IN UTAH VALLEY

Simulation Procedures

The basic distribution rule in Utah, like that of Murcia-Orihuela, is Rotation, in which each farm, typically in the order of its location on a canal, begins and terminates irrigation in each irrigation period at assigned hours. Unlike most of the canal systems in Murcia-Orihuela, however, the irrigation systems in Utah do not impose elaborate rules of crop priorities to distribute water in drought periods. In Utah the length of rotations may be varied but little else is changed with drought conditions.

Rotation is one of the basic procedures in the irrigation simulation program described in our USDA Technical Bulletin No. 1431. It can be used with other procedures, and In Utah it is used with storage water that can be ordered on demand. In simulations of irrigation procedures in Utah, water is measured by flow—cubic feet per second—so that the water available to a sector, lateral, or farm can be measured by multiplying flow by hours when the unit is assigned to receive water. Flow is considered to be uniform during any one irrigation period, but it may vary from period to period. This may not be precisely correct because of the diurnal effect of snow melt on stream flow; but it is difficult to measure this effect on specific water users, and for this reason we have not attempted to simulate it.

Each farm is supplied with the flow in the lateral for a fixed time period based on the rotation schedule. The hours assigned to each farm in the rotation are converted into a percentage of the total hours in the rotation period. Water available to a farm in its assigned time that is surplus to its needs remains in the canal and is available for use on the next farm.

Each farmer makes crop adjustments to the water he receives during drought periods. This is simulated by using the Plan or Replan subroutines.

When during low water periods farmers use reservoir water to supplement their supplies of canal water, this is simulated by the Demand procedure in combination with Rotation for canal water. The farmer can vary his demand for reservoir water from one irrigation period to another.

Program Designations With reference to table 9, Principal Distribution Rules, of Bulletin 1431, the following programs are used to simulate the Utah operating procedures:

Water Supply	Description of Procedure	Procedure Code
Stream flow	Rotation	8
Stream flow plus reservoir water	Rotation + Demand	9

Basic Data

The irrigation season consists of fourteen irrigation periods, each lasting fourteen days. Each of these can be thought of as a single two-week period or two seven-day rotations. Table A8.1 shows the mean percentage of water supply available by irrigation periods. Table A8.2 contains a frequency distribution of farms in Utah Valley and the sizes of farms used in the simulation model along with each

Table A8.1 Distribution of seasonal flow available for irrigation from the Provo River.

Irrigation Periods	April		May		June		July		Aug		Sept.		Oct.	
	1	2	3	4	5	6	7	8	9	10	11	12	13	14
% of flow	5	8	13	16	15	13	5	4	4	4	3	3	3	4

farm's proportion of the water supply. Table A8.3 shows proportions of crop acreages on farms in the Utah Valley, and table A8.4, the initial crop pattern selected for the simulated farms. Data on the crop yields, costs, and returns used in the Utah simulation are presented in table A8.5.

Table A8.2 Farm size in Utah Valley and representative farms used in the simulation.

| Farm size, irrigated acres | Farms | | Simulation Farms | | |
	Number	%	Farm No.	Acres	% water
Less than 10	640	30.5	1	18	3
10–49.9	896	42.7	2	48	9
50–99.9	325	15.5	3	98	17
100–199.9	169	8.0	4	175	24
200 and over	68	3.3	5	280	38
			6	41	8
Total	2,098	99.0			

Table A8.3 Acreages of major crops in Utah Valley, 1959.

Crops	% of Total Irrigated Acreage
Corn silage	9
Small grain	35
Alfalfa	40
Sugar beets	5
Vegetables	5
Orchards	6
Total	100

Table A8.4 Crop patterns on simulation farms, Utah Valley (in acres planted).

Crop	Farm 1	2	3	4	5	6	Total
Corn	5	8	10	18	25	15	81
Small grain	—	15	34	60	100	—	209
Alfalfa	5	15	40	70	110	18	258
Sugar beets	—	5	5	9	45	—	64
Vegetables	3	—	3	8	—	3	17
Orchards	5	5	6	10	—	5	31
Total acres	18	48	98	175	280	41	660

Table A8.5 Yields, costs, and returns per acre for crops grown in Utah Valley, Utah.

Crop	Yield	Preharvest cost[a]	Harvest cost[a]	Gross return	Full production, net return
Apples	325 bu	$360.00	$162.00	$591.00	$69.00
Peas	400 cwt	86.95	53.00	165.00	25.05
Small grain	60 bu	48.16	10.50	63.00	4.34
Corn silage	16 ton	60.15	16.00	108.00	31.85
Alfalfa	3.5 ton	33.33	28.14	77.00	15.53
Sugar beets	18 ton	119.85	40.40	252.00	91.75

[a]Preharvest and harvest costs include labor; machinery; materials such as seed, fertilizer, and sprays; real estate taxes; water; and interest on cash and land investment.

9 Conclusions

The objectives sought by the six irrigation communities in Spain and America are the same in broad outline. There are, to be sure, differences in the relative importance that each attaches to the several objectives, but these are not great, not as large as we had expected. Also, there are differences among the communities in how they implement their objective sets, but the variances in this regard are limited by the technological function of hydraulic agriculture, for this function defines in significant degree the range of operating procedures that can be used.

Irrigation technology has certain special characteristics. One is the simple fact that water, unlike the natural resources of land and minerals, for example, flows; so the status of the resource at any point in time and place is highly sensitive to changes that occur at other points in the river basin, especially points upstream. This physical trait of water-related activities has been summarized in the aphorism: "One river, one problem." In human terms it means that the location of irrigators along a stream or canal determines their social relations to a significant degree.

A second special characteristic of irrigation technology relates to the uncertainty and unpredictability of water supplies. Unregulated stream flows in arid environments are highly erratic, varying from year to year, from season to season, and in some cases from day to day and hour to hour. At the same time, the response of different crops to abundance and shortage of water varies over the irrigation season, depending on the crops' stages of growth. These physical traits make for a highly stochastic production function for irrigation agriculture rather than a deterministic one, and they induce a general sense of insecurity that is important in determining the relations among those involved in the process.

A third technical characteristic of irrigation agriculture is somewhat less general than the first two, for it applies more to traditional systems that have developed along natural channels and over natural topography than to reclamation schemes in which large blocks of land are leveled and supplied by rational networks of uniform artificial channels. In the traditional systems the problems of dividing and distributing water are complex, uniquely so for each system. How to manage a distribution system so that each irrigator receives water in the amount and at the time required by his crops; how to divide the water so that each irrigator receives the amount to which his water right or his interest in the system entitles him; and how to organize a force and a system for water delivery that will accomplish these results without great friction, at a cost irrigators will pay, and in accordance with their other objectives are questions that no irrigation community has been able to settle except by long and costly experience.

Technology, then, delimits the set of operating procedures from which a community of irrigators can choose for the purpose of gaining its objectives.

Sensible of this relationship, we can compare what has been achieved in the six communities.

LOCAL CONTROL

The most powerful conclusion that emerges from the case studies is the extent to which water users have controlled their own destinies as farmers, the extent to which the farmers of each community, acting collectively, have determined both the procedures for distributing a limited water supply and the resolution of conflicts with other groups over the development of additional supplies. With important variations to be sure, local control has been the dominant character- istic of irrigation in these regions, regardless of the nationality or religion of the farmers, the epoch, whether formal control is vested in an irrigation community or in higher levels of government, the forms of government at the higher levels, and perhaps even the legal nature of water rights. In this realm of public activ- ity—and one wonders in how many others—formal centralization of authority, where it has occurred, has not meant substantial loss of local control *de facto*. General administrative, legislative, and judicial norms laid down by higher authorities have not negated customary procedures. The norms have been either too general to accomplish this or they have been ignored by local organizatons. In his study of irrigation in medieval Valencia, Glick found that municipal, reli- gious, and royal authorities do not seek central controls but acted rather as ad- juncts to traditional cellular irrigation authorities. This continues to be the case in Valencia and in all of the communities examined.[1]

The technological characteristics of irrigation agriculture—especially the flow, stochasticity, and singularity of water supplies—create special problems of con- trol to which there are two polar responses, with a relatively small number of alternatives between them: a single leader or leadership group, which may be from outside the irrigated area, can operate the control structures and proce- dures, or all the irrigators of a water source who live within a defined service area can create and support a users' organization with authority to operate the struc- tures and procedures of water control.

Wittfogel and like-minded scholars believe that the typical response is the first one—control from outside and from on top, which can lead to despotic power in the hands of the ruler, who has the capacity to shut off the water at will, or of an agromanagerial bureaucracy that tends toward totalitarian control over water users.[2] Foreign and top control are, however, so inconsistent with the objectives of farmers to control their own destinies that they have been prepared to go to great lengths to support local cooperative organizations that have sufficient strength and coherence to be able to effect the second and alternative response to the technology of hydraulic agriculture, namely, local control.

Those who see some form of dictatorship as the typical response to water technology have underestimated the farmers' capacities to organize collectively to avoid such a result and have overestimated the facility of top control. To give credibility to the threat that he may shut off the water, a ruler must be prepared to do so, perhaps even to cut it off for periods long enough so that it hurts. Given the consequences of denying water to developed areas, a ruler who would exercise this power needs to be thoroughly despotic, and few are. It is said of El Glaoui, the ruler of the Marrakech region of Morocco under the French Protectorate, that he was despotic in just this fashion. But the United States government, although it could do so easily in the hydraulic sense, is not going to shut off the water to the farmers of the Kings River because they continue to defy federal law on family farms or to those in the South Platte-Cache La Poudre because they have refused to renegotiate their repayment contracts. Nor is the Spanish government going to close the gates on the farmers of Valencia and of Murcia-Orihuela because they have failed to abide by the national law relating to control over abstractions from streams. Once projects like Pine Flat, the Colorado-Big Thompson, and Generalísimo are built, the water behind their dams will be released to beneficiaries who can then pretty well thumb their noses at the ruler.

If farmers do not develop effective cooperative organizations or if once cohesive organizations erode, the consequence is not necessarily a switch to the alternative of top control but is more likely to be no control, that is, no sufficient response to the technological function and, as a result, ineffective irrigation agriculture. When the Strawberry Valley farmers failed to organize to take over control of the reclamation project that was built to serve them, the federal government did not seize the opportunity to exercise top control. Rather it complained that the project was not realizing its potential and offered additional inducements to the beneficiaries to establish local control.

Brunhes, it will be recalled, said that the technology of irrigation creates a psychological state of insecurity to which men will respond successfully if they are disposed toward working collectively with each other, that is, toward maintaining strong local organizations. If they are not so disposed, then they are out of harmony with their physical environment and successful irrigation agriculture will not result.

Those who emphasize outside and top control are concerned typically with the construction of hydraulic works, which frequently requires concentrations of capital and technical labor not available at the local level. From these central requirements of construction they have projected central control over irrigation without, it seems to us, looking at the problem sufficiently from the point of view of the water users. From this latter perspective we have found that the users, if they are organized, can pretty well call the tune, even where the central government has built the works. In much the same vein, Glick has observed that a historian's interpretation of a document on water control depends on whether he is interested in the subject from the view of the builder or that of the user. As an example he cites a letter of Hammurabi ordering an official to investigate an irrigation matter. Wittfogel, who is interested in the construction of hydraulic works, emphasizes the element of centralized bureaucratic authority in this document; whereas to an institutional historian like Glick, the salient feature of the letter is that the official is ordered to convoke a council of elders to resolve the matter locally. "In the former vein, irrigation cannot function without centralized control; in the latter, it cannot function without local direction of distributional arrangements, as typified in a traditional society by a body of elders who know the local custom and the immediate topographical and hydraulic problems."[3]

In addition to the general conclusion that local control is ubiquitous and powerful, several subsidiary but nonetheless important findings related to control can be drawn from the data of the six irrigation communities.

Relation of Local Organization to Community Growth and Stability

The strength and coherence of local irrigation organizations in developed regions appears to be correlated with an irrigation community's success in limiting or stabilizing growth, thereby gaining security for its members. The principle that irrigators have used universally for this purpose is time-priority: first in time, first in right; but application of the principle has varied with the operating procedures for distributing water. Where these procedures are based on prior appropriation, that principle in itself limits growth and no other procedure is needed for this purpose. If latecomers claim water this does not affect the security of those earlier in time whose beneficial needs will be met fully before any water is provided to succeeding settlers. Where, on the other hand, the basic distribution principle is that all farmers and canals receive water in proportion to the land they irrigate, an additional procedure is needed to limit growth and provide security. Otherwise latecomers could keep on joining the system, receiving water in proportion to their lands, until there was insufficient water for all. Many procedures have been adopted, all based on time-priority, including the following: to define the limits of the irrigation community and provide that no water may be delivered outside of them; to specify the canal system and provide that it may not be extended; to register the land that may be irrigated or the farm turnouts from which water can be drawn and provide that none others be used; to provide that supplemental water sources be delivered by the same procedures or through the same distribution system or to the same lands as the principal source; or some combination or variation of these.

Thus, Valencians have defined the limits of their huerta and of the service areas of their canals; they have specified their distribution networks; and within service areas, they have registered three classes of land based on time of settlement in order as follows: lands to be irrigated regularly (*regadios*), those entitled to excess water only (*extremales*), and those that are to remain dry (*secanos*). Rather than use exclusive categories like Valencia to protect early users, the farmers of Murcia-Orihuela adopted more flexible procedures that were compatible with their use of the rotation rather than the turn as their principal operating procedure. Up to a point beyond which it would be clearly inefficient, new lands were given rights to water, but the lands in each successive expansion were given less water per unit of time than older lands.

When in the sixteenth century Tibi Dam was built in Alicante, it was provided that the holders of old water rights, which were not attached to land, could sell them only to those landowners in the Huerta who, by contributing to the construction of the dam, had new rights that were attached to land. Although this rule limited the freedom of the first water users, its purpose was to stabilize the community by prohibiting transfer of old rights in the future to users who might seek to enlarge the Huerta.

Even in the South Platte-Cache La Poudre, where the appropriation principle fairly well ensures security, additional measures have been adopted for this purpose. Thus at an early stage in planning for the Colorado-Big Thompson project, the federal government agreed that no new lands were to be brought under irrigation as a result of the scheme and the Kings River farmers extracted a similar agreement from the government.

One way for an irrigation community to be secure is to control the growth of its service area. A second is to develop supplementary water supplies and to protect existing supplies against encroachment by others. Relating this second method to the vitality of local irrigation organizations, we can test two hypotheses: first, that the existence of forceful local organizations varies directly with such activity and second, and partially contradictory, that the search for additional water sources is likely to open the door to outside interests that are antagonistic to the local ones, with the result of weakening local organizations. The data from the six communities give considerable support to the first of these propositions but very little to the second one. The construction of dams with foreign capital in Valencia, Murcia-Orihuela, Colorado, Utah, and the Central Valley of California has not diminished the force of local organizations; more probably it has strengthened them.[4]

As in the case of stabilizing the size of an irrigation community, time priority has been the principle invoked by local organizations to increase the security of their water supplies. In Colorado intercommunity disputes have been settled and security of developed areas achieved with remarkable success by relying on the state courts to determine absolute priorities among those who abstract from streams, based on date of first use. The irrigation organizations of Valencia and Murcia-Orihuela have won acceptance of the principle that customary users, particularly traditionally autonomous groups of users, are entitled to preference as the basis for resolving conflicts over the development of new water supplies in the Turia and Segura valleys.

Relation of Local Organizations to Operating Procedures

One would expect that the existence of forceful local organizations would vary with the operating procedures adopted to distribute water within a community. The less automatic the procedures, the stronger would be the community organization to operate, control, and patrol the distribution system and to resolve conflicts among users. To a significant degree this is so. But it appears also that certain of the procedures adopted in each community, a different combination of procedures in each one, has required a strong local organization. One community will use procedures for dividing water among canals or for distributing it to farmers that make necessary an operating organization, whereas another will use a basic procedure that is fairly automatic for one or both of these purposes. At the same time, the second community is likely to adopt additional or supplementary procedures not used by the first one that call forth strong organization.

Thus in times of insufficient water Valencia requires a strong local organization to divide water among the principal canals and among the laterals of a single canal (the rotation of canals on the right and left banks of the river, the rotation of laterals, and the transfer of favor water among them), to divide it among the farmers of a single lateral (farm priorities, time limits, and crop priorities), and to settle disputes (the water court). In Alicante, on the other hand, a strong organization would not appear necessary to transfer water among canals, laterals, farms, and crops or to settle disputes among users, for the water market of that huerta is more automatic than are the elaborate administrative procedures of Valencia. At the same time, the institutions and procedures for the issue, auction, and collection of scrip in Alicante—for operating the water market—have themselves required a fairly strong local organization.

The procedure of prior appropriation used to divide water among canals in Colorado and Utah is so automatic once the decrees setting the order of prioritis have been agreed to, as is the procedure of dividing canal water among farmers on the basis of shares owned in mutual companies once the shares have been issued, that there would appear to be no need for strong local organizations to operate the systems. Nonetheless there are such institutions in both regions, in part because the farmers, for the purpose of mitigating the automaticity of the principal procedures, have adopted additional ones. In Colorado the farmers use different procedures for distributing their supplementary water supplies than are used for ditch water; and delivery in the same canal networks of stream flow, reservoir water, and Colorado–Big Thompson project (C-BT) water is a complex matter. We have described earlier in some detail the additional procedures adopted in Utah, in this case a result of the Mormons' desire to promote greater equality by modifying directly the usage of time priority as well as their need to develop supplementary sources.

Local Control over Conflict Resolution

The water users of our irrigation communities have managed the conflict inherent in relations among the members of a single community, as well as those with outside communities and organizations, by using a variety of alternative institutions and procedures. When any one combination has appeared to threaten local usage and local control, they typically have switched to another.

The settling of disputes, as Carl Friedrich points out, is the primordial internal function that a political order has to perform, antedating the making of rules and the application of such rules in administrative work.[5] It is performed by many institutions and procedures, not simply by the judiciary and not necessarily by judicial procedures. We shall therefore describe the principal alternative combinations of institution and procedure and then use the Kings River case (we could use any or all of the others) to show which ones the irrigators have used and for what purposes. For simplicity in describing the alternatives we assume that conflicts involve two parties. We shall call any party or institution not involved in the substance of a conflict but that enters it in order to help resolve it a third party.

There are two broad categories of procedures, depending on whether a third party is involved. If a third party is not involved, a conflict will be resolved by avoidance by one of the parties, coercion by one of the parties, or negotiation involving both parties. Avoidance occurs when one party takes no action to redress a decrement of his interest. His tactic of withdrawal, however, may induce the other party to make amends. By coercion one party imposes the outcome on the other, typically by a threat or use of force. The other party concedes. In negotiation both parties seek a mutually acceptable settlement without the intervention of a third party, but often with the aid of supporters. Negotiation is likely to be an effective form of conflict resolution where there is a clear pattern of interests that affects both parties, although the interests may be shared or in conflict; where there is a certain threshold of community and therefore of mutual confidence between the parties (negotiation is more likely to succeed between allies than adversaries); and where the issues and interests are such that each party has reason to believe that a substantial improvement might result from entering into negotiation. The outcome of successful negotiation will be a bilateral (mutual) agreement, a political bargain, a compromise, or a contract.

With the intervention of a third party, a conflict can be resolved by adjudication, legislation, arbitration, or mediation. There is an important distinction between adjudication and the other three forms, which is based on the degree to which the third party is bound by rules. Where there are no rules or only broad rules of conduct and procedure, conflict resolution will be legislative, arbitrative, or mediative. If the third party simply compromises the positions of the conflicting parties, it has engaged in arbitration or mediation, the former if the parties agree in advance to accept its judgment. If, on the other hand, the third party resolves a conflict in terms of the broader objectives of the community as a whole or of the majority of the community, it has undertaken legislation. (In some cases the results of arbitration and mediation will be in accord with broad community objectives.)

Adjudication is used to resolve conflicts where the third party achieves and explains its decisions in terms of rules of law that have been laid down in codes, statutes, or, if common law prevails, in legal precedents. Also, the procedural rules of adjudication are precise and distinctive, involving the presentation of proofs and reasoned arguments by the parties.

There is no necessary correspondence between a procedure and the institutional character of the third party. Although courts normally adjudicate, they also legislate and arbitrate on occasion, as when the U.S. Supreme Court, in cases of original jurisdiction, decides a dispute between two or more states over the allocation of the flow of an interstate river. Legislatures arbitrate when they pass bills that settle conflicts by simply compromising the positions of the parties. The Executive is likely to practice all procedures for conflict resolution in one or another of the programs it administers.

As among forms of conflict resolution, the ones used will depend on the procedure that both parties, or perhaps one of them, prefers and also on the parties' opinions of the faculties of third parties—opinions of the qualifications of third-party members: how they are chosen for office, their biases, their capacity for impartiality—and of the third party's powers to enforce its decisions.

Which of these forms have been used in the Kings River drainage basin? Before 1890 conflicts among water users on the river were settled typically by adjudication in state courts, in accordance with widely accepted rules of appropriation that had been developed by custom and enacted subsequently in statute. When in 1886 the California Supreme Court unilaterally changed these rules by recognizing riparian rights, most of the parties sought to withdraw from the courts and from third-party conflict resolution. Instead they resorted to negotiations. In 1897 the Fresno canal company, the three Mussel slough mutual companies, and the Laguna ranch negotiated an agreement allocating stream flow among them. By further negotiation this agreement was broadened to include more units and greater stream flow in 1921, 1927, 1949, and 1963. Each of these agreements provided that all pending court cases among the parties were to be dismissed or postponed and all the agreements except that of 1921 were validated by court decrees.

Thus there was a progression from adjudication, a third-party procedure, to negotiation. The threat of adjudication was an important element in the success of negotiations. The courts, by their unreasonableness in the opinion of the parties to the conflicts, impelled them toward negotiation and agreement. The agreements were approved in court decrees, to be sure, but in this the parties were using the courts, the third party, not to settle conflicts but to give supplementary authority to the settlements that had been achieved without their intervention. This procedure, it should be noted, is not the same as so-called judicial mediation, in which the court, as a third party, compels conflicting parties to reach an agreement that it subsequently ratifies in a formal decree.

At a higher level of political organization, the great majority of water users, who were losers in the state supreme court's 1886 settlement of the conflicting claims of riparian and nonriparian landowners, sought to switch the third party and the process for conflict resolution from the court and adjudication to the general assembly and legislation. Their first effort to override the court's settlement failed because once property rights had been granted to riparian claims, the protection of private property was seen by many to be sufficiently important as a broad public interest (which, it will be recalled, is the criterion for legislation) that it could not be ignored in a legislative settlement. None of the legislative proposals offered in 1886 were adequate in these terms.

The second effort in 1927, after the court had reaffirmed its support of riparian owners, succeeded. This time a broader public interest was found that would override the protection of private property if it were approved by an extraordinary majority of the legislature and by the voters in the form of a constitutional amendment. "[T]he general welfare requires that the water resources of the State be put to beneficial use to the fullest extent to which they are capable and that the waste or unreasonable use ... of water be prevented."[6]

In the meantime the water users relied on negotiation as much as they could. But in a situation where the courts had played a very large role before 1886, they could not be avoided entirely after that date. The supreme court's decision in *Lux* v. *Haggin* was so discordant with environmental conditions, however, that the courts themselves practiced avoidance without striking down the opinion. Lower-court decisions favoring riparian owners were not enforced. No judge was prepared to dry up the country, although the opinions had the effect of stopping its development. Courts ameliorated the impact of the ruling by developing other doctrines in uncommon ways—prescription, the severance of riparian water rights from riparian lands—and by limiting its application to surface flow, declaring a different doctrine for groundwater.

An unusually well informed irrigationist in Colorado, after reading the Kings River chapter in manuscript, said, "Incredible! It's still difficult to imagine the rationale for adopting the riparian doctrine after years of operating under the appropriation doctrine. Are you sure there weren't some ulterior motives that inspired the Supreme Court to opt for the riparian doctrine? Acceptance of the riparian doctrine was an affectation that none of the other western states indulged in. Why did California get into this mess? Why was the senior western state susceptible to allowing this disruptive decision to take effect?"[7]

The distance between the state supreme court and the people and the people's representatives can be explained in part by the qualifications of members of the court, if not by ulterior motives. The decision in *Lux* v. *Haggin* was four to three, the opinion being written by the Justice McKinstry. Edward Treadwell, a distinguished California water lawyer, wrote of McKinstry: "A man of higher standing, morally and intellectually, could not well have been found, but if the whole world had been sought for a man of unimpeachable character, who was still the best suited to uphold the riparian doctrine ... , no one could have done better than to have selected Justice McKinstry for that part. He was an old man already and lived to be much older. He was born and bred in the common law, and knew his Blackstone forwards and backwards. He believed honestly and sincerely in the omnipotence of the law and the infallibility of the common law of England to solve every human dispute."[8] Given these qualifications of the court as third party, the Kings River water users used, insofar as they could, alternative forms to settle conflicts between those who lived on the river and those who had brought river water to the plains.

The Kings River case includes examples of negotiation for conflict resolution in addition to those discussed above, particularly conflicts over water rights that were settled when one party negotiated purchase of the rights and facilities of the other, and the lengthy negotiations between water users and the U.S. government over Pine Flat Dam.

Arbitration was used in the 1963 contracts insofar as both parties, the water users and the federal government, agreed to be bound by a future determination of the courts on the legality of lump-sum payment to avoid acreage limitation.

The Kings River units in 1921 chose the state division of water rights as a mediator to prepare a final allocation schedule. All units submitted to the third party statements of their claims and requirements for water. They also agreed in advance to abide by the resulting schedule for the 1922 water year, and in this regard the procedure can be called arbitration.

We have noted examples of conflict resolution by the coercion of one party (such as destruction of the other party's diversion structures), but there are more examples in which obvious opportunities for coercion were converted into avoidance (such as the hesitancy of ditch riders to lock the gates of offending farmers and of the federal government to operate Pine Flat reservoir for flood control only until the water users had signed repayment contracts).

An important generalization in the literature of conflict management, especially that of the anthropologists, is that a society will make progress in the settlement of conflicts when two-party conflicts can be transformed into conflicts involving a third party that can resolve them.[9] On first consideration, experience in the Kings River appears to challenge this, for progress was made when the farmers withdrew from the courts and entered into negoitations without a third party. These Kings River data do not contravene the generalization, however, when its reasoning is examined carefully, although they do add a dimension to the relations between two-party and three-party disputes that has not been given sufficient attention. The generalization is derived from the proposition that if none of the forms involving third-party intervention are available and if negotiation fails, the parties will resort to either coercion, which may mean war in primitive societies and in international relations, or avoidance, which may mean surrender. Third-party procedures therefore enable a society to progress by avoiding war and surrender. In the Kings River case third-party procedures were available in case negotiation failed, but a compelling desire to avoid these led to the success of that procedure in which no third party was much involved. The Kings River parties, as those in the other irrigation communities, could shift back and forth among procedures in which third parties were or were not involved, thereby furthering and protecting local control of their irrigation operations.

Common Characteristics of Institutions of Local Control

The institutions of local control have certain common characteristics. They are typically cooperative or mutual organizations in which virtually all landowners have a vote. Also, the members of their representative councils, executive committees, and boards of directors, their administrative officials, and frequently their employees are irrigators with intimate knowledge of the local scene.

The qualification for voting and participating in general assemblies is based on ownership of land that receives or could receive irrigation water in all of the Spanish communities and those in the United States that are governed as irrigation districts, and on ownership of stock in the U.S. communities that have organized mutual companies. The basic principle in Spain is that each landowner is entitled to one vote, although this is modified somewhat in Orihuela, where landowners get one vote each in the election of officers but may have more than one, depending on the size of their irrigated farms, in other deliberations of the assemblies, and in Alicante, where landowners may neither vote nor participate in the general assembly if they own fewer than 4.4 irrigated acres (1.8 hectares [ha]). At the same time, the big men in Alicante (those who own a large number of old rights) are given no extra voice in the community's deliberations, although they are assessed taxes on the basis of the number of rights that they hold. By limiting in this way the voices of the very small and the very large, Alicante may have muted what would otherwise be disruptive antagonisms in a community where some members own water without land.

Contrary to the principle of one man, one vote that is practiced in farmers' cooperatives and in irrigation districts in the United States, mutual companies have adopted the corporation principle where one share has one vote. As a rule, the stockholders are farmers served by the companies in which they own stock, and the number of shares that farmers own is related principally to the areas that they irrigate. In Utah farms are small, as is the variation in their size, resulting in general and relatively equal participation by all. In Colorado the farms are larger than in Utah and the variation in their sizes is somewhat greater; but the smaller operators have not professed interests that are antagonistic to those of their larger partners, and in any case the small and medium owners are in a position to outvote the larger ones.

Local control does not necessarily mean control by the least advantaged or control for their benefit. In the California case, for example, local control has meant that the present landowners have been able to resist successfully efforts by the central government to divide up their large farms and distribute them, presumably, among landless farmers.

To conclude this discussion of local control we can say that the farmers of the six irrigation communities have met the technological requirement of control with institutions based on popular participation and native expertise, which is no mean achievement. At the same time, we can ask how many other activities in the public sector demonstrate similar characteristics of local control—for example, that centralization of authority to build works does not mean necessarily loss of local control over operating them and distributing their benefits. At the beginning of this chapter we emphasized the relation to local control of the special complexity of the technological function for irrigation agriculture. Other public activities may have similarly complex functions. The question is whether such functions have led to similar patterns of governance.

ECONOMIC GROWTH

Economic growth or efficiency for the irrigation community as a whole requires, as we have said previously, institutions that can achieve a balance between flexibility, necessary if water is to be transferred from less to more efficient uses, and security, needed if farmers and others are to make the investments of labor and capital required for economic development.

Over the long run a high degree of stability has been attained in all of the communities; they have all benefited from large investments of labor and capital, although in recent years this had been less true in Alicante than elsewhere. At the same time, it is difficult in most areas to transfer permanently the rights to use water from a less efficient to a more efficient user. This is due in part to the fact that stability and flexibility, as requirements for economic growth, are not necessarily complementary, but also to a conflict between long-run flexibility and local control. The institutions of all of the communities are based on a popular belief that to allow easy transfer of water, more so than of other means of agricultural production, is to invite foreign control over farmers' activities and that such control necessarily would be antagonistic to community objectives. Short-run flexibility is another matter, however. Water is "rented" if it is not "sold"; there is a market in water for individual rotations and even for seasons where there is scarcely any for basic water rights.

We have compared the several short-run operating procedures to determine how efficient they are in the agricultural environments of Spain, using a composite of conditions in Valencia and Murcia, and of the United States, using Colorado and Utah. In each country the two areas, though not alike, are sufficiently similar in farm sizes, crop patterns, growing seasons, water requirements, and hydrographs to justify our grouping them for the purpose of examining the major alternative water distribution rules. Nine procedures have been used. Seven of them depend on stream flow that is distributed over the irrigation season in accordance with the data in table A9.1 in the appendix following this chapter; the remaining two procedures are based on the assumption that water for the season is in storage and that farmers can draw it on demand. To examine the efficiency of these procedures we have simulated each with both 90 percent and 75 percent of the quantity of water required to achieve full production of the crop acreages that are planted. Thus the benchmark used to compare all procedures is full production with an ample water supply for all farms.

To represent each country we have used a group of seven farms and seven crops, each with four fields, so that there are 196 farm fields. The water supply varies over twenty-six irrigation periods in a crop season in Spain and fourteen in the United States. Thus the program simulates 5096 discrete farm management decisions during a single crop year in Spain and 2744 in the United States. Because the same values for crops planted are used at the commencement of each simulation (and these values are shown in the table reporting results), it might appear that crop patterns are fixed for all operating procedures and all water supplies. In fact, crops vary constantly as the simulations proceed, that is, as water is distributed. Each time water is delivered to a farm, it is applied first to those crops and fields for which it is likely to have the highest value—more specifically, those crops and fields for which dollar losses would be greatest if water were not supplied given the values of the crops, their status in the growing cycle, water requirements, and related factors. It is the use of "loss functions" that makes the simulation so powerful an analytic tool. It keeps crop patterns changing as they would in real life.

Data on the farms and crops, including irrigation water requirements and the losses that result if these requirements cannot be met due to water shortage, are in tables A9.2 to A9.5 of the appendix. Other assumptions used in the simulation program, along with a description of how it works, can be found in the authors' U.S.D.A. Technical Bulletin 1431 (revised 1974).

The nine procedures are these:

1. Shares. Each farm receives in each period a fixed percentage of the water available for the period. A farm's percentage is based on ownership of shares in the system. The number of shares owned by a farmer is normally based on the size of his farm, and in the simulations here we have assumed that this is the case. Water not used by a farm to which it is allotted is wasted. Shares is the basic procedure used for stream flow in Colorado.

2. Shares with excess water returned to canal. Same as shares procedure except that water not used by a farm is available to the next farms below should they have inadequate water during the period. Excess water is accumulated each period until it is used; but if it is not used during a period, it is wasted.

3. Rotation. Each farm has a reserved time in which to irrigate in each period; but the water delivered in this time will vary on each rotation with the instant flow in the ditch. The time assigned to a farm is normally based on farm size, and in the simulations here we have assumed this is the case. If a farmer does not take water in his assigned time, that water is available to subsequent irrigators. Rotation is the basic procedure used in Fresno, Utah, and Murcia-Orihuela.

4. Turn. Farms are served in order of location along the canal. When water reaches a farmer, he takes all he needs for the period, before the next farmer is served. Water distribution in any period begins where it stopped in the previous period. This is the basic procedure used in Valencia, although it is

abandoned in favor of farm priorities, time limits, and crop priorities when there is a drought.

5. Farm priorities. Farms are served in an order of priority based typically on time of settlement. When water reaches a farmer, he takes all he needs for the period before the farmer next in order of priority is served. Water distribution in any period begins with the first-priority farm. In the simulations here each farm has a designated priority in order from farm 1 to farm 7. The procedure of farm priorities approximates the doctrine of prior appropriation of the western United States. For the irrigation communities we have studied, however, the appropriative rights belong to the mutual companies or to irrigation districts; and the internal distribution of the water among farms is governed by other procedures. A variation of the farm priority procedure is used in Valencia, where certain farms, the so-called extremales, are second priority. They may be denied all water before first-priority farms are made to suffer significant consequences of drought.

6. Crop priorities. Crops are assigned orders of priority, based normally on economic value but sometimes on other considerations. When water is sufficient, all crops receive needed irrigations; but as shortages develop, priority crops are watered first on all farms. If water remains, it is distributed to the non-priority crops on farms by turn. In the simulations here we assume only two classes of crops: priority and nonpriority. Dry beans, apples, and potatoes have priority in Colorado-Utah; potatoes, corn, and beans have priority in Valencia-Murcia. During periods of extraordinary drought the crop priority procedure is used in Valencia, Murcia, and the New Almoradí canal of Orihuela.

7. Market. Under this procedure it is assumed that all water users bid each period for the water needed to irrigate their crops. Thus water is allocated to the highest value uses each period on the assumption that these can outbid lower value uses. The value of using water on any crop at any time is defined in terms of the loss in income that would be sustained if the crop were not watered in the current rotation, taking into account any water shortages for the crop in prior rotations. The simulation program calculates these values for each field of each crop on each farm for each rotation. The basic data for these calculations are in the tables of the appendix to this chapter. Market is the basic procedure used in Alicante.

8. Demand. Water supply for the full irrigation season is stored and available at the beginning of the season and each farm is allotted a fixed quantity for the season. The farm receives in each irrigation period the quantity of water that the crops need up to the farm's seasonal allotment. In the simulations here the water that is stored and available at the beginning of the season in each irrigation community is 90 percent or 75 percent of the water required to achieve full production. Each farm is given an allotment roughly in proportion to its size. This approximates the procedure used in Hanford for surface and groundwater, in Fresno for groundwater, and in Colorado for water that

is stored and made available to farmers by reservoir companies.

9. Demand-Plan. This is the same as demand procedure except that farmers are not limited to the areas of crops that they grow normally, which is the case for the other operating procedures. Here it is assumed that the farmers, knowing at the beginning of the season what their seasonal water supplies will be, plan the areas of their crops, within limits, so as to get the highest possible return from the available water.

We have examined the comparative efficiency of these nine operating procedures in terms of area income, that is, the income of all of the farms together. The results are displayed in tables 9.1, 9.2, and 9.3. It will be observed that under most procedures and in both water supply situations, but especially in severe drought, percentage losses in net income are greater in Colorado-Utah than in Valencia-Murcia. The principal reason for this is that irrigation is carried on the year around in Spain, allowing some lands to be double cropped. Frequently one of the crops can be brought through to harvest while the other, which matures during the months of greatest drought, will fail.

It is not surprising that the demand procedures perform best, for they are based on the availability of storage sufficient to hold an entire season's water supply so that farmers can call for water when their crops need it. The value of this storage can be estimated by measuring the amount by which the net income

Table 9.1 Simulation of Colorado–Utah irrigation systems, comparison of gross and net income from various water distribution procedures using 90 percent and 75 percent of an adequate seasonal water supply.

	Gross Income		Net Income	
	90% water	75% water	90% water	75% water
Full production (in dollars)	$188,180.25		$55,486.75	
Reduction from full production for various procedures (%)				
Shares	12.4	29.2	42.0	93.4
Shares + excess	11.0	27.7	37.1	89.3
Turn	18.0	46.4	61.0	154.4
Rotation	12.8	27.9	43.5	88.6
Priority farms	11.3	29.6	36.4	84.0
Priority crops	16.0	20.2	54.4	62.5
Market	10.8	28.3	36.4	86.6
Demand	6.2	58.5	20.9	160.5
Demand Plan	10.6	17.5	10.1	15.5

Table 9.2 Simulation of Valencia-Murcia irrigation systems, comparison of gross and net income from various water distribution procedures using 90 percent and 75 percent of an adequate seasonal water supply.

	Gross Income		Net Income	
	90% water	75% water	90% water	75% water
Full production (in pesetas)	740,250		377,600	
Reduction from full production for various procedures (%)				
Shares	32.9	43.4	61.7	81.3
Shares + excess	23.1	36.5	43.7	68.7
Turn	28.9	40.9	53.8	77.4
Rotation	23.6	36.0	44.9	67.9
Priority farms	17.9	30.0	33.1	55.0
Priority crops	19.2	33.9	37.6	66.4
Market	14.9	27.6	29.2	53.3
Demand	5.7	25.7	10.0	46.6
Demand Plan	4.9	19.1	3.1	26.0

Table 9.3 Rank order of various water distribution procedures in terms of area net income.

	Colorado-Utah		Valencia-Murcia	
Procedure	90% water	75% water	90% water	75% water
Shares	6	7	9	9
Shares + excess	5	6	6	7
Turn	9	8	8	8
Rotation	7	5	7	6
Farm priorities	3	3	4	4
Crop priorities	8	2	5	5
Market	4	3	3	3
Demand	2	9	2	2
Demand Plan	1	1	1	1

of demand procedures exceeds that of stream flow procedures and then comparing this to the costs of building the storage, which are not included here. Nor is it surprising that the demand-plan procedure is unequivocally the best in all circumstances, for with it farmers can not only call for water when their crops need it, but they also are free in each season to plan that combination of crops that will give the highest return for the available water. The poor performance of demand procedure under severe drought in Colorado-Utah may seem surprising, however. The farmers called for water as needed, exhausting the supply for all crops before the end of the season. This did not happen in Valencia-Murcia because of double cropping there. The first crop came through to harvest largely unaffected by water shortage.

Turning to the stream flow procedures, the turn is clearly the least efficient for the Colorado-Utah environment; and indeed the procedure is not used there. The procedure's poor performance is due principally to the incompatibility of water delivery and crop needs. Once drought conditions develop within a system using turn, the length of time between successive waterings becomes progressively longer and timely irrigations become more and more difficult as all farmers try to catch up on irrigating their crops once the stream reaches them. In this way the procedure wastes water. Turn is used in Valencia, however, where it is not very efficient, ranking eighth out of nine in both water supply situations. This illustrates why Valencia uses modifications of the basic turn in ordinary low water and abandons it when there is a severe water shortage, practicing instead a drought regime based on farm priorities, time limits, and crop priorities.

In Valencia-Murcia, shares is the least efficient procedure, ranking lower than it does in Colorado-Utah. In the Spanish environment many of the farms are unable to use their shares in every irrigation period and the unused water is wasted. When, however, this surplus water is made available to neighboring farms, the shares method improves considerably.

The rotation procedure used in Utah and in Murcia-Orihuela is more efficient than Valencia's turn under all conditions, and it is comparable in efficiency to the shares + excess procedure. In both cases water that is surplus to any user is made available to downstream farms and is not wasted.

Of the procedures that do not depend on full season storage, farm priorities and market are the most efficient. Although all our irrigated areas have used time priority as the basis for preferring some groups of farmers over others in their rights to water, none has assigned absolute priorities to all farms and none therefore has used farm priorities as its basic short-run procedure. Such a procedure would be so inequitable among the farmers of a close-knit irrigation community, as we shall see below where we examine the impact of operating procedures on income distribution, that irrigators have adopted it as a short-term procedure only in severe droughts, and even then with regard to small classes of farms rather than individual farms.

The market also has been unpopular with the irrigators of many communities, but not because it is in fact inequitable as a short-term operating procedure, for

Table 9.4 Differences between market and turn procedures in area net income under two water supply situations (percent losses from full production).

Procedure	Colorado-Utah		Valencia-Murcia	
	90% water	75% water	90% water	75% water
Turn	61.0	154.4	53.8	77.4
Market	36.4	86.6	29.2	53.3[a]
Difference	24.6	67.8	24.6	24.1[a]

[a]Reduction for market procedure is too high (and the resulting difference, too low) because simulation program did not eliminate new plantings during extreme drought.

this is not the case, as we shall see below. Farmers have traditionally feared the instability and loss of local control that could result from a market in water rights as a long-term procedure; and they have projected this fear to a dislike of market as a means of allocating seasonal water in the short run, although there is no necessary relation between the indirect consequences of short- and long-run market systems, as the Alicantians have discovered. The farmers of that area have used a market, including an auction, as the most efficient way to distribute their limited and erratic water supply. With 75 percent of a normal supply the market procedure in Spain would in fact perform better than the results shown in table 9.2. During years of extreme drought farmers do not plant late season crops where there is little chance of water being available to bring them through to harvest. The program we have used to simulate the market is deficient in that it has not eliminated these plantings. It has thereby wasted some water on these crops, but more importantly, considerable money—their preharvest costs—has been wasted.

We have seen, then, that the operating procedure used to distribute water in a shortage situation has significant effect on net income from agriculture in an irrigated region. Considering only the stream flow procedures of shares with the use of surplus water, turn, rotation, and market (therefore excluding shares with wasted surplus water, the two priority procedures, and the two procedures that depend on storage) the market procedure is the best in both water supply situations and in both regions; and the turn is the worst. The differences between market and turn in terms of percentage loss of area income from the income realized at full production are shown in table 9.4.

INCOME DISTRIBUTION

To examine the influence of irrigation operating procedures on income distribution among farmers and farms in an irrigation community one needs to know first the basis for allocating or defining rights to water—what we call the long-term procedure—and second, the effects on this base distribution of alternative short-term procedures for sharing the costs of drought when water is in short supply. The long-term basis for distributing water is generally the acre or hectare of irrigated land. The farmer receives water in proportion to the amount of irrigated land that he works. The relation of this to equitable distribution of income from use of the water by farmers will depend largely on the size distribution of farms.

The principle of equality of land units for allotting water has been modified, however, in each community by some form of the exclusionary principle of time priority—first in time, first in right—for priority is the means by which the irrigators have achieved community stability and economic growth. Thus the basis for dividing water among farmers in any irrigation community is largely the result of the tradeoff that the irrigation community has developed between equality of all acres in the community and the priority of these acres in terms of time of initial irrigation. In Valencia this tradeoff is represented by three classes of land with differentiated rights, in Murcia, by the fact that some farms, added to the service areas of canals at a relatively late date, have less time per hectare in a rotation than farms that began irrigating earlier. In Colorado stability was achieved by allocating stream flow to mutual companies on the basis of prior appropriation, with the result that in an average year 80 percent of the companies deliver less than 2 acre-feet of stream flow per acre, while 20 percent deliver more than 2 acre-feet. Subsequently, when the Colorado–Big Thompson project was built, this tradeoff between equality and priority was modified. Farmers were permitted to subscribe for a quantity of supplemental project water, which when added to their company water would give their lands an adequate supply, roughly 2 acre-feet/acre.

Considering as given any inequalities in the long-run allocation of water, we have simulated alternative short-run procedures, using the same basic data as in our simulations for economic efficiency, to compare in terms of equality how the procedures distribute the consequences of seasonal drought and to determine the short-run tradeoffs between income distribution and efficiency that result from each procedure. Three metrics have been used, each representing a different definition of equality. The ordinances, rules, and actions that constitute the legislative histories of the operating procedures of the six communities indicate that irrigators have not been clear on which of these definitions, or which combination of them, corresponds most closely to their objectives. The measures are as follows:

1. Average loss in net income per acre (hectare). Starting with the income per acre of each farm when there is adequate water and therefore full production, we have determined by simulation the reduction in income per acre for each farm under each procedure when only 90 percent and 75 percent of water are available. Then, using the simulation data on individual farms, we have calculated two measures for each operating procedure that enable us to compare the procedures in terms of how close they come to distributing water among farms so that the average per acre losses of all farms are equal. The first measure is the median deviation of the average losses in income per acre

Table 9.5 Simulation of Colorado-Utah irrigation systems, comparison of net income from various water distribution procedures using 90 percent (shown in boldface type) and 75 percent of an adequate seasonal water supply.

	Farm		
	1	2	3
Full production (in dollars)	2,651.40	6,230.60	6,948.00
Reduction from full production for various procedures (%)			
Shares	**48.4**	**41.8**	**37.8**
	86.6	83.6	87.6
Shares + excess	**48.4**	**29.8**	**32.3**
	86.6	84.4	87.6
Turn	**43.6**	**80.3**	**85.7**
	144.5	180.2	142.1
Rotation	**51.0**	**41.8**	**34.2**
	104.0	101.0	84.0
Priority Farms	**0.0**	**0.0**	**0.0**
	0.0	0.0	0.0
Priority Crops	**26.5**	**56.7**	**74.6**
	47.7	34.2	62.2
Market	**27.9**	**21.1**	**33.0**
	76.1	57.8	80.0
Demand	**20.4**	**23.4**	**17.8**
	122.6	119.4	133.7
Demand Plan	**10.4**	**12.5**	**12.0**
	14.3	16.7	16.0

4	5	6	7
7,618.75	3,273.00	11,755.00	17,010.00
65.3	**28.9**	**42.0**	**34.6**
102.8	92.1	98.2	93.2
55.8	**11.6**	**42.7**	**32.8**
100.5	66.5	98.2	85.6
97.4	**47.7**	**56.8**	**39.2**
148.9	185.2	122.0	170.5
67.7	**49.0**	**42.0**	**35.6**
72.1	119.4	80.1	89.5
0.0	**0.0**	**7.8**	**113.2**
2.6	1.6	52.3	236.2
35.4	**39.5**	**44.7**	**45.4**
61.2	62.2	78.3	64.6
46.2	**28.9**	**37.9**	**40.5**
107.3	75.4	86.2	94.5
19.4	**21.0**	**20.0**	**22.4**
174.7	131.1	164.0	189.0
12.4	**10.0**	**10.4**	**7.2**
18.0	15.7	15.6	14.0

Table 9.6 Simulation of Valencia-Murcia irrigation systems, comparison of net income from various water distribution procedures using 90 percent (shown in boldface type) and 75 percent of an adequate seasonal water supply.

	Farm		
	1	2	3
Full production (in pesetas)	31,000	54.050	25,500
Reduction from full production for various procedures (%)			
Shares	**91.3**	**53.6**	**148.5**
	103.7	77.0	153.4
Shares + excess	**91.3**	**52.1**	**89.8**
	103.7	75.6	137.0
Turn	**55.2**	**22.6**	**133.9**
	123.0	53.0	53.6
Rotation	**89.4**	**52.1**	**94.5**
	104.5	75.6	117.9
Priority farms	**0.0**	**0.0**	**0.0**
	0.0	0.0	7.1
Priority crops	**53.7**	**17.3**	**14.1**
	66.6	44.5	37.6
Market	**34.3**	**26.8**	**27.4**
	62.2	49.4	53.8
Demand	**5.3**	**7.4**	**100.0**
	43.9	58.6	100.0
Demand Plan	**5.6**	**8.3**	**34.1**
	28.9	36.0	47.1

4	5	6	7
47,600	118,750	16,700	84,000
91.3	**40.7**	**61.0**	**42.4**
101.3	61.9	75.6	70.7
69.0	**26.2**	**18.9**	**21.8**
86.7	55.5	29.0	46.9
84.3	**47.4**	**37.2**	**44.0**
83.1	56.4	78.9	109.7
62.7	**36.9**	**15.8**	**15.7**
86.8	56.1	35.2	46.9
10.4	**21.3**	**18.9**	**109.0**
13.9	60.4	101.1	131.7
32.7	**49.1**	**13.1**	**43.0**
85.2	77.0	32.6	69.9
29.0	**32.1**	**25.3**	**26.6**
54.6	53.7	52.9	51.3
13.7	**0.0**	**0.0**	**0.0**
87.9	29.1	0.0	34.1
13.3	**+4.3**	**+12.0**	**+3.3**
36.1	19.8	+7.3	21.4

Table 9.7 Normalized median deviations of different operating procedures, based on dollar (peseta) losses per acre (hectare) in net farm incomes.

	Colorado-Utah				Valencia-Murcia			
	90% water		75% water		90% water		75% water	
Procedure	Deviation	Rank	Deviation	Rank	Deviation	Rank	Deviation	Rank
Shares	.2360	5	.0953	2	.8691	5	.5592	6
Shares + excess	.2418	6	.1128	3	.7475	4	.6118	7
Turn	.3261	7	.2259	7	.8990	6	.3314	3
Rotation	.1695	2	.3126	8	.7384	3	.5472	5
Farm priorities	a	9	21.5643	9	1.5967	7	2.1007	9
Crop priorities	.3413	8	.1340	6	.3462	2	.2683	2
Market	.0694	1	.0396	1	.2280	1	.2341	1
Demand	.1883	4	.1131	4	4.3098	9	.7529	8
Demand Plan	.1823	3	.1337	5	2.0977	8	.5240	4

[a] Infinite because median farm has zero losses. A Gini coefficient is defined, however. See table A9.6.

of each farm; the lower the deviation, the closer the procedure to equality in these terms.[10] The second measure is the Gini coefficient of losses in income per acre. As the two measures give results that are consistent, we have used the less sophisticated one in the text and included the Gini coefficients in table A9.6 in the appendix.

2. Average loss in net income per farm. This measure assumes that equality relates to losses in farm income as a whole rather than losses in farm income per acre. The ranking of procedures will differ from that for income per acre because different farmers plant different combinations of crops. The method used for determining the median deviations for all procedures in this case is analogous to that used for the first measure. We have not used Gini coefficients here because absence of a constant unit (income per acre) makes the calculations less reliable.

3. Average loss in water supply per acre (hectare). The literature on the operating procedures of several of the irrigation communities states the equality objective in physical rather than monetary terms (that is, that all farms are to share shortages of water in proportion to their area). To evaluate alternative operating procedures with this criterion, we start with the water per acre (hectare) delivered to each farm under full production and determine by sim-

Table 9.8 Normalized median deviations of different operating procedures, based on dollar (peseta) losses per farm in net incomes.

Procedure	Colorado-Utah 90% water Deviation	Rank	75% water Deviation	Rank	Valencia-Murcia 90% water Deviation	Rank	75% water Deviation	Rank
Shares	.1859	3	.0565	1	.4551	3	.2784	4
Shares + excess	.3188	6	.0822	3	.5025	5	.3705	6
Turn	.3343	7	.1221	4	.5109	6	.2765	3
Rotation	.1908	4	.1408	6	.4889	4	.3234	5
Farm priorities	a	9	25.9911	9	2.0492	8	2.9481	9
Crop priorities	.3353	8	.1424	7	.4425	2	.2519	2
Market	.2022	5	.1405	5	.0861	1	.0449	1
Demand	.0672	1	.1652	8	3.2917	9	.5962	8
Demand Plan	.1277	2	.0619	2	1.9040	7	.4281	7

[a] Infinite because median farm has zero losses.

ulation the reduction in water per acre for each farm under each procedure when only 90 percent and 75 percent of water are available to the area as a whole. Using these data we have calculated for each procedure the median deviation and the Gini coefficient of the average farm loss in water per acre. Tables 9.5 and 9.6 show the net income of each farm when it has adequate water and achieves full production and the percentage losses in net income for each farm under each operating procedure when only 90 percent and 75 percent of adequate water are available. These are the data of the simulation runs. Tables 9.7, 9.8, and 9.9 and tables A9.6 and A9.7 of the appendix show the deviations of all procedures from perfect equality according to each of the three definitions of equality.

It will be observed from the rank orders of these tables that the priority farms procedure is the poorest; and indeed, this makes good sense for the procedure is not designed to provide equality among farms in any of the senses in which we use the term. First come, first served is its standard of justice, so that water shortages are forced entirely on the lowest priority farms.

The market procedure, on the other hand, provides overall the most equal distribution of losses. For Spain the market ranks first among all procedures for all definitions of equality. For the United States the market ranks first among all

Table 9.9 Normalized median deviations of different operating procedures, based on acre-inch (m³) losses per acre (hectare) in water delivered.

| Procedure | Colorado-Utah | | | | Valencia-Murcia | | | |
| | 90% water | | 75% water | | 90% water | | 75% water | |
	Deviation	Rank	Deviation	Rank	Deviation	Rank	Deviation	Rank
Shares	.1623	5	.0748	5	.5663	4	.3849	5
Shares + excess	.1933	6	.1147	6	.3731	2	.3380	3
Turn	.4059	7	.2832	7	1.8068	6	.2178	2
Rotation	.1263	4	.0730	4	.3784	3	.3617	4
Farm priorities	a	9	a	9	a	9	a	9
Crop priorities	.6041	8	.2196	8	1.3873	5	.6545	8
Market	.0444	3	.0333	2	.2723	1	.1321	1
Demand	.0322	1	.0306	1	2.0904	8	.4553	6
Demand Plan	.0333	2	.0336	3	2.0050	7	.4860	7

[a] Infinite because median farm has zero losses. Gini coefficients are defined, however. See table A9.7.

procedures when the criterion of equality is percentage loss in income per acre and first among stream flow procedures when the criterion is water delivered. It performs relatively poorly only when the criterion is equal percentage loss in farm income. This result was unanticipated for two reasons. First, since the rationale of the market procedure is to allocate water to farms with a high proportion of high-value crops and deny it to those with low-value crops, we expected greater differences among farm losses for the market than for certain other procedures. The contrary outcome is due in part to the particular combinations of crops run in the simulations. These crops, however, are representative of those grown in two different environments, neither of which actually uses the market procedure. An examination of the crop data in tables A9.2 and A9.3 of the appendix shows that there has been no intentional bias in favor of the market procedure. We can agree, then, with our numbers that a market procedure for distributing irrigation water ranks high in equality.

A second reason we did not anticipate the performance of the market is that this procedure is the most efficient of all the stream flow procedures, that is, it provides the largest economic growth.[11] It is a doctrine of many welfare economists that among several procedures the ones that rank high in efficiency will do poorly in distributing income equally among beneficiaries while those that do

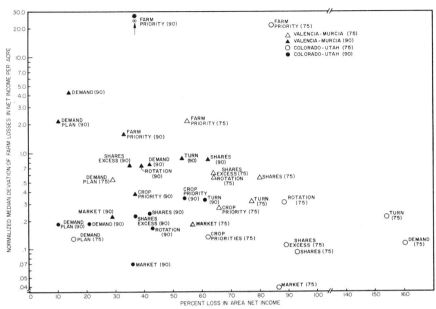

Figure 9.1 Tradeoffs between economic growth (measured by percentage losses in area net income) and distribution equality (measured by deviations of farm losses in net income per acre) for various water distribution rules, with 90 percent and 75 percent water supply in Colorado–Utah and Valencia–Murcia.

well in distributive equality will be inefficient.[12] This conventional wisdom, we discover, does not apply to a wide variety of conditions in irrigation agriculture.

The tables reveal interesting comparisons between the Spanish and American regimes. The several operating procedures provide a higher degree of equality in the Colorado-Utah environment than in Valencia-Murcia, with the exception of the market procedure when it is measured in terms of income losses per farm and of farm priorities, which is not relevant for these comparisons. Also, in Spain the deviation in median losses per acre is higher than the deviation in net farm incomes for all operating procedures except farm priorities. This indicates that farmers are able to protect their income to some extent by selective irrigation of crops during drought periods. For Colorado-Utah a similar comparison does not show a clear trend. One reason is that the American farmers do not have the opportunity to double crop.

Finally, to compare the short-term tradeoff between economic efficiency and distribution equality achieved by each procedure in each region, we have composed figures 9.1 to 9.3. The most significant of these tradeoffs we have discussed already; the purpose of the figures is to put them together in graphic presentation.

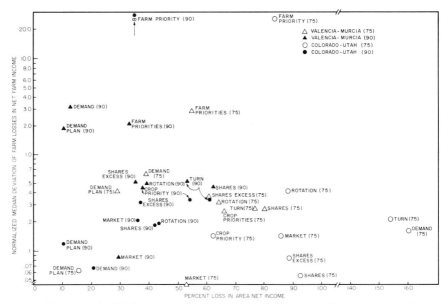

Figure 9.2   Tradeoffs between economic growth (measured by percentage losses in area net income) and distribution equality (measured by deviations of farm losses in net income) for various water distribution rules, with 90 percent and 75 percent water supply in Colorado–Utah and Valencia–Murcia.

The information developed in these studies of six irrigation communities suggests hypotheses and conclusions that relate to intellectual and scholarly interests other than local control, income distribution, and economic growth, but we have not mastered these other subjects in sufficient depth to make full use of our data. We shall simply indicate the subjects and the nature of the hypotheses and conclusions concerning each that might be developed by further examination of chapters 2 through 8.

The Process of Economic Development

There are many possible applications of the data to the study of economic development. One aspect that intrigues us is how and to what extent land speculation and corporate wealth have affected agricultural development (see chapter 5 for a definition of land speculation). Contemporary economists who are concerned with the processes of economic development have given relatively little consideration to the effects of speculation in natural resources on conditioning economic growth. This was not the case for American economic historians of the early twentieth century, with the result that much of what is known and taught today derives from their views, which were very much influenced in turn by the

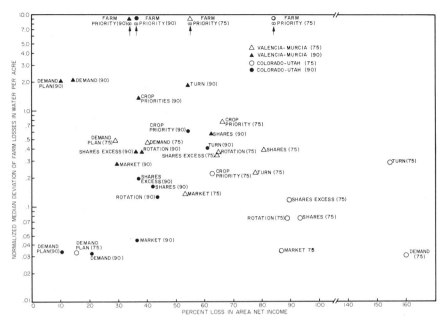

Figure 9.3   Tradeoffs between economic growth (measured by percentage losses in area net income) and distribution equality (measured by deviations of farm losses in water per acre) for various water distribution rules, with 90 percent and 75 percent water supply in Colorado–Utah and Valencia–Murcia.

political philosophy of the Progressive movement. Our data on California are especially useful in this connection.

The Progressive economic historians have claimed that land speculation and the intrusion of corporate wealth in agriculture have stultified economic growth and retarded development of the West. The speculators, they said, took a short-run view and exploited land and other natural resources without thought for future economic growth. Their activities prevented homesteaders from locating farms. By withholding land for a rise in price they created speculators' deserts, thereby dispersing economic activities over a large area and increasing private and governmental costs. Furthermore, absentee ownership was itself a prescription for retarding economic development. Among other things, it caused a rapid increase in tenancy, with all of its social costs.

Speculation in land has different consequences for economic growth than speculation in other factors of production, it was argued, because of the economic peculiarities of land as a commodity. The market in land lacks the continuity and liquidity characteristic of markets for wheat, cotton, and securities. The units of sale lack homogeneity; and since land cannot be shipped to market centers for inspection, there is widespread ignorance of the facts of supply and demand and of the movement of values. Fluidity of the land market is further limited by the complicated procedures necessary to effect a transaction in land.

In Fresno the actual consequences for economic development of land speculation and corporate wealth have been, in almost every respect, the opposite of those stated by the Progressive historians. This we have seen in chapter 5.

The Progressive economic historians have argued that land speculation and corporate wealth in agriculture, in addition to retarding economic development, have led to unjust effects on the distribution of wealth in America. They generated excessive profits and contributed to the concentration of wealth in the hands of a few. It is true, certainly, that in the San Joaquin Valley men like Chapman, Friedlander, and the Perrins made fortunes in land speculation and development; but being speculators they frequently lost fortunes, too. Chapman was ruined financially by his large investment in an imaginative scheme for the integrated development of the water resources of several streams in the valley. After 1875 he lost much of his lands to the Bank of California, to Miller and Lux, and to the Scottish capitalists who had given him backing; and he lost the Fresno Canal and Irrigation Company as well to a San Francisco bank. In the depression of 1893-94 the Perrins lost the Fresno canal company and much of their land in the area.

We need to know more about the profitability of speculation in irrigated areas before we can say anything definitive about its effects—adverse or beneficial—on the distribution of wealth and before we can compare the consequences of land speculation on the distribution of wealth to its consequences in terms of economic development. Bogue and Swierenga have used econometric techniques to calculate the rates of return to speculators in public lands in Iowa and Illinois.[13] The opportunities and problems of speculation in irrigation communities are different, to be sure, but these authors' analytical techniques can be adapted to them.

Henry George is the intellectual leader of those who have argued since the 1870s that speculative profit in land is unearned and therefore unjust because the speculator contributes nothing to the increased value that he reaps. This value is created by the economic development of the community, especially its population growth, and the speculator, if anything, retards development by such activities as withholding land while he waits for its value to rise. This argument against profits applies to the land itself, not to developments on the land. It is normally accompanied by reform proposals to nationalize land or to deprive its owners of the unearned increment by taxation—the so-called single tax. One of the principal arguments against the analysis and proposals of the single taxers has been the difficulty of separating site values and improvement values—the activities of the land speculator and those of the land developer. Based on the Fresno experience, this criticism is well taken.

Finally, the Progressive historians have argued that land speculation has injected poison into the lifestream of American politics. Here they refer to the ways in which laws for the disposal of federal and state public lands were written and administered, involving influence peddling, conflicts of interest, bribery, and other corrupt practices. In the Fresno situation would any other method of disposing of the public lands have resulted in less corruption? An alternative would have been for the government to develop the lands—to construct the irrigation systems, provide credit, recruit the colonists. But given the extraordinarily rapid rate of economic and social change and the political morality in California at the time, there would likely have been more corruption in the much larger bureaucracies that would have been needed to conduct these programs than there was in the Government Land Office.

Although we have relied on the Fresno case study to illustrate the role of land speculation in economic development, we do not mean that such speculation is uniquely Californian or American. Speculation in agricultural land has accompanied the opening to settlement of new areas in all parts of the world throughout the nineteenth and twentieth centuries.[14] We need to know more about its special role in irrigated areas outside the United States and about the respective roles of the agricultural corporate entrepreneur and the government in such areas.

The Nature of Justice in Political Economy

To a significant degree our conclusions relate to the justice of institutions—to the relations in irrigation communities among popular control, distributive shares, economic growth, and farmers' concepts of fairness. We have not evaluated these conclusions, however, in terms of any of the formal models of justice developed by logicians and political philosophers. This challenge remains, and to suggest how interesting and how relevant it could be we present here a summary of John Rawls's model from his recent book, *A Theory of Justice.*[15] Rawls derives a general conception and a model of a just, basic institutional structure that can serve as a standard for appraising existing institutions and for guiding social change related to them. The general conception is that all social primary goods, by which Rawls means liberty and opportunity, income and wealth, and the bases of self-respect, should be distributed equally unless an unequal distribution of any of these goods is to the advantage of the least favored. The model based on this general conception consists of two principles and two priority rules. The first principle holds that each person is to have an equal right to the most extensive system of equal basic liberties that is compatible with a similar system of liberty for all. By basic liberties Rawls means political liberty (the right to vote and to be eligible for public office) together with freedom of speech and assembly, liberty of conscience and freedom of thought, freedom of the person along with the right to hold personal property, and freedom from arbitrary arrest and seizure as defined by the concept of the rule of law. These liberties are all required to be equal by the first principle, since citizens of a just society are to have the same basic rights. The second principle holds that social and economic inequalities are to be arranged so that they are both to the greatest benefit to the least advantaged and attached to offices and positions that are open to all under conditions of fair equality of opportunity. Thus, while the distribution of wealth and income need not be equal, it must be to everyone's advantage and at the same time positions of authority must be accessible to all.

The first rule, which states the relations between these two principles, provides that liberty is to have priority over social and economic equality, so that liberty can be restricted only for the sake of liberty and not for the purpose of greater social and economic advantages. The second rule is that the principle relating to social and economic equality is prior to the external principle of economic growth (or efficiency) and to that of maximizing the sum of advantages. That is, justice, as defined, has priority over efficiency and welfare.

Rawls believes that instititutions modeled on his principles and rules of justice are inherently stable and that the forces making for stability increase as time passes. To achieve stability a just system needs only to bring about in its members a desire to act in accordance with its rules for reasons of justice. This can be done, says Rawls; a just system must and can generate its own support.

These principles apply mainly to the basic institutions of society, not necessarily to its lesser political and social structures. Whether or not Rawls would try to apply the principles to our irrigation communities, which are of such basic importance in arid environments, is not clear. Abstract formulae for justice need to be modified in the face of complex technological functions. Nonetheless, the relations we have found between economic equality and economic growth for different operating procedures can be examined in terms of Rawls's model, as can be our findings relating to the pervasiveness of local control in general and variations among the communities in the extensiveness of popular participation. Indeed, our findings in these matters raise questions about the Rawls model for justice in institutions. The irrigators of America and Spain have believed that stability can be achieved best by respecting seniority, or time priorities, which become then an important basis for economic inequality. Also, it would appear that they, more than Rawls, are willing to accept merit, or hard work, as a legitimate basis for inequality. The irrigators, in other words, may subscribe to a different pattern for distributive justice, one in which the distributive effects of hard work, perhaps even those of natural endowments, are believed to be deserved. The objectives of the Mormon irrigators of Utah appear to be closer to those of Rawls than the objectives of the other communities; but certainly hard work and in a special sense natural endowments were important parts of the Latter Day Saints' objective set.

Further, irrigators, in judging the justice of a system for distributing water, have paid considerable attention to the process, that is the procedures and organization, for distribution as well as to the end-state distribution pattern that results from the process. The extent to which the process is itself considered to be just—the extent to which community members are satisfied with their participation in determining the procedures and with the effectiveness of the procedures in avoiding outside control and arbitrary actions by the communities' officers—is an important factor in their overall estimation of the distributive justice of the system.[16]

Decision Theories

Any case studies of government institutions will include data that are relevant to theories of decision making, but these irrigation cases have material that is especially interesting for one aspect of that study, the role of uncertainty. In making economic and political decisions with regard to irrigation, it is necessary to give great attention to physical uncertainty because of the irregularity and unpredictability of stream flow, and also to individual and community attitudes toward this uncertainty.

There is a large literature on the description of hydrologic uncertainty, and Maass and his associates in earlier works have elaborated the notion of an economic loss function—that is, economic measures of failures to achieve planned output due to hydrologic uncertainty—as a means of applying uncertainty to the several purposes for which water resources are developed.[17] This loss function concept is basic to the simulation program used in this study.

The attitude of individuals, groups, and communities toward physical uncertainty derives in part from their perceptions of natural hazards. There is a significant body of research, most important the work of Gilbert White and his associates, on this subject.[18] They have begun to identify the factors that affect perception of such events and to describe how these influence decisions on human adjustments to hazards. A careful analysis of the decisions made in our six irrigation communities with regard to both long-term operating procedures (for example, procuring new sources of water) and short-term procedures (for example, choosing among alternative rules for distributing existing sources) could possibly contribute to the formulation of hypotheses on this important subject.

The Process of Political Development

In the last twenty years the study of political development has occupied a large number of political scientists. The results of their work have been surveyed and evaluated recently in a lengthy essay by two leaders of the group, Samuel Huntington and Jorge Dominguez.[19] Political development has dealt with the relations between modernization and certain aspects of a political system. By modernization is meant such "socioeconomic" processes as industrialization, urbanization, increasing literacy and mass media consumption, economic growth, and greater social and occupational mobility. The political factors of major interest have been the following:

1. Political institutions (the nature of the formal organizations through which society makes authoritative decisions and particularly the extent to which such institutions are democratic or authoritarian). Several dimensions of political institutions are of special importance in the relations between them and

modernization: their adaptability, autonomy, complexity, coherence, bases of legitimacy, arrangements for political participation, and the extent to which they provide for concentration or pluralism in the distribution of political power.

2. Political participation (the nature and scope of people's activities that are designed to affect governmental decision making).

3. Political culture (the values, attitudes, orientations, myths, and beliefs that people have about politics and government and particularly about the legitimacy of government).

4. Political integration (the extent to which politics is not characterized by sharp cleavages along ethnic, social, religious, class, cultural, or territorial lines).

We have been concerned with many of these political factors. However, the context in which political developers have studied them robs their findings of relevance for our study of irrigation communities. As in the case of local or central control over irrigation systems, one's perspective depends on where he stands. We have been at the center of the irrigation community, observing it, as well as the central government, from the perspective of the irrigators' objectives and attainments. The political developers stand at the center of the nation-state, observing it, as well as "parochial communities" within, from the perspective of the nation's ability to achieve modernization and political integration.

To illustrate, Huntington and Dominguez report, "In actual practice the only assertion that can conclusively be made about the political effects of modernization is that it will ultimately either destroy the traditional political institutions in the society or induce drastic changes in them so as to adapt them to the broader and more diversified demands of modern society." [20] From our perspective the resilience of the governing institutions of irrigation communities in Spain from the Middle Ages, and in the United States from early development, to this date gives little support to this conclusive assertion. Similarly, Huntington and Dominguez report that different parochial societies have responded differently to similar external stimuli. Yet we have been impressed by the similarities of the responses of irrigation communities in old Spain and new Spain, in nineteenth-century America and twentieth-century America, to the external stimulus of threats to their water rights and water supplies.

Irrigation communities apparently look different when viewed from on top, or alternatively, they are very different from other traditional and parochial societies. If the conflict between the findings of political developers and our own is due to the fact that irrigation societies are a special case, this would be presumably because of the prominent role of technology in irrigation. Yet technology has been largely ignored by those who have studied political development, being subsumed for the most part under the heading of economic factors that influence modernization. Also, we should ask the question again: Are there other public activities, with related communities and institutions, that have

similarly complex technological functions leading to similar patterns of governance?

A few political scientists have focused on lesser communities, principally in
studies of local responses to development-aid projects in underdeveloped countries. Some of their conclusions can be compared to ours. But this scholarly
work has remained outside of the mainstream of political development studies; it
is not included in the Huntington and Dominguez survey, for example.[21]

Theories of political development are largely irrelevant to the development of
political institutions for irrigation. Does one find greater relevance in the work
of social anthropologists? Their interest in irrigation has blossomed in recent
years, resulting in a number of studies of small, frequently primitive communities, the best of which in our view are those that relate the system of leadership
in the community to differentiated roles in the management and control of the
irrigation system.[22] Unlike studies in political development, those in anthropology have given attention to technology. But just as the studies of political development are deficient for our purposes in not recognizing the puissance of
parochial societies, those of anthropology are in good part deficient in not
recognizing the links of parochial societies to outside centers of power and influence—social, economic, and political links; links to societies on the same level
of organization and to those at higher levels. Similarly, the anthropological studies have largely ignored the time or historical dimension in their analysis of irrigation institutions. The fieldwork strategies and techniques of the anthropolo-
gist, emphasizing as they do participant observation, have discouraged extralocal
considerations.[23]

Our studies do link local systems to outside centers of power and they include a historical dimension. For these reasons they may be suggestive to those
anthropologists who want to break the local bonds that bind them, but we
realize our studies cannot meet the requirements of a rigorous anthropological
model. They were not designed for this purpose.

Relations between Man and His Environment

These studies of the development of irrigation in six communities are relevant to
the geographical study of the relations between man and his environment, and
it is interesting in this context to examine again the theories of Jean Brunhes,
whose turn-of-the-century analysis of irrigation systems we have found to be
perceptive. For Brunhes there are two intervening variables between natural
environment and human adjustments to it. The first is the psychology or state of
mind of the people of an area; natural hazard conditions that menace groups and
individuals create a state of psychological insecurity, which varies with the
degree and character of the hazard. The second variable is the attitude or disposition of a people toward cooperation, toward working collectively with others,
which is in turn a surrogate for various cultural factors. Although it is common

for men to seek to free themselves from a psychological state of uncertainty, they do not invariably do so, for this requires that they cooperate under fixed rules that may be quite rigorous, and for cultural reasons they may not be prepared to do this.

Although the requirements of cooperation have at times caused great strains in the communities, the irrigators in southeastern Spain and the western United States have on the whole adjusted remarkably well to their natural environments.

APPENDIX: BASIC DATA FOR COMPARISON OF IRRIGATION IN COLORADO-UTAH AND VALENCIA-MURCIA AND GINI COEFFICIENTS OF OPERATING PROCEDURES

Table A9.1 Hydrograph of stream flow for 90 percent of adequate seasonal water for Valencia-Murcia and Colorado-Utah.

	Valencia-Murcia		Colorado-Utah	
	Irrigation period	Percent of seasonal supply	Irrigation period	Percent of seasonal supply
January	1	0.0		
	2	2.0		
February	3	3.0		
	4	3.3		
March	5	6.0		
	6	6.0		
April	7	3.0	1	6
	8	6.0	2	7
May	9	6.0	3	7
	10	3.0	4	9
June	11	6.0	5	10
	12	4.9	6	12
	13	7.0		
July	14	4.0	7	10
	15	5.0	8	8
August	16	3.0	9	7
	17	6.0	10	6
			11	5
September	18	2.0	12	4
	19	5.0	13	4
October	20	4.0	14	4
	21	5.0		
November	22	4.0		
	23	3.0		
	24	0.0		
December	25	2.8		
	26	0.0		

Table A9.2 Farm sizes and crop patterns.

| | Farm | | | | | | | |
Crop	1	2	3	4	5	6	7	Total
Valencia-Murcia (in hectares planted)								
Potatoes	0.25	0.0	0.3	0.0	0.0	0.2	0.0	0.75
Corn	0.25	0.4	0.0	0.0	0.5	0.2	0.5	1.85
Beans	0.00	0.4	0.0	0.4	0.5	0.0	0.0	1.30
Peppers	0.00	0.3	0.3	0.4	0.0	0.0	0.5	1.50
Wheat	0.00	0.3	0.0	0.0	0.5	0.2	1.0	2.00
Citrus	0.25	0.0	0.0	0.3	1.0	0.0	0.5	2.05
Alfalfa	0.00	0.3	0.0	0.0	0.5	0.0	0.0	0.80
Total	0.50	1.0	0.3	0.7	2.5	0.4	1.5	10.25 [a]
Colorado and Utah (in acres planted)								
Dry beans	10	10	20	20	10	0	30	100
Apples	8	12	10	0	10	0	0	40
Potatoes	0	0	0	10	0	15	20	45
Sugar beets	0	20	20	30	0	60	80	210
Corn	12	20	40	45	20	55	80	272
Alfalfa	10	18	30	40	10	50	60	218
Wheat	0	0	0	15	0	40	60	115
Total	40	80	120	160	50	220	330	1,000

[a] Total area is 6.9 ha; the difference represents double cropping.

Table A9.3 Crop yields, costs, and returns for Valencia-Murcia (in thousands of pesetas) and Colorado-Utah (in dollars).

Crop	Yield	Price	Gross returns	Preharvest cost	Harvest cost	Total cost	Net returns
Valencia-Murcia							
Potatoes	280.0 q. m.	.2857	80.00	30.00	10.00	40.00	40.00
Corn	60.0 q. m.	.75	45.00	15.00	6.00	21.00	24.00
Beans	80.0 q. m.	.6875	55.00	19.00	7.00	26.00	29.00
Peppers	200.0 q. m.	.50	100.00	40.00	15.00	55.00	45.00
Wheat	30.0 q. m.	.75	22.50	2.40	0.60	3.00	19.50
Citrus fruit	250.0 q. m.	.52	130.00	45.00	25.00	70.00	60.00
Alfalfa	230.0 q. m.	.3478	80.00	20.00	15.00	35.00	45.00
Colorado-Utah							
Dry beans	18.5 cwt	7.00	129.50	53.00	36.00	89.00	40.50
Apples	476.0 box	2.05	975.80	521.00	238.00	759.00	216.80
Potatoes	225.0 cwt	1.50	337.50	120.00	112.00	232.00	105.50
Sugar beets	21.5 ton	14.00	301.00	127.00	57.00	184.00	117.00
Corn	90.0 bu	1.15	103.50	65.00	15.00	80.00	23.50
Alfalfa	5.0 ton	20.00	100.00	52.00	25.00	77.00	23.00
Wheat	65.0 bu	1.05	68.25	40.00	10.50	50.50	17.75

Table A9.4 Irrigation water requirements for crops in Valencia-Murcia (in cubic meters) and Colorado-Utah (in acre-inches).

	Irrigation period	Valencia-Murcia						
		Potatoes	Corn	Beans	Peppers	Wheat	Citrus	Alfalfa
January	1	0	0	0	0	0	0	0
	2	0	0	0	0	0	0	1,000
February	3	0	0	0	0	0	787	0
	4	0	0	1,250	0	0	0	0
March	5	700	0	0	0	1,000	0	1,000
	6	0	0	0	0	0	0	0
April	7	925	0	1,250	0	0	0	0
	8	0	0	0	0	1,020	0	0
May	9	812	0	0	0	0	1,000	0
	10	850	0	0	0	0	0	0
June	11	50	0	0	0	0	0	1,200
	12	0	420	0	1,000	0	0	0
	13	0	0	0	0	0	1,088	0
July	14	0	527	0	1,000	0	0	1,500
	15	0	0	0	0	0	0	0
August	16	0	727	0	1,200	0	1,088	0
	17	0	0	0	0	0	0	1,400
September	18	0	727	0	1,200	0	0	0
	19	0	0	0	0	0	0	0
October	20	0	0	0	0	0	0	1,000
	21	0	0	0	0	0	1,045	0
November	22	0	0	0	0	0	0	0
	23	0	0	0	0	0	0	0
	24	0	0	0	0	0	1,000	1,000
December	25	0	0	0	0	0	0	0
	26	0	0	0	0	0	0	0

Colorado-Utah							
Irrigation period	Dry Beans	Apples	Potatoes	Sugar Beets	Corn	Alfalfa	Wheat
1	0	0	0	0	0	12	8
2	0	0	6	6	6	0	0
3	6	12	0	0	0	0	6
4	0	0	5	7	4	0	0
5	6	0	0	0	0	12	6
6	0	12	4	5	6	0	0
7	4	0	4	6	0	0	0
8	4	0	4	0	4	12	0
9	4	0	4	5	4	0	0
10	0	12	4	5	0	0	0
11	0	0	4	6	4	0	0
12	0	0	0	0	0	12	0
13	0	6	0	4	0	0	0
14	0	0	0	0	0	0	0

Table A9.5 Estimates of percentage loss in yields from not meeting scheduled irrigations.

		Valencia-Murcia						
	Irrigation period	Potatoes	Corn	Beans	Peppers	Wheat	Citrus	Alfalfa
January	1	—	—	—	—	—	—	—
	2	—	—	—	—	—	—	10
February	3	—	—	—	—	—	10	—
	4	—	—	30	—	—	—	—
March	5	20	—	—	—	25	—	—
	6	—	—	—	—	—	—	20
April	7	15	—	30	—	—	—	—
	8	—	—	—	—	25	—	—
May	9	20	—	—	—	—	15	—
	10	20	—	—	—	—	—	—
June	11	20	20	—	—	—	—	20
	12	—	—	—	15	—	—	—
	13	—	20	—	—	—	20	—
July	14	—	—	—	10	—	—	25
	15	—	40	—	—	—	—	—
August	16	—	—	—	12	—	20	—
	17	—	—	—	—	—	—	15
September	18	—	20	—	12	—	—	—
	19	—	—	—	—	—	—	—
October	20	—	—	—	—	—	—	10
	21	—	—	—	—	—	15	—
November	22	—	—	—	—	—	—	—
	23	—	—	—	—	—	—	—
	24	—	—	—	—	—	10	10
December	25	—	—	—	—	—	—	—
	26	—	—	—	—	—	—	—

Assumptions for table:
1. Each acre (hectare) during each irrigation period receives either full water requirement or no water. Figures represent losses from no water for the period.
2. Two successive "misses" result in 100 percent loss, except for citrus and alfalfa.
3. Percentage reduction is calculated in terms of yield anticipated at the time of the water

Colorado-Utah							
Irrigation period	Dry Beans	Apples	Potatoes	Sugar Beets	Corn	Alfalfa	Wheat
1	—	—	—	—	—	35	25
2	—	—	20	20	30	—	—
3	25	25	—	—	—	—	25
4	—	—	15	20	20	—	—
5	25	—	—	—	—	30	25
6	—	20	15	15	40	—	—
7	30	—	15	20	—	—	—
8	20	—	20	—	15	30	—
9	20	—	20	15	15	—	—
10	—	25	20	15	—	—	—
11	—	—	20	25	10	—	—
12	—	—	—	—	—	20	—
13	—	5	—	10	—	—	—
14	—	—	—	—	—	—	—

shortage. Thus the percentage reduction in yield resulting from a second water shortage is based on the already reduced yield from the first one.

4. A direct relation is assumed between the physical yield of crops and economic values (except potatoes), that is, water shortage affects yield and not quality.

Table A9.6 Gini coefficients of different operating procedures, based on dollar (peseta) losses per acre (hectare) in net farm incomes.

Procedure	Colorado-Utah				Valencia-Murcia			
	90% water		75% water		90% water		75% water	
	Gini	Rank	Gini	Rank	Gini	Rank	Gini	Rank
Shares	.1289	4	.0600	2	.3575	3	.2831	4
Shares + excess	.1880	8	.0772	4	.3902	4	.3490	7
Turn	.1759	6	.1462	7	.4078	6	.2068	3
Rotation	.1222	3	.1661	8	.4052	5	.3147	5
Farm priorities	.8353	9	.7942	9	.7010	8	.5861	9
Crop priorities	.1778	7	.0873	5	.2736	2	.2040	2
Market	.0479	1	.0254	1	.1338	1	.1365	1
Demand	.1200	2	.0643	3	.7808	9	.4341	8
Demand-Plan	.1372	5	.0963	6	.5169	7	.3367	6

Table A9.7 Gini coefficients of different operating procedures, based on acre-inch (m³) losses per acre (hectare) in water delivered.

	Colorado-Utah				Valencia-Murcia			
	90% water		75% water		90% water		75% water	
Procedure	Gini	Rank	Gini	Rank	Gini	Rank	Gini	Rank
Shares	.1162	5	.0539	5	.3318	4	.2445	3
Shares + excess	.1520	6	.0873	6	.3265	3	.2889	5
Turn	.3314	7	.2011	8	.5159	6	.1325	2
Rotation	.0970	4	.0504	4	.3125	2	.2825	4
Farm priorities	.8360	9	.7801	9	.8271	9	.6784	9
Crop priorities	.3948	8	.2002	7	.5697	8	.3954	8
Market	.0307	2	.0267	3	.1773	1	.0975	1
Demand	.0247	1	.0218	1	.6654	7	.3451	7
Demand-Plan	.0890	3	.0231	2	.5008	5	.3279	6

Note: In tables A9.6 and A9.7 the Gini coefficients were developed in the following manner for each procedure: for each farm the money value of loss per acre or hectare from the value at full production (or losses in water delivered from water required for full production) was calculated. The farm losses were then summed. Each farm loss was expressed as a percentage of the sum of losses and ranked in decreasing order. The ranked percentage losses were then graphed cumulatively in the standard Lorenz fashion, except that the Y and X axes were inverted so that the Lorenz curve would take its normal position. The Lorenz curve was formed by drawing lines between these points, and the area under the curve calculated. This area was subtracted from .5 to give the area of inequality, which was then multiplied by 2 to give the Gini coefficient.

Notes

Notes to chapter 1

1. For the Beersheba wells, see Genesis, chapters 21 and 26. For the model of the Gargantuan war, see W. F. Smith (tr.), *Rabelais* (Cambridge, England: Cambridge University Press, 1934), vol. I, pp. lv–lvii.

2. Elwood Mead, *Irrigation Institutions* (New York: Macmillan, 1903), p. 52.

3. Thomas F. Glick, *Irrigation and Society in Medieval Valencia* (Cambridge, Ma.: Harvard University Press, 1969), p. 70.

4. *Ordenanzas de las aguas del azud de Alfeitami de la villa de Almoradí, 1793* (Almoradí, 1955), Art. 28.

5. Karl A. Wittfogel, *Oriental Despotism: A Comparative Study of Total Power* (New Haven, Conn.: Yale University Press, 1957).

6. Wittfogel is confusing and perhaps contradictory on irrigation in what he calls "property-based industrial civilizations." See especially pp. 12, 214–218. There are numerous critiques of Wittfogel, including Lon L. Fuller, "Irrigation and Tyranny," 17 *Stanford Law Review* 1021–42 (July 1967), who criticizes him on similar grounds and also attacks his methodology, and Glick, *Irrigation and Society*.

7. Sindicato de Regulación del Río Turia, *Reglamento,* 18 May 1934, Art. 3.

8. James Hudson, *Irrigation Water Use in the Utah Valley* (University of Chicago, Department of Geography, Research Paper No. 79, 1962).

9. Raymond L. Anderson, "The Irrigation Water Rental Market: A Case Study," 13 *Agricultural Economics Research* 54–58 (1961). One reason the farmers use "rent" rather than "sell" is to protect their water rights under the Colorado water code.

10. Pedro Díaz Cassou, *Ordenanzas y costumbres de la huerta de Murcia* (Madrid: Fortanet, 1889), p. 121.

11. David C. Major and John S. Major, "Toward an Inferential Method for Evaluating Public Works Projects in Pre-Modern China" (Staff Paper No. 361, Ralph M. Parsons Laboratory for Water Resources and Hydrodynamics, Massachusetts Institute of Technology, Cambridge, Ma., 1977).

12. For citations to these works, see the notes to the relevant chapters in this book.

13. David H. Fisher, *Historians' Fallacies: Toward a Logic of Historical Thought* (New York: Harper and Row, 1970), p. 215. In this study we do not attempt to relate an irrigation community's objectives to the community's general value structure. For a brilliant study that relates "values" to "criteria for the ranking of goals for future action" in an arid environment, see Evon Z. Vogt, *Modern Homesteaders* (Cambridge, Ma.: Harvard University Press, 1955).

14. Jean Brunhes, *L'irrigation dan la Péninsule Ibérique et dans l'Afrique du Nord* (Paris: C. Naud, 1902). Curiously, Wittfogel, although he has an immense bibliography, makes no reference to Brunhes.

Notes to chapter 2

1. From the large literature on this famous region, only a few of the principal sources used in this study are listed: Maurice Aymard, *Irrigations du midi de l'Espagne* (Paris: Lacroix, 1864); Francisco Borrull y Vilanova, *Tratado de la distribución de las aguas del río Segura* (Valencia: D. Benito Monfort, 1831); Jean Brunhes, *L'irrigation dans la Péninsule Ibérique et dans l'Afrique du Nord* (Paris: C. Naud, 1902); Eugenio Burriel de Orueta, *La huerta de Valencia, zona sur* (Valencia: Institución Alfonso el Magnánimo, 1971); Victor Fairén Guillén, *El Tribunal de las Aguas de Valencia y su proceso* (Valencia: Caja de Ahorros, 1975); Alice Foster, *The Geographic Structure of the Vega of Valencia* (Chicago: University of Chicago Libraries, 1936); Vicente Giner Boira, *El Tribunal de las Aguas de la vega de Valencia* (Valencia: Tipografía Moderna, 1960); Thomas F. Glick, *Irrigation and Society in Medieval Valencia* (Cambridge, Ma.: Harvard University Press, 1969); [François-Jacques] Jaubert de Passa, *Canales de riego de Cataluña y Reino de Valencia*, 2 vols., trans. Juan Fiol (Valencia: D. Benito Monfort, 1844); José Latour Brotóns, "La distribución de las aguas en la huerta de Valencia," *Astrea: revista de la abogacía y de la toga* (1957), also *Antecedentes de la primitiva ley de aguas* (Madrid: Domenech, 1955), Andrés Llauradó, *Tratado de aguas y riegos*, 2 vols., 2nd ed. (Madrid. Moreno y Rojas, 1884); Jaime Marco Baidal, *El Turia* (Valencia: Mari Montañana, 1960); Colin Scott Moncrieff, *Irrigation in Southern Europe* (London: Spon, 1868).

The currently effective ordinances of the canals of the huerta of Valencia are published together in Jaubert de Passa, *Canales*, Vol. II. They are as follows, with dates of approval by appropriate higher authorities: Moncada, 1268; Cuart, 1709 and Benacher y Faitenar, 1740; Tormos, 1843; Mislata, 1751 and Chirivella 1792; Mestalla, 1771; Favara, 1701; Rascaña, 1765; Robella, 1835, subsequently revised and approved in 1970.

2. Burriel, *La huerta de Valencia*, p. 229 and chapter 9.

3. For example, ibid.

4. Moncada is not to share in the extra water gained by the huerta's rotation with the pueblos castillos and there have been centuries of argument over how this rule is to be enforced. The procedure that has evolved is approximately as follows: on days when the rotation is with the huerta, Moncada's withdrawal from the river cannot exceed the average flow through its control structure on the night before the huerta's turn begins. On first consideration this might appear to restrict Moncada unduly, since the upstream pueblos are likely to withdraw as much water as they can on the last day of their rotation, when Moncada's intake is to be gauged. But this is offset by the fact that the farmers of the pueblos do not irrigate at night and the control for Moncada is the average of measurements taken at sundown and sunup.

5. The operating procedure of the Moncada canal differs from the remaining seven. Before moving to crop priorities, Moncada requires each farmer to begin and terminate his irrigation at a set day and hour that are known to the farmer and recorded in the community records. The time allowed each farmer is related to the size of his farm. Because this operating procedure is typical of the middle and low valleys of the Segura River, which are the subject of chapter 3, it is not described further here.

6. Glick, *Irrigation and Society*, pp. 240–242, gives this example and others.

7. Ibid., chapter 5, gives the details of these events.

8. The following documents relate to the Generalísimo Dam: Authorization of the dam: R.O. 16 December 1927, R.O. 9 March 1928, O.M. 3 June 1931. Confirming jurisdiction of Tribunal de las Aguas: D. 5 April 1932. Temporarily suspending concessions for river water: R.O. 13 May 1929, R.O. 3 June 1931. Organization of Confederación Hidrográfica de Júcar: D. 26 June 1934, O.M. 1 July 1935. Sindicato de Regulación del Río Turia, Reglamento 18 May 1934, approved by O.M. 4 June 1936, published in Valencia 1937. For a partisan statement on the negotiations that led to approval of the dam, see Leopoldo Hernandez, "El pantano Blasco Ibañez en Benageber" in *Las Provincias, almanaque para 1933* (Valencia, 1934), pp. 129–142.

9. Based on interviews and observations by Maass.

10. This claim is spurious in a fundamental sense. Rights to water use cannot be sold, to be sure, as they can in certain regions of Spain; but the value of water is capitalized in the value of the land to which it is attached, and the land can be sold.

11. Llauradó, *Tratado de aguas,* vol. II, p. 317; Aymard, *Irrigations du midi,* pp. 46–67; Brunhes, *L'Irrigation,* p. 71.

12. Latour Brotóns, "La distribución de las aguas," makes this point.

13. The prime mover of the hydraulic policy was Joaquin Costa, *Política hidráulica: misión social de los riegos en España* (Madrid: Biblioteca J. Costa, 1911). For the antecedents of the national water law, see Latour Brotóns, *Antecedentes.* There is a significant literature on the development of Spanish water law and administration. For a recent study that refers in turn to the earlier works, see Sebastian Baquer Martin Rotortillo, *Aguas públicas y obras hidráulicas* (Madrid: Editorial Tecnos, 1966). For convenient handbooks of legislation, see Francisco Pan Montojo, ed., *Legislación de aguas,* 10th ed. (Madrid: Gongora, 1957) and Ministerio de Obras Públicas, *Esquema del derecho de aguas español* (Madrid, 1975).

14. The following documents relate to the incription of "concessions" for canals in the huerta of Valencia: Ley de Aguas, Arts. 257, 152. Inscription orders: Rovella, O.M. 5 December 1957, modified by O.M. 9 July 1962; Favara, O.M. 20 November 1961; Rascaña, 7 July 1962; Mislata, 1 June 1965; Mestalla, 29 November 1965; Tormos, 29 September 1966; Cuart, 16 May 1967; Moncada, provisional order. Decision of supreme court, 21 September 1963. See also Burriel, *La huerta de Valencia,* pp. 207–209, 379–380.

15. Burriel, *La Huerta de Valencia,* p. 208.

16. Brunhes, *L'irrigation,* pp. 95–108.

17. Foster, *The Geographic Structure,* pp. 63–65.

Notes to chapter 3

1. The following are the principal sources used in this study. Relating to both Murcia and the low valley: *Homenaje a la economía de Alicante y Murcia* (Bilbao: Banco de Vizcaya, Revista Financiera, 1953); Andrés Llauradó, *Tratado de aguas y riegos,* 2nd ed., 2 vols. (Madrid: Moreno y Rojas, 1884).

Relating to Murcia: José Antonio Ayala, *El regadío murciano en la primera mitad del siglo XIX* (Murcia: Junta de Hacendados de la Huerta de Murcia,

1975); Maurice Aymard, *Irrigations du midi de l'Espagne* (Paris: Lacroix, 1864); Juan Belando y Melendez, *El río Segura y la huerta de Murcia* (Murcia: El Albun, 1878); Pedro Díaz Cassou, *Ordenanzas y costumbres de la huerta de Murcia* (Madrid: Fortanet, 1889, republished 1971 by Junta de Hacendados de la Huerta de Murcia with an introduction by Joaquín Cerdá Ruiz-Funes), *La huerta de Murcia* (Madrid: Fortanet, 1887), and *Proyecto de ordenanzas para la huerta de Murcia* (Murcia: El Diaria de Murcia, 1881); Junta de Hacendados de la Huerta de Murcia, *Memorias, 1913–14* (Murcia: El Tiempo, 1914), *Memoria, 1933–36* (Murcia: El Tiempo, 1936), and office records of this organization; Rafael de Mancha, *Memoria sobre la población y los riegos de la huerta de Murcia* (Murcia: Mariano Bellido, 1836); Mariano Ruiz-Funes García, *Derecho consuetudinario y economía popular de la provincia de Murcia* (Madrid: Jaime Ratés, 1916).

Relating to huertas of the low valley: Rafael Altamira y Crevea, *Derecho consuetudinario y economía popular de la provincia de Alicante* (Madrid: Huérfanos del S.C. Jesús, 1905); Juan Roca de Togores y Albuquerque, *Memoria sobre los riegos de la huerta de Orihuela*, 1831 (printed in [François-Jacques] Jaubert de Passa, *Canales de riego de Cataluña y Reino de Valencia*, vol. II (Valencia: D. Benito Monfort, 1844); J. Rufino Gea, *La acequia de Molino* (Orihuela: Tipografía de la Lectura Popular, 1903); printed ordinances: *Orihuela 1836* (Orihuela, 1946), *Callosa de Segura*, n.d. (Callosa de Segura, 1958), *Las aguas del Azud de Alfeitami de la villa de Almoradí*, 1793 (Almoradí, 1955), *Catral*, 1899 (Orihuela, 1899), *Acequia de Cox*, 1865 (Alicante, 1944), *Las villas de Dolores y S. Fulgencio*, 1875 (Alicante, 1877); office records of the following organizations: Juzgado Privativo de Aguas de Orihuela, Juzgado Privativo de Aguas del Azud de Alfeitamí, Sindicato de la Acequia de Cox, Sindicato de Riego de Catral.

Selected decrees and ministerial orders: organization of Confederación Hidrográfica del Segura: decrees of 21 May 1934 and 7 December 1935; organization and functions of Comisaría de Aguas del Segura: decree of 7 December 1935; concessions and allocations of water: R.O. of 12 April 1913, decrees of 7 December 1935, 14 April 1942, 25 April 1953, O.M. of 25 April 1953.

2. O.M. 25 April 1953, Art. 1.

3. See Díaz Cassou, *La huerta de Murcia*, p. 297. Similarly the irrigators of Valencia recorded dimensions of their canal divisors in case they should have to be rebuilt. See Thomas F. Glick, "Levels and Levelers: Surveying Irrigation Canals in Medieval Valencia," 9 *Technology and Culture* 165–180 (1968).

4. In some cases—the laterals that serve the medium high and low lands in the first division of the New Almoradí canal, for example—the rotation by tanda is customary rather than statutory, in the sense that it is known to all farmers and practiced by them, but is not a matter of record.

5. In some, particularly open laterals, water is distributed by turn rather than rotation (each farmer takes what he needs without limit of time when the water reaches him). In some other sectors, especially during that period of the sector's time when only high lands can irrigate, farmers open their gates simultaneously and take whatever water they can get.

6. The Dolores distribution system, which is below Orihuela, uses an alternative procedure for activating its rotation, a procedure that, although less flexible than that of Murcia and Orihuela proper, is probably more consistent with the water shortage that results from Dolores's need to rely on Orihuela's return flow. Effective dates are fixed in the ordinances. Thus the rotation system begins on

April 27 each year and ends on September 30. From October 1 until the end of February water is distributed without rotation or turn but subject to certain constraints relating to the scheduling of deliveries, and from March 1 until the rotation period begins it is delivered to each farmer in turn but without a time limit.

7. In some canal sectors, in parts of the Callosa canal, for example, a farmer who elects to use surplus water may not necessarily take all he needs. He cannot open his headgate for a period of time longer than that to which he would be entitled in the regular rotation. Ordinances for Callosa, Art. 145; Almoradí, Art. XV; Murcia, Art. 152.

8. Ordinances for Orihuela, Art. 146; Callosa, Art. 146.

9. Ordinances for Murcia, Art. 153.

10. Díaz Cassou, *Ordenanzas y costumbres,* pp. 123–124. Ordinances for Murcia, Art. 158; Callosa, Art. 153; Almoradí, Arts. XXV, XXVI.

11. Ordinances for Callosa, Art. 145.

12. Most of the data for this section are from field interviews and records in the Junta de Hacendados of Murcia on the extreme droughts of 1838, 1856, 1913–14, 1934–5, 1953, and 1968.

13. Aymard, *Irrigations du midi,* p. 220.

14. Regulations governing the assemblies of the supply canal communities: ordinances for Murcia, Arts. 127–142; Orihuela, Arts. 62–66, 81–83, 89, 226; Callosa, Arts. 62–68, 86–87, 227. Those governing their administration: ordinances for Murcia, Arts. 100–114; Orihuela, Arts. 26–38, 81, 85, 124, 132, 139; Callosa, Arts. 26–38, 86, 90, 125, 132, 139.

15. Regulations governing the assemblies of the Junta of Murcia and the Juzgados of Orihuela and Callosa: ordinances for Murcia, Arts. 128–142; Orihuela, Arts. 30, 71–73, 78–79; Callosa, Arts. 30, 73, 78, 83–84. Those governing their administration: ordinances for Murcia, Arts. 160–163; Orihuela, Arts. 31–38, 71–76; Callosa, Arts. 13–38, 73–81.

16. Regulations governing the water courts: ordinances for Murcia, Arts. 164–178; Orihuela, Arts. 166–185; Callosa, Arts. 167–186.

17. Emilio Diez de Revenga Torres, *Notas sobre el Consejo de Hombres Buenos de la huerta de Murcia* (Murcia: Junta de Hacendados de la huerta de Murcia, 1975) p. 21.

18. Díaz Cassou, *La huerta de Murcia,* p. 303.

19. Almoradí ordinances.

20. Ordinances of Orihuela, Art. 32; Callosa, Art. 32; Almoradí, Art. I.

21. Ordinances of Orihuela, Art. 35; Callosa, Art. 35; Almoradí, Art. I.

22. See, for example, R.O. 12 April 1913.

23. The earlier decree of 14 April 1942 had included in its first category all irrigations established without limitations prior to 1925.

24. Junta de Hacendados de la Huerta de Murcia, *Memorias,* 1913–14, p. 45.

25. In this connection, see the prediction of Ruiz-Funes, writing in 1916, that the new organization would fail, p. 134.

Notes to chapter 4

1. The following are the most important sources used in this study. Secondary sources on Alicante irrigation: Rafael Altamira y Crevea, "Alicante: Mercado de agua en la huerta" in Joaquín Costa (ed.), *Derecho consuetudinario y economía popular de España* (Barcelona: Manuel Soler, 1902), vol. II, and *Derecho consuetudinario y economía popular de la provincia de Alicante* (Madrid: Asilo de Huérfanos, 1905); Maurice Aymard, *Irrigations du midi de l'Espagne* (Paris: Lacroix, 1864); Jean Brunhes, *L'irrigation dans la Péninsule Ibérique et dans l'Afrique du Nord* (Paris: C. Naud, 1902); Francisco de Estrada, *Reseña histórica sobre las aguas con que se riega la huerta de Alicante* (Alicante: Pedro Ibarra, 1860); Antonio López Gómez, "Riegos y cultivos en la huerta de Alicante," 12 *Estudios geográficos* 701–771 (November 1951); Andrés Llauradó, *Tratado de aguas y riegos*, 2nd ed., 2 vols (Madrid: Moreno y Rojas, 1884); Francisco Verdú, *Discurso sobre las aguas que sirven al riego público de la huerta de Alicante* (Alicante: n.p., 1739).

Primary sources on Alicante irrigation: *Boletín del sindicato de riegos de la Huerta de Alicante*, 1950–1961; Rafael Viravens y Pastor, *Crónica de la ciudad de Alicante* (Alicante: Carratala y Gadea, 1876); *Estatutos para el govierno de la ciudad de Alicante concedidos por Carlos II en 1669* (Orihuela: Jayme Mesnier, 1699); "Estatutos y reales ordenanzas de 1741 para el buen govierno, administración y distribución del agua del pantano proprio del real patrimonio, que sirve al riego de la huerta de la ciudad de Alicante," in Vicente Branchat, *Tratado de los derechos y regalías del real patrimonio en el reyno de Valencia*, vol. III (Valencia: de Orga, 1784); *Reglamento para el aprovechamiento de las aguas de riego de la huerta de Alicante aprobado en 1849* (reimp., Alicante: Guijarro, 1930); *Reglamento para el sindicato de riegos de la huerta de Alicante aprobade en 1865* (reimp. Alicante: Progreso, 1910).

Primary sources on Riegos de Levante: Ministerio de Obras Públicas, Tribunal de Aguas de Riegos de Levante, *Memoria de 1942* (Alicante, 1942), *Estudio para la distribución del agua de riego* (Alicante, 1942), *Censo de regantes, margen izquierda* (Alicante, 1942), and *Reglamento especial de las juntas de regantes* (Alicante, 1943); Comunidad de Riegos de Levante, *Ordenanzas, reglamento para el sindicato de riegos, y reglamento para el jurado de riegos* (Elche, 1948).

2. Throughout we shall follow the convention in Alicante of capitalizing Huerta when it refers to that city.

3. This figure does not include some 1500 ha of irrigated land in the Baccarat sector of Alicante that is separate from the traditional Huerta, both topographically and administratively. There are in addition some 300 irrigated ha, which, although joined to the traditional Huerta topographically, are not under the jurisdiction of its irrigation community. If more water were available, about 500 additional ha could be brought under irrigation using the present canal distribution system and an additional 1500 ha by means of new but modest distribution works. Manuel Sanchez Buades, secretary of the Sindicato de Riegos de la Huerta de Alicante, "Informe" presented to the Consejo Económico Sindical Provincial (Alicante, June 1961, typescript).

4. From Sanchez Buades, "Informe."

5. Calculated on the following assumptions: two simultaneous *dulas* at 128 l/s each; seventeen rotations—eleven winter at twenty-one days each and six summer at fourteen days each; no *agua doble*.

6. For the history of these efforts at regulation, see Altamira, "Alicante," pp. 143-145.

7. The fractional units of 2/3 and 1/3 are needed for summer rotations.

8. The ordinances provide also that irrigators in the zone between Tibi Dam and the Alicante Huerta elect one delegate, but they have failed to do so.

9. See in this connection, Thomas F. Glick, "Medieval Irrigation Clocks," 10 *Technology and Culture* 424-428 (1969).

10. 1865 *Reglamento,* Articles 36, 34, 16, 25.

11. On the nature of royal patrimony, see Branchat, *Tratado de los derechos,* Vol. I.

12. It was in this period that the independent jurisdiction of the Valencia water court was seriously challenged and successfully defended. See Francisco Borrull y Vilanova, *Tratado de la distribution de las aguas del rio Turia* (Valencia: D. Benito Monfort, 1831).

13. *Boletín de Sindicato de Riegos de la Huerta de Alicante* (No. 206, February 1957), p. 4.

14. *Boletín de Sindicato,* (Número extraordinario, 30 July 1950).

15. These figures do not include Levante's small service area on the right bank of the Segura River.

16. Outside of Alicante, where water is delivered at 50 rather than 150 l/s, the quota is one hour for 10 tahullas.

17. 1849 *Reglamento,* Art. 25.

18. Dominance of local custom in water distribution is the principal theme of Altamira's studies of the Alicante water market. Altamira, "Alicante."

19. 1865 *Reglamento,* Art. 36 (1).

20. See, for example, Brunhes, *L'irrigation,* pp. 82, 95–108, although his argument does not follow precisely the one given here.

Notes to Chapter 5

1. There is a huge literature on the development of irrigation in the Central Valley. The sources that have been used most frequently are these: Frank Adams, *Delivery of Water to Irrigators* (Washington, D.C.: U.S. Dept. of Agriculture, Experiment Sta. Bulletin 229, 1910), *Irrigation Resources of California and their Utilization* (Washington, D.C.: U.S. Dept. of Agriculture, Experiment Sta. Bulletin 254, 1913), and *Irrigation Districts in California* (Sacramento: Calif. Dept. of Public Works, Div. of Engineering and Irrigation, Bulletin 21, 1929); Alta Irrigation District, *Annual Report* (Dinuba, annual); Joe S. Bain, Richard E. Caves, and Julius Margolis, *Northern California Water Industry* (Baltimore: Johns Hopkins Press, 1966); Hubert H. Bancroft, *Chronicles of the Builders of the Commonwealth,* vol. III: Agriculture—California (San Francisco: History Co., 1892); Harry Barnes, *Use of Water from Kings River, California* (Sacramento: Calif. Dept. of Engineering, Bulletin 7, 1918); J. B. Benedict and J. B. Lippincott, "Review of the Reports on the Kings River Multiple Purpose Project of the U.S. Army Engineers and the U.S. Bureau of Reclamation for the Lemoore Canal and Irrigation Co." (Ms 1940, Water Resources Center Archives, Univ. of Calif., Berkeley); James L. Brown, *The Mussel Slough Tragedy* (n.p., 1958).

Calif. Dept. of Engineering, *Irrigation Districts in California, 1887-1915* (Bulletin 2, Sacramento, 1916); Calif. Dept. of Public Works, Div. of Water Rights, *Kings River Investigation: Water Masters Reports, 1918-1923* (Bulletin 2, Sacramento, 1923); Calif. Dept. of Public Works, Div. of Engineering and Irrigation, *Irrigation Requirements of Calif. Lands* (Bulletin 6, Sacramento, 1923), *Ground Water Resources of the Southern San Joaquin Valley* (Bulletin 11, Sacramento, 1927), *Irrigation Districts in California* (Bulletin 21, Sacramento, 1929, and periodically thereafter until 1964), Reports on costs and charges for irrigation water, as follows: Bulletin 8, 1925; Bulletin 34, 1930; Bulletin 36, 1930 (Sacramento); Calif. Dept. of Public Works, Div. of Water Resources, *Report of Kings River Water Master, 1918-1930* (Bulletin 38, Sacramento, 1931); Moses J. Church, "Irrigation in the San Joaquin Valley" (Ms 1883, Bancroft Library, Univ. of Calif., Berkeley); Victor M. Cone, *Irrigation in the San Joaquin Valley, California* (Washington, D.C.: U.S. Dept. of Agriculture, Experiment Sta. Bulletin 239, 1911); *History of Fresno County* (San Francisco: Wallace W. Elliott & Co., 1882), *History of Tulare County* (San Francisco: Wallace W. Elliott & Co., 1883); Fresno Irrigation District, *Annual Report* (Fresno, annual); *General Directory of Fresno County, California, for 1881* (Fresno: Fresno Republican, 1881); Isaac Friedlander, Estate papers, 1872-1881, in Jane Foster papers, Calif. Historical Society, San Francisco.

Paul Gates, *History of Public Land Law Development* (Washington, D.C.: Government Printing Office, 1968); Carl E. Grunsky, *Irrigation Near Fresno, California* (Washington, D.C.: U.S. Geological Survey, Water Supply Paper 18, 1898); William Hammond Hall, Letter Books, 1877, Calif. Historical Society, San Francisco, and *Report of the State Engineer, 1880,* part IV, "Irrigation"; and same for 1881, part IV "The Irrigation Question" (Sacramento: State Printing Office, 1880, 1881); S. T. Harding. "History of Kings River Water Conservation District from Presentation of Organization Petition on June 1924 to May 1928 (Ms, Water Resources Center Archives, Univ. of Calif., Berkeley), "History of Work on Kings River 1938-1952" (Ms, Water Resources Center Archives, Univ. of Calif., Berkeley), *Water in California* (Palo Alto: N-P Publications, 1960); Harry J. Hogan, *The 160 Acre Limitation* (Ph.D. thesis, George Washington University, Washington, D.C., 1972); Walter L. Huber, "Engineering Report upon Fresno Irrigation District with Special Reference to the Proposal of the District to Acquire the System of Fresno Canal and Land Corp." (1921, Ms, Water Resources Center Archives, Univ. of Calif., Berkeley); "Engineering Report Upon Consolidated Irrigation District with Special Reference to the Proposal of the District to Acquire the System of Consolidated Canal Co." (1922, Ms, Water Resources Center Archives, Univ. of Calif., Berkeley); Wells A. Hutchins, *Delivery of Irrigation Water* (Washington, D.C., U.S. Dept. of Agriculture, Technical Bulletin 47, 1928), *Commercial Irrigation Companies* (Washington, D.C., U.S. Dept. of Agriculture, Technical Bulletin 177, 1930), *Irrigation Districts, Their Organization, Operation and Financing* (Washington, D.C.: U.S. Dept. of Agriculture, Technical Bulletin 254, 1931), *Mutual Irrigation Companies in California and Utah* (Washington, D.C.,: U.S. Farm Credit Admn., Bulletin 8, 1936), and others, *Irrigation-Enterprise Organizations* (Washington, D.C.: U.S. Dept. of Agriculture, Circular 934, 1953), *The California Law of Water Rights* (Sacramento: State Printing Office, 1956), *Irrigation Water Rights in California* (Calif. Agricultural Experiment Sta. Circular 452, rev., 1967).

Irrigation Districts Assoc. of Calif., *Western Water News* 1950-1969; Charles L. Kaupke, *Forty Years on Kings River* (prepared for Kings River Water Assoc., Fresno, 1957); Kings River Pine Flat Assoc., *Report on Kings River Project* (Fresno, 1943); Kings River Water Assoc., *Administrative Agreement and Water*

Right Indenture dated May 3, 1927; Agreements Supplementing and Amending [same]; and *Monthly Diversion Schedules* (Fresno, 1949), *Watermaster Report* (Fresno, annual); Lewis Publishing Co., *Memorial and Biographical History of the Counties of Fresno, Tulare, and Kern, California* (Chicago: Lewis Publishing Co., 1890); Joseph B. Lippincott, *Storage of Water on Kings River, California* (Washington, D.C.: U.S. Geological Survey, Water Supply Paper 58, 1902); Arthur Maass, *Muddy Waters: The Army Engineers and the Nation's Rivers* (Cambridge, Ma.: Harvard University Press, 1951), and Hiller B. Zobel, "Anglo-American Water Law: Who Appropriated the Riparian Doctrine?" 10 *Public Policy* 109–156 (1960); W. A. McAllister, *A Study of Railroad Land Grant Disposals in California* (Ph.D. dissertation, Univ. of Southern Calif., 1940); Elwood Mead, *Report of Irrigation Investigations in California* (Washington, D.C.: U.S. Dept. of Agriculture, Experiment Sta. Bulletin 100, 1901); Eugene L. Menefee and Fred A. Dodge, *History of Tulare and Kings Counties, California* (Los Angeles: Historical Record Co., 1913); Mary Montgomery and Marion Clawson, *History of Legislation and Policy Formation of the Central Valley Project* (U.S. Dept. of Agriculture, Bureau of Agricultural Economics, Berkeley, 1946); Charles V. Moore and Trimble R. Hedges, *Economics of On-Farm Irrigation Water Availability and Costs, and Related Farm Adjustments* (Calif. Agricultural Experiment Station, Giannini Foundation Research Reports 257, 258, 261, 263, 1962–63); Gerald D. Nash, "Henry George Reexamined: William S. Chapman's Views on Land Speculation in Nineteenth Century California," 33 *Agricultural History* 133 (1959).

James D. Schuyler, "Report on the Property and Business of the Consolidated Canal Co. of Fresno County, Calif." (1902, Ms, Water Resources Center Archives, Univ. of Calif., Berkeley); Wallace Smith, *Garden of the Sun: A History of the San Joaquin Valley, 1772–1939* (Los Angeles: Lymanhouse, 1939); I. Teilman and W. H. Shafer, *The Historical Study of Irrigation in Fresno and Kings Counties in Central California* (Fresno: Williams & Son, 1943); Virginia E. Thickens, "Pioneer Agricultural Colonies of Fresno County," 25 *Calif. Historical Society Quarterly* 17–38, 168–177 (1946); Thomas H. Thompson, *Official Historical Atlas Map of Fresno County* (Tulare, 1891), *Official Historical Atlas of Tulare County* (Hanford, 1892); U.S. Congress, House of Representatives, *Central Valley Project Documents,* part 1–House Doc. 84–416 (1956); part 2–House Doc. 85–246 (1957); U.S. Dept. of the Army, Corps of Engineers, *Report on Kings River* (Washington, D.C.: U.S. House Doc. 76–630, 1940), *Sacramento-San Joaquin Basin Streams*–comprehensive report (Washington, D.C.: U.S. House Doc. 81–367, 1949); U.S. Dept. of the Army, *Report on Allocation of Costs of Kings River and Tulare Lake Project, California* (Washington, D.C.: U.S. House Doc. 80–136, 1947); U.S. Dept of the Interior, Bureau of Reclamation, *Kings River Project in California* (Washington, D.C.: U.S. House Doc. 76–631, 1940), *Central Valley Basin: Comprehensive Report* (Washington, D.C.: U.S. Senate Doc. 81–113, 1949), *North Fork Kings River Development* (Washington, D.C.: U.S. House Doc. 81–537, 1950), Contracts for Kings River Project: Interim Contract (No. 14-06-200-2365, Dec. 1953); O & M Contract (No. 14-06-200-692A, Dec. 1963); Master Agreement Supplementing and Amending Water Right Indenture and Administrative Agreement (September 1963)–all mimeo; U.S. Dept. of the Interior, Office of the Secretary, *Excess Land Provisions of the Federal Reclamation Laws and the Payment of Charges* (Washington, D.C., 1956, Pts. 1–2); Paul Vandor, *History of Fresno County* (Los Angeles: Historical Record Co., 1919); Ben R. Walker, *The Fresno County Blue*

Book (Fresno: A. H. Crawston, 1941); Lilbourne A. Winchell, *History of Fresno County and the San Joaquin Valley* (Fresno: A. H. Crawston, 1933).

2. Thompson, *Atlas Map of Fresno County,* p. 13.

3. Henry George, who named Chapman as California's chief land speculator, said that he controlled only 350,000 acres in 1871. Henry George, *Our Land and Land Policy* (New York: Doubleday & McClure, 1901, p. 71).

4. Vandor, *History of Fresno County,* p. 183.

5. Teilman and Shafer, *Historical Study of Irrigation,* p. 24.

6. Calif. Immigrant Union, *Supplement to All About California and The Inducements to Settle There* (San Francisco: Calif. Immigrant Union, 1876), p. 5.

7. *General Directory of Fresno County, California, for 1881,* pp. 111–112.

8. *E. D. Porter et al.* v. *Fresno Canal and Irrigation Co.,* 6 Opinions and Orders Railroad Commission of Calif. 133 (3 February 1915).

9. *M. V. Stirewalt et al.* v. *Consolidated Canal Co.,* 9 Opinions and Orders Railroad Commission of Calif. 857 (29 April 1916); 10 ibid. 692 (21 August 1916).

10. *Falbrook Irrigation District* v. *Bradley,* 164 U.S. 112 (1896).

11. The following calculation gives acre-feet of water per month for one acre under each rule:

Fresno Irrigation District:

$$\frac{1 \text{ (cfs)} \times 86400 \text{ (seconds*)}}{10 \text{ (acres)}} \qquad \begin{aligned} &= 8640 \text{ cf/acre/run} \\ &= 0.20 \text{ af}^\dagger/\text{acre/run} \end{aligned}$$

Fresno Canal Company:

$$\frac{4 \text{ (cfs)} \times 86400 \text{ (seconds*)} \times 15 \text{ (days}^{\dagger\dagger})}{640 \text{ (acres)}} \qquad \begin{aligned} &= 8100 \text{ cf/acre/run} \\ &= 0.19 \text{ af}^\dagger/\text{acre/run} \end{aligned}$$

* 24 hrs. = 86400 seconds
† 43200 cf. = one af. Although the correct figure is 43560, it is customary to define an acre foot as 1 cfs flowing continuously for 12 hrs, or 43200 cf
†† Normally 2 runs per month

12. Hutchins, *Mutual Irrigation Companies,* p. 113.

13. The terms used to describe the procedures of the Fresno and Consolidated irrigation districts—rotation and demand—are those used in the area. These terms have somewhat different meanings in the typology that we have used in chapter 9.

14. Teilman and Shafer, *Historical Study of Irrigation,* pp. 39–42.

15. Barnes, *Use of Water,* pp. 39, 46.

16. Ibid., pp. 38–39.

17. See, for example, Nash, "Henry George Reexamined."

18. Benjamin E. Lloyd, *Lights and Shades in San Francisco* (San Francisco: A. L. Bancroft, 1876), p. 115.

19. *Bank of Calif.* v. *Fresno Canal and Irrigation Co.,* Thirteenth District Court, Fresno County, April 1878, plaintiff's and defendant's briefs and court opinion, in custody of Fresno County Clerk; 58 Cal. 202 (July 1878) on appeal.

20. There is both a need and an opportunity for economic historians to examine speculation in greater detail, using the econometric methods that Bogue and Swierenga have used to study the rate of return of land speculators in Iowa and Illinois. See Allen G. and Margaret B. Bogue, " 'Profits' and the Frontier Land Speculator," 17 *Journal of Economic History* 1–24 (1957); Robert P. Swierenga, *Pioneers and Profits: Land Speculation on the Iowa Frontier* (Ames: Iowa State University Press, 1968).

21. Teilman and Shafer, *Historical Study of Irrigation,* p. 49.

22. Mead, *Report of Irrigation Investigations,* pp. 38–42.

Notes to chapter 6

1. The principal sources for this chapter are cited in note 1 of chapter 5.

2. William Hammond Hall, *Report of the State Engineer, 1880,* pt. IV, "Irrigation," (Sacramento: State Printing Office, 1880), p. 6.

3. Elwood Mead, *Report of Irrigation Investigations in California* (Washington, D.C.: U.S. Dept. of Agriculture, Experiment Sta. Bulletin 100, 1901), pp. 33–34, 54–55, 61–62.

4. Cal. Stats. 1850, p. 219.

5. These basic differences have been stated nakedly. They have been modified by principles of "reasonable use," "beneficial use," and the long-standing common law doctrine of prescription.

6. *Moyer* v. *Preston,* 6 Wyo. 308, 318, 44 Pac. 845, 847 (1896).

7. *Coffin* v. *Left Hand Ditch Co.,* 6 Colo. 443, 446–447 (1892).

8. *Drake* v. *Earhart,* 2 Idaho 750, 753–754, 23 Pac. 541, 542 (1890). See also *Stonewell* v. *Johnson,* 7 Utah 215, 225–226, 26 Pac. 290, 291.

9. *Hill* v. *King,* 8 Cal. 336, 338 (1857)

10. *Lux* v. *Haggin,* 69 Cal. 255, 10 Pac. 674 (1886).

11. Ibid., 384–385, 10 Pac. 749.

12. Quoted in S. T. Harding, *Water in California* (Palo Alto: N-P Publications, 1960), p. 39.

13. Quoted in Wells A. Hutchins, *The California Law of Water Rights* (Sacramento: State Printing Office, 1956), pp. 53–54.

14. See Arthur Maass and Hiller B. Zobel, "Anglo-American Water Law: Who Appropriated the Riparian Doctrine?" 10 *Public Policy* 109 ff. (1960).

15. For cases see Hutchins, *California Law,* pp. 298–343.

16. For cases see ibid., pp. 192–194.

17. For California cases on groundwater see ibid., pp. 426–465.

18. 200 Cal. 81, 252 Pac. 607 (1926).

19. Calif. Const., art. XIV, sec. 3.

20. Hall, *Report,* pp. 117-161; Mead, *Report of Irrigation Investigations,* pp. 53-59, 276-282.

21. Harry Barnes, *Use of Water from Kings River, California* (Sacramento: California Dept. of Engineering, Bulletin 7, 1918), p. 112.

22. There is sufficient documentation on the riparian suits in opinions of the California Supreme Court. Because the riparian doctrine was new and the relations between riparian, prescriptive, and appropriative rights undefined, that court heard appeals from the county courts in most cases. On the other hand, the supreme court denied most appeals from the county courts in suits among appropriators. Because appropriation had been the accepted method of acquiring water rights until 1883, there were many fewer legal questions remaining to be settled concerning that doctrine. As a consequence the documentation for Kings River is poor. The county court decrees are not published, and in any case they contain little of the court's reasoning and not many facts. A compilation of the important county court decrees, inadequate unfortunately, can be found in Mead, *Report of Irrigation Investigations,* pp. 58-60, 277-282. The supreme court opinions in the riparian cases are these: *Heilbron* v. *Last Chance Water Ditch Co.,* 75 Cal. 117, 17 Pac. 65 (1888); *Last Chance Water Ditch Co.* v. *Heilbron,* 86 Cal. 1, 26 Pac. 523 (1890); *Lower Kings River Water Ditch Co.* v. *Heilbron,* 75 Cal. xvii, 17 Pac. 69 (1888); *Heilbron* v. *Emigrant Ditch Co.,* 75 Cal. xvii, 17 Pac. 68 (1888); *Lillis* v. *Emigrant Ditch Co.,* 95 Cal. 553, 30 Pac. 1108 (1892); *Heilbron* v. *Peoples Ditch Co.,* 75 Cal. xvii, 17 Pac. 69 (1888); *Lillis* v. *Peoples Ditch Co.,* 3 Cal. Unreported Cases 494, 29 Pac. 780 (1892); *LIllis* v. *Peoples Ditch Co.,* Cal. unreported, 34 Pac. 715; *Heilbron* v. *Fowler Switch Canal Co.,* 75 Cal. 426, 17 Pac. 535 (1888); *Heilbron* v. *Centerville and Kingsburg Irrigation Ditch Co.,* 76 Cal. 8, 17 Pac. 932 (1888); *Heilbron* v. *Kings River and Fresno Canal Co.,* 76 Cal. 11, 17 Pac. 933 (1888); *Heinlen* v. *Fresno Canal and Irrigation Co.,* 68 Cal. 35, 8 Pac. 513 (1885); *Heilbron* v. 76 *Land and Water Co.,* 80 Cal. 189, 22 Pac. 62 (1889); 96 Cal. 7, 30 Pac. 802 (1892).

23. W. H. Shafer in I. Teilman and Shafer, *The Historical Study of Irrigation in Fresno and Kings Counties in Central California* (Fresno: Williams & Son, 1943), pp. 48-49.

24. Teilman in ibid., p. 22.

25. Calif. Dept. of Public Works, Division of Water Rights, *Report,* Pt. IV (Sacramento, 1922), pp. 61-62.

26. *Administrative Agreement; Water Right Indenture; Agreement Supplementing and Amending Administrative Agreement Dated May 3, 1927* (Fresno: Kings River Water Assoc., 1949).

27. Charles L. Kaupke, *Forty Years on Kings River* (prepared for Kings River Water Assoc., Fresno, 1957), p. 46. The statement is not entirely accurate, since there remained questions about the rights of the canals in the Centerville bottoms and the allocation of river channel losses between Piedra and the several points of diversion. In 1952 the Centerville canals joined to organize the Kings River Water District, which signed the indenture in 1963 and went on its schedule; and a definite procedure for allocating river channel gains and losses was worked out during the same period.

28. By assuming that all stored water is used as B water, we allocate a greater percentage of total water to B water than in the earlier simulation and a lesser percentage to pumped water (see table 5.7).

29. Principal sources for this discussion of negotiations are the following documents and the references cited therein: U.S. Dept. of the Interior, Office of the Secretary, *Excess Land Provisions of the Federal Reclamation Laws and the Payment of Charges,* 2 parts (Washington, D.C.: Dept. of the Interior, 1956); Arthur Maass, *Muddy Waters: The Army Engineers and the Nation's Rivers* (Cambridge, Ma.: Harvard University Press, 1951); U.S. Dept. of the Interior, Bureau of Reclamation, Contracts for Kings River Project: Interim Contract (No. 14-06-200-2365, Dec. 1953); O & M Contract (No. 14-06-200-692A, Dec. 1963); Master Agreement Supplementing and Amending Water Right Indenture and Administrative Agreement (September 1963), all mimeo; Irrigation District Assoc. of Calif., *Western Water News* 1950-1969. Unless otherwise cited, quotations are from documents easily identified in these sources.

30. For several years the negotiations were carried on by Kings River Conservation District, discussed below.

31. *San Francisco Chronicle,* 12 November 1951. Hunter was unopposed for reelection in 1952. In 1954 he lost to B. F. Sisk, a Democrat, who has remained in Congress to this day.

32. U.S. Dept. of the Interior, Bureau of Reclamation, *North Fork Kings River Development* (Washington, D.C.: U.S. House Doc. 81-537, 1950), p. 95.

33. See Arthur Maass, *Muddy Waters,* chapter 5.

34. *San Francisco Chronicle,* 11 November 1951.

35. The best study, which includes a full bibliography of others, is Harry J. Hogan, *The 160 Acre Limitation* (Ph.D. thesis, George Washington University, Washington, D.C., 1972).

36. Ibid., p. 135.

37. This point is made by Alden Bigler Davis, *The Excess Land Law in the Central Valley of California* (Ph.D. Thesis, University of California, Berkeley, 1961), p. 20.

Notes to chapter 7

1. U.S. Agricultural Census Reports, 1964 and 1969.

2. Robert G. Hemphill, *Irrigation in Northern Colorado* (Washington, D.C.: U.S. Dept. of Agriculture, Bulletin 1026, May 1926), pp. 27-31.

3. R. J. Tipton, "More Efficient Use of Water," *One Hundred Years of Irrigation in Colorado* (Colorado Water Conservation Board and Colorado A. & M. College, 1952), p. 41.

4. David Boyd, "Irrigation Near Greeley," *Water Supply Paper No. 9* (Washington, D.C.: U.S. Geological Survey, Dept. of the Interior, 1897), pp. 27-28.

5. Ibid., p. 61.

6. Section 6, Article XVI, *Constitution of the State of Colorado* (1876).

7. R. L. Anderson and L. M. Hartman, *Introduction of Supplemental Irrigation*

Water (Ft. Collins, Colo.: Colorado State University Agricultural Experiment Station, Tech. Bulletin 76, 1965), p. 3.

8. For an account of origin and formation, see J. M. Dille, *A Brief History of the Northern Colorado Water Conservancy District and the Colorado–Big Thompson Project* (Loveland, Colo.: NCWCD, 1958).

9. See Elwood Mead, *Irrigation Institutions* (New York: Macmillan, 1903), pp. 145–146.

10. This activity has been reported by Raymond L. Anderson, "The Irrigation Water Rental Market: A Case Study," 13 *Agricultural Economics Research* 54–58 (1961) and "Operation of the Irrigation Water Rental Market in the South Platte Basin," 42 *Journal of Farm Economics* 1501–1502 (1960).

11. As told to Anderson by one of the original directors.

12. Dille, *A Brief History,* p. 31.

Notes to chapter 8

1. Early irrigation development in Utah has been described in three very good studies published near the turn of the present century. These are Charles H. Brough, *Irrigation in Utah* (Baltimore: Johns Hopkins Press, 1898), George Thomas, *The Development of Institutions Under Irrigation* (New York: Macmillan, 1920); and Elwood Mead (ed.), *Report of Irrigation Investigations in Utah* (Washington, D.C.: U.S. Dept. of Agriculture, Experiment Sta. Bulletin 124, 1903). See also Leonard J. Arrington and Dean May, " 'A Different Mode of Life': Irrigation and Society in Nineteenth-Century Utah," 49 *Agricultural History* 3–20 (1975).

2. Quoted in William R. Palmer, "Utah Water Courts," 33 *Reclamation Era* 233 (November 1947).

3. Quoted in Roy Huffman, *Irrigation Development and Public Water Policy* (New York: Ronald Press, 1953), p. 42.

4. James Hudson, *Irrigation Water Use in the Utah Valley, Utah* (Chicago: University of Chicago Press, 1962).

5. M. Leon Hyatt, Gaylord V. Skogerboe, Frank W. Haws, and Lloyd H. Austin, *Hydrologic Inventory of the Utah Lake Drainage Area* (Logan, Utah: Utah Water Research Laboratory, Utah State University, 1969), p. 135.

6. U.S. Census of Irrigation, 1960, State Table 4, p. 337.

7. Hudson, *Irrigation Water Use,* pp. 124–125.

8. Hyatt et al., *Hydrologic Inventory,* p. 135.

9. Mead, *Report,* p. 127.

10. Wells A. Hutchins, *The Utah Law of Water Rights* (Salt Lake City: State Engineer of Utah and Economic Research Service, U.S. Department of Agriculture, 1965), pp. 69–70.

11. Hudson, *Irrigation Water Use,* p. 236.

12. Ibid., p. 139.

13. *A Method of Evaluating Irrigation Benefits of Watershed Protection, Ameri-*

can Fork-Dry Creek Watershed, Utah (Washington, D.C.: Interim Report of Study, Economic Research Service, U.S. Dept. of Agriculture, April 1960), p. 6.

14. See, for example, Hudson, *Irrigation Water Use,* chapter 7.

15. Thomas, *Development of Institutions,* p. 152.

16. U.S. Reclamation Service, *Fourth Annual Report* (Washington, D.C.: Government Printing Office, 1905), p. 333.

17. "Federal Reclamation by Irrigation," Report Submitted to the Secretary of the Interior by the Committee of Special Advisers on Reclamation (U.S. Senate Document 68-92, 1924).

18. Ibid., pp. 106–107.

19. Ibid., p. 196.

20. U.S. Reclamation Service, *Annual Report for Fiscal Year 1925,* (Washington, D.C.: Government Printing Office, 1925), pp. 8–9.

21. Fact Finders' Report, pp. 146–147, supra note 17.

22. Public Law 80-462; Senate Report 80-878; House Report 80-1492.

23. Thomas, *Development of Institutions,* pp. 83–84, 110–111; Lowry Nelson, *The Mormon Village* (Salt Lake City: University of Utah Press, 1952).

24. Brough, *Irrigation in Utah,* p. 19.

25. Thomas, *Development of Institutions,* p. 111.

26. Hudson, *Irrigation Water Use,* p. 91.

27. Ibid., p. 235.

Notes to chapter 9

1. Thomas F. Glick, *Irrigation and Society in Medieval Valencia* (Cambridge, Ma.: Harvard University Press, 1970). For a fascinating study of how the villages of a small oasis in eastern Iran restricted the influence of those in a neighboring village who provided them with investment that was essential for the repair of the village ganat, see Brian Spooner, "Irrigation and Society: the Iranian Plateau," in Theodore E. Downing and McGuire Gibson (eds.), *Irrigation's Impact on Society* (Tucson: University of Arizona Press, 1974). One gains a highly imperfect sense of how water is distributed in irrigated areas by reading the vast literature on national and state water codes and laws or the equally abundant and prolix literature on the legal nature of water rights. There is a difference between legal concepts of water rights and water practice, and many students of irrigation have overstressed the importance of rights, about which they can write at length without leaving their desks. Glick makes a similar point in *The Old World Background of the Irrigation System of San Antonio, Texas,* Southwestern Studies, Monograph No. 35 (El Paso: University of Texas, 1972).

2. See N. D. Gulhati and William Charles Smith, "Irrigation Agriculture: An Historical Review," in R. M. Hagan, H. R. Haise, and T. W. Edminister (eds.), *Irrigation of Agricultural Lands* (Madison, Wi.: American Society of Agronomy, 1967).

3. Thomas F. Glick, book review, 3 *Journal of Interdisciplinary History* 416–420 (1972).

4. On the other hand we have entertained the possibility that the federal government's entry into Strawberry Valley, Utah, exacerbated differences between the prospective irrigators of the Highline canal and farmers irrigating from the older canals.

5. Carl J. Friedrich, *Man and His Government* (New York: McGraw-Hill, 1963), p. 423.

6. California Constitution, Article XIV, Section 3.

7. Letter to Maass from R. L. Anderson, 3 March 1975.

8. Edward F. Treadwell, *The Cattle King* (New York: Macmillan, 1931), pp. 90–93.

9. See as examples, Laura Nader, "Conflict: Anthropological Aspects," *International Encyclopedia of the Social Sciences* (New York: Macmillan and Free Press, 1968); Klaus-Friedrich Koch, *War and Peace in Jalémó: The Management of Conflict in Highland New Guinea* (Cambridge, Ma.: Harvard University Press, 1974).

10. Actually we use a normalized median deviation, as follows:

$$\text{M.D.} = \frac{1}{n} \cdot \frac{\sum\limits_{i=1}^{n} \left| v_i - v_m \right|}{v_m}$$

11. The differences between market and farm priorities in Colorado-Utah are insignificant.

12. For a recent example of welfare economics in this context, see Martin Bronfenbrenner, *Income Distribution Theory* (Chicago: Aldine-Atherton, 1971), pp. 6–12.

13. Chapter 5, note 20.

14. Lewis Cecil Gray, "Land Speculation," IX *Encyclopaedia of the Social Sciences* (New York: Macmillan, 1933), p. 68.

15. John Rawls, *A Theory of Justice* (Cambridge, Ma.: Harvard University Press, 1971), esp. pp. 60–63, 261–263, 302–303, and 498.

16. Robert Nozick raises this criticism and others in his critique of Rawls. See Nozick, *Anarchy, State, and Utopia* (New York: Basic Books, 1974), chapter 7, "Distributive Justice."

17. See Arthur Maass, Maynard M. Hufschmidt, Robert Dorfman, Harold A. Thomas, Jr., Stephen A. Marglin, and Gordon Maskew Fair, *Design of Water Resource Systems* (Cambridge, Ma.: Harvard University Press, 1962); Maynard M. Hufschmidt and Myron B. Fiering, *Simulation Techniques for Design of Water Resource Systems* (Cambridge, Ma.: Harvard University Press, 1966); Myron B. Fiering, *Streamflow Synthesis* (Cambridge, Ma.: Harvard University Press, 1967).

18. Gilbert F. White and J. Eugene Haas, *Assessment of Research on Natural Hazards* (Cambridge, Ma.: MIT Press, 1975); Ian Burton, Robert W. Kates, and Gilbert F. White, *The Environment as Hazard* (New York: Oxford University Press, 1975).

19. Fred I. Greenstein and Nelson Polsby (eds.), *Handbook of Political Science* (Reading, Ma.: Addison-Wesley, 1975), vol III, pp. 1–114.

20. Ibid., p. 48.

21. See monographs and reports of Cornell University, Center for International Studies, Rural Development Committee (Norman Uphoff, Chairman), and the work of John D. Montgomery: "Allocation of Authority in Land Reform Programs: A Comparative Study of Administrative Processes and Outputs," 17 *Administrative Science Quarterly* 62–75 (1972); *Technology and Civic Life: Making and Implementing Development Decisions* (Cambridge, Ma.: The MIT Press, 1974).

22. As examples of recent interest in irrigation: Symposium on Irrigation Civilizations, 1968 Annual Meeting of American Anthropological Association; Symposium on Irrigation's Impact on Society, 1972 Annual Meeting of Southwestern Anthropological Association; Symposium on Irrigation and Communal Organization, 1973 Annual Meeting of American Anthropological Association. Papers for the 1953 symposium were edited by Julian Steward and Published under the title *Irrigation Civilizations: A Comparative Study* (Washington, D.C.: Pan American Union, 1955). Those of the 1972 symposium have been edited by Theodore E. Downing and McGuire Gibson and published as anthropological papers of the University of Arizona, No. 25 (Tucson, Az.: 1974). The papers published in this last volume include references to most of the community studies, but not to the study that from our point of view is the best of them all: Jacques Berque, *Structures sociales du haut-atlas* (Paris: Presses Universitaires de France, 1955). Berque gives special attention to the stratification of leadership roles, as do Eva and Robert Hunt in their studies of the Cuicatec region of Mexico (1972 symposium and a paper presented at the 1973 symposium and published as "Canal Irrigation and Local Social Organization," 17 *Current Anthropology* 389–411, 1976).

23. In addition to the anthropological work, there are recent studies of individual irrigation systems by agricultural economists, agricultural engineers, rural sociologists, and others. For a good bibliography, see E. Walter Coward, Jr., "Irrigation Institutions and Organizations: An International Bibliography," (Ithaca, N.Y.: Cornell International Agriculture Mimeograph 49, 1976). A number of these studies focus on problems that concern us in this book, especially Richard B. Reidinger, "Institutional Rationing of Canal Water in Northern India: Conflict Between Traditional Patterns and Modern Needs," 28 *Economic Development and Cultural Change,* 79–104 (1974); and Ramon H. Myers, "Economic Organization and Cooperation in Modern China: Irrigation Management in Xing-Tai County, Hobei Province," *The Polity and Economy of China: The Late Professor Yuji Muramatsu Commemoration Volume* (Tokyo: Keizai Shinposha, 1975).

Recently Max K. Lowdermilk and his associates at Colorado State University have undertaken a major research project on local water management in arid lands of less developed countries (financed by the U.S. Agency for International Development). Some preliminary findings have been published in *Water Management Research in Arid and Sub-Humid Lands of Less Developed Countries,* Annual Technical Report to U.S. Agency for International Development (Ft. Collins, Colorado: Water Management Research Project, Colorado State University, Dec. 31, 1976), especially appendixes 40 and 42.

Acknowledgments

Those to whom we are indebted for teaching us about irrigation and farm life in the six huertas, principally farmers and officers of irrigation communities, are legion. We hope to see many of them again soon. Here we record the names of only a few of the irrigation community officers and others who were especially helpful and hope that their colleagues and constituents will understand that our respect and appreciation extends equally to them.

Valencia: Vicente Giner Boira; also José Latour Brotóns, Thomas F. Glick, Juan Gabriel Velamazan Gomez, and José María Martín Mendiluce for documentation and basic data.

Murcia-Orihuela: José María Gil Egea, Guillermo Pastor Moscardó, Manuel Alegría Mazeres, Emilio Bregante Palazón, and Francisco Martínez Lineares; also Justo Llácer Barrachina and Juan Torres Fontes for documentation and basic data.

Alicante: Manuel Sánchez Buades and José Bovard Eberle; also Vicente Ramos for documentation.

California: Howard Keck, Edgar Waldron, Albert Lowe, J. C. Bishop, Robert L. Naylor, and George B. Clarke; also Robert E. Leake, Jr., Norman D. Sturm, Gerald J. Giefer, Maude K. Swingle, H. L. Masini, and Fred Jinbo for documentation and basic data.

Colorado: Norman Collins, Ernest Meyer, and Lawrence Cox, J. R. Barkley, and Earl Phipps.

Utah: Gaylord V. Skogerboe.

For assistance in writing the simulation program we are indebted to Ron L. Smith and Charles Jackson; in calculating the Gini coefficients, to Thomas Shemo; and in preparing the manuscript, to Marian Stanwood Adams and Doris McMurray.

The maps have been drawn by artist Garry Fujiwara, who grew up on an irrigated farm near Fresno.

Maass's research in Spain was supported in part by fellowships from the John Simon Guggenheim Memorial Foundation, the Social Science Research Council, and the Commission for Educational Exchange between the United States and Spain.

George A. Pavelis and Harry Steele of the Economic Research Service, U.S. Department of Agriculture, and Dean Don K. Price, Jr., of the John Fitzgerald Kennedy School of Government, Harvard University, have been sympathetic sponsors of our work.

Publishing a large book with a great many tables and figures is costly. The authors are indebted to the Harza Engineering Company of Chicago for a subvention that allows this book to be offered to the public at what we believe to be a reasonable price. We salute the interest of this company in research and scholarship in a field in which it is highly regarded for engineering practice.

    Photo credits: 12, top, Vicente Giner Boira; 12, left, Ayuntamiento de
Valencia; 12, right, Francisco Almela y Vives; 13, top, reproduced initially in
Francisco Borrul y Vilanova, *Tratado de la distribución de las aguas del río
Turia,* 1831; 13, bottom, reproduced initially in the journal, *Le Tour du Monde,*
vol. 6, 1862; 54, top and bottom, Junta de Hacendados de la Huerta de Murcia;
55, top right, Guillermo Pastor Moscardó; 55, bottom, Confederación Hidrográfica del Segura; 102, top, Antonio Joseph Cavanilles, *Observaciones sobre el
Reyno de Valencia,* vol. 2, 1797; 102, bottom left, and 103, top, Sindicato de
Riegos de la Huerta de Alicante; 102, bottom right, Manuel Sanchez Buades;
103, bottom, Richard Reidinger; 148, top, U.S. Bureau of Reclamation and
Fresno Irrigation District; 149, top, U.S. Army Corps of Engineers; 149, bottom,
from promotional pamphlet of Calif. Immigrant Union, 1873; 276, top, and
277, top, Raymond L. Anderson; 277, bottom, U.S. Bureau of Reclamation;
326, top and bottom, U.S. Bureau of Reclamation.

Index